SOCIAL GROUPS AND PRODUCTION IN MYCENAEAN ECONOMIES

sidestonepress

SOCIAL GROUPS AND PRODUCTION IN MYCENAEAN ECONOMIES

Papers from the Langford Conference,
Florida State University, Tallahassee,
24-25 February 2023

DANIEL J. PULLEN (ED)

Published by Sidestone Press, Leiden
www.sidestone.com
E-mail: info@sidestone.nl
Phone: (+31)(0)71-7370131

Lay-out & cover design: Sidestone Press
Cover: View of Kalamianos and Saronic Gulf. Photo: D. J. Pullen © SHARP. Pottery from Petsas House, Mycenae. Photo: K. Shelton.

ISBN 978-94-6426-332-9 (softcover)
ISBN 978-94-6426-333-6 (hardcover)
ISBN 978-94-6426-334-3 (PDF e-book)

DOI: 10.59641/yy367bk

FSU
FLORIDA STATE UNIVERSITY

Contents

Acknowledgements

The contributions to this volume were originally delivered at the Spring 2023 Langford Conference entitled "Social Groups and Production in Mycenaean Economies," held at Florida State University in Tallahassee, 24–25 February 2023. I would like to thank the George and Marian Langford Family Endowment in the Department of Classics at Florida State University for funding the conference. Karmel Hawkins and Julia Yarboro from the Classics Department's office spent much time and effort to make the conference a smooth-sailing operation. My doctoral student Jami Craig was invaluable in the preparations and running of the conference, including coordinating volunteers among the other graduate students, and I thank her. I would also like to thank my colleagues and graduate students in the Classics Department, especially Tim Stover, Sarah Craft, Andrea de Giorgi, and Jim Sickinger, who pitched in and helped in many ways to make the conference the success that it was.

I would like to thank the authors for their timely responses and most of all for their high-quality contributions to this volume. This publication is generously supported by the George and Marian Langford Family Endowment in the Department of Classics at Florida State University. I thank the chair of the Classics Department, Tim Stover, for his support of this publication. I would like to thank my good friends and colleagues Dimitri Nakassis, William Parkinson, and Michael Galaty for their advice and comments throughout the preparation of the conference and this volume.

Daniel J. Pullen
Tallahassee
August 2024

Contributors

Daniel J. Pullen (dpullen@fsu.edu) is Professor Emeritus of Classics at Florida State University. He co-directs (with Tom Tartaron) the Saronic Harbors Archaeological Research Project, investigating the Mycenaean harbor town of Kalamianos. He also participates in the Diros Regional Project's Ksagounaki Excavations exploring the open-air Final Neolithic settlement and cemetery associated with the Alepotrypa Cave. His research interests include landscape archaeology, emergence of complex societies, and socio-political and economic organization in the Aegean Neolithic and Bronze Age.

Natalie Abell (ndabell@umich.edu) is Associate Professor of Mediterranean Archaeology in the Department of Classical Studies at the University of Michigan. Many of her current publication projects are focused on northwestern Kea, as part of the ongoing study of material from John Caskey's excavations at Neolithic Kephala and Bronze Age Ayia Irini. She is also a senior staff member of the Kea Archaeological Research Survey (directed by Joanne Murphy). Her research interests include exchange, economy, mobility, and craft production in the Bronze Age Aegean and beyond.

Peter M. Day (p.m.day@sheffield.ac.uk) is Emeritus Professor of Archaeological Materials at the University of Sheffield and Research Associate at the Institute of Nanoscience and Nanotechnology, NCSR Demokritos, Athens. He specializes in analytical approaches to archaeological ceramic assemblages, integrating macroscopic, microscopic and chemical techniques. His research examines questions of production, exchange, technological practice and identity in a variety of contexts, focusing on the Neolithic, Bronze Age and early Medieval periods of the Mediterranean. Recent fieldwork and publications focus on the southern Aegean, Sicily, Sardinia and south-western Iberia. Currently, he leads both archaeological and ethnographic projects examining tradition, technological change, and transmission in the ceramic material culture of displaced and mobile populations.

Jan Driessen (jan.driessen@uclouvain.be) is Professor Emeritus of Aegean archaeology at the UCLouvain in Belgium and Marion Rawson Visiting Scholar at the University of Cincinnati. He directs the excavations of the Minoan settlement at Sissi on Crete and co-directs the excavations at Pyla-Kokkinokremos on Cyprus. He is especially interested in Bronze Age social structure and the effects of natural and manmade disasters on human communities.

Michael L. Galaty (mgalaty@umich.edu) is Professor of Anthropology and Classical Studies and Director and Curator of European Archaeology for the Museum of Anthropological Archaeology at the University of Michigan. He has co-directed archaeological projects in Albania, Greece, Kosovo, and the United States. His research interests include the rise of complex societies, in the Bronze and Iron Age Balkans in particular, regional archaeological survey, and the scientific analysis of pottery.

Eleftheria Kardamaki (elkardamaki@yahoo.gr) studied archaeology at the National and Kapodistrias University in Athens, Greece and did her Ph.D. at the Ruprecht-Karls-University in Heidelberg. Since 2011 she has been working on research projects with a focus on ceramic investigations of the Late Bronze Age in the Aegean. In 2023 she became a scientific collaborator at the University of Heidelberg and has undertaken the study of the pottery from the NW Lower Town of Tiryns.

Sarah C. Murray (sc.murray@utoronto.ca) is Associate Professor of Classics at the University of Toronto. Her research concerns the archaeological evidence for economic and social developments during the Late Bronze and Early Iron Ages in the Aegean. She is co-director of the Bays of East Attica Regional Survey, an archaeological project based around the bay of Porto Rafti in Greece.

Dimitri Nakassis (dimitri.nakassis@colorado.edu) is Professor in the Department of Classics at the University of Colorado - Boulder. His research focuses on the Mycenaean societies of the Late Bronze Age Aegean and the diachronic study of Greek rural landscapes. He is the author of *Individuals and Society in Mycenaean Pylos* (2013) and the co-editor of the forthcoming publication of the inscribed documents from "Palace of Nestor" at Pylos. He is also co-director of the Western Argolid Regional Project, an archaeological survey in southern Greece.

William A. Parkinson (wparkinson@fieldmuseum.org) is Curator of Anthropology at the Field Museum of Natural History and Professor of Anthropology at University of Illinois at Chicago. He and Attila Gyucha co-direct the Körös Regional Archaeological Project. Bill also co-directs the Southern Mani Archaeological Project with Chelsea Gardner and Rebecca Seifried. His research explores the social dynamics of early village societies and the emergence of early states.

Kim Shelton (sheltonk@berkeley.edu) is Director of the Nemea Center for Classical Archaeology at the University of California Berkeley. She directs the excavations at the Sanctuary of Zeus, Ancient Nemea, the Petsas House, Mycenae, and the TAPHOS chamber tomb project at Aidonia. As a specialist in ceramics and the political economy of the prehistoric Aegean, her research is focused on workshop dynamics and their relationship to the market economy of pottery, the regional needs of a diverse population, and the Mycenaean palatial administration. Her research on ancient Greek ritual and religion explores the earliest manifestations of Greek religious ritual through permanent architectural establishments and ritual paraphernalia from the Bronze Age to the Archaic periods. She has worked at Mycenae for more than 30 years with the Archaeological Society of Athens.

Thomas F. Tartaron (tartaron@sas.upenn.edu) is Associate Professor of Classical Studies at the University of Pennsylvania. He is Executive Director of the Center for the Analysis of Archaeological Materials (CAAM) in the Penn Museum and Associate Curator in the Museum's Mediterranean Section. He has participated in numerous excavations and regional surveys in Greece, Cyprus, Iraq, and the United States. Currently, he is carrying out cross-cultural ethnoarchaeological research in Greece, Cyprus, and India, collecting oral histories from elder fishermen and women to better understand coastal life in antiquity.

Getting beyond elite versus non-elite in Mycenaean economies

Daniel J. Pullen

Introduction

As archaeologists, we are obsessed with elites. For a discipline that purports to study human societies, we often focus on but a (presumably) small portion of those societies. Some of the reasoning for this obsession is that by their very nature, elites are thought to be more easily observable than non-elites through their patterns of distribution and consumption of material goods visible in the archaeological record. Aegean Prehistory is no exception to this general obsession, with our interests in palatial centers, exotica and long-distance trade, and the emergence of social complexity — which by the latter we often mean the emergence of elites. To be sure, the appearance of elites usually does mean the transformation of social, political, and economic structures into something different, and often into a hierarchically based structure. But too often we look at the material manifestations of these transformations, such as relative wealth and access to resources, and not at the transformations themselves. We assume that greater wealth and access to resources, for example, are indications of elite individuals or groups without understanding the roles that wealth and resource access might have in the emergence and expression of being a member of the elite portion of society. Steps to correct this situation have been made, such as Sarah Murray's questioning of the role of elites in the ancient economy and how we use terminology and categorization (Murray 2017, 2023). Her reanalysis of the exotica in the Perati cemetery (Murray 2018) is a great model for re-evaluating our assumption that elites controlled foreign trade and contacts as a means for marking themselves from others — she actually looked at the distribution and context of those exotic, foreign items, and found that the majority of foreign items were scarabs, amulets, and other prophylactic items, and that they have no correlation with the wealth of the tombs. Instead, she demonstrates that imported objects do not necessarily relate to elite "self-fashioning" or politically driven exchange among elites in many contexts.

The main goal of this volume is to look at social groups involved in economic activity who are not members of the palace-based institutions and "elites" in Late Bronze Age Mycenaean societies. This is not to say that examining palatial and other elites is not important — rather, we wish to consider a fuller range of the members of a society, their organization, their institutions, and their contributions to the economies of those societies. While we are interested in the non-elites, we still need to ascertain what we mean by palatial institutions and palatial elites if we are to understand those who are not part of those groups in the Mycenaean world. We must question our terminology, methodology,

ORCID 0000-0002-3911-9645
Department of Classics,
Florida State University
dpullen@fsu.edu

In *Social Groups and Production in Mycenaean Economies. Papers from the Langford Conference, Florida State University, Tallahassee, 24-25 February 2023*, edited by D. Pullen (2025), 11–20. Leiden: Sidestone Press.

and assumptions, and how we make use of them if we are going to make progress in understanding the past.

Nakassis (2013) has demonstrated that individuals named in the Linear B tablets at Pylos often recur in different contexts, suggesting that an individual could be involved in more than one role in the Pylian political economy. Some roles seem to be directly associated with the palace, while other roles seem to be associated with the regions, district capitals, and institutions outside the palace. This implies that individual actors operated at multiple levels within the hierarchy of the Pylian state (see, for example, Nakassis 2012). While we would not want to assume similar patterns among the Late Bronze Age states without direct evidence, in this instance the assumption of multiple roles played by an individual is well grounded in anthropological theory of the social persona. Indeed, it would be surprising to find that individuals did not play multiple roles in their interactions with others. It is likely, then, that local elites, interacting occasionally with the palace centers (with those interactions recorded in the Linear B tablets), also interacted with individuals and institutions in their own communities (with those interactions *not* recorded); in economic interactions, this would have involved market exchange, and not just at the local level: the tablets themselves even refer to wages and a few texts record "purchases" (the *o-no* tablets) of materials from named individuals (see Bennet and Halstead 201: 275-278 for a recent discussion of the *o-no* tablets). One of the characteristics of markets is not only that they facilitate the horizontal integration of many actors, but also that they provide opportunity for relationships to emerge between actors at different levels, that is, vertical integration. We would go so far as to suggest that one of the roles these elite individuals played was that of merchant, facilitating trade and exchange not only on the regional level within a Late Bronze Age kingdom but also at a larger scale, such as the Aegean merchants referred to in the Ugaritic texts. The presence of sets of weights in wealthy tombs (e.g., the lead weights found in the Vapheio tholos tomb, Schon 2015) could be seen to corroborate this suggestion of elite involvement in trade and exchange. But it need not be only elites who are involved in these activities. As Natalie Abell (2014, 2020) and others have shown, technologies and craftspeople can be organized independent of elites, and the processes of technological adoption and adaption can readily be a bottom-up enterprise not directed from those above. In a recent study of non-elite elements in the Pylos Linear B tablets dealing with land tenure, Susan Lupack (2024) shows that many professions, including craftspeople, own or lease land, with the plots sometimes of sizeable nature. What is especially interesting is her attempt to untangle the web of economic and personal relationships within the community (*damos*) through the multiple leasing arrangements with multiple plots of land.

A major problem is the lack of clearly identifying what we mean by "elites." Nosch identified a common conception of Mycenaean elites as an undefined aristocracy which includes senior officials, priests and other dignitaries, and the king and the royal family[1] (Nosch 2007: 299; cf. Nakassis 2013: 166: "in the traditional model of the Mycenaean state, members of the elite are defined as palatial officials"). As Nakassis and others have demonstrated, there are problems with this conception when we recognize that the "palace" is not the only institution of authority nor does it control the economy as in the now discredited top-down, redistributive economy espoused by Finley nearly 50 years ago (Finley 1973) and still featured in much recent scholarship outside the discipline of Aegean prehistory (see Nakassis 2024 for a critique of these views; see also chapters by Galaty and Parkinson and by Murray in this volume). Lupack, echoing Legarra Herrero (2016; see below), notes that the elite are not homogenous, but rather she identifies three different "spheres" of power in Messenia, each "distinct but often overlapping": the palatial administration, the sanctuaries and their religious personnel, and those who govern the sixteen districts (*damoi*) into which Late Bronze Age Messenia is divided (Lupack 2024: 2). This observation of Lupack fits firmly within the recent trend of scholars in Aegean prehistory who have shown that there is great variety and complexity to societies and their economies, not just those of the Late Bronze Age mainland with large portions of economic activity outside the purview of the "palaces" (to list but a few such studies: Voutsaki and Killen 2001; Galaty and Parkinson 2007; Pullen 2010; Galaty, Nakassis, and Parkinson 2011; Parkinson, Nakassis, and Galaty 2013; Nakassis, Galaty, and Parkinson 2016).

Still, however, the term "elite" is not often defined or explicitly conceptualized in discrete terms that can be analyzed. I would argue that our use (and overuse and abuse and misuse) of the term "elites" (and the corollary term "non-elite") as a "black box" of social and economic actors and action is seriously due for more rigorous examination. Borja Legarra Herrero (2016) is one of the few Aegean scholars to directly query the concept of "elites" and how they are used in Mediterranean archaeology and history of the Bronze and Iron Ages. As he shows, elites are most often invoked as the "catalysts for change," in that they are identified as the agents who adopt and adapt new technologies, materials, and ideas. Legarra Herrero criticizes the blanket application of a generic concept of "elite" without consideration of cultural or historical contexts, and suggests that often our conceptions of elites are based in part on modern concepts of elites and their behavior. For example, he finds fault

1 "Eine undefinierte Aristokratie, um höhere Beamte, Priester und andere Würdenträger und, vor allem, um den König und die königliche Familie."

with the idea that foreign items are linked to elites and their identification through their becoming "value-laden exotica," just as Murray did for Perati (see above). Instead, Legarra Herrero argues for the need to study "the complex relationship between elites, group agency, ideology, and connectivity in a clearly defined cultural context and through precise definitions of the terms based on archaeological evidence" (Legarra Herrero 2016: 38).

One social group that has the greatest potential for study is that of the household. The household is often presumed to have a role in economic activity. But we greatly lack any idea of what constitutes a "household," let alone how it might be defined, in Mycenaean Greece. Defining a household is still a topic of discussion in archaeology in general, as Cameron Wesson noted in 2008: "my review of one of the seminal anthropological volumes on the subject [Netting, Wilk, and Arnold 1984] reveals no less than *3 pages* devoted to definitions of the household" (Wesson 2008: 10, emphasis added). But as Wesson continues, "there is general agreement that the household is a basic social unit that involves both social and physical reproduction of the group's members" and "households are further defined by the productive activities performed by those members" (2008: 10). Wilk and Rathje (1982: 618), in one of the first attempts to theoretically address the concept of households, identified "Households [as] the level at which social groups articulate directly with economic and ecological processes. ... In fact, we can define the *household* as the most common social component of subsistence, the smallest and most abundant activity group." Most scholars emphasize that the "household is the minimal unit of economic production" (Wesson 2008: 11), but it "is not necessarily a corporate social unit bound together by kinship or other ties" (Ashmore and Wilk 1988: 3).

Jan Driessen first proposed the relevance of the Lévi-Straussian concept of the House (sociétés à maison; Lévi-Strauss 1983) for Aegean archaeology at the 2007 Political Economies conference (Driessen 2010). The House as a form of social and economic organization has great appeal; archaeologists working in Crete embraced it, producing several good studies. Fewer scholars working in Mainland Greece have explored the concept, in large part because of the paucity of good (or any) archaeological data on households. For example, of the 20 chapters in Relaki and Driessen's 2020 volume *Oikos* (Relaki and Driessen 2020), only one discusses the Late Bronze Age mainland, and that contribution by Kalliopi Efkleidou utilizes mortuary data to examine the possibility of House societies in mainland Greece. Corien Wiersma (2020) utilized the idea of House-centric societies, sometimes also called proto-House societies, in her examination of EH III through LH I mainland Greek societies. She sees an increasing importance of property and kinship to transmit property through the generations in the mortuary data of this period as indicative of moving from supposedly "egalitarian" kin-based societies to ranked societies — that is, characteristics of House-centric societies. Nakassis picks up, chronologically as it were, from where Wiersma leaves off, in the palatial Mycenaean period for his recent discussion of House societies (Nakassis 2022). As he points out, House societies are often thought of as transitional from kin-based societies of the earlier Middle Helladic period and the later hierarchical, stratified societies at the "state level" of the palatial period, in which state-level social organization is thought to be incompatible with Houses. Thus, there has been little attention paid to House societies during the palatial Mycenaean period because of preconceived notions of later Bronze Age social structure being highly centralized, hierarchical, and palatially dominant, by definition incompatible with Houses. One of the great values of Nakassis' article is how he emphasizes that the emergence of palaces and the palatial elite "entail structural transformations and reconfigurations rather than the imposition of essentially foreign systems" (Nakassis 2022: 135). The historical dynamic of development, change, and transformation are all too often ignored in our static ideas of Mycenaean social, political, and economic organization.

Even if the House is not a suitable model for explaining Mycenaean economies, the household remains as a prime construct to explore sociopolitical and economic organization in a society. This is not to say households are uniform in structure and organization, but they are, as noted above, often the basic social unit in a society. We need to approach the concept of the household with a more critical eye and evaluate the data to see whether we can identify the structure of organization and relationships of the social group that forms a household.

Generally, it is assumed that a household maps onto a "domestic" structure (though Driessen's work on the sociétés à maison has shown that we shouldn't immediately conclude that), and thus by identifying the activities that occur within and surrounding those structures one can talk about the production and consumption patterns of a household. But we have appallingly few domestic structures in Mycenaean archaeology with good contextual and stratigraphic data (see Shelton's contribution in this volume for a notable exception). The next few comments are based on Pascal Darcque's invaluable 2005 compilation *L'habitat mycénien*.[2]

- Of the hundreds of known Mycenaean sites, only 36 have provided direct evidence for structures that can be studied to any significant degree.
- Of those 36 sites, only 11 produced 5 or more buildings that could be studied in any detail: Mycenae, Tiryns, Thebes, Nichoria, Malthi, Thermon, Asine, Midea,

2 Undoubtedly these figures could be adjusted to reflect recent work, but the overall picture would not, I think, change all that much.

Korakou, Gla, and Chrysso (to which we can now add Iklaina, Mitrou, Dimini, Kanakia, and Lazarides, among others).
- Darcque lists 183 buildings for the entire Mycenaean world, from LH I through LH IIIC, out of which 626 rooms can be measured. This of course includes the palaces and other potentially non-domestic structures.
- 89 of those 183 buildings are found at the three palatial sites of Mycenae, Tiryns, and Thebes, plus Gla. (To this, our work at Kalamianos can add 55 buildings that can be measured to an extent similar to the measurements of Darcque and some 195 measurable rooms.)

How can we identify households with such a small sample size? Jamie Aprile's use of intra-site distributional data at Nichoria is one of the few such studies that have attempted to look at household-level economic data (Aprile 2013). She went beyond the published reports into the excavation archives to gain a fuller picture of the assemblages within structures. While her emphasis was on examining the economic relationships between Nichoria and the palatial center at Pylos, and she makes several assumptions about "elites" versus non-elites, I think her approach is one that could be followed at other sites. In this volume, both Kim Shelton and Natalie Abell attempt to fill out the picture of economic activity at the level of the household. Shelton's work at Mycenae's Petsas House shows how much information about a household one can glean from careful excavation and recording, multiple types of analyses on a wide variety of material remains, and detailed contextual analysis. Abell's work at Ayia Irini on Kea is a good example of using comparative data from several structures (and sites) to generate a picture of the variety of ceramic and textile production strategies in play at the same time.

This volume

This volume is the outcome of the Langford Conference on "Social Groups and Production in Mycenaean Economies," held at Florida State University in Tallahassee in February 2023. The inspiration for that conference lay in the many conversations I have had over the years with Dimitri Nakassis, Bill Parkinson, Mike Galaty, and others, following on the 2007 Langford conference on Political Economies of the Aegean Bronze Age (collected papers in Pullen 2010). The charge of the 2007 conference was to take an explicitly comparative approach to the political economies in the Aegean, and to more carefully examine the variation between Crete and the Mainland, but also within those areas and through time. Subsequently, sessions organized by Nakassis, Parkinson, and Galaty on Aegean Bronze Age economies presented at the annual meetings of the Archaeological Institute of America in 2009, 2012, and 2014 and published in the *American Journal of Archaeology* on redistribution (Nakassis, Parkinson, and Galaty 2011), markets (Parkinson, Nakassis and Galaty 2013), and in the *Journal of Mediterranean Archaeology* on reciprocity (Nakassis, Galaty, and Parkinson 2016) in the Aegean Bronze Age, as well as a session at the 2018 meeting of the European Association of Archaeologists in Barcelona on merchants, markets, and exchange, built some of the groundwork for the 2023 conference. But more specifically it was discussions with Nakassis about the concept of House societies in the Mycenaean world, first presented by Driessen at the 2007 Langford Conference (Driessen 2010) for the Aegean setting, in conjunction with his contribution to a recent volume edited by Juan Carlos Moreno García (Nakassis 2022), that got me thinking we should explore other social and kin groups in Mycenaean societies through another Langford conference. While I personally think that the household — not the same as House societies à la Lévi-Strauss (Lévi-Strauss 1983) — is a critical level of analysis we need to explore for looking at Mycenaean economies, I charged the contributors to look at the full range of possible social, kin, and non-kin groups from individual actors to the palatial elites and their involvement in production, consumption, and distribution in the Late Bronze Age Greek mainland.

In his contribution to this volume **Dimitri Nakassis** examines the Linear B evidence for socioeconomic organization in Mycenaean palatial societies. His analysis identifies some of the terminology used in the tablets to describe social structure and institutions as the palatial officials sought to oversee components of the political economy. Immediately we are confronted with the situation whereby we can identify groups and types of elites, even the names of some individuals, yet the non-elite are often not recorded other than numerically. Scholars, Nakassis argues, have assumed a uniformity of the status of the non-elite, even to the degree of presuming widespread slavery — indeed he faults many scholars of simplifying or "flattening" the lives of the non-elites, just as the palatial authorities did. The non-elite are not, in fact, uniform. He concludes that despite the large number of individuals named in the tablets in various capacities, the administrators depended more on households for the operation of the economy. These households likewise were not uniform, Nakassis maintains, but vary in size and complexity and included both elite and non-elite members. It is by examining non-elite membership in these households that we can begin to flesh out the lives of non-elites in Mycenaean society. Nakassis' contribution sets the stage, then, for looking at the contributions of households and non-elites to the economies of Mycenaean societies.

The structural transformation and reconfiguration of social organization, especially the House in Minoan Crete from the LM IB to LM IIIA2, is explored in depth by **Jan Driessen** in this volume. He argues that the Minoan House as he defines it is a "bottom-up, archaeological data-driven hypothesis," one that is culturally and historically specific; he thus avoids the problems such as those that Nakassis (2022) identified in trying to make the archaeology of Minoan Crete fit into the Levi-Straussian model of the House. In particular, Driessen looks at Minoan Crete after the extensive LM IB troubles that left the island unrecognizable physically and socially, to see what effects the new "more individualizing types of elites" of LM II found at Knossos and elsewhere might have on Minoan social organization. He suggests continuity in occupation by the same intergenerational units that comprise the Minoan Houses at several sites, despite the different sequences in rebuilding and building anew, whereby new, smaller structures of LM II are followed by larger complexes in LM IIIA (e.g., at Sissi). Can those larger complexes be considered Houses?

We have made progress in looking at social and political variability across time and space in the Aegean. The 2007 Langford Conference on Political Economies, many of whose contributors continue to work on this topic and are represented in the current volume, made important contributions to the notion of variability within the Aegean. The influence of the 2007 Langford conference was clear at the 2019 Political Geographies of the Aegean Bronze Age conference, organized by Jan Driessen and Gert-Jan van Wijngaarden, where most participants accepted the notion of variability within Mainland polities (van Wijngaarden and Driessen 2022). Still, there continue to be holdouts who take a "One-Ring-to-Rule-Them-All" view of a politically and socially unified Mycenaean world (e.g., Kelder 2010; Eder and Jung 2015). This viewpoint unfortunately obscures the great variability and historical trajectories apparent in the archaeological record, and stifles detailed examination of the ancient economy if it doesn't fit this monolithic, top-down model. **Michael Galaty and William Parkinson**, in their contribution to this volume, tackle head-on this view and its misconceptualization of the archaeological record. They demonstrate that economic *non*-integration of Mycenaean polities is quite clear in archaeological data and the Linear B evidence: there is virtually no evidence for inter-polity or foreign trade by the palaces in the Linear B evidence. The Mycenaean economies are not centralized or specialized in themselves, as has been shown repeatedly in the rejections of Finley's model. In sum, as Galaty and Parkinson conclude, there is no evidence for one "economically integrated Mycenaean state" — in fact the evidence is for the opposite.

Sarah Murray examines whether non-palatial organizations that are not households or other kin-based groups function as part of Mycenaean economies. She explores the utility of the economic concept of the "firm" (a "hierarchical, non-state organization that [is] vertically integrated and encompasses multiple stages of production and/or distribution within [its] unified structure") in Aegean archaeology. She argues for its usefulness as a framework to look at economic actors at a wide range of scales and to fill conceptual gaps between palace-level and individuals or household-level economic activity. Murray's contribution is the first to explicitly use these concepts in Aegean archaeology, and is part of the recent trend that recognizes the great variety in organization, institutions, actors, and economic modes in ancient economies. Unfortunately, as Murray and several other contributors to this volume argue, Finley's (1973) outmoded picture of static, monolithic states in the Late Bronze Age Aegean as centralized, palatial bureaucracies engaged in extensive redistribution still prevails outside the discipline of Aegean prehistory (and even sometimes within — see the chapter by Galaty and Parkinson in this volume). Murray offers several significant insights and compelling suggestions about institutions and organization of economic activity, including the suggestion of guilds and cooperatives (see also Shelton's contribution for the possibility of guilds). And in the spirit of the 2007 Langford Conference, Murray makes extensive use of comparative material, especially with the novel use of later historical examples.

One area of the ancient economy where some of us have explored the role of non-palatial actors is that of merchants in the broadest sense. It is clear to several scholars of prehistoric Aegean political economy that market exchange was one of the primary modes of exchange operating in the Late Bronze Age Aegean world (see the papers in Parkinson, Nakassis and Galaty 2013). Even some of the realms of craft production with significant palatial interest, such as metalworking and textiles, must have had a non-palatial component in their production and distribution to the populace beyond the palatial elite and their followers. Market exchange does not mean that there must be physical marketplaces, since those activities can take place in locations that lack archaeologically identifiable characteristics, such as along roads; the frequency of markets is also a factor in whether there is a need for formal marketplaces. Market exchange can be supported by infrastructures other than physical marketplaces, such as harbor installations or roads. Tom Tartaron and I have suggested that the establishment of the harbor town at Mycenaean Kalamianos on the Saronic Gulf was intended to take advantage of and compete in the increasing variety of trade in the Saronic Gulf, including local, medium, and long-distance trade (Pullen and Tartaron 2007; Pullen 2020). The well-known Mycenaean road systems in the Argolid include segments that seem to function more for local circulation of people and goods, than for other functions such as defense of borders. Road systems, like small maritime worlds, link communities, facilitating horizontal integration among the inhabitants of different communities. **Tom Tartaron** continues his explorations of Mycenaean maritime economies (Tartaron 2013) in his contribution by focusing on the people and communities who linked the various networks of the coastscape, landscape, and seascape through the anchorages, harbors, and ports. Tartaron utilizes the concepts of network theory to examine the types of links and connections. He argues for "strong links" among the maritime communities in the Saronic Gulf, but "weak links" between coastal sites such as Kalamianos and the Argive (palatial) centers. Thus, maritime communities often have strong links forming coastal "small worlds," but these communities at least in the Mycenaean world are part of larger-scale systems in the palatial period.

Examining ancient economies from a theoretical point of view is extremely important, but we also must test how our ideas fit the archaeological data. The pervasiveness of ceramics in the archaeological record and the detailed attention ceramics receive from archaeologists provide a good "test case" for examining the role of social and kin groups in the production of goods in Mycenaean economies. For this reason, I have included contributions from several scholars who work directly with ceramic production, at various scales, including at the household level and at a near industrial scale at a palatial center. The three detailed discussions of pottery communities by Natalie Abell, Kim Shelton, and Peter Day and Eleni Kardamaki are linked through their consideration of historical contingencies, context, and variability at multiple scales in operation in ceramic production and composition. Long-enduring traditions in how pots are made are considered in all three papers. All three eschew the old static, top-down model of Mycenaean economies and instead utilize analytical programs (especially Day and Kardamaki), geographic comparisons of adaptation and resistance to technological changes (Abell), and detailed contextual analysis of one workshop (Shelton) to construct bottom-up approaches to ceramic production and consumption. With these bottom-up approaches all three contributions put people into the production and distribution of pottery. As these three papers demonstrate, there is so much more involved when we identify a ceramic workshop or invoke ceramics as a component of a Mycenaean economy.

Natalie Abell's contribution uses the concepts of communities and their set, or "constellation," of practices within the framework of networks in the Aegean during the later Middle Bronze Age and early Late Bronze Age. In line with the theme of variability, she shows how different social groups can operate in different ways within one economic activity — ceramic production — which can lead to significant differences in material culture. Abel explores how craft communities in the Cycladic Islands reacted differently among themselves to the "Minoanization" phenomenon, and how differently they reacted from Mainland societies. The relative lack of shared knowledge between the Cycladic and Mainland craft communities is at odds with the geographic proximity and intense metallurgical interactions. She explores why this difference through the lens of knowledge brokers, and indicates some interesting avenues to explore.

The Petsas House at Mycenae is well known as the location of a major ceramic workshop dating to the earlier palatial period. **Kim Shelton** digs deep into the evidence for the organization of the social group working and living in the building. Shelton argues the organization of the potters was changing from a multigenerational, family-based group producing for domestic use by others to a more hierarchical or stratified group with professional craftspeople and non-kin related individuals who produced on a larger scale and for a more specialized market that probably included a foreign dimension. That the household was successful is indicated by the wealth displayed in the construction and decoration of the domestic areas of the structure, yet at the same time room for the large-scale production and storage (and marketing?) of the ceramic products formed an integral part of the overall structure. Shelton has identified a whole continuum in scale of economic actors, from individuals whose forming and painting styles can be recognized to the larger group of workers constituting the workshop, and to the household itself as economic actor. Shelton argues in part based on the great variety of shapes in very large quantities in production and in storage, along with evidence for experimentation and innovation, that the workshop operated with a high degree of independence from the palace; indeed, the palace was but one customer. She also argues for a relatively high socio-economic status for the individuals in charge of the workshop as it responds to consumer and market demands, with some products targeted for overseas consumption (e.g., pictorial style kraters painted for Cypriot consumers). She suggests guilds or some other professional groups were at work in the Petsas House, much like Murray postulates in her paper.

Using four regionally and contextually diverse cases of ceramic crafting communities, **Peter Day and Eleftheria Kardamaki** examine the dynamics of ceramic vessel production and consumption as the craftspeople respond to tradition and change demand. They are especially interested in the patterns of production over the *longue durée*, in the degree to which long established patterns of traditions are disrupted and transformed (or not), such as the adoption of Mycenaean fineware shapes and decoration. Instead of a top-down approach to ceramic production, they construct a bottom-up approach that considers the great variety in historical traditions, contexts of ceramic production, and changing demands and need by those consuming the ceramic products. Day and Kardamaki emphasize the *social* aspect of the *chaînes opératoires* and how this approach of "ways of practice" can lead to a better understanding of the members of these potting communities. The long-lasting technical traditions involved are explicitly linked by them to membership in the potting community through the transmission of knowledge; learning these ways of doing is fundamental to being part of the group. Their discussion of the transmission of knowledge fits very well with Abell's idea of knowledge brokers.

The contributions of this volume

The papers in this volume do not claim to be the final word on social groups, elites, non-elites, and production in Mycenaean economies, but they do make important contributions to these topics and raise new issues. Several important and interrelated themes are evident in these papers, themes that merit greater attention in our future work: the questioning of our terminology, methodology, and assumptions; the dimensions of complexity, variability, and scale; and dynamism of temporal change. These themes are found not just in the study of Mycenaean economies, but indeed can be invoked in other fields in the archaeology of the Aegean and elsewhere.

Perhaps one of the most fundamental contributions is the call to question our terminology. This call for more precise definitions of our concepts and terms — or even just for definitions — is not new to this volume, but characterizes much recent research in Aegean archaeology. Several of those scholars who have recently voiced these calls to question our terminology are represented in this volume. Too many of our concepts mask great complexity behind simple terms, such as "the economy," "control of production," or "elite"; this situation derives in part from a lack of precision in our terminology. One of the main contributions of many of the papers is to tease apart the tangled webs of these complex ideas. For instance, it is clear we need to move away from the simple dichotomies of elite versus non-elite and examine the wide continuum of actors in the economy at various scales and in various configurations. The elite are not a monolithic entity, nor for that matter are the non-elite. There are other dimensions along which people can be organized in the economies than the simple distinction of those in charge vs. those not, such as supra-household groups including the Minoan House, guilds, or firms. When we consider the full range of the economies of Mycenaean polities, a focus on elites (whether palatial or not) leaves out much of what goes on. Our use of certain terms, such as slave, or assumptions, such as women's roles in the economy, often are biased by modern notions of these terms and need reassessment.

Intimately related with complexity is variability — gone are the days of simplistic, monolithic models that are often top-down and do not recognize the great range of possibilities and configurations. Several scholars in this volume call for models that recognize bottom-up approaches based on archaeological data in specific cultural and historical contexts and that do not try to make the data fit monolithic or over-generalizing models. Over the last couple of decades we have seen a shift from monolithic models and interpretations of Bronze Age societies, in their political organization, social organization, and economic activities, to approaches which uses multiple scales of analysis and that emphasize social and political variability across time and space. Generalizing models are still very useful — take for instance the comparison by Parkinson and Galaty of Minoan and Mycenaean social-political organization (Parkinson and Galaty 2007). They showed that there are some fundamental differences in how societies on Crete are organized as more heterarchical and corporate from how societies on the Bronze Age mainland are organized as more hierarchical and networked. But as Parkinson and Galaty in their subsequent work have shown, *within* the world of Mycenaean[3] polities there is great variation in social, political, and economic organization.

The palimpsest of archaeological data can be at odds with our desire for a historical or temporal dimension to our studies. Equally problematic can be the over-reliance on data that represent but a short segment of time; the study of Mycenaean economies is especially fraught, given that evidence from the Linear B tablets which originate from the final months of the palatial administration at Pylos is extrapolated to characterize the entirety of the Late Bronze Age (and all the palatial centers). This results in a static, unchanging continuous present for the several centuries of the palatial Mycenaean phase. As many of the contributors to this volume have shown, looking at the structural transformations of socio-political and economic organization can be more informative, and help us to understand the variability we see among the different Late Bronze Age polities. Issues of adoption, adaptation, resilience and perseverance can be brought out in our studies when we consider the diachronic dimension to societies and their economies.

Our understanding of Mycenaean society and the people who participated in the economy has come a long way since the centralized, redistributive palace model of Moses Finley (1973). We now understand that the Late Bronze Age Aegean was not a monolithic unit, but that there was a multitude of actors, groups, and institutions involved in the economies of the different polities, and which changed through time. Though much remains to be done, the contributors to this volume show us many innovative and thought-provoking ways to proceed. We hope the readers will agree.

3 The very term "Mycenaean" is a generalizing one, and unfortunately our usage of it to describe the various societies and cultures of the Late Bronze Age mainland (and sometimes beyond) and the chronological period they occupy often obscures the great regional and temporal variability we see in the archaeological record. I do not, however, foresee us giving up using the term "Mycenaean" any more than we might give up the old tripartite Early, Middle, and Late Helladic chronological scheme with all its implied evolutionary baggage.

Bibliography

Abell, N., 2014. Migration, Mobility, and Craftspeople in the Aegean Bronze Age: A Case Study from Ayia Irini on the Island of Kea. *World Archaeology* 46: 551–568.

Abell, N., 2020. Rethinking Household-Based Production at Ayia Irini, Kea: An Examination of Technology and Organization in a Bronze Age Community of Practice. *American Journal of Archaeology* 124: 381–416.

Aprile, J., 2013. The New Political Economy of Nichoria: Using Intrasite Distributional Data to Investigate Regional Institutions. *American Journal of Archaeology* 117: 429–436.

Ashmore, W., and R. R. Wilk, 1988. Household and Community in the Mesoamerican Past. In *Household and Community in the Mesoamerican Past*, edited by R. R. Wilk and W. Ashmore, 1–27. Albuquerque: University of New Mexico Press.

Bennet, J., and P. Halstead, 2014. O-no! Writing and Righting Redistribution. In *KE-RA-ME-JA: Studies Presented to Cynthia W. Shelmerdine*, edited by D. Nakassis, J. Gulizio, and S. A. James, 271–282. Philadelphia: INSTAP Academic Press.

Darcque, P., 2005. *L'Habitat mycénien: Formes et fonctions de l'espace bâti en Grèce continentale à la fin du IIe millénaire avant J.-C.* Bibliothèque des Écoles françaises d'Athènes et de Rome 319. Paris: École française d'Athènes.

Driessen, J., 2010. Spirit of Place: Minoan Houses as Major Actors. In *Political Economies of the Aegean Bronze Age: Papers from the Langford Conference, Florida State University, Tallahassee, 22–24 February 2007*, edited by D. J. Pullen, 35–65. Oxford: Oxbow Books.

Eder, B., and R. Jung, 2015. <Unus pro omnibus, omnes pro uno>: The Mycenaean Palace System. In *Tradition and Innovation in the Mycenaean Palatial Polities*, edited by J. Weilhartner and F. Ruppenstein, 113–140. Mykenische Studien 34. Vienna: Austrian Academy of Sciences.

Finley, M. I., 1973. *The Ancient Economy*. Berkeley: University of California Press.

Galaty, M. L., and W. A. Parkinson, eds., 2007. *Rethinking Mycenaean Palaces II: Revised and Expanded Second Edition*. Monograph 60. Los Angeles: University of California at Los Angeles, Cotsen Institute of Archaeology.

Galaty, M. L., D. Nakassis, and W. A. Parkinson, eds., 2011. Forum: Redistribution in Aegean Palatial Societies. *American Journal of Archaeology* 115: 175–244.

Kelder, J. M., 2010. *The Kingdom of Mycenae: A Great Kingdom in the Late Bronze Age Aegean*. Bethesda, MD: CDL Press.

Legarra Herrero, B., 2016. An Elite-Infested Sea: Interaction and Change in Mediterranean Paradigms. In *Of Odysseys and Oddities: Scales and Modes of Interaction Between Prehistoric Aegean Societies and Their Neighbours*, edited by B. Molloy, 25–51. Oxford: Oxbow Books.

Lévi-Strauss, C., 1983. *The Way of the Masks*. London: Jonathan Cape Ltd.

Lupack, S., 2024. How Elitist Were Typical Mycenaean Communities? Investigating Relative Status in Mycenaean Damoi Through the Landholders of the Pylos Ep and Ea Series. *Oxford Journal of Archaeology* 43: 226–236.

Murray, S. C., 2017. *The Collapse of the Mycenaean Economy: Trade, Imports, and Institutions, 1300–700 BCE*. Cambridge: Cambridge University Press.

Murray, S. C., 2018. Imported Exotica and Mortuary Ritual at Perati in Late Helladic IIIC East Attica. *American Journal of Archaeology* 122: 33–64.

Murray, S. C., 2023. Eastern Mediterranean Bronze Age Trade in Archaeological Perspective: A Review of Interpretative and Empirical Developments. *Journal of Archaeological Research* 31: 395–447.

Nakassis, D., 2012. Prestige and Interest: Feasting and the King at Mycenaean Pylos. *Hesperia* 81: 1–30.

Nakassis, D., 2013. *Individuals and Society in Mycenaean Pylos*. Mnemosyne Supplements 358. Leiden: Brill.

Nakassis, D., 2022. Communities, 'Houses', and Political Organisation in the Mycenaean World. In *From House Societies to States: Early Political Organisation from Antiquity to the Middle Ages*, edited by J. C. Moreno García,123–140. Multidisciplinary Approaches to Ancient Societies 3. Oxford: Oxbow Books.

Nakassis, D., 2024. Before the Economy? Growth, Institutions, and the Late Bronze Age. In *Models, Methods, and Morality - Assessing Modern Approaches to the Greco-Roman Economy*, edited by S. Murray and S. Bernard, 151–184. Cham, Switzerland: Springer Nature: Palgrave/MacMillan. DOI:10.1007/978-3-031-58210-3_6.

Nakassis, D., M. L. Galaty, and W. A. Parkinson, eds., 2016. Discussion and Debate: Reciprocity in Aegean Palatial Societies: Gifts, Debt, and the Foundations of Economic Exchange. *Journal of Mediterranean Archaeology* 29: 61–132.

Netting, R. McC., R. R. Wilk, and E. J. Arnold, eds., 1984. *Households: Comparative and Historical Studies of the Domestic Group*. Berkeley: University of California Press.

Nosch, M.-L. B., 2007. Eliten und Elitenbildung in der Mykenologie. In *Keimelion: Elitenbildung und Elitärer Konsum von der Mykenischen Palastzeit bis zur Homerischen Epoche. The Formation of Elites and Elitist Lifestyles from Mycenaean Palatial Times to the Homeric Period. Akten des internationalen Kongresses vom 3. Bis 5. Februar 2005 in Salzburg*, edited by E. Alram-Stern and G. Nightingale, 299–310. Veröffentlichungen der Mykenischen Kommission 27, Österreichische Akademie der Wissenschaften Philosophisch-Historische Klasse

Denkschriften 350. Wien: Verlag der Österreichischen Akademie der Wissenschaften.
Parkinson, W. A., and M. L. Galaty, 2007. Primary and Secondary States in Perspective: An Integrated Approach to State Formation in the Prehistoric Aegean. *American Anthropologist* 109: 113–129.
Parkinson, W. A., D. Nakassis, and M. L. Galaty, eds., 2013. Forum: Crafts, Specialists, and Markets in Mycenaean Greece. *American Journal of Archaeology* 117: 413–459.
Pullen, D. J., ed., 2010. *Political Economies of the Aegean Bronze Age: Papers from the Langford Conference, Florida State University, Tallahassee, 22–24 February 2007.* Oxford: Oxbow Books.
Pullen, D. J., 2020. Merchants, Ports, and Market Exchange: Strategies for Coping in an Interconnected Mycenaean World. In *Communication Uneven. Acceptance of and Resistance to Foreign Influences in the Connected Ancient Mediterranean*, edited by J. Driessen, 189–202. Aegis 20. Louvain-la-Neuve: Presses universitaires de Louvain.
Pullen, D. J., and T. F. Tartaron, 2007. Where's the Palace? The Lack of State Formation in the Late Bronze Age Corinthia. In *Rethinking Mycenaean Palaces II: Revised and Expanded Second Edition*, edited by M. L. Galaty and W. A. Parkinson, 146–158. Monograph 60. Los Angeles: University of California at Los Angeles, Cotsen Institute of Archaeology.
Relaki, M., and J. Driessen, eds., 2020. *Oikos. Archaeological Approaches to House Societies in the Bronze Age Aegean.* Aegis 19. Louvain-la-Neuve: Presses universitaires de Louvain.
Schon, R., 2015. Weight Sets: Identification and Analysis. *Cambridge Archaeological Journal* 25: 477–494.
Tartaron, T. F., 2013. *Maritime Networks in the Mycenaean World.* Cambridge: Cambridge University Press.
van Wijngaarden, G. J., and J. Driessen, eds., 2022. *Political Geographies of the Bronze Age Aegean: Proceedings of the Joint Workshop of the Belgian School at Athens (EBSA) and the Netherlands Institute at Athens (NIA), May 28 to 31, 2019.* BABESCH Supplement 43. Leuven: Peeters.
Voutsaki, S., and J. Killen, eds., 2001. *Economy and Politics in the Mycenaean Palace States. Proceedings of a Conference held on 1–3 July 1999 in the Faculty of Classics, Cambridge.* Cambridge Philological Society Supplementary Volume 27. Cambridge: Cambridge Philological Society.
Wesson, C. B., 2008. *Households and Hegemony: Early Creek Prestige Goods, Symbolic Capital, and Social Power.* Lincoln: University of Nebraska Press.
Wiersma, C., 2020. House(centric) Societies on the Prehistoric Greek Mainland. *Oxford Journal of Archaeology* 39: 141–158. DOI:10.1111/ojoa.12190.
Wilk, R. R., and W. L. Rathje, 1982. Household Archaeology. *American Behavioral Scientist* 25: 617–639.

Reading Between the Lines

Textual Evidence for Socioeconomic Organization in the Late Bronze Age

Dimitri Nakassis

Abstract
Despite the volume of recent research on economic organization in Mycenaean palaces, there remains little consensus on what the appropriate scale of analysis is, and in particular, what the dominant unit of production and consumption was. Although Linear B texts certainly cannot resolve this issue on their own, they do provide critical context in two ways. They directly provide emic terminology for the various institutions that participated in the workings of palatial administration, and they indirectly suggest the existence of organizational units that are not explicitly named but can be understood to underlie economic or administrative systems monitored by palatial officials. This paper reviews the textual evidence adduced thus far, and attempts to show that it can be taken further. Reading further between the lines, we can see that Linear B administrations relied not so much on specific individuals as on households of various sizes and levels of complexity that included members of both the elite and the non-elite.

Introduction
Despite the massive quantity of research on economic organization in the Late Bronze Age, there remains little consensus on what the appropriate scale of analysis is and what the dominant unit of production and consumption was. As Jan Driessen (2010: 35) observes, "any political economy is a reflection of the *social* organization of production, exchange and consumption… it is not possible to talk about *Minoan* political economy so long as no serious progress is made on its societal organization." The same could certainly be said of Mycenaean society and economy: so much of the discussion has focused on the economic role of the palaces and the political elite that other social dimensions of economic production and consumption have remained largely unexamined. In short, to make progress in our understanding of economic systems, we need to do a better job of comprehending social structures.

Although Linear B texts certainly cannot on their own detail all the social structures at work, they do provide critical context in two ways: first, they can directly supply emic terminology for the various structures and institutions that interfaced with the palatial administration. Secondly, and I will argue more importantly, they can indirectly or obliquely suggest organizational units that are not explicitly named or described in any detail, but can be understood to underlie political economies. I will argue that reading further between the lines, we can observe that Linear B administrations relied on households of various sizes and levels of complexity. I suggest moreover that these

ORCID 0000-0002-0783-2702
Department of Classics,
University of Colorado
Boulder
dimitri.nakassis@colorado.edu

In *Social Groups and Production in Mycenaean Economies. Papers from the Langford Conference, Florida State University, Tallahassee, 24-25 February 2023*, edited by D. Pullen (2025), 21–34. Leiden: Sidestone Press.

households included members of the elite and the non-elite and thus a focus on these structures sheds light on the lives of upper- and lower-status individuals.

Between a rock and a hard place: institutions and individuals

The failure to theorize Mycenaean society derives from the historical development of its study. Post-war, post-decipherment syntheses focused on the institutional titles in Linear B texts. A bureaucratic hierarchy surmounted by the king (*wa-na-ka, wanax*) was constructed and mapped onto society, which thus became a mirror image (or perhaps better, a projection) of palatial administration (see Figure 2.1). This model, which was based on the presumed economic monopoly enjoyed by palatial institutions, began to collapse in the late 1980s. On the one hand, Paul Halstead (1988; 1992) observed that the economic control exerted by the palaces was partial and directed at specific activities and industries. On the other hand, there was renewed attention to non-palatial institutions, especially the village community (*da-mo, dāmos*), and its relationship to the palatial center (Deger-Jalkotzy 1983; de Fidio 1987, 1992; Halstead 2001; cf. Lupack 1999).

Stronger criticism of the managerial model of Mycenaean society tended to focus on individuals and agency (Shelmerdine 2011; Nakassis 2013a), for two

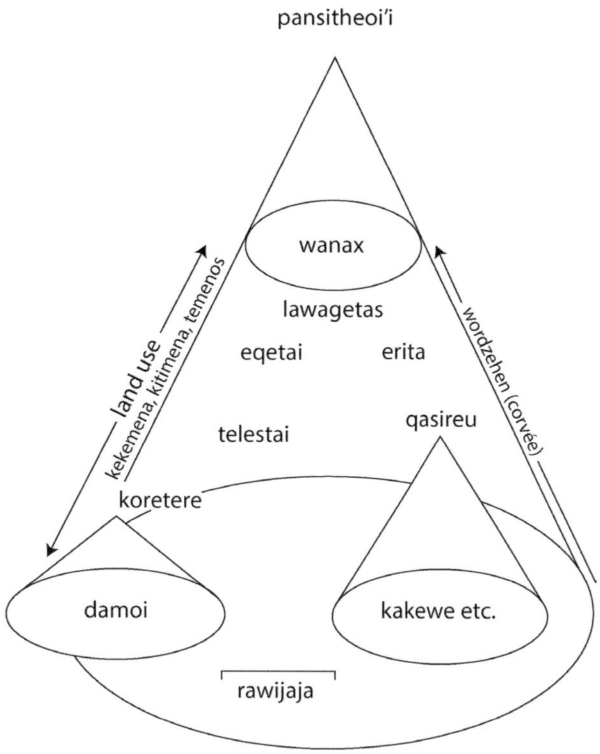

Figure 2.1. "The Mycenaean social hierarchy in Linear B tablets" of Klaus Kilian (1988: 273) (redrawn by D. Nakassis).

reasons. One is the nature of the evidence: the commonest type of word in Linear B are the personal names of individuals, mostly men, who interfaced with the palatial administration and who were responsible for a variety of activities under that purview. The second is the traditional opposition of agency and structure: when faced with a model in which society was entirely subordinated to, and indeed determined by, a managerial order, it was perhaps reasonable to observe that social relationships are never determined by institutions but are a dynamic process involving knowledgeable agents and social structures. Indeed, my own work was strongly influenced by anthropological and sociological theorizations of the structure-agency relation (Nakassis 2013b). Yet in leaning into the importance of individual Pylians, this work tended to portray them as typically Mediterranean "competitive aggrandizers in a zero-sum political game" (Nakassis 2013a: 177), resulting in an extremely shallow theory of the individual and of society.

Thus, the addition of individual agency to the understanding of Pylian (and by extension Mycenaean) society arguably accounts much better for the evidence at our disposal, but the resulting synthesis is nevertheless vulnerable to a variety of criticisms (Nakassis 2013a: 177; 2022: 123–124; 2023). Indeed, neither the managerial nor the structure-and-agency models of Mycenaean society have made any meaningful attempt to theorize social organization in the way that Driessen (2010) has advocated for Crete: the former because it views non-palatial structures as effectively irrelevant in the face of overwhelming palatial power, the latter because of its narrow focus on using the named individuals that crowd our texts to oppose the former model.

Careful analysis of the textual evidence suggests that it is not entirely correct to understand the personal names of individuals in the text as persons, since names certainly function, at least much of the time, as an administrative shorthand (Nakassis 2023). That is to say, not only do names primarily indicate the responsible party for a task (rather than the person who is actually doing the work), but they also must have stood in for or indicated larger groups of persons, especially in cases where a single person is responsible for a wide variety of activities (Nakassis 2022). For example, the Knossian collector named *we-we-si-jo* was responsible for 33 flocks in nine different places in central Crete; the Pylian collector *a-ke-o* for 28 flocks in at least twelve different places in both provinces of Messenia. Such persons must have had extensive networks of kin or dependents to carry out so many administrative tasks concurrently across such a large expanse (Nakassis 2013a: 157–160).

In short, scholars of Mycenaean society have thought a great deal about the governing institution and its elite without giving nearly as much consideration to the social units and structures that provided the basis for the constitution of social life (but see Lupack 2011). This is understandable, given the nature of our evidence; the fact that virtually all the texts are written by and for the palatial administration makes it difficult to investigate other institutions and non-elite groups (Bennet and Shelmerdine 2008: 308). To break the impasse that we find ourselves in, however, we must make progress in precisely this area, reading between the lines to tease out more from the texts than they reveal at first sight.

Institutions in the texts

As Koenraad Verboven and colleagues (2007: 47) once observed, "there is no point trying to read between the lines if you do not know what is *on* the lines." Before proceeding to the thornier task of studying social units that are only obliquely mentioned in the texts, a brief review of those institutions that are directly mentioned is therefore in order. To begin with, we should note that there are no clearly recognizable or distinguishable terms for the palace (as a physical structure or as an institution) or for religious establishments (but see further below), as there were in other contemporary Late Bronze Age societies. Other institutions for which we do have emic terminology are not well-attested, but have been subjected to extensive analyses by textual scholars (Carlier 2016; Shelmerdine 2008, with references).

The institution most amply documented in our texts is the *dāmos* (*da-mo*; plural *dāmoi*). At Pylos, *dāmoi* contribute staples for a feast (PY Un 718), manage agricultural estates (PY E- series) and in that capacity engage in a dispute with the priestess Eritha over the status of her land-holding (PY Ep 704.5–6; cf. Eb 297); men in the *dāmos* (*o-pi-da-mi-jo, opidāmioi*) are responsible for fattening pigs (PY Cn 608), presumably for sacrifice (Piquero Rodríguez 2019: 166–170, 211–212). Michel Lejeune (1965: 6) defined the *dāmos* as a local administrative entity with an agricultural function ("une entité administrative locale à vocation agricole"), but this description seems somewhat too restrictive, and most scholars have since understood *dāmoi* as village communities, although how autonomous they were from the palace remains debated (Carlier 2016: 668, 672; De Fidio 1987: 149; De Fidio 1992: 196; Killen 1998; Lupack 2011: 214; Halstead 2001: 50).

The difficulties in analyzing the *dāmos* are typical, given the evidence at our disposal. It seems to have been an important institution, but because our texts are written by palatial administrators, the evidence points primarily towards the function of the institution as it applied to palatial interests, not the meaning of the institution to the community. Some scholars have argued that *dāmoi* were complex corporate entities that engaged in a range of activities dealing with property and other economic activities, rather than being mere appendages of the palatial administration at a local level (Lupack 2011: 214, with references). The fact that four personal names and one official title are compounded with *dāmos* (García Ramón 2006: 48–50; 2010: 76–87; cf. Palaima 1999: 372–373) may corroborate the notion that the term was not purely administrative in function but had some wider social currency (see Table 2.1).

We can therefore probably conclude that a communal village institution is an important component of the social order. But it is difficult to go further than this: the evidence gives us some insight into the internal operation of the *dāmos* but not how it contributes to the formation of social life (see Lupack 2011: 212–215, with references). Thus, the *dāmos*, while extensively studied and analyzed, remains something of a black box for an analysis of Mycenaean society.

Other institutions named in the tablets differ from the *dāmos* in that they are always associated with names. They are also of special interest because they have been interpreted as kinship or residential groups. Two can be discussed together as a pair: *geronsiā* (*ke-ro-si-ja*) and *g*^{w}*asilēwiā* (*qa-si-re-wi-ja*). The latter seems to indicate a work group under the supervision of a local chief (*qa-si-re-u, g*^{w}*asileus*, cf. βασιλεύς), with the name of the chief indicated in the genitive. John Killen (1987) has convincingly argued that these are "industrial" units associated with bronzeworking and other forms of production. A very similar pattern can be observed for the *geronsiāi*: these too consist of groups of men, each defined by its association with a man's name in the genitive, apparently the head of the group. Of the four heads of *geronsiai* recorded at Pylos, three appear in the Jn series, two as smiths (*ka-ke-we, k*^{h}*alkēwes*) and one as a *g*^{w}*asileus*; additionally, one of

Linear B	Lexical type	Interpretation	Rough translation	Sites attested
a-ko-da-mo	Name	*Ark*^{h}*odāmos*	*Dāmos*-leader	Thebes
a-ko-ro-da-mo	Name	*Akrodāmos*	Highest-in-the-*dāmos*	Knossos, Thebes
e-ke-da-mo	Name	*Ek*^{h}*edāmos*	*Dāmos*-holder	Knossos, Pylos
e-u-ru-da-mo	Name	*Eurudāmos*	Wide-*dāmos*	Knossos
da-mo-ko-ro	Title	*dāmokoros*	*dāmos*-nourisher	Knossos, Pylos

Table 2.1. Personal names and title compounded with *dāmos* in Linear B.

the men assigned to a *geronsiā* is possibly a smith in the Jn series (Nakassis 2013a: 93).

Sigrid Deger-Jalkotzy (1998–1999: 76) has suggested that the Late Bronze Age g^{w}*asileus* was "a chieftain and leader of his kin group," the g^{w}*asilēwiā*. She considers the *geronsiā* "a (governing) body consisting of 'senior,' that is to say the most distinguished members of a kin group, who were perhaps the representatives of descent groups" (Deger-Jalkotzy 1998–1999: 76–77). There is little reason to believe that these terms represent kin groups, however: the only evidence is that one *geronsiā* head, a man named *a-pi-qo-ta* (probably *Amp*^{h}*ik*^{wh}*oitās*), is listed as a g^{w}*asileus* alongside his (unnamed) son (PY Jn 431.6). This has suggested to many scholars that the title of g^{w}*asileus* was hereditary (e.g., Carlier 1995: 358). Yet this fact on its own cannot plausibly suggest that the groups headed by such men were kin-based, and in the absence of additional evidence, Deger-Jalkotzy's interpretation should be rejected.[1]

Two additional emic terms that seem to point to kinship or co-residence can also be considered together: **wo-(i-)ko* (*woikos*) and **do (dō)*, the Late Bronze Age equivalents of *oikos* and *dō*, words that can both be rendered as "house" in alphabetic Greek (Nakassis 2022: 130–131). Like the g^{w}*asilēwiai*, these houses appear in the tablets as productive units, and like the g^{w}*asilēwiai*, they are always headed by an individual whose name appears in the genitive. At Knossos (As 1519.11), there is a *woikos* of **ma-ri-ne-u*, usually considered to be a man's name, but also possibly the name of a deity; at Thebes there is a *woikos* of the goddess Potnia. The semantic and functional differences between *woikos* and *dō* are uncertain, but a single scribe at Thebes (Hand 303) uses both terms in a single series of tablets (the Thebes Of series), implying an important difference between the terms (see Nakassis 2022: 131, with references). In any case, it is possible that these terms reflect Houses or House-like structures (in the Lévi-Straussian sense) that a number of scholars have identified as important social units in Bronze Age Crete (Driessen 2010; Relaki and Driessen 2020). Unfortunately, while terms like *woikos* and *dō* are strongly suggestive of the types of institutions that we are interested in, they are not well-attested: the former is attested twice (once at Knossos, once at Thebes), the latter five times (at Thebes only).

With the exception of the *dāmos*, which is identified with a toponym, these other institutions are associated with named persons or deities: the g^{w}*asilēwiā*, the *geronsiā*, the *woikos* and the *dō* are all associated with a personal name in the genitive. As observed above, the fact that multiple, spatially disparate responsibilities are sometimes assigned to a single person also suggests that personal names constituted an administrative shorthand for socioeconomic units, perhaps households, of varying size and complexity. Is it possible, then, that a personal name in the Linear B texts is effectively shorthand for a House or a household?

To answer in the affirmative, we should be able to explain why *woikos* and *dō* appear where they do, and not elsewhere. That is, what motivates the use of these terms, and can we explain why they are so rarely used? One possibility is that they are being used in a technical sense in a specific context; outside of this context, the difference between them would not matter, thus obviating the need to specify one way or the other (i.e., why write "the House of *a-ke-o*" if "*a-ke-o*" will communicate the relevant information more efficiently?). Indeed, with one exception (KN As 1519.11), these terms appear in a single set of tablets from Thebes (the Of series); clearly for the author of these documents, the difference between *woikos* and *dō* was significant, unfortunately for reasons that we do not understand (see Nakassis 2022: 130–131, with references). It is also noteworthy that in every case where these terms are used, they appear in the allative case (*-de*), indicating motion toward a place. The allative in Linear B is always, with one exception, appended to the end of a placename or some other indication of place (Lejeune 1961). The exception, *qa-ra*$_2$*-to-de* (TH Of 37.1), is probably a mistake (or shorthand) for *qa-ra*$_2$*-to do-de* (*K*^{w}*allantos dō(n)de*), "to the house of [the man named] K^{w}allans" (Montecchi 2013: 27; Ventris and Chadwick 1973: 576). One might argue, then, that these terms were only used where the scribe needed to specify the physical location to which materials were being sent (in addition, perhaps, to indicating personal responsibility); an additional motivating factor might be that the technical difference between *woikos* and *dō* must have been critical to some administrative contexts. If this is so, then we would not expect these terms to be used regularly, increasing the possibility that the names of individuals in Linear B texts actually refer to households, some of which were of considerable size and complexity.

Households and the women of Pylos

One area where personal names have not been closely scrutinized to draw inferences about social organization are adjectives formed from personal names. These formations were studied closely by John Killen (1983), who showed that Mycenaean had a specific suffix (*-eios, -eiā*; *-e-jo, -e-ja*) for these adjectives: for example, the feminine plural *a-so-qi-je-ja* (*Asōk*^{w}*ieiai*) from the man's name *a-so-qi-jo* (*Asōk*^{w}*ios*). This suffix is distinct from the standard way of producing adjectives from nouns (*-ios, -iā, -i-jo, -i-ja*), which as Killen (1983: 66) observes, is used to form ethnics, possessives, and patronymics.

1 Deger-Jalkotzy (1998–1999: 76) argues that "The later semantic developments of these terms [*qa-si-re-u, ke-ro-te,* and *ke-ro-si-ja*] lead to the conclusion that in the Mycenaean period, too, there existed societies which were based on *kin groups* (*sibs*) which were subdivided into descent groups," but none of these words in the first millennium BCE has to do with kin groups.

Figure 2.2. Pylos Aa 777. Courtesy of The Pylos Tablets Digital Project, Palace of Nestor Excavations, The Department of Classics, University of Cincinnati.

These *-eiā* adjectives are used to describe workgroups in the Pylos Aa, Ab, and Ad series, which consist of leaf-shaped tablets that record the composition of groups of women and girls (Aa) and the payment of staples (grain and dried figs) to these groups (Ab); the Ad series lists corresponding groups of men and boys (see Figure 2.2). John Chadwick (1988; cf. Olsen 2014: 69) enumerates 49 such groups, which are identified by one or more modifiers: professional activity (26 groups), ethnic (13 groups), association with a person (6 groups), and/or some other indicator (9 groups). At least nineteen of these groups are associated with textile manufacture (finishers, sewers, linen-workers, etc.); there are five groups responsible for other domestic activities, like grinding flour. The ethnics are perhaps the most well-known dimension of these tablets, since many refer to places in the eastern Aegean: there are groups from Asia (Lydia), Knidos, Miletos, Lemnos, Zephyros (Halikarnassos), and perhaps Chios, but also from other places closer to Pylos itself, like Kythera and **ti-nwa-to*, which seems to be located in (or near) the Further Province of the Pylian polity (Chadwick 1988: 83–84).

It is often argued that the workers referred to in these tablets were enslaved, despite the fact that none of them is explicitly designated as such. The arguments for this status are as follows:

1. The work assigned to these women is considered "menial" (Ventris and Chadwick 1973: 156, 418; Chadwick 1988: 90; Killen 2006: 90; Olsen 2014: 111) and they are allocated staples, which are assumed to be rations upon which these groups were entirely dependent for their subsistence (Chadwick 1988: 90; Palmer 1989: 91–92; Olsen 2014: 111). Chadwick draws particular attention to the work of the attendants (*a-pi-qo-ro, ampʰikʷoloi*), flour-grinders (*me-re-ti-ra*$_2$, *meletriai*), bath attendants (*re-wo-to-ro-ko-wo, lewotrokʰowoi*), and the various textile workers.
2. These Linear B texts bear a close resemblance to the workgroups composed of women and children (*geme*$_2$*-dumu*) known from Ur III documents (Gelb 1972); Assyriologists had generally concluded that these groups were fully dependent in practical and perhaps legal terms, which Aegeanists considered analogical support for a similar status of the groups at Pylos (Chadwick 1988: 62; Palmer 1989: 144; Killen 2006: 92).
3. The groups are not evenly spread over Messenia, but are concentrated at specific sites, especially Pylos and Leuktron, the capital of the Further Province, perhaps suggesting a need to maintain control over these groups (Olsen 2014: 112–113; cf. Chadwick 1988: 91).
4. Many of the women are described with ethnics that seem to point to origins in the eastern Aegean, suggesting that they were either migrants (Tritsch 1958) or enslaved. Women described as Milesian would have been, on this latter theory, acquired "in the slave-market of Miletos" (Chadwick 1988: 92; Killen 2006: 91; Olsen 2014: 111–112). This would differentiate them from the group described as *ra-wi-ja-ja*, interpreted by Chadwick (1988: 83) and others (see Aura Jorro 1993: 233–234) as *lāwiai*, captives (more literally "women taken as plunder," cf. Attic λεία).
5. The groups are all treated identically in the tablets, such that "if we can ascertain the servile, servant or free status of some of the workgroup women we can extrapolate from them to ascertain the status of all" (Olsen 2014: 113; Olsen 2015: 115–116; so too Killen 2006: 94 n. 9; cf. Chadwick 1988: 90).

In the most recent comprehensive discussion of this issue, Barbara Olsen concludes that all these groups were enslaved, because the tasks themselves are "for all purposes perpetual and 'uncompletable' labor" (Olsen 2014: 113; cf. Olsen 2015: 115–116), coupled with the location of these groups in major administrative centers, their reliance on subsistence rations provided by the palace, and the fact that their children are also monitored in the tablets.

This is a reasonable and popular interpretation; indeed, it has come to be regarded almost as a fact.[2] Yet it rests on shaky foundations, because the evidence has been somewhat cherry-picked in order to come to a satisfactory conclusion and plausible hypotheses have passed into verifiable truths.[3] While it is possible that one group of these women is described as plunder (*ra-wi-ja-ja*), it is also the case that two groups of these women are described as wage-earners (*e-ke-ro-qo-no*, *enkʰērokʰʷoinoi*, cf. ἐπίχειρα). This interpretation is universally accepted (Aura Jorro 1985: 211–212; Chadwick 1988: 79; Rougemont 2009: 104–105). In contrast, scholars have been uncertain about the interpretation of *ra-wi-ja-ja* (Killen 2006: 90–91); indeed, Aura Jorro (1993: 233–234) concludes that the term lacks a satisfactory Greek interpretation. One of the groups of wage-earners (see Figure 2.1) is assigned the task of general housework (*pa-wo-ke*, *panworges* [Chadwick 1998: 82]), which presumably falls into the category of menial, repetitive work. The fact that some of these workers are apparently paid wages in the form of staples for their labor (cf. Nakassis 2010: 131) would seem to invalidate the notions that (a) the staples allocated to these groups are all subsistence rations, (b) the labor assigned to these women is especially appropriate for the enslaved (Fischer 2008: 83), and most importantly (c) administrative uniformity implies homogeneity of status.

It is difficult in the extreme to determine what allocations of staples in Linear B texts imply: in general, they can be understood as rations, handouts, wages, payments, allocations on the occasion of religious festivals, and more (Bennet and Halstead 2014; de Fidio 1989; James 2002–2003; Killen 2001, 2004; Nakassis 2012a; Palmer 1989; cf. Prentice 2010: 91–95). As Rosemary Prentice (2010: 94; cf. Steinkeller 2015: 29–30) has observed in her study of pre-Sargonic Lagash, the repeated use of the term "rations" to characterize the allocation of staples has the unfortunate effect of characterizing their distribution negatively (rations are normally understood as subsistence support, not as distributions made in circumstances of plenty) as well as the recipients (recipients of rations are normally understood as "'deprived' persons"). This is exactly what has happened in the case of the Pylos Ab tablets: standard monthly payments of staples to workgroups were interpreted as rations, not unreasonably, but without subsequent scholarship reevaluating that hypothesis.[4]

In fact, we seem to have the payment of wages (to the *e-ke-ro-qo-no*) in the Ab series as well as, perhaps, the allocation of rations (to the *ra-wi-ja-ja* and others, assuming that they are indeed captives) recorded in such a way that they are indistinguishable from each other. This is unsurprising, because labor is typically recruited by multiple means in Linear B texts without being subjected to any additional administrative differentiation (Nakassis 2012a). Indeed, there is no reason for tablet-writers to vary their treatment of differently recruited groups, if the status of these groups is irrelevant to the context of these documents, as it seems to be here (Chadwick 1979: 26; cf. Nosch 2003: 21). Rather, the interest of tablet-writers is in calculating the correct quantities of grain and figs that are allocated to clearly identified groups (Chadwick 1988: 90), regardless of their legal status or the type of labor that they engaged in. Finally, it does not follow that menial labor (however defined) was undertaken exclusively or primarily by the enslaved. Not only do we have wage-earners amongst these groups, but many of the women in these groups are involved in textile production, and it seems likely that the vast majority of textile workers at Knossos were not enslaved (Killen 2006: 90).[5]

The internal evidence for slavery is thus hardly conclusive, and rather suggests that the women in these workgroups should not be interpreted monolithically. Arguments by analogy to the Assyriological evidence now point to this same conclusion: recent reevaluations of Ur III *geme$_2$-dumu* work groups have concluded that these female laborers probably occupied a variety of legal and social statuses (Lafont 2016: 161–164, 169; Steinkeller 2015: 24–26; cf. Studevent-Hickman 2008; Steinkeller 2015: 7 n. 12 on

2 The literature is enormous. Those who argue for servile status include Carlier 1983: 20; Chadwick 1976: 79; Chadwick 1988: 89–93; Efkleidou 2002–2003: 284; Efkleidou 2004: 215–217; Garlan 1988: 26–27; Killen 2006: 89–94; Killen 2024: 429–431; Olsen 2014: 109–113; Olsen 2015: 115–116; Palmer 1963: 118; Shelmerdine 2024: 304; Ventris and Chadwick 1973: 156, 410. Contrary positions are held by Billigmeier and Turner 1981: 4; Tritsch 1958; Uchitel 1984; Fischer 2007: 24–30; Fischer 2008: 77–84. A middle road is represented by Nosch 2003. I note that I too (Nakassis 2013a: 14) wrote that "It is likely that these people were entirely dependent upon the palace for their subsistence; some of them, moreover, may have been war captives."

3 For example, the young men (*ko-wo*) and young women (*ko-wa*) mentioned in these documents are commonly assumed to be the children of the women (e.g., Chadwick 1988: 62), although that is certainly not the only possibility: see Del Freo 2001–2002.

4 There is also argumentative ambiguity across different authors: while some conclude that the staples allocated in the Ab series are subsistence rations and not wages because the recipients are low status (e.g., Palmer 1989: 92), others argue that the fact that these women are allocated rations proves their low status (e.g., Olsen 2014: 110).

5 I have avoided getting into more detail, which would turn this paper into an overly technical treatise about the groups in the Aa, Ab, and Ad series, but in general I would say that these tablets tend to be read too literally and without sufficient awareness of the fact that these are primarily administrative texts whose broader context we understand poorly. One example is the assumption that these groups are full-time laborers; this is indeed a possibility, but there is nothing in our texts that requires that these women work either year-round or for full workdays. Many conclusions drawn from these tablets are not in my view reliable inferences from the texts, but rather affirm *a priori* assumptions about the status of these groups.

terminological complexity; cf. Lion 2016: 358, on female textile workers in Nuzi). Some women in these groups are described as hired labor who were paid salaries, just like the Pylian wage-earners (Lafont 2016: 164; see too Prentice 2010: 91–95; Steinkeller 2015: 26–30).

It therefore seems that the evidence is consistent with a variety of statuses for the Pylian women. With this established, we can investigate whether any of these groups belong to other social units. Five groups are certainly designated with *-e-ja* adjectives formed from masculine personal names: *ka-ru-ti-je-ja* (from the name **ka-ru-ti-jo, Karustios*), *pa-ke-te-ja* (from *pa-ke-ta*, perhaps *Sp*^{h}*agetās*), *a-so-qi-je-ja* (from *a-so-qi-jo, Asōk*^{w}*ios*), *we-we-si-je-ja* (from *we-we-si-jo*), and **to-sa-me-ja* (from **to-sa-mo*). Of the names from which these adjectives are formed, only one is directly attested at Pylos: *we-we-si-jo* appears three times as one of the smiths (*ka-ke-we, k*^{h}*alkēwes*) in the Jn series; in one case he is associated with the female deity Potnia (Nakassis 2013a: 405).[6]

A slightly different case is presented by the adjective *a-da-ra-te-ja, Adrasteiā* (Aa 785, Ab 388). This could be interpreted in two ways: as an *-e-ja* adjective of the same type as those listed above, formed from the man's name Adrastos, or a feminine personal name (Killen 1983: 72). The latter is possible formally and contextually, since on both tablets where it appears, it is followed by MUL 1 (one woman). There is a good parallel with *me-ki-to-ko-ri-ta* (Ab 575), almost certainly to be interpreted as the personal name *Megistokritā* based on its formal qualities, also followed by MUL 1 (Nakassis 2013a: 309–310). As noted by Killen (1979: 177), the term *Adrasteiā* is notable because although the personal name Adrastos is not directly attested at Pylos, the patronymic is (*a-da-ra-ti-jo, Adrastios*, "son of Adrastos"). Two high-status officials (followers; singular *e-qe-ta*, ^{h}*ek*^{w}*etās*) are described as the sons of Adrastos: they are named Dikonalos (*ḍi-ko-na-ro*) and Aigotās (*a*$_3$*-ko-ta*). Interestingly, groups of men described by the ethnic *a-pu*$_2$*-ka-ne* in military coastguard (*o-ka*) texts are exclusively associated with these sons of Adrastos, which suggests that the sons were responsible for furnishing these men (Nakassis 2012a: 272). This pattern suggests a hypothetical "House of Adrastos" (Figure 2.3): headed by a shadowy figure unattested directly in our texts, his sons are high-ranking officials who seem to supply men for coast-guarding operations; a single woman possibly associated with him appears as a recipient of staples at Pylos. This connection suggests the possibility that the groups associated with men's names in the Aa/Ab/Ad series were furnished by specific households.

John Killen, in an analysis of similar workgroups from Thebes, suggested that groups described in this way (i.e.,

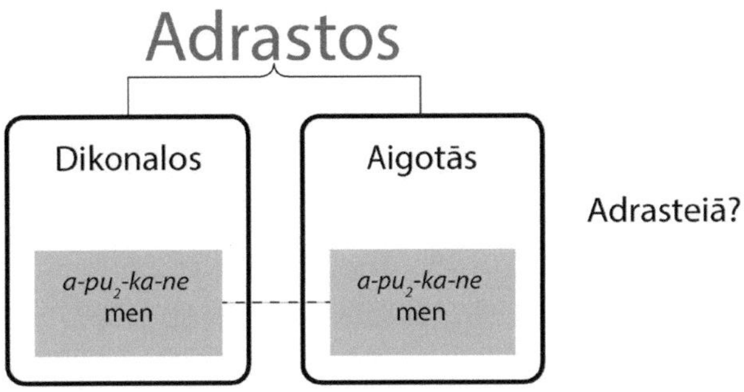

Figure 2.3. A hypothetical illustration of the "House of Adrastos" (drawn by D. Nakassis).

with the *-e-ja* adjective) "denote workgroups 'owned' by 'collectors'" (Killen 1979: 176), whom he interprets as "members of the nobility, the royal family, or the like who were allocated part of the productive capacity of the kingdom for their own benefit (hence their appearance as 'owners' of flocks, weaving workgroups, etc.)" (Killen 1979: 177; cf. Killen 1995: 213–214). In the case of these Theban work groups, Killen imagines a situation similar to the one at Knossos, where individuals such as *pe-ri-qo-ta* appear as "collectors" of flocks of sheep as well as "owners" of workgroups (described as *pe-ri-qo-te-jo* [masc. pl.]). Indeed, Rougemont (2009: 377) has suggested that the fact that these workgroups were supported by the center could strengthen Killen's hypothesis that they were allocated by the palace to the collectors for their benefit.

This is certainly a plausible scenario, but it may be worth exploring alternatives. To begin with, the Pylian working groups are not associated with collectors. They are instead linked to men who either do not appear at Pylos at all, or if they do, are not associated with animal husbandry or textile production: *we-we-si-jo* is only attested at Pylos as a smith and Adrastos is only known as the father of high-ranking military officials. The only links to collectors are fairly tenuous: they concern the repetition of certain personal names associated with collectors that recur in specific contexts across multiple palatial sites. This enigmatic pattern was first noted by Killen (1979: 176–179) and studied further by Jean-Pierre Olivier (2001), who termed these men "international collectors" (see Rougemont 2009: 278–289). For example, *we-we-si-jo* is the name of a collector at Knossos and there are *we-we-si-je-ja* women at Pylos. One other work group from Pylos might be associated with these "international" collectors: Killen (1979: 179) noted that the term *di-ko-na-re-ja* (presumably an *e-ja* adjective formed from the man's name *di-ko-na-ro*, the name of the Pylian officer and son of Adrastos discussed above) appears on a tablet from Tiryns in a landholding context (Ef 3). Perhaps, then, the woman from the house of Adrastos (if that is the correct interpretation of *a-da-ra-te-ja*) can be connected to these "international" collectors (Olivier 2001: 145, 148–149).

6 One group, described as *ka-pa-ra*$_2$*-de*, seems unlikely to be connected to a smith named *ka-pa-ra*$_2$ (Chadwick 1988: 79; on the smith, see Nakassis 2013a: 274).

At a maximum, two of the six groups can be associated with collectors in this way; if we set *Adrasteiā* aside, only one of the five Pylian work groups is associated with the "international" collectors.

It is far from clear what the relationship is between these work groups and the individuals with whom they are associated. In the case of Pylos, there is no obvious reason why we should imagine that the palatial authority allocated work groups for the benefit of four otherwise unknown men (**ka-ru-ti-jo, *pa-ke-u, a-so-qi-jo, *to-sa-mo*), as Killen (1979: 176–177; 1995: 213–214) has argued was done for collectors. In the case of *we-we-si-jo,* we have no compelling evidence that he was a member of the Pylian nobility; at most we would characterize him as a member of a broad elite group that interfaced regularly with the administration (Nakassis 2013a: 156–176). Only in the case of Adrastos do we have good reason to suspect that he belonged to "the nobility, the royal family, or the like" (Killen 1979: 177), but as we have seen there is only a single woman associated with him (Aa 785, Ab 388) and it seems strange (if not impossible) for the palace to allocate a single woman for his benefit. Perhaps therefore we should entertain the possibility, mentioned above, that these work groups were furnished to the palace by specific households. Certainly there are other cases where laborers were apparently provided by specific individuals, such that it seems to constitute a regular administrative practice of the Pylian state (Nakassis 2012a). Additionally, there are reasons to suspect that the sons of Adrastos were engaged in this practice, as mentioned above.

It seems unlikely, in any case, that the work groups associated with these named individuals were enslaved. Tablet-writers had well-established conventions for referring to the enslaved: they are consistently described as the slaves (masc. *do-e-ro*, fem. *do-e-ra*) "of" a person in the genitive, usually a genitive personal name, but titles are also attested (Killen 2006: 89–90). On the rare occasions where adjectives are used to describe enslaved persons, they are always of the *-ios* (*-i-jo*) type (Killen 1983: 84–86). Although the use of the special adjective (*-eios, -eiā*; *-e-jo, -e-ja*) does not exclude servile status — as Killen (1983: 86–88) convincingly argues, its main purpose seems to be its exclusive use for adjectives formed from personal names — we would nevertheless expect a different administrative formula for groups of enslaved women. As Chadwick (1988: 90) famously observed, "the fact that they [the women] are not specifically described as *do-e-ra* [enslaved] is of little consequence, for anyone handling these documents would have known their status." If we were certain that their status was uniform, then Chadwick would be absolutely correct, but as we have seen this is not certain and indeed seems on balance unlikely.

Building houses from dried clay

As John Bennet and Cynthia Shelmerdine (2008: 308) observe, Linear B texts tell us remarkably little about the lives of non-elite members of Mycenaean society. It is difficult to infer "where they spent their lives, under what conditions, and what else they did when not carrying out tasks for the palatial authorities" (Bennet and Shelmerdine 2008: 308). They are also usually anonymous, most often appearing in the Linear B texts as non-individuated groups of workers. Unfortunately, the manner in which the non-elite was recorded by the authors of the Linear B texts has influenced scholarly treatments: the non-elite has been understood as remarkably uniform in its composition, certainly in comparison to the elite, who can be grouped into subtypes (e.g., Driessen 1992: 197–200) or even identified individually by name (Nakassis 2013a). In the case of the Pylian workgroups, past scholarship has indeed insisted upon the uniformity of their status, with the result that they have generally been interpreted as enslaved. It is remarkable how popular this interpretation has been, despite the lack of clarity from the textual evidence. The near-automatic association of low status, humble labor, and institutional support with enslavement does not enrich our study of these people: it rather flattens their lives. It does so, moreover, in a specific way: it reduces their (complex) identities to a single point on a single axis, and thus replicates the managerial view of Pylian society in which the only thing that matters is one's standing in the palatial hierarchy. The centrality of these women to the traditional schema can be illustrated by the fact that Klaus Kilian's (1988: 293) figure depicting Mycenaean social hierarchy places the *ra-wi-ja-ja* at the very bottom (see Figure 2.1 above) — remarkably, given that the word is of uncertain meaning, appears only three times in the entire corpus, and refers to some 40 people at a single site!

The radical simplification of the lives of the non-elite is thus intimately entangled with the traditional understanding of Mycenaean society purely as a projection of palatial power. Yet in the Pylos Aa, Ab, and Ad series, which are considered emblematic of palatial control, we seem to see a combination of different methods for recruiting labor: some groups were hired, others were probably furnished by households, and yet other groups were, perhaps, enslaved. These variations in status and in the modalities of recruitment are to be expected given the complexity of palatial operations (Nakassis 2021), of course. Yet for the study of the non-elite, the simple observation that they are not uniform is important. If we want to investigate the lives of everyday Pylians, we need to be able to characterize them, rather than treating them as an undifferentiated mass. We certainly do not want to ignore the traumas they may have experienced (Hall 2015: 44), but neither do we want to deprive them of identity and agency. One possible axis of differentiation is cultural:

as Nikoloudis (2008: 53) has observed, even if the ethnic identities of these groups are not accessible to us, the use of ethnics in these documents is consistent with a broader pattern of the "physical presence and interaction in the Mycenaean world of culturally diverse population groups and individuals." Yet another may be membership in, or affiliation with, households.

The emic terminology for households (*woikos, dō*) is not attested in the texts at Pylos, but I have argued that names must in some cases have indicated socioeconomic units that exceeded a single individual. Thus, while personal names record the administrative responsibility of individuals, they also plausibly reflect the labor of their household. The most extreme example of the way that names indicate households are the use of theonyms: deities like Potnia and Hermes, when they operate as economic actors, are treated in the same way as collectors (Killen 1976: 124; cf. Killen 1996: 81; Lupack 2008: 96–100). The goddess Potnia is associated with land (at Pylos), flocks (at Knossos and Pylos), fleeces (at Knossos), craft producers (an unguent-boiler and smiths, at Pylos), and personnel (at Knossos and Pylos), all indicated by an adjective (*po-ti-ni-ja-we-jo*) that is similar to the *-e-jo* formation whose use we have seen with the female workgroups at Pylos (on the unusual form of this adjective, see Piquero Rodríguez 2019: 397–398, with references). The name Potnia in the texts can clearly refer to what we could call a household, or what Lupack (2008) calls a sanctuary.

Thus, what for us are quite different institutions are, in the Linear B tablets, administratively uniform. This homogeneity means that there can be a debate about whether the name **ma-ri-ne-u* refers to a deity or an "international collector" (Lupack 2008: 106–110; Rougemont 2009: 286–287). The fact that tablet-writers are parsimonious in their use of writing explains, at least in part, why there are so few instances of emic terms for institutions beyond the *dāmos*. The lack of terminology for the temple, for example, seems to derive from the fact that the name of the deity typically stands in for their household. At the same time, it also illustrates why reading between the lines is necessary: a literal reading of the Linear B texts would probably conclude that non-palatial institutions were unimportant (as Finley [1973: 28–29] effectively does), and a literal interpretation of the personal names in the texts would impede the recognition of the households that populate our texts.

The evidence suggests that some households were large or complex enough to handle a wide variety of administrative tasks and could even furnish labor (such as working women and fighting men) in support of palatial priorities, suggesting that they were internally heterogeneous and hierarchically organized. Indeed, if the *we-we-si-je-ja* women are associated with the Pylian smith named *we-we-si-jo*, then houses could perhaps also be nested: *we-we-si-jo* is in one text (PY Jn 431.18) associated with the house of Potnia (*po-ti-ni-ja-we-jo*).[7] These households thus appear to be not only significant to palatial operations but also to the lives of some members of the non-elite. These social units were apparently not limited to the nobility, but were hierarchically ranked and had internal hierarchies that cut vertically across different status- and age-groups. The nature of the affiliation of the non-elite to these households must, given the nature of our evidence, remain open. It is possible that some were poorer members or clients of the household in need of supplementary income (cf. Gallant 1991: 139, 164–165). But there is no reason to doubt that the information given to us about these groups by tablet-writers was meaningful, even if their reasons for recording it and the context surrounding it are obscure to us.

Reading between the lines gives us some faint but critical insights into these social units. Although they were recorded in the texts because of their significance to palatial operations, they must have had a real-world impact of the lives of the people that were affiliated with them. Future work will need not only to shed light on the internal constitution and operation of these households, but also to integrate them into our models of Late Bronze Age society and economy in a manner that is commensurate with their importance.

Acknowledgements

I thank Daniel Pullen for the invitation to participate and the other participants at the Langford colloquium for their feedback, and Kostas Vlassopoulos for a helpful discussion on Mycenaean slavery.

Bibliography

Aura Jorro, F., 1985. *Diccionario griego-español: Diccionario micénico*. Vol. 1. Madrid: Consejo Superior de Investigaciones Científicas.

Aura Jorro, F., 1993. *Diccionario griego-español: Diccionario micénico*. Vol. 2. Madrid: Consejo Superior de Investigaciones Científicas.

Bennet, J., and P. Halstead, 2014. O-no! Writing and Righting Redistribution. In *KE-RA-ME-JA: Studies Presented to Cynthia W. Shelmerdine*, edited by D. Nakassis, J. Gulizio, and S. A. James, 271–282. Philadelphia: INSTAP Academic Press.

Bennet, J., and C. W. Shelmerdine, 2008. Mycenaean States: Economy and Administration. In *The Cambridge Companion to the Aegean Bronze Age*, edited by C. W. Shelmerdine, 289–309. Cambridge: Cambridge University Press.

7 On whether Weberian patrimonialism applies to the Mycenaean world, see Nakassis 2012b: 20.

Billigmeier, J. C., and J. A. Turner, 1981. The Socio-Economic Roles of Women in Mycenaean Greece: A Brief Survey from Evidence of the Linear B Tablets. *Women's Studies* 8: 3–20.

Carlier, P., 1983. La femme dans la société mycénienne d'après les archives en Linéaire B. In *La Femme dans les sociétés antiques: Actes des colloques de Strasbourg (mai 1980 et mars 1981)*, edited by E. Levy, 9–32. Strasbourg: Association pour l'étude de la civilisation romaine.

Carlier, P., 1995. Qa-si-re-u et qa-si-re-wi-ja. In *Politeia: Society and State in the Aegean Bronze Age. Proceedings of the 5th International Aegean Conference, University of Heidelberg, Archäologisches Institut. 10–13 April 1994*, edited by R. Laffineur and W.-D. Niemeier, 355–364. Aegaeum 12. Liège: Université de Liège, Histoire de l'art et archéologie de la Grèce antique; Austin: University of Texas at Austin, Program in Aegean Scripts and Prehistory.

Carlier, P., 2016. La società micenea. In *Manuale di epigrafia micenea: Introduzione allo studio dei testi in lineare B*, edited by M. Del Freo and M. Perna, 657–676, Padova: libreriauniversitaria.it edizioni.

Chadwick, J., 1976. *The Mycenaean World.* Cambridge: Cambridge University Press.

Chadwick, J., 1979. The Use of Mycenaean Documents as Historical Evidence. In *Colloquium Mycenaeum: Actes du sixième colloque international sur les textes mycéniens et égéens tenu à Chaumont sur Neuchâtel du 7 au 13 septembre 1975*, edited by E. Risch and H. Mühlestein, 21–33. Neuchâtel: Université de Neuchâtel.

Chadwick, J., 1988. The Women of Pylos. In *Texts, Tablets and Scribes: Studies in Mycenaean Epigraphy and Economy Offered to Emmett L. Bennett, Jr.*, edited by J.-P. Olivier and T. G. Palaima, 43–95. Minos Supplement 10. Salamanca: Ediciones Universidad de Salamanca.

De Fidio, P., 1987. Palais et communautés de village dans le royaume mycénien de Pylos. In *Tractata Mycenaea: Proceedings of the Eighth International Colloquium on Mycenaean Studies, Held in Ohrid (15–20 September 1985)*, edited by P. Ilievski and L. Crepajac, 129–149. Skopje: Macedonian Academy of Sciences and Arts.

De Fidio, P., 1989. Razioni alimentari e tenori di vita nel mondo miceneo. In *Studia Mycenaea (1988)*, edited by T. G. Palaima, C. W. Shelmerdine, and P. Hr. Ilievski, 9–38. Živa Antika Monographies 7. Skopje: University of Skopje.

De Fidio, P., 1992. Mycènes et Proche-Orient, ou le théorème des modèles. In *Mykenaïka: Actes du IXe Colloque international sur les textes mycéniens et égéens*, edited by J.-P. Olivier, 173–196. Bulletin de correspondance hellénique, Supplément 25. Paris: de Boccard.

Del Freo, M., 2001–2002. Les rameurs d'*a-po-ne-we*. *Studia Minora Facultatis Philosophicae Universitatis Brunensis* 6–7: 83–90.

Deger-Jalkotzy, S., 1983. Zum Charakter und zur Herausbildung der mykenischen Sozialstruktur. In *Res Mycenaeae: Akten de VII. Internationalen Mykenologischen Colloquiums in Nürnberg vom 6.–10. April 1981*, edited by A. Heubeck and G. Neumann, 89–111. Göttingen: Vandenhoeck and Ruprecht.

Deger-Jalkotzy, S., 1998–1999. Working for the Palace: Some Observations on PY An 261. In *A-NA-QO-TA: Studies Presented to J. T. Killen*, edited by J. Bennet and J. Driessen. *Minos* 33–34: 65–81.

Driessen, J., 1992. 'Collector's Items.' Observations sur l'élite mycénienne de Cnossos. In *Mykenaïka: Actes du IXe Colloque international sur les textes mycéniens et égéens*, edited by J.-P. Olivier, 197–214. Bulletin de correspondance hellénique Supplément 25. Paris: de Boccard.

Driessen, J., 2010. Spirit of Place: Minoan Houses as Major Actors. In *Political Economies of the Aegean Bronze Age: Papers from the Langford Conference, Florida State University, Tallahassee, 22–24 February 2007*, edited by D. J. Pullen, 35–65. Oxford: Oxbow Books.

Efkleidou, K., 2002–2003. The Status of 'Outsiders' within Mycenaean Pylos: Issues of Ethnic Identity, Incorporation, and Marginality. *Minos* 37–38: 269–291.

Efkleidou, K., 2004. Slavery and Dependent Personnel in the Linear B Archives of Mainland Greece. M.A. thesis, University of Cincinnati.

Finley, M. I., 1973. *The Ancient Economy*. Berkeley: University of California Press.

Fischer, J., 2007. Freie und unfreie Arbeit in der mykenischen Textilproduktion. In *Unfreie Arbeit: Ökonomische und kulturgeschichtliche Perspektiven*, edited by M. E. Kabadayi and T. Reichardt, 1–37. Hildesheim: Georg Olms Verlag.

Fischer, J., 2008. Sklaverei und Menschenhandel im mykenischen Griechenland. In *Menschenraub, Menschenhandel und Sklaverei in antiker und moderner Perspektive: Ergebnisse des Mitarbeitertreffens des Akademievorhabens (Mainz, 10. Oktober 2006)*, edited by J. Deißler, 45–84. Forschungen zur antiken Sklaverei 37. Stuttgart: Franz Steiner Verlag.

Gallant, T. W., 1991. *Risk and Survival in Ancient Greece: Reconstructing the Rural Domestic Economy.* Stanford: Stanford University Press.

García-Ramón, J.-L., 2006. Zu den Personennamen der neuen Texte aus Theben. In *Die neuen Linear B-Texte aus Theben: Ihr Aufschlusswert für die mykenische Sprache und Kultur. Akten des internationalen Forschungskolloquiums an der Österreichischen Akademie der Wissenschaften, 5.–6. Dezember 2002*, edited by S. Deger-Jalkotzy and O. Panagl, 37–52.

Veröffentlichungen der Mykenischen Kommission 23, Mykenische Studien 19. Vienna: Verlag der Österreichischen Akademie der Wissenschaften.

García-Ramón, J.-L., 2010. Reconstructing IE Lexicon and Phraseology: Inherited Patterns and Lexical Renewal. In *Proceedings of the 21st Annual UCLA Indo-European Conference,* edited by S. W. Jamison, H. C. Melchert, and B. Vine, 69–106. Bremen: Hempen Verlag.

Garlan, Y., 1988. *Slavery in Ancient Greece, Revised and Expanded Edition,* translated by J. Lloyd. Ithaca: Cornell University Press.

Gelb, I. J., 1972. The Arua Institution. *Revue d'Assyriologie et d'archéologie orientale* 66: 1–32.

Hall, E., 2015. *Introducing the Ancient Greeks*. London: Bodley Head.

Halstead, P. J., 1988. On Redistribution and the Origin of Minoan-Mycenaean Palatial Economies. In *Problems in Greek Prehistory: Papers Presented at the Centenary Conference of the British School of Archaeology at Athens, Manchester, April 1986,* edited by E. B. French and K. A. Wardle, 519–530. Bristol: Bristol Classical Press.

Halstead, P. J., 1992. The Mycenaean Palatial Economy: Making the Most of the Gaps in the Evidence. *Proceedings of the Cambridge Philological Society* 38: 57–86.

Halstead, P. J., 2001. Mycenaean Wheat, Flax and Sheep: Palatial Intervention in Farming and its Implications for Rural Society. In *Economy and Politics in the Mycenaean Palace States: Proceedings of a Conference held on 1–3 July 1999 in the Faculty of Classics, Cambridge,* edited by S. Voutsaki and J. Killen, 38–50. Cambridge Philological Society Supplementary Volume 27. Cambridge: Cambridge Philological Society.

James, S. A., 2002–2003. The Thebes Tablets and the Fq Series: A Contextual Analysis. *Minos* 37–38: 397–417.

Kilian, K., 1988. The Emergence of *Wanax* Ideology in the Mycenaean Palaces. *Oxford Journal of Archaeology* 7: 291–302.

Killen, J. T., 1976. Linear B a-ko-ra-ja/-jo. In *Studies in Greek, Italic, and Indo-European Linguistics, Offered to Leonard R. Palmer on the Occasion of His Seventieth Birthday,* edited by A. Morpurgo Davies and W. Meid, 117–125. Innsbrucker Beiträge zur Sprachwissenschaft 16. Innsbruck: Institut für Sprachwissenschaft der Universität Innsbruck.

Killen, J. T., 1979. The Knossos Ld(1) Tablets. In *Colloquium Mycenaeum: Actes du sixième colloque international sur les textes mycéniens et égéens tenu à Chaumont sur Neuchâtel du 7 au 13 septembre 1975,* edited by E. Risch and H. Mühlestein, 151–182. Neuchâtel: Université de Neuchâtel.

Killen, J. T., 1983. Mycenaean Possessive Adjectives in -e-jo. *Transactions of the Philological Society* 113: 66–99.

Killen, J. T., 1987. Bronzeworking at Knossos and Pylos. *Hermathena* 143: 61–72.

Killen, J. T., 1995. Some Further Thoughts on 'Collectors.' In *Politeia: Society and State in the Aegean Bronze Age. Proceedings of the 5th International Aegean Conference / 5e Rencontre égéenne internationale, University of Heidelberg, Archäologisches Institut, 10–13 April 1994,* edited by R. Laffineur and W.-D. Niemeier, 213–226. Aegaeum 12. Liège: Université de Liège, Histoire de l'art et archéologie de la Grèce antique; Austin: University of Texas at Austin, Program in Aegean Scripts and Prehistory.

Killen, J. T., 1996. Thebes Sealings and Knossos Tablets. In *Atti e memorie del secondo Congresso internazionale di micenologia, Roma-Napoli, 14–20 ottobre 1991,* edited by E. De Miro, L. Godart, and A. Sacconi, 71–82. Incunabula Graeca 98. Rome: Gruppo editorial internazionale.

Killen, J. T., 1998. The Rôle of the State in Wheat and Olive Production in Mycenaean Crete. *Aevum* 72: 19–23.

Killen, J. T., 2001. Religion at Pylos: The Evidence of the Fn Tablets. In *Potnia: Deities and Religion in the Aegean Bronze Age. Proceedings of the 8th International Aegean Conference / 8e Rencontre égéenne internationale. Göteborg, Göteborg University, 12–15 April 2000,* edited by R. Laffineur and R. Hägg, 435–443. Aegaeum 22. Liège and Austin: Université de Liège and University of Texas at Austin.

Killen, J. T., 2004. Wheat, Barley, Flour, Olives and Figs on Linear B Tablets. In *Food, Cuisine and Society in Prehistoric Greece,* edited by P. Halstead and J. C. Barrett, 155–173. Sheffield Studies in Aegean Archaeology 5. Oxford: Oxbow Books.

Killen, J. T., 2006. The Subjects of the Wanax: Aspects of Mycenaean Social Structure. In *Ancient Greece: From the Mycenaean Palaces to the Age of Homer,* edited by S. Deger-Jalkotzy and I. S. Lemos, 87–99. Edinburgh Leventis Studies 3. Edinburgh: Edinburgh University Press.

Killen, J. T., 2024. Lists of Personnel. In *The New Documents in Mycenaean Greek,* edited by J. Killen, 426–491. Cambridge: Cambridge University Press.

Lafont, B., 2016. Women at Work and Women in Economy and Society during the Neo-Sumerian Period. In *The Role of Women in Work and Society in the Ancient Near East,* edited by B. Lion and C. Michel, 149–173. Berlin: de Gruyter.

Lejeune, M., 1961. La postposition -δε en mycénien. *Revue de philologie, de littérature et d'histoire anciennes* 35: 195–206.

Lejeune, M., 1965. Le *DAMOS* dans la société mycénienne. *Revue des études grecques* 78: 1–22.

Lion, B., 2016. Work and Gender in Nuzi Society. In *The Role of Women in Work and Society in the Ancient Near*

East, edited by B. Lion and C. Michel, 354–370. Berlin: de Gruyter.

Lupack, S., 1999. Palaces, Sanctuaries, and Workshops: The Role of the Religious Sector in Mycenaean Economics. In *Rethinking Mycenaean Palaces: New Interpretations of an Old Idea,* edited by M. L. Galaty and W. A. Parkinson, 25–34. Monograph 41. Los Angeles: University of California at Los Angeles, Cotsen Institute of Archaeology.

Lupack, S., 2008. *The Role of the Religious Sector in the Economy of Late Bronze Age Mycenaean Greece.* British Archaeological Reports International Series 1858. Oxford: Archaeopress.

Lupack, S., 2011. A View from Outside the Palace: The Sanctuary and the *Damos* in Mycenaean Economy and Society. *American Journal of Archaeology* 115: 207–217.

Montecchi, B., 2013. *Luoghi per lavorare, pregare, morire: Edifici e maestranze edili negli interessi delle élites micenee.* Firenze: Firenze University Press.

Nakassis, D., 2010. Reevaluating Staple and Wealth Finance at Mycenaean Pylos. In *Political Economies of the Aegean Bronze Age: Papers from the Langford Conference, Florida State University, Tallahassee, 22–24 February 2007,* edited by D. J. Pullen, 127–148. Oxford: Oxbow Books.

Nakassis, D., 2012a. Labor Mobilization in Mycenaean Pylos. In *Études mycéniennes 2010: Actes du XIIIe colloque international sur les textes égéens, Sèvres, Paris, Nanterre, 20–23 septembre 2010,* edited by P. Carlier, C. de Lamberterie, M. Egetmeyer, N. Guilleux, F. Rougemont, and J. Zurbach, 269–283. Pisa and Roma: Fabrizio Serra.

Nakassis, D., 2012b. Prestige and Interest: Feasting and the King at Mycenaean Pylos. *Hesperia* 81: 1–30.

Nakassis, D., 2013a. *Individuals and Society in Mycenaean Pylos.* Mnemosyne Supplements 358. Leiden: Brill.

Nakassis, D., 2013b. Structuration and the State in Mycenaean Greece. In *Agency in Ancient Writing,* edited by J. Englehardt, 231–247. Boulder: University Press of Colorado.

Nakassis, D., 2021. The Extractive Systems of the Mycenaean World. In *Ancient Taxation: The Mechanics of Extraction in Comparative Perspective,* edited by J. Valk and I. Soto Marín, 93–127. New York: New York University Press.

Nakassis, D., 2022. Communities, 'Houses', and Political Organisation in the Mycenaean World. In *From House Societies to States: Early Political Organisation from Antiquity to the Middle Ages,* edited by J. C. Moreno García, 123–140. Multidisciplinary Approaches to Ancient Societies 3. Oxford and Philadelphia: Oxbow Books.

Nakassis, D., 2023. People Like Us? Individuals and Individualism in the Late Bronze Age Aegean. In *Πολυμήχανος: Man of Many Ways. Papers in Honour of Professor Jan Driessen,* edited by C. Langohr and Q. Letesson, 81–87. Aegis 25. Louvain-la-Neuve: Presses universitaires de Louvain.

Nikoloudis, S., 2008. Multiculturalism in the Mycenaean World. In *Anatolian Interfaces: Hittites, Greeks and Their Neighbours. Proceedings of an International Conference on Cross-Cultural Interaction, September 17–19, 2004, Emory University, Atlanta, GA,* edited by B. K. Collins, M. R. Bachvarova, and I. C. Rutherford, 45–56. Oxford: Oxbow Books.

Nosch, M.-L., 2003. The Women at Work in the Linear B Tablets. In *Gender, Cult, and Culture in the Ancient World from Mycenae to Byzantium: Proceedings of the Second Nordic Symposium on Gender and Women's History in Antiquity, Helsinki 20–22 October 2000,* edited by L. Larsson Lovén and A. Strömberg, 12–26. Studies in Mediterranean Archaeology Pocketbook 166. Sävedalen: Paul Åströms Förlag.

Olivier, J.-P., 2001. Les 'collecteurs': Leur distribution spatiale et temporelle. In *Economy and Politics in the Mycenaean Palace States: Proceedings of a Conference held on 1–3 July 1999 in the Faculty of Classics, Cambridge,* edited by S. Voutsaki and J. Killen, 139–160. Cambridge Philological Society Supplementary Volume 27. Cambridge: Cambridge Philological Society.

Olsen, B., 2014. *Women in Mycenaean Greece: The Linear B Tablets from Pylos and Knossos.* London and New York: Routledge.

Olsen, B., 2015. The Worlds of Penelope: Women in the Mycenaean and Homeric Economies. *Arethusa* 48: 107–138.

Palaima, T. G., 1999. Mycenaean Militarism from a Textual Perspective. Onomastics in Context: *lāwos, dāmos, klewos.* In *Polemos: Le contexte guerrier en Égée á l'âge du Bronze. Actes de la 7e Rencontre égéenne internationale Université de Liège, 14–17 avril 1998,* edited by R. Laffineur, 367–379. Aegaeum 19. Liège and Austin: Histoire de l'art et archéologie de la Grèce antique and the Program in Aegean Scripts and Prehistory.

Palmer, L. R., 1963. *The Interpretation of Mycenaean Greek Texts.* Oxford: Clarendon Press.

Palmer, R., 1989. Subsistence Rations at Pylos and Knossos. *Minos* 24: 89–124.

Piquero Rodríguez, J., 2019. *El léxico del griego micénico: Index Graecitatis; Étude et mise à jour de la bibliographie.* Nancy: Association pour la Diffusion de la Recherche sur l'Antiquité.

Prentice, R., 2010. *The Exchange of Goods and Services in Pre-Sargonic Lagash.* Alter Orient und Altes Testament 368. Münster: Ugarit-Verlag.

Relaki, M., and J. Driessen, eds., 2020. *Oikos: Archaeological Approaches to House Societies in the Bronze Age Aegean*. Aegis 19. Louvain-la-Neuve: Presses universitaires de Louvain.

Rougemont, F., 2009. *Contrôle économique et administration à l'époque des palais mycéniens (fin du IIe millénaire av. J.-C.)*. Bibliothèque des Écoles françaises d'Athènes et de Rome 332. Athens: École française d'Athènes.

Shelmerdine, C. W., 2008. Mycenaean Society. In *A Companion to Linear B: Mycenaean Greek Texts and their World*. Vol. 1, edited by Y. Duhoux and A. Morpurgo Davies, 115–158. Bibliothèque des cahiers de l'Institut de Linguistique de Louvain 120. Louvain-la-Neuve: Peeters.

Shelmerdine, C. W., 2011. The Individual and the State in Mycenaean Greece. *Bulletin of the Institute of Classical Studies* 54: 19–28.

Shelmerdine, C. W., 2024. Mycenaean Society and Political Systems. In *The New Documents in Mycenaean Greek*, edited by J. Killen, 290–306. Cambridge: Cambridge University Press.

Steinkeller, P., 2015. Labor in the Early States: An Early Mesopotamian Perspective. In *Labor in the Ancient World*, edited by P. Steinkeller and M. Hudson, 1–35. Dresden: ISLET-Verlag.

Studevent-Hickman, B., 2008. The Workforce at Umma: Some New Questions. In *The Growth of an Early State in Mesopotamia: Studies in Ur III Administration*, edited by S. Garfinkle and C. Johnson, 141–147. Biblioteca del Proximo Oriente Antiguo 5. Madrid: Consejo Superior de Investigaciones Científicas.

Tritsch, F. J., 1958. The Women of Pylos. In *Minoica: Festschrift zum 80. Geburststag von Johannes Sundwall*, edited by E. Grumach, 406–445. Deutsche Akademie der Wissenschaften zu Berlin. Schriften der Sektion für Altertumswissenschaften 12. Berlin: Akademie Verlag.

Uchitel, A., 1984. Women at Work: Pylos and Knossos, Lagash and Ur. *Historia* 33: 257–282.

Ventris, M., and J. Chadwick, 1973. *Documents in Mycenaean Greek, 2nd ed.* Cambridge: Cambridge University Press.

Verboven, K., M. Carlier, and J. Dumolyn, 2007. A Short Manual to the Art of Prosopography. In *Prosopography Approaches and Applications: A Handbook*, edited by K. S. B. Keats-Rohan, 35–69. Oxford: Unit for Prosopographical Research, Linacre College, University of Oxford.

A House Divided?

Social Structure Before, During and After the Mycenaean Administration at Knossos

Jan Driessen

Abstract

The previous Langford conference in 2007 (see Pullen 2010) presented an occasion to engage with the House Society model as proposed by Lévy-Strauss and to apply it to Minoan Crete. In the meantime, numerous anthropological studies have discussed the model for traditional societies and there is also a wide application by archaeologists — with varied success. A workshop at the UCLouvain in 2018 presented an occasion to submit the applicability and pertinence of the concept for the Cretan Bronze Age context to a critical analysis. It became obvious that in fact very few societies strictly adhered to the Lévy-Straussian model, which in fact acted more as a straitjacket rather than stimulating further research. A bottom-up appreciation of archaeological data allows a better time-and space-contingent definition of the main characteristics of what a 'House' represented within the specifically Cretan context during its main Bronze Age phases (EM-LM I), and it are these characteristics which guide the present attempt to trace the development of the Minoan *House* through the troubled times of LM IB and afterwards. It will be argued that a few earlier Minoan *Houses* survived the troubles seemingly unscathed while new elites were established during the Knossian administration (LM II-IIIA2), occupying more modest dwellings that probably reflect initial nuclear families. While the old *Houses* may not have survived the LM IIIA2 destruction of the palace, the newly created elites appear to have developed into *Houses*, especially outside Knossos. To what extent funerary evidence agrees with this hypothesis is also discussed.

Introduction

The identification of the basics of social structure and kinship relations of an ancient society that has left us with mostly accountancy records is not without obstacles since it remains hard to leave one's Eurocentric comfort zone and approach the archaeological material with a bottom-up perspective that is as little as possible contaminated by present conceptions nor based on extrapolations and inferences from other contemporary societies. Purely archaeological approaches to kinship (Ensor 2013; Johnson and Paul 2016) have, however, shown that relevant hypotheses can be formulated that, occasionally, even find confirmation through advances in bioarchaeological research (e.g., Alt et al. 2016).

The 2007 Langford meeting (Pullen 2010) presented a first occasion to overcome a long-lasting frustration as to my understanding of Minoan social structure and an opportunity to propose an alternative way of appreciating Cretan settlement and house evidence to obtain, if not a better, then at least a more mitigated understanding of the basics of Minoan social structure

ORCID 0000-0001-6146-5010
UCLouvain and Department of Classics, University of Cincinnati
jan.driessen@uclouvain.be

In *Social Groups and Production in Mycenaean Economies. Papers from the Langford Conference, Florida State University, Tallahassee, 24-25 February 2023*, edited by D. Pullen (2025), 35–46. Leiden: Sidestone Press.

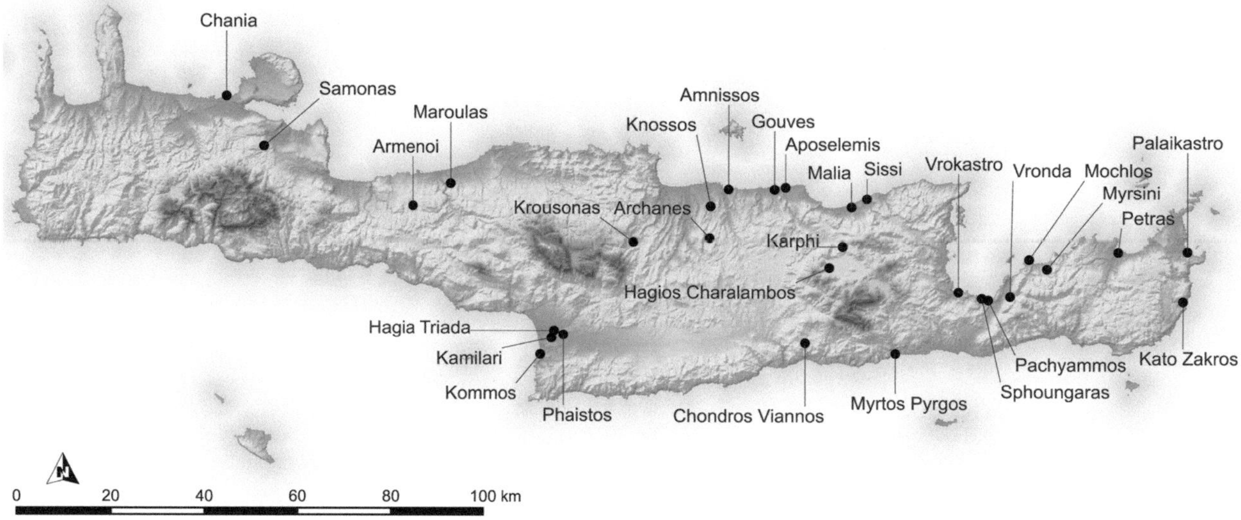

Figure 3.1. Crete: Sites Mentioned in the Text (©TALOS-N. Kress, with permission).

and organization (Driessen 2010a). At the time, I was much influenced (perhaps overenthusiastically) by anthropological studies on what are known as *House Societies*, an extended social group of which the identification went back to Franz Boas' study in the late 1890s of the *numayma* of the Kwakiutl of British Columbia, explicitly dubbed *House Society* in the 1970s by Claude Lévi-Strauss in his book *The Way of the Mask* when discussing the Tlingit (Lévi-Strauss 1983). In anthropology, House/house-centric/house-based societies have been studied extensively and it was only a question of time before their relevance would filter down into archaeology. Important edited volumes such as that by Carsten and Hugh-Jones (1995), Joyce and Gillespie (2000), and Beck (2007) have explored the use of the concept more widely, including in archaeology, and since then the *House* (in italics with capital H as I will refer to it) has been identified (often convincingly) in several ancient and less ancient societies (e.g., Sissons 2010; Wynne-Jones 2013; Chiang 2015; Nelson-Hurst 2015; Artursson 2015; Thomas 2016; Kuo 2021). While several studies have used the *House* concept in Aegean archaeology (González-Ruibal 2006; González-Ruibal and Ruiz-Gálvez 2016; Driessen 2012, 2017, 2018; Relaki 2009; Apostolaki 2015), in 2018, Maria Relaki and I felt that the time was ripe to examine the validity of the concept primarily where Minoan Crete was concerned in a three-day workshop published as *Oikos. Archaeological Approaches to House Societies in Aegean Prehistory* (Relaki and Driessen 2020). At the meeting, a few papers touching other societies were presented, including one by Kalliopi Efkleidou (2020) who looked for the evidence of *Houses* in tombs of the Mycenaean Argolid, a theme which touched the focus of the present meeting *Social Groups and Production in Mycenaean Economies*. Since then, Corien Wiersma (although presented at *Oikos*) has treated the topic in the *Oxford Journal of Archaeology* (Wiersma 2020) for the Early and Middle Helladic periods and Dimitri Nakassis (2022) explored the Mycenaean side in the edited volume *From House Societies to States: Early Political Organisation* (Moreno Garcia 2022), also paying attention to Linear B terms as well as to those termed "collectors." And finally, Tina Kalantzopoulou (2022) has investigated whether the concept could be used for Cretan mountain communities.

Not all scholars who participated in the *Oikos*-workshop agreed with our hypothesis to regard Minoan Crete as a *House Society* while others recognized such a system only at specific moments during its long Bronze Age history. I partly think that this disagreement is largely a result of adhering too closely to the Lévi-Straussian definition as if it would or should be a fixed screenplay which societies followed or had to strictly observe cross-culturally and at all times, as Nakassis (2022: 126) already observed when referring to Watanabe's (Watanabe 2004: 160) "ready-made formulations." But both in the introduction to the *Oikos* volume with Maria Relaki (Driessen and Relaki 2020) and in a co-authored paper with Quentin Letesson for the same volume (Letesson and Driessen 2020), we attempted to go beyond the Lévi-Straussian definition or rather to present a definition of the *House* which was both culturally and historically specific for Minoan Crete. That is, we attempted to recognize archaeological patterns first and then combine these observations to create a hypothetical model for the social structure that best corresponded with these patterns. Whether we call this the Minoan *House* rather than another term such as *"oikos," "do,"* or *"kotona"* (or *gens, genos, stratos*) is less relevant although it would perhaps have been more appropriate since it would have sidestepped a too strict identification with the Lévi-Straussian concept. Others have proposed to use the term "social house" to distinguish between the social unit and the physical structure (cf. also Nelson-Hurst 2015: 259). Suggesting alternative terms is rarely successful, however, as the discussion surrounding the Minoan "palace," court centers/compounds/complexes, etc., shows, but again, as long as we know what we really mean with a term, it should be acceptable. At the outset of this paper then, I think it is necessary to repeat what a Minoan *House* represents, to avoid misunderstanding. It remains a bottom-up, archaeologically data-driven hypothesis. This also means that, at this moment, we cannot convincingly prove the existence of a Lévi-Straussian *House Society* because we simply do not have access to all necessary criteria including kinship, alliance formation and the maintenance of property (outside that of the residential structure itself), sufficient reasons to stick to a Minoan *House* (already Driessen 2010a, 2012, 2015, 2017, 2018).

The Minoan *House*

Our starting point was the large to exceptionally large size of residential structures, with dwellings on Crete that, since the advanced Neolithic period, often exceed 100 m^2 or more (Figure 3.1). Using the (granted) simplistic equation of 1 person equals 10 m^2, it suggested that extended social groups occupied these residential structures (cf. Coupland and Banning 1996).

A second characteristic is the intergenerational use of both the residential structure and/or the location, giving it a sense of permanence. This is suggested by the use and/or palimpsestic rebuilding of structures throughout several ceramic periods, most often illustrated by a vertical succession at the very spot rather than a horizontal displacement (see Haggis 2013). The close link with the place is often accentuated through foundation deposits or buried offerings.

A third characteristic is that a clear investment in the design and appearance of certain residential structures can be observed; some Minoan scholars have even assumed that innovations in architecture first took place within residences before being applied to palatial architecture (Schoep 2004, 2007). This attention to architecture is accentuated by special materials, room fittings, etc., but also e.g., by house models, miniatures, foundation deposits, and so on.

A fourth characteristic is that the dwelling acts as a nexus of interactions that perpetuates a sense of identity and this is mainly through the presence of meeting or reception rooms (*polythyra*) on the one hand, and cultic features (lustral basins, pillar crypts, etc.) on the other hand. Both show the importance of several residences as the foci for a larger social unit and, basically, as "miniature palaces." This also implies a potential public or semi-public role of these residences for non-residents, also suggested by their access and circulation systems (Letesson 2014) and implies that the boundaries of the household did not coincide with those of the physical structure. Moreover, it stresses the semi-public character of the building which also served to host visitors (ξενία?) through, for example, feasts as indicated by feasting equipment and a much larger than necessary supply of cups.

A fifth feature is that several residences also acted as independent economic actors as suggested by the presence of evidence for craft production. Some of the crafts involved formed part of what are called "maintenance activities" (Monton-Subias and Sanchez-Romero 2008), including limited cooking and textile production; others, however, seem to be organized at a larger scale and may have provided a more extensive group with the necessary ceramics and metals. Architectural specialists may also be included amongst these crafts and, although only indicated by proxy evidence, farmers and shepherds. Trade and mercantile activities too could be a *House*-related affair and Steve Karacic (2015) has proposed that the Prepalatial longboats could well have been manned by *House* members in their voyages to acquire obsidian and metals. Doniert Evely (2000: 550) too has stressed how most evidence for crafts comes from dwellings and not from palaces and this only changes in LM IB when the Kato Zakros palace also focusses heavily on production.

Two additional features seem to strengthen this corporate view of society. One is funerary, the other external group involvement in public building and feasting. As is well known, the primary method of body disposal in Minoan society (up to a point) was collective, something that agrees well with the *House Society* hypothesis, since we can perhaps assume that "Gathered in Death" also means "Gathered in Life" (Schmitt, Déderix, and Crevecoeur 2018). Collective burial probably expressed a corporate identity, with tombs being houses and an "enduring material referent for a particular social group" (Thomas 2016: 8). Collective tombs hence prioritized groups and group solidarity over individuals and their glorification (Driessen 2010b). At this moment of research, we are not able to state yet that people buried together in a Circular or House tomb shared blood or other ties but advances in DNA and isotope analyses may soon improve this (cf. Skourtanioti et al. 2023). But the close location of tombs to settlements should be stressed and this is especially the case for House Tombs (Vavouranakis 2007). The other is public building and feasting, which likewise suggest the involvement of different, largely equivalent groups. This has been confirmed by a detailed study of mason's marks on ashlar (Devolder 2018) and by the identification of different groups within the ceramic deposits such as that of the Protopalatial Lakkos Deposit at Petras (Haggis 2007), the Knossos Palace deposits (Macdonald and Knappett 2007), and the Neopalatial Sissi deposits (Caloi 2018; Mathioudaki 2022). Both features illustrate a clear bottom-up direction in collective action.

The *House Society* hypothesis for Crete implies a high degree of equality between the different *Houses* but also an internal hierarchy within the *Houses*, perhaps based on age, gender or ritual status (cf. Puglisi 2020). Why the *House* on Crete? I have argued that it was a typical Cretan solution since only a sizeable, internally differentiated, long-living enduring corporate group would be able to respond to the simultaneous and intergenerational demands on labor investment that were required by the agropastoral economy of the island (Driessen 2018; Driessen and Letesson 2023): *simultaneity* as implied by the relatively short harvesting periods of the Mediterranean triad and various tasks of herding; *intergenerationally* because especially olives and vines but also flock maintenance required a multi-year investment. Moreover, insularity and male absence for trade surely played a role.

The *House* then was the best environmentally adapted solution for this agropastoral insular society. I feel strengthened in this hypothesis by the results of a recent paleogenetic analysis (Skourtanioti et al. 2023) which is based on a Cretan sample of 66 individuals from different sites and periods (Early Neolithic Aposelemis (6 samples); Middle Bronze Age Hagios Charalambos (28), Late Bronze Age Chania (27), Aposelemis (3) and Krousonas (2)). Not only do their results effectively illustrate the arrival of the so-called WES (Western Eurasian Steppe) ancestry, also found on the Mainland, especially at Late Bronze Age Chania and hence a phase of mixing between different population groups, but more importantly, they were also able to illustrate a very high degree of consanguinity at Middle Bronze Age Hagios Charalambos, which suggested a relatedness to the degree of first cousins. This marital system, also present in the Cyclades, seems a result of endogamy, the practice of marrying within a special group, and hence likely to prevent the inherited farmland within families from being divided, in order to ensure a continuity of the family in one place, hence precisely what we would expect for a *House*.

This in, a nutshell, is our present hypothesis. Within this general framework, however, we should leave sufficient room for variety, development, and change. Accepting the *House* as the main social actor certainly does not exclude the presence of other social systems or of regional or temporal variety. Jeunesse and colleagues (2021) have shown how, on the island of Sumba in Indonesia, the western part of the island is largely organized in tribes, forming egalitarian *House Societies* with a council of elders in each village, while the eastern part of the island comprises different chiefdoms with royal, hereditary lineages. Sumba is an island somewhat larger than Crete and one of the rare contemporary contexts where even today megalithic monuments are still produced. An identical material culture exists all over the island despite there being 24 different ethnic groups and eight different languages and hence two political and social systems. The geographical separation between the two systems is not absolute and they are mixed within their respective core regions. Both systems use megalithic tombs for collective burials, but they serve all *House* members in the *House Society*, whereas they only receive the royal lineage in the chiefdoms (Adams and Kusumawati 2011). These last tombs are larger and more extensively decorated. Because informants are available, we can acquire an understanding of the social differences.

The House after Late Minoan IB

In earlier papers, I primarily explored the *House Society* system for the Minoan periods (also Driessen and Letesson 2023), while here the focus is on the post-LM IB periods, taking up O. Dickinson's challenge, who, in a review of Relaki and Papadatos (2018), noted that the *House Society* model

> "... represents a praiseworthy attempt to conceive of Minoan Society as potentially more 'different' than has been usual, and to provide a setting for the marked 'communal' element in Minoan culture....One might also hope to learn whether, if it formed the bedrock of Minoan society, it is thought to have survived the Late Minoan I collapse of the original Minoan civilization" (Dickinson 2020: 580).

A first problem we must tackle is whether the end of collective burials also meant the end of the social system as represented by the Minoan *House*. It is well known that collective tombs already become rare during the Neopalatial period with only a handful examples still in use (Kamilari, Myrtos Pyrgos, and Sissi) and during the same phase, large cemeteries with individual body depositions such as at Sphoungaras, Pachyammos, and elsewhere seem to become if not the rule, then more preeminent. Especially for LM IB, however, funerary evidence is notoriously lacking and this, as we already argued (Driessen and Macdonald 1997: 35–83), illustrates just one of the considerable societal changes that Crete was going through in the period after the Santorini eruption. Together with the going-out-of-use of all palaces and their central courts as venues for staged collective, regional feasting and ritual integration, the abandonment of vernacular venues such as peak sanctuaries and cave shrines, the change from a prime female to a male divinity, and the gradual diminishing in the architectural and decorative investment of private residences, these changes are quite upsetting, perhaps even world-changing, affecting the core of Minoan society and thus undoubtedly also its social basis. The bottom-up direction of collective action seems clearly to become less important, if not largely eradicated. When the smoke of the LM IB fires eventually clears, the island was unrecognizable (*contra* Whitelaw 2022: 62 who, I believe, overemphasizes continuity). All main Neopalatial settlements and cult places had gone up in fire and/or were in ruins, many abandoned forever, and apart from the Knossos palace, no public buildings remained. The recent publication of the volume *One State Many Worlds* (D'Agata et al. 2022) is of immense help to get a better grasp of the relevant period. Did the Minoan *House* as attested in the previous periods survive the troubles? As before, we have two strands of evidence: settlement and funerary data.

There is considerable discussion on what precisely happened at Knossos between the LM IB and LM II periods. Macdonald (2005) has argued for some changes to have taken place in the palace already during LM IB, continuing with major changes in LM II. The same process — Neopalatial buildings (whether or not partly damaged in LM IA by Santorini-eruption related events) patched up and reused in LM IB–LM II — can also be seen elsewhere at Knossos, as in the Unexplored Mansion, the South House, and the Royal Villa (Hatzaki 2011: 258). The detailed biographies of the South House and the Royal Villa remain somewhat obscure but at least that of the Unexplored Mansion is clear (Popham at al. 1984): built in LM IA and possibly damaged by earthquake in that same period, it was extensively reused during LM II when there is evidence for cult activity but also for metal production. The house was extensively damaged by fire at this moment and the reuse afterwards is much more limited. The biography of House X at Kommos, is quite similar (Shaw and Shaw 2012; Rutter 2017): built in LM IA, it remained occupied throughout without suffering a wholesale destruction until it was given up in early LM IIIA2. Most of its floor deposits date to LM II so we may perhaps assume some disturbance then since there were considerable modifications afterwards and some rooms were given up. The same thing happened with Maison Epsilon at Malia. The first rooms of this complex were found when a road between the palace and the national road was cut in the 1930s, but its true excavation took place in the fifties (Deshayes and Dessenne 1959), followed by smaller investigations later (Pelon 1967, 1970; Bradfer-Burdet 2003, 2004, 2006). Although there was a Protopalatial predecessor, Neopalatial Epsilon also included a lustral basin, two large reception rooms, a columnar court, a frescoed room, plastered floors and ashlar. The quality of some finds (especially the lamps) is also surprising. It was an elite complex, undoubtedly. Pelon's study has shown that there were four main phases, the first being Protopalatial and the last Postpalatial whereas phase IIIB is dated to LM IB–LM II, when the building was simply reused after some minor LM IA disturbance, hence, closely paralleling the history of the Unexplored Mansion and House X at Kommos. After its abandonment in LM II, its ruins were only reoccupied after an interruption in LM IIIB, a reoccupation which took place especially in the most eastern and western rooms.

These three cases in three different settlements have in common that we have no reason *not* to assume that the same intergenerational social unit occupied the building between LM IA and LM II, i.e., for at least 100 years or four generations (Rutter 2017: 237). Moreover, each of these buildings is quite large, with 205 m^2 ground floor space for Kommos X, 460 m^2 for the Unexplored Mansion and 1370 m^2 for Neopalatial Epsilon. It is very possible that something similar happened with Building 1 at Palaikastro, which was also largely reused without much change from LM I to LM II (MacGillivray and Sackett 2019). Using our rule of thumb, this would mean respectively about 20, 46 and 137 residents. Even if these numbers are exaggerated, it may imply that some social units were able to maintain themselves throughout the period of troubles and even though, apart from that of Knossos, no other palace survived.

On the other hand, several other buildings either at Malia and Knossos or in other sites seem to be newly built LM II constructions, and Whitelaw (2022: 55) has noted the blatant reduction in size of individual dwellings after the Neopalatial period. Indeed, newly constructed residential buildings, often with fewer than five rooms, have been recognized at Knossos, at Malia (in Quartier Nu), at Sissi, and at Mochlos and Chania. At Knossos, for example, the Gypsum House, located behind the Stratigraphical Museum next to the LM II–IIIA dancing circles (of which the function remains debated), was constructed in LM II (Warren 1983: 63–65). It got its name because of the ample use of gypsum for slabs, bases, staircases etc. Although only a part of the building was excavated (the rest remains hidden in the baulk), it comprised four rooms including an entrance room, a frescoed main room as well as two rooms to the west. The material found in it would also suggest that this was an elite dwelling but of relatively small size and it did not seem to survive the LM II period. The same goes for a house excavated near the South-West House (S.VII) (Macdonald 2011, 2022: 121, figs. 6–10), built and destroyed by fire in LM II. The presence of fine gypsum floor slabs, a polythyron, and pillars suggests it was a house of some standing but again it cannot have been very large. The same may apply to a house recently excavated at Gypsades which was occupied in LM II but also suffered a destruction (Morgan 2015: 34–35). Likewise, the LM II remains we found beneath Quartier Nu at Malia and at Sissi are those of small buildings (Driessen and Farnoux 1994) and the same seems true for the building constructed on top of the LM IB house at Chania's Agia Aikaterini Square (Hallager and Hallager 2016). At Mochlos too, the houses constructed somewhat later, in LM IIIA, are small, rarely comprising more than five rooms (Brogan, Smith, and Soles 2002; Soles and Davaras 2011). The only thing all these contexts have in common is a typical Knossian pottery assemblage so we can assume their occupants formed part of the new regime. But we clearly seem to have a contrast with, on the one hand, large complexes that show a continuity from the previous period into the next, and, on the other hand, newly built residences of small size. These small, new houses often did not survive the period, nor do they comprise specifically larger rooms that could be used for receptions or as a ritual focus. This suggests they belonged to more introverted, nuclear families. Is it then possible that in some settlements some *Houses* survived the LM IB troubles but elsewhere they did not, and new elites progressively established themselves? This may be the case, but perhaps something else is also going on. As we will see below, both at Sissi and at Malia, the small LM II structures were followed by large complexes, and this seems also to be the case elsewhere in the Cretan countryside. The restudy of the remains on a hill at Kephali Chondros Viannos showed that the core of this complex was an original central residence with Knossian characteristics continuously inhabited between LM II and LM IIIA2 when it suffered a fire destruction (Platon 2022). This central residence counts about 10 rooms, and it was against its walls that all other rooms were constructed afterwards in LM IIIA2 and IIIB (Platon 2022: 282–283). Does Chondros illustrate a new process of a gradually expanding social group and the recreation or renaissance of a larger corporate unit, in a sense announcing what happened, e.g., at Late Geometric Vronda (Gaignerot-Driessen 2016: 149)? This process — the recreation of larger corporate units — is a phenomenon which we can observe immediately after the fall of Knossos in LM IIIA2.

One of the most persisting problems facing Minoan archaeologists is not in which period to place the destruction of the palace at Knossos, but rather when precisely within the Late Minoan IIIA period this happened: at the beginning, the middle, or the end? Our pottery resolutions do not allow this conundrum to be solved for the moment. While Evans had suggested Late Minoan II, i.e., around 1400 BCE, Popham modified this into early LM IIIA2 (around 1375 BCE), with Raison proposing 1350 BCE and Macdonald (2005) going down to 1325 BCE (Driessen 2008). Does this really matter? We think so. Deciding when the destruction happened in the 14th century BCE is important for our historical thinking. Just one example: the megaron and other buildings at Hagia Triada are said to have been constructed in LM IIIA2 but we have no way of deciding whether this was *before* or *after* the destruction of Knossos.[1] The same goes for most of the larger building complexes in the excavation of which I was involved: Quartier Nu at Malia and Building CDE at Sissi (Driessen 2017 for a more detailed analysis). Both buildings preserved plenty of good floor assemblages *in situ* and both complexes were constructed on top of the ruins of earlier buildings. We may envisage that this reflects both a structural concern and an attempt to link with the past. For Quartier Nu, we assume that, because of its regularity, a core building to the east was first laid out early in LM IIIA2 but soon after the complex developed around a small central court which carries the thus far only Bronze Age pebble mosaic found on Crete. In its first phase, when a kitchen/tower still functioned to the east, the entire complex may have functioned as a single unit. After an earthquake destruction, however, the west side may have been abandoned (as was the east kitchen/tower), and only the east part was reused till this burned down late in LM IIIB. If this interpretation is correct, we would have a repetition of what we saw at Chondros Viannos, the gradual extension of a core building into a multiroom complex. At Sissi, Building CD may also have started off with a core building, which was expanded into a much larger complex CDE in early LM IIIB. This too, however, suffered from an earthquake accompanied by fire after which the south wing was given up, but the north wing continued till the advanced LM IIIB period.

Does this turn Nu and Sissi CDE into *Houses*, as existed in earlier Minoan times? If we recall the six characteristics mentioned earlier, they do answer most of the requirements. The buildings have a large size in common, each counting about 30 rooms, quite surprising for the period. But although there is also a vertical stratigraphy with the palimpsestic rebuilding on the same spot, it seems that we have relatively modest core buildings which only develop later into larger complexes by horizontally adding additional spaces and functions. In both cases, however, the complexes were intentionally placed on earlier structures as if they wanted to create a link with a longer genealogy. We also have a few foundation deposits stressing the importance of the construction. Both complexes include halls that could serve for larger numbers of people, including non-residents, and in both cases, there is sufficient ritual equipment to claim that they also had a cultic function (Gaignerot-Driessen 2014). Moreover, pits associated with both complexes also show that feasting was a major element in the social relations of the residents and potentially also included non-residents (Driessen, Farnoux, and Langohr 2008). Architectural elaboration, however, seems much reduced although the presence of house-related imagery such as the large house model and pebble mosaic at Malia Quartier Nu and the hut-models found at Sissi may be relevant here, stressing their emblematic use.

The archaeological evidence, taken broadly, hence seems to suggest different developments. On the one hand, there exist old corporate groups residing within large

1 Privitera (2016: 153) mentions for example that the Casa VAP was built "at the very beginning of LM IIIA2" with changes in the house taking place "at an advanced stage of LM IIIA2" and that the Hagia Triada painted sarcophagus dates to the "ripe LM IIIA2" (2016: 155).

complexes in a few major settlements that survived the LM IB destructions but seem to have disappeared with the LM IIIA2 destruction of the palace. On the other hand, new, small-scale social units develop into larger corporate groups. These seem to have started before the destruction of the Knossos palace but continued and even thrived afterwards, at least till the end of the 13th century BCE. This also seems to imply that there was a renaissance of a type of Minoan *House* different undoubtedly from the earlier type. It also seems to imply indeed that the *House* model was very much a social solution that was closely linked to the Cretan environment and economy.

How to make this settlement evidence agree with funerary data is not easy since there is little evidence for truly collective tombs during the Final and Postpalatial periods on Crete, and, as mentioned, collective tombs are more commonly associated with Lévi-Straussian *House Societies*.[2] To explain the absence of collective tombs it is often suggested that corporate identity was largely given up to the advantage of individual status, expressed through precious grave gifts such as jewelry, bronze weapons, and vases. This privatization of luxury goods by a minority would hence betray a considerable change in the sociopolitical system. This should perhaps be mitigated. That there is a change cannot be denied but it was perhaps less world-shocking than assumed. For a start we should note with Galanakis (2022: 148) that six out of 11 Neopalatial funerary locations at Knossos show *continuity*, paralleling the settlement evidence of the Unexplored Mansion and other buildings mentioned above. It should also be remembered that even the Tlingits, a tribe that Lévi-Strauss used to back up his *House Society* theory, practiced individual inhumation usually within *House*-related burial plots. Can we conjecture something similar for Crete? Galanakis (2022) has also noted how rare it is to find tombs on Crete during the Final and Postpalatial period that were used for more than a few individuals, and this is in some contrast with the Mainland where there is good evidence for collective burials. Two remarks are in order here. Although our evidence is fragmented, it seems probable that each major settlement on Crete had *multiple* burial grounds during this period and each ground could have belonged to a specific *House*. At Knossos, burial grounds are found at Gypsades, Zafer Papoura, Ailias, Sellopoulo, and Mavrospelio, but the same may be true for e.g., Palaikastro, Chania, Malia, Archanes, and Phaistos, all sites where several burial plots have been identified that were in use at the same time. We can even wonder if cemeteries that are located at some distance from each other, such as that of Mochlos-Limenaria and Myrsini, with respectively 31 and 12 tombs, could have belonged to separate groups residing in the same settlement (Smith 2020). The same may be the case for Karphi, Vrokastro, and in the Messara where quite a lot of small cemeteries cluster in the same general area (Girella 2020). I would not go as far as Naglak and Terrenato (2020: 33–34) who assumed that an entire cemetery of 600 graves in Osteria dell'Osa near Gabii should be attributed to a single *House*. On Crete, spatial clustering of tombs *within* large cemeteries can already be noted at earlier Sphoungaras and this is also the case at Zafer Papoura and Armenoi. In this last cemetery, Eleni Papadopoulou (2017) has recognized three separate clusters while the Maroulas cemetery has two groups of tombs apparently used simultaneously. Tomb clustering is evidently an argument used to conjecture the existence of a *House Society* on the Mycenaean Mainland but on its own (i.e., without relevant settlement data) I would remain careful about such conclusions.

Finally, we can ask who the people were residing in these new, gradually expanding Final and Postpalatial complexes. I would agree with Dimitri Nakassis (2022) that their occupants may have been those who are known from our Linear B studies as "collectors," some kind of elite with multiple interests, variously interpreted as stakeholders, aristocrats, or nobles. Perhaps *House* representatives would be a better term and Landenius Enegren (2008) already suggested that the collector names could express household/clan affiliations, in the manner of the second personal name recorded in the genitive case in early Mesopotamian texts (the pre-Sargonic Farah administrative lists). Although collectors are regularly mentioned with their names, often they also occur in the adjectival form and perhaps interpreting these as "of the *House* of Wewesijojo," helps us to understand them better as indicating decentralized elite Houses. Neither at Sissi nor at Malia do these large "collector" complexes stand on their own and smaller buildings also exist, occupied at the same time. These may have comprised dependent nuclear families, retainers, allies, or neighbors of some sort. And this mixture of large and small households seems also the case at Gouves, Amnissos, Samonas, Palaikastro, and Chania, simply judging from the sizes of the residential evidence.

Conclusion

What I have suggested in this paper is that the specific social structure as represented by the Minoan *House* partly survived the troubles of the LM IB period in some of the main settlements but that, during Late Minoan II, new more individualizing types of elites established themselves or were created in both the capital and the countryside, perhaps filling up a power vacuum left by the elimination

2 This said, we may miss part of our LM II–IIIA evidence since later interferences clearly happened. At Sissi, within the ruins of a Neopalatial House tomb, a LM II–IIIA1 shaft grave was installed; this was used twice, the last burial being disturbed, the earlier one, of a woman, remaining intact (Driessen and Mouthuy 2022). In the same ruins, however, we also found a pit with redeposited human bones and LM IIIA2 miniature vases, as well as a box with the remains of at least six people and LM IIIA vases, including a conical cup, a piriform jug, a jar, and a pyxis lid while nearby were primary depositions.

of earlier groups. While both the old and new elites may have been obliterated in the capital together with central authority with the destruction of the palace at Knossos in LM IIIA2, the countryside elites seem to be at the basis of the development of new corporate groups. Why is this? Largely, I suspect, because it was the best, most adapted or most engrained social system to the Cretan environment and mixed economy in which flock keeping, cereals, vines and olives demanded an intergenerational labor investment by a larger corporate group that acted as one, and organized its own internal specialization which could not be assured by the smaller social units or households. But the insular involvement surely also played a role since comparative ethnographic work has shown that in such situations men are often absent for trade, forcing those who stay behind to form more extensive groups in which females played a major role and ensured economic production. Extensive corporate groups, however, are detrimental to central authority and it may be suggested that, from the outset, the Knossian Linear B administration may not have been entirely favorable to their presence even if it needed these to be operational. Later, external dominators such as the Romans, the Venetians, Ottomans, and the modern Athenian state have each tried to eliminate such groupings. This said, the Cretan *Soï* still survives today (Herzfeld 1983; Daskalopoulou 2018).

Acknowledgements

It was with immense pleasure that I came back to Tallahassee, almost to the day 16 years after the first Langford meeting on the Political Economy of the Bronze Age took place in 2007, and I thank Dan Pullen for the invitation and him, his colleagues, and students for their warm welcome. Thanks also to Quentin Letesson, Dimitri Nakassis and Maria Relaki for comments on the manuscript.

Bibliography

Adams, R. L., and A. Kusumawati, 2011. The Social Life of Tombs in West Sumba, Indonesia. *Archaeological Papers of the American Anthropological Association* 20: 17–32.

Alt, K. W., S. Zesch, R. Garrido-Pena, C. Knipper, A. Szécséni-Nagy, C. Roth, C. Tejedor-Rodriguez, P. Held, I. Garcia-Martinez-de-Kagràn, D. Navitanuck, H. Arcusa Magallón and M.A. Rojo-Guerra, 2016. A Community in Life and Death: The Late Neolithic Megalithic Tomb at Alto de Reinoso (Burgos, Spain). *PLoS One* 2016 Jan 20: 11(1):e0146176. DOI:10.1371/journal.pone.0146176.

Apostolaki, E., 2015. On the Household Structure of Neopalatial Society. In *Minoan Archaeology: Perspectives for the 21st Century. Proceedings of the International PhD and Post-Doc Conference at Heidelberg, 23–27 March* 2011, edited by S. Cappel, U. Günkel-Maschek and D. Panagiotopoulos, 223–239. Aegis 8. Louvain-la-Neuve: Presses universitaires de Louvain.

Artursson, M., 2015. The Long-House as a Transforming Agent. Emergent Complexity in Late Neolithic and Early Bronze Age Southern Scandinavia 2300–1300 BC. In *The Bell Beaker Transition in Europe*, edited by M. M. Prieto Martinez and L. Salanova, 69–76. Oxford: Oxbow Books.

Beck, R. A., Jr., ed., 2007. *The Durable House: House Society Models in Archaeology*. Center for Archaeological Investigations, Occasional Paper 35. Carbondale: Southern Illinois University.

Bradfer-Burdet, I., 2003. Malia. Quartier Epsilon. *Bulletin de correspondance hellénique* 127: 452–455.

Bradfer-Burdet, I., 2004. Malia. Quartier Epsilon. *Bulletin de correspondance hellénique* 128–129.2.1: 960–968.

Bradfer-Burdet, I., 2006. Malia. Quartier Epsilon. *Bulletin de correspondance hellénique* 130: 756–757.

Brogan, T., R. A. K. Smith, and J. S. Soles, 2002. Mycenaeans at Mochlos? Exploring Culture and Identity in the Late Minoan IB to IIIA1 Transition. *Aegean Archaeology* 6: 89–118.

Caloi, I., 2018. Inaugurating the Court-Centred Building? A MM IIIB Feasting Deposit at Neopalatial Sissi, North-Central Crete. *Studi micenei ed egeo-anatolici n.s.* 4: 7–39.

Carsten, J., and S. Hugh-Jones, eds. 1995. *About The House — Levi-Strauss and Beyond.* Cambridge: Cambridge University Press.

Chiang, C.-H., 2015. "Houses" in the Wansan Society, Neolithic Taiwan. *Journal of Anthropological Archaeology* 39: 151–163.

Coupland, G., and E. B. Banning, eds. 1996. *People who Lived in Big Houses: Archaeological Perspectives on Large Domestic Structures.* Monographs in World Archaeology 27. Madison, Wisconsin: Prehistory Press.

D'Agata, A. L., L. Girella, E. Papadopoulou, and D. G. Aquine, eds. 2022. *One State, Many Worlds: Crete in the Late Minoan II–IIIA2 Early Period. Proceedings of the International Conference held at Khania,* Μεγάλο Αρσενάλι, *21st – 23rd November 2019*. Studi micenei ed egeo-anatolici n.s. Supplemento 2. Rome: Edizioni Quasar.

Daskalopoulou, S., 2018. Territorialités et structure des familles linéaires d'Anoyia. *HAL Open Science* 01856047. https://hal.science/hal-01856047.

Deshayes, J., and A. Dessenne, 1959. *Fouilles exécutées à Malia: Exploration des maisons et des quartiers d'habitation (1948–1954).* Études crétoises 11. Paris: Geuthner.

Devolder, M., 2018. The Functions of Masons' Marks in the Bronze Age Palace at Malia (Crete). *American Journal of Archaeology* 122: 343–365.

Dickinson, O. T. P. K., 2020. Review of M. Relaki and Y. Papadatos, eds. *From the Foundations to the Legacy of Minoan Archaeology. Journal of Greek Archaeology* 5: 577–580.

Driessen, J., 2008. Chronology of the Linear B Texts. In *A Companion to Linear B: Mycenaean Greek Texts and their World*, edited by Y. Duhoux and A. Morpurgo Davies, 69–79. Bibliothèque des cahiers de l'Institut de Linguistique de Louvain 120. Louvain-la-Neuve: Peeters.

Driessen, J., 2010a. Spirit of Place: Minoan Houses as Major Actors. In *Political Economies of the Aegean Bronze Age: Papers from the Langford Conference, Florida State University, Tallahassee, 22–24 February 2007*, edited by D. J. Pullen, 35–65. Oxford: Oxbow Books.

Driessen, J., 2010b. The Goddess and the Skull: Some Observations on Group Identity in Prepalatial Crete. In *Cretan Offerings: Studies in Honour of Peter Warren*, edited by O. Krzyszkowska, 107–117. British School at Athens Studies 18. London: The British School at Athens.

Driessen, J., 2012. A Matrilocal House Society in Pre- and Protopalatial Crete? In *Back to the Beginning: Reassessing Social and Political Complexity on Crete during the Early and Middle Bronze Age*, edited by I. Schoep, P. Tomkins, and J. Driessen, 358–383. Oxford: Oxbow Books.

Driessen, J., 2015. For an Archaeology of Minoan Society. Identifying the Principles of Social Structure. In *Minoan Archaeology: Perspectives for the 21st Century. Proceedings of the International PhD and Post-Doc Conference at Heidelberg, 23–27 March 2011*, edited by S. Cappel, U. Günkel-Maschek, and D. Panagiotopoulos, 149–166. Aegis 8. Louvain-la-Neuve: Presses universitaires de Louvain.

Driessen, J., 2017. Understanding Minoan In-House relationships on Late Bronze Age Crete. In *Minoan Architecture and Urbanism: New Perspectives on an Ancient Built Environment*, edited by Q. Letesson and C. J. Knappett, 80–104. Oxford: Oxford University Press.

Driessen, J., 2018. Beyond the Collective... The Minoan Palace in Action. In *From the Foundations to the Legacy of Minoan Archaeology: Studies in Honour of Professor Keith Branigan*, edited by M. Relaki and Y. Papadatos, 291–313. Sheffield Studies in Aegean Archaeology 12. Oxford: Oxbow Books.

Driessen, J., and A. Farnoux, 1994. Mycenaeans at Malia? *Aegean Archaeology* 1: 54–64.

Driessen, J., A. Farnoux, and C. Langohr, 2008. Favissae. Feasting Pits in LM III. In *Dais: The Aegean Feast. Proceedings of the 12th International Aegean Conference/ 12e Rencontre égéenne internationale, University of Melbourne, 25–29 March 2008*, edited by L. Hitchcock, R. Laffineur, and J. Crowley, 197–205. Aegaeum 29. Liège: Université de Liège, Histoire de l'art et archéologie de la Grèce antique and Austin: University of Texas at Austin, Program in Aegean Scripts and Prehistory.

Driessen, J., and Q. Letesson, 2023. The Gathering. Collectivity and the Development of Bronze Age Cretan Society. *Journal of Archaeological Research* 32: 1–58. DOI:10.1007/s10814-023-09183-1.

Driessen, J., and C. F. Macdonald, 1997. *The Troubled Island: Minoan Crete before and after the Santorini Eruption*. Aegaeum 17. Liège: Université de Liège, Histoire de l'art et archéologie de la Grèce antique;. Austin: University of Texas at Austin, Program in Aegean Scripts and Prehistory.

Driessen, J., and O. Mouthuy, 2022. The LM II–IIIA2 Kingdom of Knossos as Reflected by its Linear B Archives. In *One State, Many Worlds: Crete in the Late Minoan II–IIIA2 Early Period. Proceedings of the International Conference held at Khania,* Μεγάλο Αρσενάλι, *21st – 23rd November 2019*, edited by A. L. D'Agata, L. Girella, E. Papadopoulou, and D. G. Aquine, 71–84. Studi micenei ed egeo-anatolici n.s. Supplemento 2. Rome: Edizioni Quasar.

Driessen, J., and M. Relaki, 2020. House Rules.... In *Oikos. Archaeological Approaches to House Societies in the Bronze Age Aegean*, edited by M. Relaki and J. Driessen, 1–6. Aegis 19. Louvain-la-Neuve: Presses universitaires de Louvain.

Efkleidou, K., 2020. Looking for Houses in the Tombs: The Evidence for House Societies in the Mycenaean Argolid. In *Oikos: Archaeological Approaches to House Societies in the Bronze Age Aegean*, edited by M. Relaki and J. Driessen, 289–308. Aegis 19. Louvain-la-Neuve: Presses universitaires de Louvain.

Ensor, B., 2013. *The Archaeology of Kinship: Advancing Interpretation and Contributions to Theory*. Tucson: University of Arizona Press.

Evely, R. D. G., 2000. *Minoan Crafts: Tools and Techniques. An Introduction*. Studies in Mediterranean Archaeology 92. Jonsered: Paul Åströms Förlag.

Gaignerot-Driessen, F., 2014. Goddesses Refusing to Appear? Reconsidering the Late Minoan III Figures with Upraised Arms. *American Journal of Archaeology* 118: 489–520.

Gaignerot-Driessen, F., 2016. *De l'occupation postpalatiale à la cité-état grecque: le cas du Mirambello (Crète)*. Aegaeum 40. Leuven-Liège: Peeters.

Galanakis, Y., 2022. Neither Minoan nor Mycenaean: The Burial Record of Knossos and the Materialisation of a New Social Order, 1600–1400. In *One State, Many Worlds: Crete in the Late Minoan II–IIIA2 Early Period. Proceedings of the International Conference held at Khania, Μεγάλο Αρσενάλι, 21st – 23rd November 2019*, edited by A. L. D'Agata, L. Girella, E. Papadopoulou, and D.G. Aquine, 139–178. Studi micenei ed egeo-anatolici n.s. Supplemento 2. Rome: Edizioni Quasar.

Girella, L., 2020. Middle Minoan III—Late Minoan IIIB Tombs and Funerary Practices in South-Central Crete.

In *Death in Late Bronze Age Greece*, edited by J. M. A. Murphy, 248–281. Oxford: Oxford University Press.

González-Ruibal, A., 2006. House Societies vs. Kinship-Based Societies: An Archaeological Case from Iron Age Europe. *Journal of Anthropological Archaeology* 25: 144–173.

González-Ruibal, A., and M. Ruiz-Gálvez, 2016. House Societies in the Ancient Mediterranean (2000–500 BC). *Journal of World Prehistory* 29: 383–437.

Haggis, D. C., 2007. Stylistic Diversity and Diacritical Feasting at Protopalatial Petras: A Preliminary Analysis of the Lakkos Deposit. *American Journal of Archaeology* 111: 715–775.

Haggis, D. C., 2013. Destruction and the Formation of Static and Dynamic Settlement Structures in the Aegean. In *Destruction: Archaeological, Philological and Historical Perspectives*, edited by J. Driessen, 63–87. GRAAL: Groupe de recherches en archéologie et anthropologie de Louvain 1. Louvain-la-Neuve: Presses universitaires de Louvain.

Hallager, E., and B. P. Hallager, eds. 2016. *The Greek-Swedish Excavations at the Agia Aikaterini Square, Kastelli, Khania, 1970–1987, 2001, 2005 and 2008: Results of the Excavations under the Direction of Yannis Tzedakis and Carl-Gustaf Styrenius. Volume V.1 and 2: The Late Minoan IIIA: I and II Settlements.* Skrifter utgivna av Svenska Institutet i Athen 4° 47:5: 1–2, Stockholm: Svenska Institutet i Athen.

Hatzaki, E., 2011. Defining "Domestic" Architecture and "Household" Assemblages in Late Bronze Age Knossos. In *ΣΤΕΓΑ: The Archaeology of Houses and Households in Ancient Crete*, edited by K. T. Glowacki and N. Vogeikoff-Brogan, 247–262. Hesperia Supplement 44. Athens: American School of Classical Studies at Athens.

Herzfeld, M., 1983. Interpreting Kinship Terminology: The Problem of Patriliny in Rural Greece. *Anthropological Quarterly* 56: 157–166.

Jeunesse, C., N. Bec-Drelon, B. Boulestin, and A. Denaire, 2021. Aspects de la gestion des dolmens et des tombes collectives actuels dans les sociétés de l'île de Sumba (Indonésie). *Préhistoires méditerranéennes* 9.2: 165–179. DOI:10.4000/pm.3098.

Johnson, K. M., and K. S. Paul, 2016. Bioarchaeology and Kinship: Integrating Theory, Social Relatedness, and Biology in Ancient Family Research. *Journal of Archaeological Research* 24: 75–123.

Joyce, A. R., and S. D. Gillespie, eds., 2000. *Beyond Kinship: Social and Material Reproduction in House Societies.* Philadelphia: University of Pennsylvania Press.

Kalantzopoulou, T., 2022. *Taking the High Road: Prehistoric Habitation and Exploitation in the Mountains of East Crete. New Evidence from an Extensive Survey.* Aegis 22. Louvain-la-Neuve: Presses universitaires de Louvain.

Karacic, S. T., 2015. All Aboard: The Longboat and a Heterarchical Interpretation of the Mochlos Cemetery. In *Minoan Archaeology: Perspectives for the 21st Century. Proceedings of the International PhD and Post-Doc Conference at Heidelberg, 23–27 March 2011*, edited by S. Cappel, U. Günkel-Maschek, and D. Panagiotopoulos, 167–180. Aegis 8. Louvain-la-Neuve: Presses universitaires de Louvain.

Kuo, S.-C., 2021. The House Society of Paiwan Tribe in Southern Taiwan. *Academia Letters 2021* DOI:10.20935/AL3734.

Landenius Enegren, H., 2008. *The People of Knossos: Prosopographical studies in the Knossos Linear B archives.* Boreas: Uppsala Studies in Ancient Mediterranean and Near Eastern Civilizations 30. Uppsala: Uppsala University Library.

Letesson, Q., 2014. From Building to Architecture: The Rise of Configurational Thinking in Bronze Age Crete. In *Spatial Analysis and Social Spaces: Interdisciplinary Approaches to the Interpretation of Prehistoric and Historic Bult Environments*, edited by E. Paliou, L. Undine and S. Polla, 49–90. Topoi: Berlin Studies of the Ancient World 18. Berlin and Boston: Walter de Gruyter.

Letesson, Q., and J. Driessen, 2020. 'On the House': A Diachronic Look on the Configuration of Minoan Social Relationships. In *Oikos: Archaeological approaches to House Societies in the Bronze Age Aegean*, edited by M. Relaki and J. Driessen, 7–24. Aegis 19. Louvain-la-Neuve: Presses universitaires de Louvain.

Lévi-Strauss, C., 1983. *The Way of the Masks*. London: Jonathan Cape Ltd.

Macdonald, C. F., 2005. *Knossos*. London: The Folio Society Ltd.

Macdonald, C. F., 2011. LM IB Phases at Mochlos and the Single Phase of LM IB at Knossos: A Response to Kellee Barnard and Thomas Brogan. In *LM IB pottery: Relative Chronology and Regional Differences. Acts of a Workshop Held at the Danish Institute at Athens in Collaboration with the INSTAP Study Center for East Crete, 27–29 June 2007*, edited by T. M. Brogan and E. Hallager, 451–456. Monographs of the Danish Institute at Athens 11.1-2. Athens: The Danish Institute at Athens.

Macdonald, C. F., 2022. Architectural Continuity, Renovation and Innovation in the Town and Palace of Knossos, LM IB–IIIA1. In *One State, Many Worlds: Crete in the Late Minoan II–IIIA2 Early Period. Proceedings of the International Conference held at Khania, Μεγάλο Αρσενάλι, 21st – 23rd November 2019*, edited by A. L. D'Agata, L. Girella, E. Papadopoulou, and D. G. Aquine, 117–128. Studi micenei ed egeo-anatolici n.s. Supplemento 2. Rome: Edizioni Quasar.

Macdonald, C. F., and C. Knappett, 2007. *Knossos: Protopalatial Deposits in Early Magazine A and the South-West Houses*. British School at Athens Supplementary Volume 41. London: The British School at Athens.

MacGillivray, J. A., and L. H. Sackett, eds. 2019. *Palaikastro Building 1*. British School at Athens Supplementary Volume 48. London: The British School at Athens.

Mathioudaki, I. 2022. Reconstructing the Neopalatial Pottery Sequence at Sissi. In *Excavations at Sissi. V. Preliminary Report on the 2017–2019 Campaigns*, edited by J. Driessen, 524–574. Aegis 21, Louvain-la-Neuve: Presses universitaires de Louvain.

Monton-Subias, S., and M. Sanchez-Romero, eds., 2008. *Engendering Social Dynamics: The Archaeology of Maintenance Activities*. British Archaeological Reports International Series 1862. Oxford: Archaeopress.

Moreno Garcia, J. C., ed., 2022. *From House Societies to States: Early Political Organisation from Antiquity to the Middle Ages*. Multidisciplinary Approaches to Ancient Societies 3. Oxford: Oxbow Books.

Morgan, C., 2015. The Work of the British School at Athens. *Archaeological Reports* 61: 34–48.

Naglak, M. C., and N. Terrenato, 2020. Central Italian Elite Groups as Aristocratic Houses in the Ninth to Sixth Centuries BCE. In *Roman Law before the Twelve Tables*, edited by S. W. Bell and P. J. du Plessis, 25–40. Edinburgh: Edinburgh University Press.

Nakassis, D., 2022. Communities, 'Houses', and Political Organisation in the Mycenaean World. In *From House Societies to States: Early Political Organisation from Antiquity to the Middle Ages*, edited by J. C. Moreno García, 123–140. Multidisciplinary Approaches to Ancient Societies 3. Oxford: Oxbow Books.

Nelson-Hurst, M. G., 2015. The (social) house of Khnumhotep. In *The World of Middle Kingdom Egypt (2000–1550 BC)*, edited by G. Miniaci and W. Gratjetzki, 257–272. Middle Kingdom Studies 1, London: Golden House Publications.

Papadopoulou, E., 2017. LM III Mortuary Practices in West Crete: The Cemeteries of Maroulas and Armenoi near Rethymnon. *Studi micenei ed egeo-anatolici n.s.* 3: 131–157.

Pelon, O., 1967. La Maison Epsilon reconsidérée. *Bulletin de correspondance hellénique* 91: 494–512.

Pelon, O., 1970. *Fouilles exécutées à Malia: Exploration des maisons et des quartiers d'habitation (1963–1966). 3. Le Quartier E.* Études crétoises 16. Paris: Geuthner.

Platon, L., 2022. Kephali Chondros, Viannos. The Post-Neopalatial Settlement. In *One State, Many Worlds: Crete in the Late Minoan II–IIIA2 Early Period. Proceedings of the International Conference held at Khania, Μεγάλο Αρσενάλι, 21st – 23rd November 2019*, edited by A. L. D'Agata, L. Girella, E. Papadopoulou, and D. G. Aquine, 281–292. Studi micenei ed egeo-anatolici n.s. Supplemento 2. Rome: Edizioni Quasar.

Popham, M. R., J. H. Betts, M. Cameron, H. W. Catling, E. A. Catling, D. Evely, R. A. Higgins and D. Smyth, 1984. *The Minoan Unexplored Mansion at Knossos*. British School of Archaeology at Athens Supplementary Volume 17. Oxford: Thames and Hudson.

Privitera, S., 2016. The Tomb, the House, and the Double Axes: Late Minoan IIIA2 Hagia Triada as a Ritual and 'Mythical' Place. In *Metaphysis: Ritual, Myth and Symbolism in the Aegean Bronze Age. Proceedings of the 15th International Aegean Conference, Vienna, 22–25 April 2014*, edited by E. Alram-Stern, F. Blakolmer, S. Deger-Jalkotzy, R. Laffineur, and J. Weilhartner, 149–156. Aegaeum 39. Leuven-Liege: Peeters.

Puglisi, D., 2020. Rites of Passage in Minoan Palatial Crete and their Role in structuring a House Society. In *Oikos: Archaeological approaches to House Societies in the Bronze Age Aegean*, edited by M. Relaki, and J. Driessen, 63–80. Aegis 19. Louvain-la-Neuve: Presses universitaires de Louvain.

Pullen, D. J., ed., 2010. *Political Economies of the Aegean Bronze Age: Papers from the Langford Conference, Florida State University, Tallahassee, 22–24 February 2007*. Oxford: Oxbow Books.

Relaki, M., 2009. Rethinking administration and seal use in Third Millennium Crete. *Creta Antica* 10: 353–372.

Relaki, M., and Y. Papadatos, eds., 2018. *From the Foundations to the Legacy of Minoan Archaeology: Studies in Honour of Professor Keith Branigan*. Sheffield Studies in Aegean Archaeology 12. Oxford: Oxbow Books.

Relaki, M., and J. Driessen, eds., 2020. *Oikos: Archaeological Approaches to House Societies in the Bronze Age Aegean*. Aegis 19. Louvain-la-Neuve: Presses universitaires de Louvain.

Rutter, J. B., 2017. *House X at Kommos: A Minoan Mansion near the Sea. Part 2. The Pottery*. Prehistory Monographs 57. Philadelphia: INSTAP Academic Press.

Schoep, I., 2004. Assessing the Role of Architecture in Conspicuous Consumption in the Middle Minoan I–II Periods. *Oxford Journal of Archaeology* 23: 243–269.

Schoep, I., 2007. Architecture and Power: The Origins of the Minoan 'Palatial Architecture'. In *Power and Architecture: Monumental Public Architecture in the Bronze Age Near East and Aegean*, edited by J. Bretschneider, J. Driessen, and K. van Lerberghe, 213–236. Orientalia Lovaniensia Analecta 156. Leuven: Peeters Publishers.

Schmitt, A., S. Déderix, and I. Crevecoeur, eds., 2018. *Gathered in Death: Archaeological and Ethnological*

Perspectives on Collective Burial and Social Organisation. Aegis 14. Louvain-la-Neuve: Presses universitaires de Louvain.

Shaw, M. C., and J. W. Shaw, eds., 2012. *House X at Kommos: A Minoan Mansion near the Sea. Part 1. Architecture, Stratigraphy, and Selected Finds*. Prehistory Monographs 35. Philadelphia: INSTAP Academic Press.

Sissons, J., 2010. Building a House Society: The Reorganization of Maori Communities Around Meeting Houses. *Journal of the Royal Anthropological Institute* 16: 372–386. DOI:10.1111/j.1467-9655.2010.01630.x.

Skourtanioti, E., H. Ringbauer, G. A. Gnecchi Ruscone, R. A. Bianco, M. Burri, C. Freund, A. Furtwängler, N. F. Gomes Martins, F. Knolle, G. U. Neumann, A. Tiliakou, A. Agelarakis, M. Andreadaki-Vlazaki, P. P. Betancourt, B. P. Hallager, O. A. Jones, O. Kakavogianni, A. Kanta, P. Karkanas, E. Kataki, K. Kissas, R. Koehl, L. Kvapil, J. Maran, P. J. P. McGeorge, A. Papadimitriou, A. Papathanasiou, L. Papazoglou-Manioudaki, K. Paschalidis, N. Polychronakou-Sgouritza, S. Preve, E.-A. Prevedorou, G. Price, E. Protopapadaki, T. Schmidt-Schultz, M. Schultz, K. Shelton, M. Wiener, J. Krause, C. Jeong, and P. W. Stockhammer, 2023. Ancient DNA reveals admixture history and endogamy in the prehistoric Aegean. *Nature Ecology & Evolution* 7: 290–303. DOI:10.1038/s41559-022-01952-3.

Smith, R. A. K., 2020. The Power of the Dead. In *Death in Late Bronze Age Greece*, edited by J. M. A. Murphy, 282–299. Oxford: Oxford University Press.

Soles, J. S., and C. Davaras, eds., 2011. *Mochlos IIC: Period IV. The Mycenaean Settlement and Cemetery: The Human Remains and Other Finds*. Prehistory Monographs 32. Philadelphia: INSTAP Academic Press.

Thomas, J., 2016. House Societies and the Beginning of the British Neolithic. In *Dialogue: Tradition and Interaction in the Mesolithic*, edited by J. Thomas, J. Debert, and M. Larsson, 3–10. British Archaeological Reports International Series 2809. Oxford: Archaeopress.

Vavouranakis, G., 2007. *Funerary Landscapes East of Lasithi, Crete, in the Bronze Age*. British Archaeological Reports International Series 1606. Oxford: Archaeopress.

Warren, P. M., 1983. Knossos: Stratigraphical Museum Excavations, 1978–1982. Part I. *Archaeological Reports* 29: 63–87.

Watanabe, J., 2004. Some Models in a Muddle: Lineage and House in Classic Maya Social Organization. *Ancient Mesoamerica* 15: 159–166.

Whitelaw, T. M., 2022. Knossos during LM II-IIIB: Dynamism and Development. In *One State, Many Worlds: Crete in the Late Minoan II-IIIA2 Early Period. Proceedings of the International Conference held at Khania, Μεγάλο Αρσενάλι, 21st – 23rd November 2019*, edited by A. L. D'Agata, L. Girella, E. Papadopoulou, and D. G. Aquine, 35–70. Studi micenei ed egeo-anatolici, n.s. Supplemento 2. Rome: Edizioni Quasar.

Wiersma, C., 2020. House(centric) Societies on the Prehistoric Greek Mainland. *Oxford Journal of Archaeology* 39: 141–158. DOI:10.1111/ojoa.12190.

Wynne-Jones, S., 2013. The Public Life of the Swahili Stonehouse, 14th-15th Centuries AD. *Journal of Anthropological Archaeology* 32: 759–773.

Not a Great Kingdom

Mycenaean Economic Variation as a Measure of Nonintegration

Michael L. Galaty
William A. Parkinson

Abstract

Recently, some Aegean archaeologists have begun to talk openly about a Mycenaean "Great Kingdom," perhaps led by Mycenae. Presumably, this kingdom spanned all of southern Greece and integrated the various palace-states, socially, politically, and economically. The evidence cited for a single Great Kingdom includes: 1) architectural similarities; 2) Linear B parallels; 3) the preeminence of Mycenae; 4) descriptions in Homer; 5) references to Ahhiyawa in Eastern Mediterranean texts; and 6) a tacit implication that bigger political formations are always better.

In this paper, we address the Great Kingdom thesis and question the evidence used to construct it. That the Mycenaeans were linked socially across space is indisputable: they shared a language, writing system, and various other cultural behaviors. Social interaction (and shared ontogenies) can explain some of these similarities, but the jump from social interaction to political integration is a large one. We suggest that political integration of the Mycenaean states would have required economic integration, and vice versa. In fact, the primary reason to integrate politically would have been to facilitate economic integration. However, evidence for economic integration within and between Mycenaean states is lacking. Mycenaean economic structures and behaviors are marked not by similarity and redundancy, as might be expected if they were managed from the top down, but rather by differentiation and variability. Seeing how different Mycenaean states might have functioned together economically, let alone politically, is difficult, at best, and this undermines the Great Kingdom thesis.

To support our position, we compare economic data from various Mycenaean states. We describe and compare different Mycenaean economic systems, based on Linear B and archaeological data. Ultimately, this exercise mitigates against a Great Kingdom and reinforces the traditional interpretation, that the Mycenaean states operated independently, as networked social entities that sometimes cooperated, but most often simply ignored one another.

ORCID 000-0001-7754-8347
University of Michigan
Museum of Anthropological
Archaeology
mgalaty@umich.edu

ORCID 0000-0001-7721-1381
Field Museum of Natural
History *and* University of
Illinois at Chicago
wparkinson@fieldmuseum.org

Introduction

In 2010, Jorrit Kelder published *The Kingdom of Mycenae: A Great Kingdom in the Late Bronze Age Aegean*, in which he argued that the Mycenaean states were part of a larger, integrated political formation, i.e., a Great Kingdom or an "empire," with a capital at Mycenae, circa 1500–1200 BCE (Kelder 2010; see also, more recently, Kelder and Waal 2019). Surprisingly, *The Kingdom of Mycenae* was scarcely reviewed in academic journals, and it seems that few Aegean archaeologists gave its controversial thesis much

In *Social Groups and Production in Mycenaean Economies. Papers from the Langford Conference, Florida State University, Tallahassee, 24-25 February 2023*, edited by D. Pullen (2025), 47–58. Leiden: Sidestone Press.

thought, or attention.[1] This inattention was a mistake, made by those of us who reject the notion of a Mycenaean Great Kingdom, because the idea has gained an alarming degree of traction recently.

Kelder was not, of course, the first archaeologist to refer to a Mycenaean Empire — Hooker did so repeatedly in his 1976 book *Mycenaean Greece* (Hooker 1976) — but he has certainly been the most persistent. He is joined by Birgitta Eder and Reinhard Jung, who published a paper called "Unus pro omnibus, omnes pro uno: The Mycenaean Palace System" in 2015, in which they critiqued many of Kelder's conclusions (e.g., that Crete was *not* part of the Mycenaean Great Kingdom), and at the same time argued for an even more expansive, integrated pan-Mycenaean cultural and political system (Eder and Jung 2015). The main problem with Eder and Jung's paper is that they conflate cultural and political systems; the so-called Mycenaean "koine" is taken to be evidence for a Mycenaean super-state, and vice versa. They also privilege evidence from texts, including both those from the Eastern Mediterranean as well as Linear B — as does Kelder — and assert that "the idea of a unified political system in Mycenaean Greece has gained considerable support in recent years from scholars working with the evidence provided by Linear B tablets" (Eder and Jung 2015: 116, citing the example of Olivier 2006, who presented the concept of a Mycenaean Empire, before rejecting it; see also Palaima 2012). One of the strongest supporters of a unified Mycenaean political-administrative system, both before *The Kingdom of Mycenae* was published and since, is well-known Assyriologist Nicholas Postgate. Postgate (2001, 2014, see p. 412 where he cites Kelder 2010; see also Tartaron 2008: 108, who is open to Postgate's ideas about the Mycenaeans, but, ultimately, strongly reaffirms regionalism [see Tartaron 2010]) asserts that similarities in Linear B, from palace to palace, must have been the result of a unified, pan-Mycenaean administrative system. However, it is hard not to see this as "projecting" models of Mesopotamian political organization — and discussions about city-states and empires in that context — onto the Aegean.

Many scholars cite Kelder (2010), alongside other books on Mycenaean archaeology, without taking a position, one way or the other, on the idea of a Mycenaean Great Kingdom (e.g., Iacono et al. 2022: 406). Others are Hittite/Anatolian philologists, historians, and archaeologists (e.g., Beckman, Bryce, and Cline 2012; Blackwell 2014; Roosevelt et al. 2018), who refer to his book in passing, as an authoritative reference on the Mycenaeans, while at the same time giving tacit approval to the idea of a Mycenaean Great Kingdom, which was equal to or in competition with the Hittites. Interestingly, Kelder has recently begun working with Eberhard Zangger, who has strongly advocated for a Luwian Empire, which until now has purportedly remained unknown to archaeology (see Hajnal, Zangger, and Kelder 2022). The existence of one Great Kingdom, the Mycenaean, helps prove the existence of the other, the Luwian, along similar geopolitical lines.

Rebutting the evidence for a Mycenaean Great Kingdom

The arguments made in support of a Mycenaean Great Kingdom, by Kelder (2010) and by Eder and Jung (2015), focus on: 1) similarities from palace to palace; 2) the use of Linear B; 3) the preeminence of Mycenae; 4) descriptions in Homer; 5) references to Ahhiyawa (the Achaeans) in Eastern Mediterranean texts; and 6) an implicit assumption that bigger political formations are always better. We briefly discuss each of these in turn, before turning more specifically to economics.

Similarities between states

Elsewhere, we have argued that despite their shared cultural traits, the Mycenaean states were characterized by significant political-economic variability (cf. Galaty and Parkinson 2007; Galaty et al. 2010; Parkinson and Galaty 2010). This variability is an artifact of very different geographical settings — for example, Pylos is in southwestern Messenia and Mycenae is in the Argolid, with access to different maritime networks (Tartaron 2013) — and different short- and long-term "historical trajectories" (Parkinson and Galaty 2007). Different Mycenaean states in different areas experienced different ontogenetic conditions and development. Shared origins and cultural transmission, with Minoan Crete and between individual states, led to shared practices and styles, in art and architecture for example, thus Renfrew and Cherry's (1986) formulation of Bronze Age "peer polities" in Crete and in general. But this does not mean that political-economic systems were also shared, let alone integrated across borders. Indeed, Minoan political systems were seemingly very different as compared to Mycenaean systems (cf. the "corporate" – "network" distinction: Parkinson and Galaty 2007), and Mycenaean systems were very different as compared to each other, i.e., Late Minoan II-III ("Mycenaean") Knossos was very different from Late Helladic III Pylos was very different from Late Helladic III Mycenae (Galaty and Rutter 2022). This we can say based on archaeology alone, Linear B aside. Economic variability, within and between Mycenaean states, mitigated against pan-Mycenaean political integration;

1 Robert Consoli (https://squinchpix.blogspot.com/2014/12/much-have-itravelled-in-realms-of-gold.html?q=kelder) and Dimitri Nakassis (https://englianos.wordpress.com/2013/08/21/political-unity-in-the-lba/) both wrote blog posts regarding Kelder's thesis. The only published review we could find is Woudhuizen (2010) in *Bibliotheca Orientalis*.

the former disallowed the latter, or made the latter less attractive and, therefore, less likely.

It is often said that the architecture of the Mycenaean palaces is similar from state to state. Indeed, the megarons at different palaces are quite comparable in terms of layout and, seemingly, function. However, this too is most likely the result of shared origins and/or parallel evolution. When there are differences, they often stem from variable degrees of Minoan influence. For example, Early Mycenaean Pylos and Agios Vasileios versus all other palaces, both early and late, were court-centered; the megaron was "imposed" on Pylos, whereas Agios Vaseilios was destroyed before this could happen. Similar architecture at various (late) Mycenaean palaces does not reflect the presence of a single, integrated political system, no more than similar Classical architecture in Athens and Washington D.C. means that Greece and the United States are politically integrated. In fact, when we look at Mycenaean central places, side by side, they are quite dissimilar, reflecting common ancestry, perhaps, and differentiation with modification through time. If we look at the wider landscape, there are additional, obvious differences between, for example, Mycenae and Pylos: at Mycenae, the so-called "mansions," the Grave Circles, the walls, shrines, temple, and Lion Gate; at Pylos, the Northeastern Building, the archive room, the so-called Queen's Megaron, and the port facility at Romanou. These different buildings and infrastructure projects reflect very different regional site and landscape histories, but also materialize very different political-economic systems, ones in which goods were made, stored, and distributed — and power was manifested — very differently.

Similarities in Linear B

Supporters of the Great Kingdom thesis have argued, based on similarities in the structure of Linear B from state to state, that a single system of administration must have been in place. They point to a shared dialect, identical signs and ideograms, similar terminology, for instance, for taxation and officials, and posit that Mycenaean Greek was used as a *lingua franca*. They often cite Postgate (2001, 2014) in support of this interpretation of Linear B, based on Near Eastern parallels. We would argue — again, as with architectural similarities — that the similarities in Linear B stem from a single, shared source, Late Minoan Knossos, and the subsequent spread of Linear B, over time — probably relatively quickly — to all other palaces from that source, perhaps via Pylos. Linear B should be seen as a technology, a tool, one that was adopted fully formed by palatial authorities and then adapted to different regional political-economic systems by specially trained scribes. This explains the absence of literature, histories, and letters; Linear B was implemented for economic purposes only. Ultimately, using Linear B to argue for a pan-Mycenaean system of administration, let alone political integration, is akin to arguing that because computers are used for record-keeping in various cities across the modern world, they must all be administered together, from a single source.

One of the primary arguments in support of a Great Kingdom, made by Kelder (2010, Kelder and Waal 2019) in particular, is that the duties of the *wanax*, the "king," and the *lawagetas*, who was some kind of second-in-command, are difficult to define with certainty and seem to sometimes duplicate one another. Kelder (2010, Kelder and Waal 2019) therefore posits that the wanax was a peripatetic ruler, who operated out of Mycenae, travelling from palace to palace, overseeing his kingdom. Day-to-day duties were handled by the lawagetas. There are numerous problems with this interpretation of the wanax, but Linear B aside, we would note that there is no archaeological evidence whatsoever for this kind of administrative system, tying individual Mycenaean states to Mycenae. If the Mycenaean economy was structured such that surplus goods and finished products were destined for transfer to Mycenae, then the tablets should reflect this. And yet, there are almost no tablets anywhere, from any palace, that record the names of, let alone the transfer of anything, to another Mycenaean state. The tablets from each state for the most part only record the names of places within that state; the economies reflected in the tablets are regional economies. Moreover, as Nakassis (2013) has demonstrated for Pylos, the economy was highly localized and personal, depending on a multitude of named individuals, who participated for a wide variety of reasons and filled numerous roles. Thus, the tablets reflect political-economic systems that met local social as well as fiscal needs. Even those individuals, the so-called "collectors," who had wide-ranging duties, held multiple titles, and occasionally display "international" interests (e.g., in the textile and perfume trades), as described in Linear B, primarily at Pylos, undertake mostly local, even colloquial, activities, such as the raising of sheep (Kyriakidis 2010).

Homer and the preeminence of Mycenae

Even today, Mycenae may appear to be the preeminent Mycenaean center, the wealthiest, the biggest, and the best of the palatial capitals. However, there is no evidence, from Linear B or archaeology, to suggest Mycenae controlled or was integrated with any other Mycenaean state. The geography of Greece would seem to mitigate strongly against such control — with, for example, vassal states sending tribute to Mycenae — let alone integration. If such relationships existed, we would expect to see them reflected in the Pylian Linear B corpus, but they are not, and it is difficult to see exactly how Mycenae would have enforced its rule over long distances and rough terrain. As importantly, it is difficult to understand why Mycenae

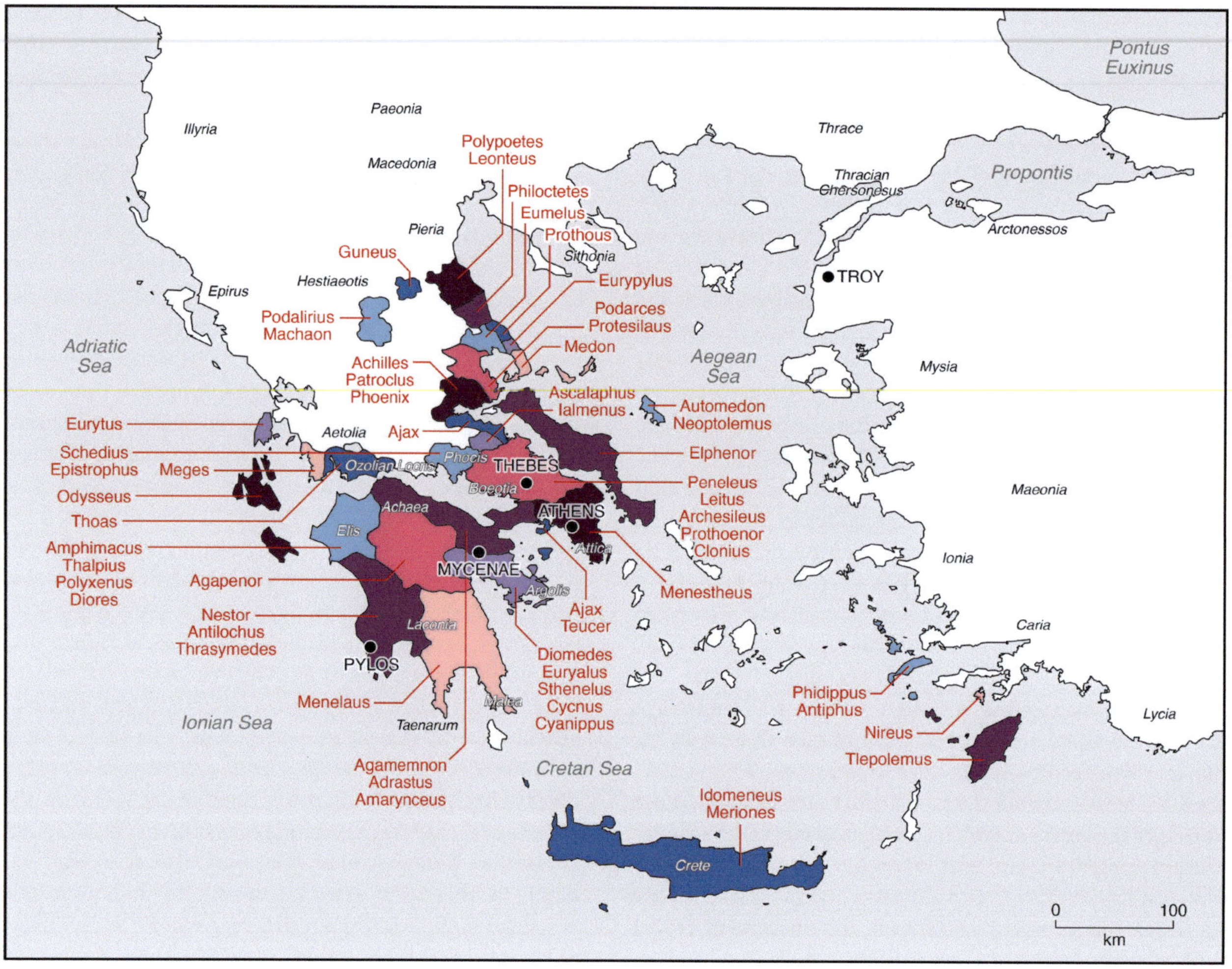

Figure 4.1. Map of Mycenaean territories based on attestations in the *Iliad*. Modified from a map by Carlos Parada, Greek Mythology Link (1997). Bruce Worden.

would have wanted to create and then hold a Great Kingdom. What factors, whether push or pull, would have led to such an outcome?

The short answer is, there are none. As a result, proponents of the Mycenaean Empire thesis, particularly classical scholars, often cite Homer, naming Mycenae the seat of a High King, with Agamemnon at the helm. In fact, Homer makes it clear that Agamemnon was at best a first among equals and was a temporary war leader only. His title as wanax derives from that role as much as, or more than, it does from his rule over Mycenae. Much of the narrative action in the *Iliad* is driven by other kings and warriors, like Achilles, who rebel against Agamemnon's leadership. When Mycenaean territories are mapped based on the *Iliad*, Agamemnon's kingdom looks rather small, smaller than others, by far (Figure 4.1). This fits the archaeology: Mycenae was one kingdom among many. Mycenae's king was one king among many. The best he could do was encourage participation in a joint venture, attacking Troy, in the name of honor, with the promise of plunder. Force was not involved, economics were not involved, the incentives to participate in the war were primarily social. Homer argues against the existence of a Great Kingdom, not for one.

References to Ahhiyawa (the Achaeans) in Eastern Mediterranean texts

Perhaps the main evidence cited by Kelder (2010) and others in support of a Mycenaean Great Kingdom comes from references to Ahhiyawa in Eastern Mediterranean texts. Even if Ahhiyawa can be equated with the Achaeans, and the Achaeans can be equated with the Mycenaeans, which seems possible, we do not know to which Mycenaean state the name "Ahhiyawa" referred. Thus, when a Hittite king wrote a letter, it is unclear to whom he thought he was writing. That the term Ahhiyawa described a real Great Kingdom of all the Mycenaeans, with which eastern rulers regularly communicated, seems like the least likely explanation among many possible explanations.

First, it is a mistake to assume that just because Eastern Mediterranean kings used the term Ahhiyawa, that this was what the "Mycenaeans" called themselves. Throughout human history, external powers, when interacting with non-integrated political systems represented by disparate peoples, often misnamed them and tried to force integration on them. This was done to Native American peoples by European nations repeatedly, who used names like "Sioux" and "Chippewa" to refer to groups who shared languages, and may have interacted socially and sometimes economically, but were not politically integrated. The fact that the name Ahhiyawa — Achaean, one small Greek group among many — is used in Eastern Mediterranean texts, as opposed to the name for Mycenae — Mukanu, as attested in Egyptian texts — works *against* the thesis of a Mycenaean Great Kingdom.

Second, it also seems clear that the Ahhiyawans were minor players. Sherratt's (2001) use of the term "potemkim" to refer to them is in our estimation not far off the mark. They are described as Great Kings but not necessarily treated as such. It may be that emissaries from the East were occasionally sent to Ahhiyawa, bearing gifts, one brother king to another, but this was a seemingly rare occurrence — once in a generation? — and to be honest, *all* the foreign items from all Mycenaean Greece could have arrived there via a single diplomatic mission. It seems that Amenhotep III sent a delegation early in the 14th century BCE, recorded in stone after the fact. The Egyptians knew the names of several Mycenaean — and Minoan — states, including Mycenae, but also Messenia. However, this record also argues against a Mycenaean Great Kingdom. If Mycenae were the capital of a Great Kingdom, why go to these other places? The itinerary may make some geographic sense, but it does not make any sense if this was a diplomatic mission to a Great Kingdom, led by Mycenae.

All that said, there is no question that different Mycenaean states traded with other Mediterranean states. But the nature of that trade remains an open question, one recently addressed in detail by Murray (2017). Was it sponsored by palatial elites, handled by merchants, or a mix of the two? If international trade was in fact under the purview of the palaces, we would expect some mention of it in the Linear B tablets. There is none. If Mycenae was the capital of a Great Kingdom, we would expect some mention of international trade in its Linear B documents to the exclusion of all others. There is none. We would expect foreign goods to come to Mycenae to the exclusion of other states, with perhaps some measure of redistribution. This is not the case. It could be argued that more foreign prestige goods have been recovered from Mycenae than from the other Mycenaean states, but there are numerous, obvious problems with this argument, relating to differential preservation, taphonomy, and archaeological recovery rates. Moreover, as demonstrated by Cline (2007), it seems that different palaces cultivated different international trade partners over time, for example Mycenae with the Egyptians and Tiryns the Cypriots, with almost no eastern imports to Pylos at all. This being the case, it seems almost impossible to sustain an argument for a Great Kingdom based on international trade patterns.

A tacit implication that bigger political formations are always better

By the Late Bronze Age, Mycenae may well have controlled the Argolid and Pylos may have controlled all of Messenia, but their rule, at Pylos in particular (Cosmopoulos 2019; Cosmopoulos et al. 2019), appears to have been short-lived and precarious. Each of the palaces was destroyed at slightly different times, over the course of a relatively short amount of time. The cause or causes of the collapse remain opaque, but if there were a Great Kingdom, and the collapse was the result of an uprising, we would have expected Mycenae to be destroyed first, and the other palaces to have survived. This is not what appears to have happened.

A larger problem for the Great Kingdom thesis, however, is that its proponents never discuss its formation, as correctly noted in the blog post by Consoli, cited above (note 1). If a Great Kingdom existed, when and how was it forged, and why is there no evidence for the formation process? If a Great Kingdom was created through the consolidation of various independent polities, this must have been through war, but there is no evidence for this whatsoever. What evidence exists for the destruction of sites prior to 1200 BCE, e.g., from Iklaina or Agios Vasileios (see Eder and Jung 2015: 124–125), either has not been subjected to absolute dating (Iklaina is the sole exception; Cosmopoulos et al. 2019), or points to consolidation on a local level.[2] It seems much more likely that if there was a war of consolidation, prosecuted by Mycenae, that this happened circa 1200 BCE, and failed. As we ask above, though, if this were the case, why were all the palaces destroyed and abandoned, not just that at Mycenae? The evidence looks much more like a systemic collapse that reverberated throughout the eastern Mediterranean, rather than the takeover of a capital city.

We would assert, strongly, that political independence is a particularly Greek trait. It may be a human trait. We are predisposed to dislike and distrust political domination, above all when it is forced upon us. Small modular city-states are the norm throughout Greek history — and throughout

2 The lack of absolute dates from Mycenaean sites continues to be a vexing problem. As a case in point, the recent 326-page edited volume on "synchronizing" the destructions of the Mycenaean palaces (Jung and Kardamaki 2022) *does not report a single radiocarbon date.*

the wider Mediterranean — through the Classical Age, down to the era of Greek independence. There is a reason why the rallying cries of the Greek revolution and its aftermath were "filiki" and "omonoia." There was, in effect, no Greek Sargon. Even when Philip II and, later, Rome "conquered" Greece, the city-states still maintained a large degree of independence through a variety of means, and they were certainly not fully integrated politically or economically.

Given these historical realities, some scholars have taken to calling the Mycenaean Great Kingdom a "confederation," without ever actually defining what they mean by confederation. The term confederation has a very specific technical-anthropological definition. A confederation is a loose political formation composed of independent polities that agree to an alliance and to cooperate in times of common need. The key to confederacy is that the alliance is defined in legal terms, which are meant to preserve the sovereignty of the participating, independent entities. The whole goal of a confederacy is to *avoid* political domination and integration, not promote it, which runs completely counter to the whole notion of a Mycenaean Great Kingdom. Historical confederacies, like the Haudenosaunee (i.e., the "Six Nations" or Iroquois) confederacy, whose Great Law of Peace was recorded on a wampum belt, or the League of Lezhë, whereby Skanderbeg unified the Albanian tribes in response to Ottoman invasion, bear almost no resemblance to the Mycenaean states. Confederation is an exceedingly poor euphemism for "empire," even an imagined one.

Ultimately, many of the scholars who argue for a Mycenaean Great Kingdom seem to think that somehow, inevitably bigger is better. A bigger state is better than a smaller state, and an empire is surely better, i.e., more liable to be successful, in the long run. This amounts to a badly misdirected evolutionary argument, masquerading as archaeological systematics, since evolutionary change does not "prefer" one state of being over any other. So we should ask, is bigger always better? This question is an important one for our understanding of the past and how and why ancient states formed. It is an important one for understanding modern history. And it is a critical one for understanding current events. However, not all or even most ancient states were big and a trend towards growth, versus stasis, may have been unproductive over the long term.

The American experience seems to argue against growth for growth's sake, otherwise why not conquer Canada and Mexico? When presented with the opportunity for empire, after WWII for example, the United States rejected occupation and growth. In fact, given the evidence at hand, the Mycenaeans seem to have been a lot more like the United States than they were like, for example, Russia. The United States has a shared history and culture, like the Mycenaeans, but no one state has absolute power over any other, and our economic systems remain relatively decentralized. Nevertheless, globally, there is a tilt towards autocracy and away from democracy. We would argue that this is exactly what Homer warns us about: choosing autocratic leadership à la a Great Kingdom versus independence, and freedom. We do not see evidence for a Mycenaean Great Kingdom, but we do see evidence for a trend towards autocracy indicated in the archaeology of the Mycenaeans, in the Linear B, and in Homer. The Mycenaean *wanakes* may have wanted to get bigger, but that impulse failed circa 1200 BCE. The *Iliad* is not just a love story, or a war story, it is a parable about power, unchecked power. Not much has changed in the almost 3000 intervening years. Power needs to be confronted, or autocratic impulses appear and spread. That is the lesson of the Mycenaeans, a lesson we would best heed.

Economic nonintegration

As the above makes clear, the strongest evidence against a unified Mycenaean state comes from the variation exhibited between the different Mycenaean polities. This is something many archaeologists have written about from many different perspectives: geographic, political, ideological, and, of course, economic. In this last part of the paper, we try to delineate some of these differences, with economic concerns in mind.

In 2014 we published an Aegaeum paper with Daniel Pullen and Rebecca Seifried that explored the differences in mortuary landscapes and regional settlement distributions between Messenia and the Argolid (Galaty et al. 2014). This exercise was built on observations that scholars like Bennet (1994) and Voutsaki (1998) had made many years ago about the distribution of tombs in Messenia and the Argolid. There are many small tholos tombs in Messenia, and they are widely distributed, whereas there are fewer, larger tholos tombs in the Argolid, concentrated at Mycenae, and many more chamber tombs. We are not sure how the recently excavated tholoi at Pylos change this picture, but the overall pattern suggests that political power was distributed very differently in Messenia versus the Argolid.

Looking at the distribution of settlements, the Least Cost Path (LCP) system that connected settlements in Messenia is circulatory, linking all settlements more-or-less equally (as described by Lukerman back in 1972). The Argolid's path system, by contrast, is dendritic, centered around Mycenae. These different path systems reflect different growth histories, linked to very different mortuary customs, and, we would argue, very different political systems. Pylos would eventually become Messenia's central place, but only late in Late Helladic IIIB. Sites like Iklaina remained competitors until late in the game (Cosmopoulos 2019). By contrast, the densely packed Argolid was home to at least two, maybe more palatial centers and several other competing settlements. The political process there unfolded quite differently and culminated in a very different "landscape of power" compared to Messenia.

In dual-processual terms (Blanton et al. 1996), the Argolid exhibits a much more network-focused orientation, likely because of the up-close, intensive interactions between elites from several nearby settlements. This is indicated not only in the density of the settlements and tombs in the Argolid, but also in the complex road networks that connected the sites, as well as the monumental stone architecture at the centers. By contrast, Messenia seems to have been more corporately oriented, having less concern about peer-to-peer competition and more of a focus on cultivating buy-in through feasts and festivals.

These different regional trajectories are also indicated in long-distance trade networks. If the Mycenaean polities constituted a unified state, whether extractive or redistributive, the expected pattern would be a fall-off from the primary center to the secondary and tertiary centers. Instead, we see a high degree of regional, or even site-based, variability, with different sites in the Argolid, Crete, and Messenia each establishing their own trading partners and preferences for exotic goods from specific regions (Cline 2007; Parkinson 2010). This picture also reinforces the idea that the political landscape in the Argolid was much more wealth-based and focused on alliance formation and networking than in Messenia, something we attribute to historical and geographic differences in the formation of the different, independent polities.

This variability in aspects of socio-political organization is also reflected in economic organization. Mycenaean regional economies were not all-encompassing and controlled by palatial elites. There were multiple mechanisms of exchange, as attested in both the Linear B tablets and archaeologically. Some industries and items were of great interest to the palace, and others less so, and to a great extent these things varied in different polities. Mycenaean centers also did not operate hyper-specialized, integrated economies, in which each settlement made one thing and one thing only, as was the case, for example, in the Inka state (D'Altroy and Earle 1985). Each individual polity — and, probably, each individual settlement of a certain size — was largely self-sufficient in terms of the production of the staple and wealth goods needed to function, and any goods a household needed but did not have or could not produce on its own could be acquired, perhaps through market exchange (Parkinson, Nakassis, and Galaty 2013). This situation led to variability within and between states in terms of how economies were organized and operated, but it also would have made the inter-regional exchange of goods and services insignificant or unnecessary.

Foreign trade, when it occurred, also appears to have been handled largely outside the purview of the palaces. As a result, neither inter-polity nor international commerce are recorded in Linear B texts, the former because it did not happen to any great extent, or at least not with any regularity, and the latter because it was effectively "anarchic" and not monitored by the palace. Both point to the lack of an integrated, unified economy.

Given Greek geography, and given the above (very brief) description of Mycenaean political economy, we might ask, again, what incentive there was for one Mycenaean state to attempt to conquer any other state, let alone all others? As we have argued elsewhere (e.g., Galaty et al. 2010; Galaty, Nakassis, and Parkinson 2016; Galaty and Parkinson 2007; Parkinson and Galaty 2007, 2010; Parkinson, Nakassis, and Galaty 2013; Nakassis, Parkinson, and Galaty 2011), the Mycenaean states were connected in many ways that did not require political hegemony or a unified economy. These could have included: intermarriage, kin relationships (real and fictive), reciprocal gift exchanges, shared labor exchanges, religious festivals, sports events, feasting, merchant activity, trade partnerships, joint ventures, livestock roundups, markets and marketing, and so on. All of these would have established and maintained a Mycenaean cultural "koine," for lack of a better term; but none required political or economic integration. In fact, since most economic activities in Mycenaean states appear to have operated without palatial, or any other kind of political intervention, it is hard to see why and how palatial agents would have had the need and means to control the economy *in toto*, be it that of their own state or that of a different state.

There is no direct archaeological or Linear B textual evidence to support the idea of pan-Mycenaean political integration to take advantage of or to create pan-Mycenaean economic systems. The different regional Mycenaean economies (plural) themselves could not be integrated, both within and between states, because they each functioned very differently, in different environments and at different scales, obviating the need for political integration. An integrated system is one in which the loss of one subsystem causes all other subsystems, and the system itself, to destabilize. Thus, an integrated economy encompassing a single, unified Mycenaean state could not survive the removal of a regional economic component. However, this does not appear to have been the situation for Mycenaean states. For example, if the palace at Pylos had stopped making perfumed oil, the larger Mycenaean economic system likely would not have been terribly affected. Specialized perfume production, while important at Pylos, was not integrated into the wider Mycenaean economic system.

Perhaps the best example of a non-integrated Mycenaean economic subsystem, which was not subject to political control, comes from the bronze industry. If ever there were a resource and industry seemingly worth monopolizing, it would be bronze and the manufacture of bronze implements, like tools and weapons, but, according to the Pylos tablets, the industry was mostly decentralized (Smith 1992/1993). Numerous independent smiths received allotments of bronze, which were worked, and then a portion of the finished products were remanded to the palace (according to the so-called *ta-ra-si-ja* system).

This interpretation of the Linear B data receives archaeological confirmation through the work of Aulsebrook (2022), who demonstrated that seemingly identical metal vessels, made by different workshops, reflect different production steps, with different costs, in both labor and material. This would have made metal-working a very difficult industry to centralize, oversee, and integrate. The Mycenaean palaces did not support the standardized, mass production of goods, in attached factories. Even simple goods, like pottery, that were easily mass-produced. Mycenaean mass-produced pottery was, for example, outsourced at Pylos, to a so-called royal potter, who seems to have worked elsewhere, not at the palace proper (Galaty 2010).

Interestingly, the tablets do not record the initial acquisition of bronze (e.g., in ingot form), which must have originated outside the state and probably outside of Greece, so presumably the palace acquired it on the open market, from merchants, like any other consumer (Aprile 2013). Bronze working was not integrated into the larger economy, palatial or otherwise. Destabilization of the bronze economy occurred only, it seems, when the Mediterranean bronze trade, which was external to Pylos, faltered, late in Late Helladic IIIB, prompting a recall of "temple" bronze (Baumbach 1983, but see also Palaima 1995). It is likely that this type of external economic disruption, in this case, contraction in the supply of bronze, affected all the Mycenaean states, but not because they were politically integrated; rather, because they all depended on outside sources of bronze.

But it was not just specialized crafts that were not integrated into the broader Mycenaean world, even at the regional level; activities as basic as agricultural production were also not fully integrated into Mycenaean economic systems. Many of the tax assessments in the Pylos Linear B texts are recorded as unpaid, so evidently failures did happen, or, alternatively, people just refused to pay. The tax system itself was not economically and politically integrated in ways that made regular, predictable tax collection necessary. Mycenaean economies were not centralized or specialized in ways that demanded tight, regional integration of production, distribution, and taxation. Mycenaean elites at different palaces essentially ran their own economic enterprises, which were mostly wealth-financed, employing local labor, managed by local leaders, and occasionally they skimmed a bit off the top in the form of "taxes," much of which went to support religious activities. Here again, we see variability. The exception is "Mycenaean" Knossos, which seems to have administered a wool industry for off-island export and economic gain (Killen 1964). The wool industry was integrated into Knossos's political system in ways scarcely, or never, achieved on the Mainland.

Conclusion

As we have tried to demonstrate, the evidence for a Mycenaean Great Kingdom with a unified, integrated political economy is mostly circumstantial and lacking. What evidence there is, comes from text sources that are external to Greece, written by individuals who almost certainly had not been to Ahhiyawa. There are no references in the Linear B documents to a Great Kingdom, even if we work hard to read between the lines. Interpreting the wanax as a peripatetic Great King, who kept multiple palaces in multiple states, with lawagetai at their beckon call, feels to us like special pleading. Perhaps the strongest argument against the possibility or desirability of a single politically integrated state is, as we have outlined, the absence or difficulty of creating an economically integrated state. If the latter did not exist or could not be brought into existence, why go through the trouble of conquering the other Mycenaean states? When, in fact, the Mycenaean states themselves did not or could integrate their own, local economies, to any great extent.

Ultimately, that scholars like Kelder (2010) and Eder and Jung (2015) have presented a different interpretation of Mycenaean political organization is not, in and of itself, a problem. We should welcome differences of opinion in scholarly debate, especially about how obscure ancient societies were organized. The problem is that many of us ignored the argument and chuckled to ourselves, hoping that its proponents would lose steam and the whole thing would just go away. Clearly, that has not happened and now the Great Kingdom thesis demands real testing, using hard archaeological data.

While many Aegean prehistorians can envision relationships between different Mycenaean polities resulting in ad hoc alliances or even temporary confederations, the hardest part to swallow about the idea of a unified Mycenaean state is that it is inherently static. The following quote is from an Annales-based critique of Marcus' (1992) "dynamic model" by Iannone (2002: 68):

> "The crux of the problem lies in the fact that Mayanists, like other archaeologists throughout the world, have often been guilty of employing a rather rigid dichotomy between centralizing and decentralizing structures (i.e., essentialism). Specifically, there has been a tendency to assign the ancient Maya state to one or the other of these categories with little regard to the differences in temporal and spatial scales that are the

focus of individual analyses. As a result, we have often painted a rather simplistic picture of what was clearly a rather fluid and complex social amalgamation."

This is why many of us have such a visceral reaction to the notion of a unified Mycenaean state — it is simplistic and essentializing.

But what is most disconcerting about the idea of a Great Kingdom is that it is not at all new. Instead, notions of highly centralized Mycenaean states, whether unified or not, sets the conversation back almost a century, when Mycenaean economic systems were understood to be top-down and monolithic, situated at the distant periphery of the larger, more mature states of Egypt and the Near East. In the years since, Mycenaean archaeologists and Linear B specialists have worked together to tease apart the nuances of Bronze Age social organization and interaction and understand the dynamic, complex political and economic relationships that linked these polities and societies. The Great Kingdom thesis takes us backward not forward. Let's move forward.

Bibliography

Aprile, J., 2013. The New Political Economy of Nichoria: Using Intrasite Distributional Data to Investigate Regional Institutions. *American Journal of Archaeology* 117: 429–436.

Aulsebrook, S., 2022. Forging Ahead or Foiled Again? A New Direction for Cross-Craft Analysis with Case Studies from Late Bronze Age Metalworking in the Aegean. In *Sympozjum Egejskie: Papers in Aegean Archaeology 3*, edited by S. Aulsebrook, K. Żebrowska, A. Ulanowska, and K. Lewartowski, 99–112. Turnhout: Brepols.

Baumbach, L., 1983. An Examination of the Evidence for a State of Emergency at Pylos c. 1200 B.C. In *Res Mycenaeae: Akten des VII. internationalen Mykenologischen Colloquiums in Nürnberg vom 6.–10. April 1981*, edited by A. Heubeck and G. Neumann, 28–40. Göttingen: Vandenhoeck and Ruprecht.

Bennet, J., 1994. Space Through Time: Diachronic Perspectives on the Spatial Organization of the Pylian State. In *Politeia: Society and State in the Aegean Bronze Age. Proceedings of the 5th International Aegean Conference, University of Heidelberg, Archäologisches Institut. 10–13 April 1994*, edited by W.-D. Niemeier and R. Laffineur, 587–602. Aegaeum 12. Liège: Université de Liège, Histoire de l'art et archéologie de la Grèce antique; Austin: University of Texas at Austin, Program in Aegean Scripts and Prehistory.

Beckman, G. M., T. R. Bryce, and E. H. Cline, 2012. *The Ahhiyawa Texts*. SBL - Writings from the Ancient World Series 28. Leiden: Brill.

Blackwell, N. G., 2014. Making the Lion Gate Relief at Mycenae: Tool Marks and Foreign Influence. *American Journal of Archaeology* 118: 451–488.

Blanton, R. E., G. M. Feinman, S. A. Kowalewski, and P. N. Peregrine, 1996. A Dual-Processual Theory for the Evolution of Mesoamerican Civilization. *Current Anthropology* 37: 1–14.

Cline, E. H., 2007. Rethinking Mycenaean International Trade with Egypt and the Near East. In *Rethinking Mycenaean Palaces II: Revised and Expanded Second Edition*, edited by M. L. Galaty and W. A. Parkinson, 190–200. Monograph 60. Los Angeles: University of California at Los Angeles, Cotsen Institute of Archaeology.

Cosmopoulos, M., 2019. State Formation in Greece: Iklaina and the Unification of Mycenaean Pylos. *American Journal of Archaeology* 123: 349–380.

Cosmopoulos, M., S. E. Allen, D. J. Riebe, D. Ruscillo, M. Liston, and C. Shelton, 2019. New Accelerator Mass Spectrometry 14C Dates from the Mycenaean site of Iklaina. *Journal of Archaeological Science: Reports* 24: 888–899.

D'Altroy, T. N., and T. K. Earle, 1985. Staple Finance, Wealth Finance, and Storage in the Inka Political Economy. *Current Anthropology* 26: 187–206.

Eder, B., and R. Jung, 2015. <Unus pro omnibus, omnes pro uno>: The Mycenaean Palace System. In *Tradition and Innovation in the Mycenaean Palatial Polities*, edited by J. Weilhartner and F. Ruppenstein, 113–140. Mykenische Studien 34. Vienna: Austrian Academy of Sciences.

Galaty, M. L., 2010. Wedging Clay: Combining Competing Models of Mycenaean Pottery Industries. In *Political Economies of the Aegean Bronze Age: Papers from the Langford Conference*, edited by D. J. Pullen, 230–247. Oxford: Oxbow Books.

Galaty, M. L., and W. A. Parkinson, 2007. Introduction 2007: Mycenaean Palaces Rethought. In *Rethinking Mycenaean Palaces II: Revised and Expanded Second Edition*, edited by M. L. Galaty and W. A. Parkinson, 1–17. Monograph 60. Los Angeles: University of California at Los Angeles, Cotsen Institute of Archaeology.

Galaty, M. L., and J. B. Rutter, 2022. Event, Process, Transition, Transformation: Concluding Remarks and Data Regarding Crete's Monopalatial Period. In *One State, Many Worlds: Crete in the Late Minoan II–IIIA2 Early Period. Proceedings of the International Conference held at Khania,* Μεγάλο Αρσενάλι, *21st – 23rd November 2019*, edited by A. D'Agata, L. Girella, E. Papadopoulou, and D. E. Acquini, 425–451. Studi micenei ed egeo anatolici, n.s., Supplemento 2. Rome: Edizioni Quasar.

Galaty, M. L., W. A. Parkinson, J. F. Cherry, E. H. Cline, P. N. Kardulias, R. Schon, S. Sherratt, H. Tomas, and D. Wengrow, 2010. Interaction Amidst Diversity: An Introduction to the Eastern Mediterranean Bronze Age. In *Archaic State Interaction: The Eastern Mediterranean in the Bronze Age*, edited by W. A. Parkinson and M. L. Galaty, 29–51. Santa Fe, NM: School for Advanced Research Press.

Galaty, M. L., W. A. Parkinson, D. J. Pullen, and R. Siefried, 2014. Mycenaean –scapes: Geography, Political Economy, and the Eastern Mediterranean World System. In *PHYSIS: L'Environment naturel et la relation homme-milieu dans le monds égéen protohistorique. Actes de la 14e Rencontre égéenne internationale, Paris, Institut National d'Histoire de l'Art (INHA), 11-14 décembre 2012*, edited by G. Touchais, R. Laffineur, and F. Rougemont, 449–456. Aegaeum 37. Leuven/Liège: Peeters.

Galaty, M. L., D. Nakassis, and W. A. Parkinson, 2016. Introduction. In *Discussion and Debate: Reciprocity in Aegean Palatial Societies: Gifts, Debt, and the Foundations of Economic Exchange*, edited by D. Nakassis, M. L. Galaty, and W. A. Parkinson. *Journal of Mediterranean Archaeology* 29: 61–70.

Hajnal, I., E. Zangger, and J. Kelder, eds., 2022. *The Political Geography of Western Anatolia in the Late Bronze Age*. Archaeolingua Series Minor 45. Budapest: Archaeolingua.

Hooker, J. T., 1976. *Mycenaean Greece*. London: Routledge and Kegan Paul.

Iannone, G., 2002. Annales History and the Ancient Maya State: Some Observations on the "Dynamic Model." *American Anthropologist* 104: 68–78.

Iacono, F., E. Borgna, M. Cattani, C. Cavazzuti, H. Dawson, Y. Galanakis, M. Gori, C. Iaia, N. Ialongo, T. Lachenal, A. Lorrio, R. Micó, B. Molloy, A. Nafplioti, K. Peche-Quilichini, C. Rihuete Herrada, and R. Risch, 2022. Establishing the Middle Sea: The Late Bronze Age of Mediterranean Europe (1700–900 BC). *Journal of Archaeological Research* 30: 371–445.

Jung, R., and E. Kardamaki, eds., 2022. *Synchronizing the Destructions of the Mycenaean Palaces*. Mykenische Studien 36 / Denkschriften der philosophisch-historischen Klasse 546. Vienna: Austrian Institute of Archaeology.

Kelder, J. M., 2010. *The Kingdom of Mycenae: A Great Kingdom in the Late Bronze Age Aegean*. Bethesda, MD: CDL Press.

Kelder J. M., and W. Waal, eds., 2019. *From 'Lugal.Gal' to 'Wanax': Kingship and Political Organisation in the Late Bronze Age Aegean*. Leiden: Sidestone Press.

Killen, J. T., 1964. The Wool Industry of Crete in the Late Bronze Age. *Annual of the British School at Athens* 59: 1–15.

Kyriakidis, E., 2010. 'Collectors' as Stakeholders in Mycenaean Governance: Property and the Relations Between the Ruling Class and the State. *Proceedings of the Cambridge Philological Society* 56: 140–177.

Lukerman, F. E., 1972. Settlement and Circulation: Pattern and Systems. In *The Minnesota Messenia Expedition: Reconstructing a Bronze Age Environment*, edited by W. A. McDonald and G. R. Rapp, Jr., 148–170. Minneapolis: University of Minnesota Press.

Marcus, J., 1992. Dynamic Cycles of Mesoamerican States. *National Geographic Research & Exploration* 8: 392–411.

Murray, S. C., 2017. *The Collapse of the Mycenaean Economy: Trade, Imports, and Institutions, 1300–700 BCE*. Cambridge: Cambridge University Press.

Nakassis, D., 2013. *Individuals and Society in Mycenaean Pylos*. Leiden: Brill.

Nakassis, D., W. A. Parkinson, and M. L. Galaty, 2011. Redistribution in Theoretical and Cross-Cultural Perspective. *American Journal of Archaeology* 115: 177–184.

Olivier, J.-P., 2006. De 'l'empire mycénien' et de sa nécéssaire fiscalité. In *Fiscality in Mycenaean and Near Eastern Archives: Proceedings of the Conference Held at Soprintendenza Archivistica per la Campania, Naples, 21–23 October 2004*, edited by M. Perna, 183–188. Studi egei e vicinorientali 3. Paris: de Boccard.

Palaima, T. G., 1995. The Last Days of the Pylos Polity. In *Politeia: Society and State in the Aegean Bronze Age. Proceedings of the 5th International Aegean Conference, University of Heidelberg, Archäologisches Institut. 10–13 April 1994*, edited by W.-D. Niemeier and R. Laffineur, 623–633. Aegaeum 12. Liège: Université de Liège, Histoire de l'art et archéologie de la Grèce antique; Austin: University of Texas at Austin, Program in Aegean Scripts and Prehistory.

Palaima, T. G., 2012. Security and Insecurity as Tools of Power in Mycenaean Palatial Kingdoms. In *Études myceniennes 2010: Actes du XIIIe colloque international sur les textes egeens, Sevres, Paris, Nanterre, 20–23 septembre 2010*, edited by P. Carlier, Ch. de Lamberterie, M. Egetmeyer, N. Guilleux, F. Rougemont, and J. Zurbach, pp. 345–356. Pisa: Biblioteca di Pasiphae.

Parkinson, W. A., 2010. Beyond the Peer: Social Interaction and Political Evolution in the Bronze Age Aegean. In *Political Economies of the Aegean Bronze Age: Papers from the Langford Conference, Florida State University, Tallahassee, 22–24 February 2007*, edited by D. J. Pullen, 11–34. Oxford: Oxbow Books.

Parkinson, W. A., and M. L. Galaty, 2007. Primary and Secondary States in Perspective: An Integrated Approach to State Formation in the Prehistoric Aegean. *American Anthropologist* 109: 113–129.

Parkinson, W. A., and M. L. Galaty, 2010. Introduction: Interaction and Ancient Societies. In *Archaic State*

Interaction: The Eastern Mediterranean in the Bronze Age, edited by W. A. Parkinson and M. L. Galaty, 3–28. Santa Fe, NM: School for Advanced Research Press.

Parkinson, W. A., D. Nakassis, and M. L. Galaty, 2013. Crafts, Specialists, and Markets in Mycenaean Greece. Introduction. *American Journal of Archaeology* 117: 413–422.

Postgate, J. N., 2001. System and Style in Three Near Eastern Bureaucracies. *Economy and Politics in the Mycenaean Palace States: Proceedings of a Conference held on 1–3 July 1999 in the Faculty of Classics, Cambridge*, edited by S. Voutsaki and J. T. Killen, 181–194. Cambridge Philological Society Supplementary Volume 27. Cambridge: Cambridge Philological Society.

Postgate, J. N., 2014. Wool, Hair and Textiles in Assyria. In *Wool Economy in the Ancient Near East and the Aegean: From the Beginnings of Sheep Husbandry to Institutional Textile Industry*, edited by C. Breniquet and C. Michel, 401–427. Oxford: Oxbow Books.

Renfrew, C., and J. F. Cherry, eds., 1986. *Peer Polity Interaction and Socio-political Change*. Cambridge: Cambridge University Press.

Roosevelt, C., C. Luke, S. Ünlüsoy, J. M. Marston, P. Pavúk, M. Pieniążek, J. Mokrisova, C. Scott, N. Shin, and F. G. Slim, 2018. Exploring Space, Economy, and Interregional Interaction at a Second-Millennium B.C.E. Citadel in Central Western Anatolia: 2014–2017 Research at Kaymakçı. *American Journal of Archaeology* 122: 645–688.

Sherratt, S., 2001. Potemkin Palaces and Route-based Economies. In *Economy and Politics in the Mycenaean Palace States: Proceedings of a Conference held on 1–3 July 1999 in the Faculty of Classics, Cambridge*, edited by S. Voutsaki and J. T. Killen, 214–238. Cambridge Philological Society Supplementary Volume 27. Cambridge: Cambridge Philological Society.

Smith, J. S., 1992–1993. The Pylos Jn Series. *Minos* 27–28: 167–259.

Tartaron, T. F., 2008. Aegean Prehistory as World Archaeology: Recent Trends in the Archaeology of Bronze Age Greece. *Journal of Archaeological Research* 16: 83–161.

Tartaron, T. F., 2010. Between and Beyond: Political Economy in Non-palatial Mycenaean Worlds. In *Political Economies of the Aegean Bronze Age: Papers from the Langford Conference, Florida State University, Tallahassee, 22–24 February 2007*, edited by D. J. Pullen, 161–193. Oxford: Oxbow Books.

Tartaron, T. F., 2013. *Maritime Networks in the Mycenaean World*. Cambridge: Cambridge University Press.

Voutsaki, S., 1998. Mortuary Evidence, Symbolic Meanings and Social Change: A Comparison Between Messenia and the Argolid in the Mycenaean Period. In *Cemetery and Society in the Aegean Bronze Age*, edited by K. Branigan, 41–58. Sheffield Studies in Aegean Archaeology 1. Sheffield: Sheffield Academic Press.

Woudhuizen, F. C., 2010. Review of J. M. Kelder, "The Kingdom of Mycenae. A Great Kingdom in the Late Bronze Age Aegean." *Bibliotheca Orientalis* LXVIII.1–2: 140–145.

Mycenaean Economic Institutions: A Firm's Eye View

Sarah C. Murray

Abstract

The major categories of economic unit present in discourse on the Mycenaean economy include individuals, palaces, households, and non-palatial entities distinct from households or kin-based units. The latter category is difficult to handle analytically, because the textual evidence at our disposal provides a primarily palace-eye view of the economy, while extant archaeological evidence is not particularly forthcoming regarding the nature or existence of economic units between state-level and household- or individual-level scales. In economic thought, many such mid-level entities are categorized as firms: hierarchical non-state organizations that are vertically integrated, encompassing multiple stages of production and/or distribution within a unified structure. While theories of the firm have been brought sporadically to bear on historical Greco-Roman economies, they have not been formally applied in the study of Aegean prehistory. This paper aims to fill that gap, considering whether non-palatial institutions in the Mycenaean economy might be usefully conceptualized as firms. I first review the normal economic conditions under which firms generally come into being. I argue that conditions conducive to the emergence of firms were present in the Mycenaean Bronze Age, then identify some entities apparent within the available corpus of Mycenaean textual and archaeological evidence that resemble firms. I also discuss evidence for non-state entities that seem structurally distinct from firms, and suggest that the economic landscape of Mycenaean states could have included other integrated organizations such as cooperatives and guilds. I conclude that thinking comparatively about such organizations as they are defined according to modern theories of the firm might be useful more generally in developing a systematic yet flexible reconstruction of elusive Mycenaean economic structures at a range of scales between the individual and the state.

Introduction

Recent research has made clear that the Bronze Age Aegean economy was a dynamic "mosaic of elements" far more diverse in its constituent parts than older models allowed (Earle 2011: 237). Less clear is the precise demeanor of these constituent parts. There are many established methodological and theoretical toolkits in archaeological thought through which we may interrogate entities like states, individuals, and households. On the other hand, non-state economic organizations are challenging to query. The evidence available from which to begin reconstructing their nature or existence is far from ideal. Moreover, models for interrogating such organizations are not very well developed,

ORCID 0000-0002-0229-9224
Department of Classics,
University of Toronto
sc.murray@utoronto.ca

In *Social Groups and Production in Mycenaean Economies. Papers from the Langford Conference, Florida State University, Tallahassee, 24-25 February 2023*, edited by D. Pullen (2025), 59–78. Leiden: Sidestone Press.

because archaeologists have less-often investigated the historical role of such entities. In this paper, I aim to assess whether economic theories of the firm might be helpful in filling some relevant gaps in the evidence and sketching out some possibilities regarding the nature of mid-level economic institutions in the Mycenaean Aegean.

Why the firm? Models and complexity in the Mycenaean economy

In his work on the ancient economy, the influential twentieth-century Greek historian Moses Finley consistently reconstructed the Mycenaean state as presiding over a redistributive economic system that closely resembled those of Near Eastern states, with strong control over resource distribution and producers' activities (Finley 1973: 135). Subsequent study of the Mycenaean Linear B texts, which formed the primary basis for Finley's understanding of the Mycenaean state, and new archaeological discoveries have repeatedly demonstrated thoroughgoing flaws in Finley's reconstruction, making his model a common *Prügelknabe* for Aegean prehistorians. Nonetheless, the basic parameters of his characterization of LBA Aegean states as centralized, bureaucratic, and redistributive have proven durable, especially outside of specialist circles (e.g., Snodgrass 1986; Osborne 1996: 3; Jung 2016: 563).

As Nakassis discusses elsewhere, the durability of Finley's model almost certainly relates in part to its utility for Greek historians, who may find a narrative that effectively severs Bronze Age developments from Iron Age institutions convenient for a variety of practical and ideological reasons (Nakassis 2024). However, I suspect that this explanation is unlikely to account entirely for the continuing appeal of Finley's model. After all, the last fifty years have seen a great swell of interest in connecting the historical narrative of the Bronze Age Aegean to that of first millennium Greece, especially through detailed study of the years following the demise of Mycenaean states (ca. 1200–1050 BCE) and the Early Iron Age (ca. 1050–700 BCE) (Kotsonas 2016: 260–264). The strength of this trend indicates that scholars are no longer systematically eager to demur from the challenge of engaging Bronze Age Aegean sociopolitical structures with those of historical Greece.

I suggest that another factor impacting the endurance of a Finleyan model for the Mycenaean economy might be the absence of a coherent, viable alternative put forward by scholars who do not agree with its parameters. Research advances within the field of Aegean prehistory have definitely made clear that the Mycenaean economy was not a static, monolithic economic system dominated by the palatial elites, but rather a complex and many-faceted, overlapping set of institutions that developed organically through time. While shedding light on the reality that things were more complicated is a step in the right direction, doing so leaves us at something a loss when it comes to imposing analytical order on the resulting landscape of "complex networks of institutions and individuals" that is now correctly reconstructed as comprising Mycenaean economic systems (Nakassis 2022: 664). What kinds of institutions are we talking about? How did institutions and individuals articulate? How did non-palatial institutions relate to the palatial bureaucracy?

While Finley's model of the Mycenaean economy was probably too simple, part of the appeal of such a model was that it set out a clear vision of the economy's logic and organizing features that could be coherently explained and easily understood. This is, in a way, the merit of all models: they abstract complex systems by sacrificing some degree of detail and nuance pursuant to clear communication. Of course, it is salutary to jettison old models once it becomes clear that their contours not only simplify, but fail to accurately recreate the shape of reality that may be perceived based on available evidence. However, in order for scholarship to move forward, it is also necessary to generate new, analytically powerful frameworks for understanding that can replace and improve upon older ones.

In the case of the Mycenaean economy, scholars have done an exemplary job of demonstrating that a Finleyan model does not fit the evidence regarding the function of Aegean Bronze Age states (papers in Voutsaki and Killen 2001; Pullen 2010). Although some scholars remain unconvinced by this criticism, it seems generally accepted that the reality was far more complex than a centralized command economy, with many sectors of production and exchange residing outside of palatial control and little uniformity of economic management even within the industries managed at least in part by palatial agents. Beyond merely critiquing Finley's model, scholars of the Aegean Bronze Age have put forth compelling new ideas about how the Mycenaean economy might be more usefully conceptualized in a way that recognizes complexity while accommodating the abstraction necessary for clear communication. Papers from a previous Langford conference edited by Pullen leveraged theories of political economy to clarify additional dynamism between political and economic concerns in Aegean Bronze Age societies (Pullen 2010). A series of edited collections by Galaty, Nakassis, and Parkinson interrogated the complex transactional environment within Bronze Age economies, demonstrating that redistribution, reciprocity, and market exchange were present and internally variable through space and time (Galaty, Nakassis, and Parkinson 2011; Parkinson, Nakassis, and Galaty 2013; Nakassis, Galaty, and Parkinson 2016). More recently, Driessen and others have posited that the household constituted the core unit of Aegean Bronze Age economies, drawing on work by Levi Strauss and others to generate a powerful explanatory model that is logically conducive to abstraction and comparative analysis (Driessen 2010; Driessen 2018; Driessen and Letesson 2023; Nakassis 2022).

These productive vectors of scholarship have most often drawn from or engaged with ideas in anthropological archaeology. In this paper, I aim to build upon such work through engagement with concepts from economic thought instead. In particular, I draw from frameworks developed in the area of neoinstitutional (or new institutional) economics, especially the theory of the firm. New institutional economics is distinct from classical or neoclassical economic thought in that it recognizes the social frictions inherent to economic systems that preclude the smooth balancing of the price mechanism in market economies. One of its main intellectual projects concerns reconstructing the optimal configuration of "institutions" that might assuage such frictions and thereby guarantee smooth functioning and economic growth. Institutions, defined very broadly, are the rules, both formal and informal, present in a given human environment that serve to generate regularities of behavior (Greif 2006: 30; Nye 2008). They may usefully be considered as social processes that are generative of coordination among economic agents, especially insofar as they reduce the transaction costs associated with unpredictability and information asymmetries, which encourages exchange.

In general, institutional economics centers the transaction in considering the optimal configuration of economic environments. In neoinstitutional view, economic systems in which considerable frictions make transacting costly are less likely to function well and facilitate growth, because the costs associated with transacting are sufficiently high to preclude parties from exchanging, effectively sludging up the moving parts of the market (North 1994: 359–364; Platteau 2008). Thus, a primary function of institutions is to reduce transaction costs. For example, it is assumed that parties wishing to engage in any exchange of goods will want to gather information about goods and services, and seek assurances in the face of subsequent disputes about ownership. Institutions assuage such concerns by facilitating information sharing and providing systems of property rights, thus reducing the individual costs and concerns accruing among transactors and easing frictions within the economic system.

Neoinstitutional principles, especially those developed by the economic historian Douglass North and his students, have become popular interpretative tools amongst scholars studying historical Greco-Roman economies (papers in Scheidel, Saller, and Morris 2007; Bang 2009). Applying such concepts to premodern societies and their organizational characteristics is now a well-established strategy with a demonstrated track record of generating analytical clarity (Greif 2006; Lo Cascio 2018; Terpstra 2019). At the same time, institutional thinking, like any theoretical toolkit, is not without flaws. It has been subjected to well-argued critiques by both economists and historians for many decades (Granovetter 1985; Bowes 2021; Viglietti 2021). From a humanistic point of view, it is especially problematic insofar as it tends to collapse nearly every aspect of society into the logic of the rational economic actor — such that anything encouraging us to trust other transactors — friendship, religious affiliation, business attire — is swallowed up into the logic of encouraging smooth exchange.

However, there are several reasons we might expect that institutional thinking might be helpful for studying Mycenaean economic systems. First, given that much of the evidence available from which to reconstruct Mycenaean economic systems concerns transactions, it seems inherently plausible that ideas from institutional thinking might be productively applied to this particular set of data. Second, institutional economics contains a strongly historical element, in that it is concerned to explain how and why institutions change over time as wider social or environmental conditions governing the costliness of transacting alter (North 2005; North, Wallace, and Weingast 2009). It is certain that the palatial Mycenaean economic system came into being at a certain historical moment, and ceased to function at a later historical moment. Thus, scholars have a powerful intellectual remit to explain why and how this system came into being and eventually dissolved. Thinking through static systems has not been conducive to generating such explanations. Perhaps institutional thinking may offer some new and productive possibilities concerning the historical development of Mycenaean economic systems. Third, institutional thinking encourages comparative analysis, providing an analytically valid framework within which to draw comparative logic from data-rich scenarios into service for filling in the evidentiary gaps we face in the study of Bronze Age economies.

The aim is not to generate a totalizing model at odds with recent reconstructions of the Mycenaean economy that posit a strong role for households, individuals, center-periphery dynamics, and political economy. Rather, I merely wish to demonstrate that applying some ideas from institutional thinking to the evidence from the Aegean Bronze Age might provide an additional layer of insight into the historical development and structure of its economies, especially about the potential motivations and strategies of different economic actors, that have not been enlightened by previous approaches.

It is of course impossible to produce a full reinterpretation of the Mycenaean economy along institutionalist lines in the current context. Here, I focus on institutionalist theories of the firm and the extent to which their logic might shed interesting new light on Mycenaean economic structures. A firm is a hierarchical non-state social organization that encompasses multiple stages of production and/or distribution of a given product within a unified structure. Such vertical integration effectively swallows up what would normally require many individual transactions (say, between producers and distributors) into a series of long-term contractual agreements that bind multiple individual agents within a larger economic unit (Joskow 2004; 2008: 12–14). Put another way, the firm is viewed as the place "where coordination through prices is replaced by coordination through authority" in cases where hierarchy (through the formation of routines) is seen to offer better efficiencies than markets (Garrouste and Saussier 2008: 26).

My focus on firms is inspired in part by Pullen's prescient comments in a recent paper. Discussing individuals' economic agency beyond engagement with the palace centers, Pullen notes that their activities would almost certainly have involved market exchange. He goes on to surmise that such exchange would have provided an "opportunity for relationships to emerge between actors at different levels, that is, **vertical integration**" (Pullen 2020: 191 (emphasis added)). A primary definitional feature of firms is that they are vertically integrated, so in essence these comments amount to a hypothesis that firms, or organizational characteristics similar to those of firms, were present in the Aegean Bronze Age. While vertically integrated firms have been identified in Classical Aegean contexts (e.g., Lytle 2016), to my knowledge no systematic study of Mycenaean economic activity from this point of view has been undertaken. This paper takes on the challenge posed by Pullen's compelling hypothesis and attempts to identify such instances of vertical integration in the evidence from the Aegean Bronze Age. Doing so promises analytical progress: many non-state, supra-household economic organizations are categorized as firms in economic thought, so theories of the firm have potential to bridge a current conceptual gap between our understanding of palace-level and individual or household-level economic units (Coase 1937; Garrouste and Saussier 2008).

Key concepts and definitions: Firms and entrepreneurs

Why do firms exist? If market economies always worked efficiently, balancing supply and demand in perfect harmony to determine fair prices, there would be no need for firms. Firms come into being when factors arise that incentivize actors in an economic system to organize upstream and downstream economic activities through integration. This can occur for a variety of reasons. A firm might come into being when the costs of transacting in the market, such as gathering information about where products can be acquired, assembling resources needed to make a complex product, or trusting transaction partners, are higher than the costs associated with organizing contracts within a firm. A rise in transaction costs is usually associated with either technological innovation or a change in the overall economic environment. These new features interrupt the normal functioning of markets and cause high levels of uncertainty regarding prices, supply, and demand (Coase 1937; Garrouste and Saussier 2008; cf., Granovetter 1985). Alternatively, firms may come into existence when there are economies of scale to be achieved by combining inputs into a single production process, or when there are significant advantages to be gained from vertical integration and coordination of different stages of production.

Thus, both negative and positive conditions may precipitate the emergence of firms: problems with or dysfunction within the market, or the lure of lucrative opportunities to be gained through integration. By organizing across sectors, and by virtue of an explicitly hierarchical internal organization, a firm is able to coordinate changing information about prices and information about new technologies or production methods. Firms also benefit from shouldering risk and hazards arising from uncertainty. In doing so, they may profit from novel technologies that individuals may not possess the capital or risk appetite to engage with. Overall, firms mitigate and profit from changing or novel economic circumstances.

Since households and house societies have been discussed widely in archaeological literature (papers in Moreno García 2022; Driessen and Letesson 2023), and share some key characteristics with firms, it is useful to here briefly delineate a distinction between a household and a firm. Both firms and family- or household-based groups benefit from solidarity among members and a structure of authority that is conducive to decision making. The household oversees many upstream and downstream economic activities within the boundaries of single organization rather than in an open market subject to the price mechanism. However, economists view house- or kin-based units as functionally and organizationally distinct from firms, especially because of distinctions that are seen to impact their performance in managing dynamic economic environments. First, and most obviously, a family-based unit coheres naturally, but is very limited as far as scale and scalability are concerned. Second, the stages of economic production overseen by a household are usually associated with agricultural production, and thus involve multiple, inter-related, seasonalized, localized, and difficult to observe activities (Cook, Klein, and Iliopoulos 2008: 301–304). This makes coordination and the allocation of incentives difficult to manage, and creates challenges for decision making. Weak property rights and a corporate structure that hinders rapid, responsive decision-making and tends to suffer from conflict amongst peer group members with diverging interests can also lead to poor outcomes for household-based economic organizations (Cook and Iliopoulos 2000).

This brings us to the role of the individual at the top of the hierarchy of a firm and the detailed reconstruction of how firms come into being (since, e.g., high transaction costs themselves cannot generate firms). The introduction of a firm is usually attributed to the agency of an entrepreneurial individual. Entrepreneurs are individuals possessing a specific skill — identifying new opportunities and developing strategies to build on existing realities in order to realize them, especially when uncertainty creates a hindrance to predicting the precise outcomes (Schumpeter 1934; Langlois and Robertson 1995; Casson 1997; Foss and Klein 2005). They are seen as pragmatic agents who behave strategically and bypass collective traditional constraints on behavior to protect their own interests and enhance their own individual wealth or standing (Kirzner 1973; Foss and Klein 2008).

An important point to emphasize as a preface to the following discussion is that, whenever they exist, firms are not antithetical to or opposed against the existence and independence of markets and political organizations. On the contrary, the relationships between firms, states, and markets are of fundamental interest to economists working on theories of the firm (e.g., Williamson 1975). It is clear that some types of transaction are carried out in both contexts, e.g., often take place in markets as well as within firms simultaneously within a given environment, belying the notion that economies form simple systems that can be entirely parsed through a single unitary logic or rationality (Ménard 2004). Overall, analysis of firms or firm-like behavior in Bronze Age economic contexts ought to remain similarly open to complexity.

Mycenaean economic organization: Evidence for firms or firm-like behavior

Is there any compelling textual or archaeological evidence to support the possibility that organizations along the lines of devolved mercantile firms existed in the Aegean Bronze Age? In what follows, I outline a few points of evidence in the Mycenaean Linear B texts that may indicate that firms, or structures resembling them, were present in the Mycenaean economy and discuss whether there is archaeological evidence that might support the existence of such units.

Entrepreneurial individuals

In order to reconstruct firms, it is important to first identify the presence of entrepreneurial individuals, since such individuals are crucial engines for the identification of the opportunity to profit from vertical integration and the action required to generate systems that can capitalize on such opportunities. Of immediate interest is one category of people that appears regularly in the corpus of Linear B tablets and who seem to have economic functions that reside somewhere in between the palatial and household level: collectors.

The conventional term collector is applied to named individuals involved in a range of activities that are most often related to the textile industry (Bennet 1992; Driessen 1992). Collectors do not have official titles, like other categories of elite administrators, but they clearly occupy an important position within the economy. Their activities are heterogeneous, including shearing and herding flocks, distributing wool allotments to workers, and collecting finished cloth for delivery to the palace (Rougement 2009: 374–387). Collectors are among a select group of individuals who occasionally receive *o-no* payments, probably in return for services rendered to the palace (Bennet and Halstead 2014). These peculiarities have previously led to speculation that collectors could have been individuals who operated on their own behalf rather than as state agents (Bennet 1992; Kyriakidis 2010; Nakassis 2013: 168–169). To this we may add that collectors appear to act in ways that are consistent with what we would expect for the head of a vertically integrated mercantile firm, insofar as they coordinate multiple stages of production and coordinate between producers and consumers. This is consistent with Nakassis' assessment, that collectors were "involved in a large number of activities" and "made extensive use of personal or institutional networks to administer their responsibilities," while going further to specify that the nature of these activities involved vertical integration of production in a manner that bears strong resemblance to what we would expect to see in a firm-like organization (Nakassis 2022: 132–13). Nakassis argues that the collectors may also be associated with houses. Such a scenario is not incompatible with the idea that collectors operated in firm-like ways. Early Modern mercantile firms were almost all organized as family firms anchored in households (e.g., Arrighi 1994: 98).

An objection to this conceptualization might be that collectors' activities are supervised by the palaces, perhaps indicating subordination as opposed to independence. Extant records about collectors' activities tie them directly to palaces, and there is little doubt that their activities were — at some juncture and in some cases — subsumed within the palatial management system (Bennet 1992: 80). However, it has been surmised that such records only record a tiny fraction of collectors' activities (Pullen 2020: 191). The logic of institutions provides some basis for arguing that the existence of records documenting transactions with collectors itself undermines the argument that they operated under palatial control. In institutional thought, writing would be considered a useful technology for reducing anxiety, and thus transaction costs, among exchange partners. It does so by generating permanent records that assuage anxiety over property rights. At least in principle, this technology should be used especially in transactions that create special anxiety. In other words, if the collectors were internal agents wholly integrated within the palatial organization, it would not be necessary to record their dealings with the palace, at least from the point of view of institutional thinking, because such dealings would be governed by internal political hierarchies, rather than subject to the uncertainties of exchange in a market. Thus, it may be the case that the presence of recorded transactions signals not palatial control but palatial interest in affairs that are anxiety-inducing in particular because they are beyond palatial control.

Reconstructing a Mycenaean firm: Distributed mercantile production

If we accept that collectors could have been acting as heads of firms or behaving in firm-like ways, the obvious next set of questions concern the logic, structure, and impetus for such organizations and behaviors. In general, the activities of Mycenaean collectors most strongly resemble the activities of entrepreneurs at the head of distributed mercantile firms that govern so-called putting-out or cottage industries (Littlefield and Reynolds 1990; Banaji 2020). In such industries, the firm organizes delivery of raw materials to a scattered agricultural labor force, instructs workers regarding which and how many products to deliver, and oversees the marketing, sale, and distribution of final products. This form of industrial organization was particularly widespread in several regions of Europe during the Medieval and Early Modern periods, especially in the textile and ironworking industries. Beginning in the thirteenth and fourteenth centuries, demand for European craft products experienced a surge arising from the expansion of global trade (Arrighi 1994: 91). Across the continent, entrepreneurial merchants identified both the challenges and potential profits presented by the new economic scenario and organized distributed mercantile firms in order to leverage these conditions to their own benefit. Such firms became dominant in the seventeenth, eighteenth, and nineteenth centuries. Their proprietors shouldered the risks and costs involved in transporting and selling a large quantity of goods in distant, unpredictable markets, in turn benefiting from high profits accruing from the sale of European products abroad, where such products were dear (Landes 1969; Klima 1974; Kriedte, Medick and Schlumbohm 1981).

Far from being unique to early modern Europe, devolved mercantile firms of this nature appear in various times and places where similar conditions obtain. For example, increased tourism in Mexico's Yucatan peninsula resulted in the rise of distributed hammock-making firms in the 1980s (Littlefield 1979; Littlefield and Reynolds 1990). Such firms delivered yarn and wages to a scattered agricultural workforce through a series of middlemen based in rural villages. Participating villagers delivered finished hammocks, which the wholesale firms then sold on to tourists at a sizeable profit. Economic historians have observed that this sort of mercantile firm tends to arise in particular circumstances: when demand increases, but the organization of labor precludes the generation of sufficient supply to meet that demand through normal market forces. Such devolved firms are especially advantageous when producers occupy marginal agricultural territory and are eager for opportunities to earn extra income. They are likewise best suited to operate in sectors like the textile industry, where there are high labor to capital input ratios and where technologies of production are easily decentralized (Mantoux 1961; Medick 1981; Fischer 1973).

The presence of such conditions in the Mycenaean situation could indirectly support an interpretation positioning "collectors" as agents that operated in firm-like ways. One of the changes in material culture that marks the onset of the Late Bronze Age in the Aegean is an increase in the presence of long-distance imports from the northern Balkans, Europe, and the eastern Mediterranean, and a slightly later quantitative increase of Mycenaean exports elsewhere. Trade relationships arising in the late Middle Bronze Age and early Late Bronze Age are especially evident in the form of opulent exotica deposited in tombs at sites like Kolonna on Aegina and Mycenae (Kilian-Dirlmeier 1997; Voutsaki 2001; Wright 2008). Mycenaean exports, especially represented by ceramic vessels, some of which may have contained value-added agricultural products, are increasingly conspicuous at eastern Mediterranean sites starting in the LH IIIA period (Papadimitriou 2012).

The advent of new trade routes that could have been generative of increased demand for craft products is thus generally evident in the archaeological record of the early Mycenaean period on the Greek mainland. The opening of such new trade routes and relationships would have increased the costs of transacting, but also presented opportunities for those willing to engage in risky business — transactions that required dealing with unknown strangers, committing goods for export to unfamiliar markets, and sending goods away on long, risky maritime voyages. Monroe's (2010) reconstruction of the "sunk costs" represented in the Uluburun ship's wrecked cargo provides one sense of the potential risks involved in long-distance exchange in the Late Bronze Age, though this probably represents something approaching a maximum. Locally, an increase in demand for craft products was probably not easily met, because the population was likely dispersed throughout the landscape in small agricultural settlements. Industries suitable to organization through vertically integrated firms — those with high labor to capital input ratios and little need for centralized technologies — were certainly present, for example, in the case of the textile industry. Given these economic realities, we might not be surprised to find something resembling a vertically integrated mercantile firm organized by entrepreneurial individuals in the Late Bronze Age Aegean.

The presence of mercantile-minded entrepreneurial actors has been more thoroughly explored in the context of eastern Mediterranean regions, especially Cyprus, where recent reconstructions identify a society driven by entrepreneurial individuals and groups focused on metal manufacture and distribution (Knapp and Meyer 2023), and Ugarit, where textual and archaeological evidence support the idea that wealthy merchants facilitated both royal and non-royal transactions in the port of Ras Shamra (Calvet 2000). Regarding the apparently strong entrepreneurial spirit of Late Bronze Age Cypriots, it is interesting to note that a collector known as *Kuprios* (*ku-pi-ri-jo*) was present at Knossos in connection with the oil industry (Rougement 2009: 262–277, 401–422). While we cannot be certain that this individual was from Cyprus, considerable circumstantial evidence has indicated that Cypriots were likely engaged as agents or arbiters of exchange in some contexts within the Mycenaean economy (Sherratt 2003; Hirschfeld 2010) and that individuals knowledgeable about Cypriot practices were present at some Aegean sites (e.g., Vetters 2014). The possible presence of a Cypriot agent entangled within Mycenaean economic affairs is interesting to consider alongside the considerable comparative historical evidence that foreign entrepreneurs often occupied special status as residents in the territories of trading partners, as their presence was necessary to facilitate exchange that lifted all boats. In Early Modern cases, such visitors were often present in foreign trade hubs for decades, eventually becoming permanent members of local society through the social capital gained from generating wealth and opportunity for local communities (Braudel 1984: 125). Perhaps the textual attestation of the Knossian *Kuprios* could represent a fleeting glimpse of a resident foreign Bronze Age merchant. Burns' suggestion that elite houses on the outskirts of Mycenaean palatial sites could have been home to these kinds of wealthy merchants is also interesting to consider along these lines (Burns 2007).

Ta-ra-si-ja production and distributed mercantile firms

Additional evidence for the presence of firm-like organizations in the Mycenaean state exists in the form of Linear B records that indicate the structure of production systems. Of obvious interest in this regard is the *ta-ra-si-ja* system of resource management, documented in Linear B texts from Knossos and Pylos in connection with the production of textiles, metal artifacts, and (possibly) chariots (Killen 2001). *Ta-ra-si-ja* transactions record allocations of raw materials to scattered laborers who produced finished products. Texts recording the *ta-ra-si-ja* system make clear that the system worked a lot like the putting-out system described above, with distribution of raw materials to scattered laborers by agents who later returned to those same laborers to collect finish goods for distribution to a willing consumer. In the cases documented in Linear B records, the immediate customer would have been the palatial centers; however, these goods may ultimately have been destined for trading partners outside of the region via longer-distance trade networks. While laborers were compensated with money in the Early Modern case, in the non-monetized Mycenaean economy, their compensation must have taken different forms — e.g., Nosch has argued that textile workers in the Knossos tablets were compensated in kind, with extra wool (Nosch 2000).

Overall, the textual record makes rather likely the existence of a vertically integrated organizational system, whether strongly governed by the palatial centers, under the control of middlemen, or managed by independent agents, that is nearly identical to known types of distributed mercantile firms recorded in historical contexts. The archaeological record is compatible with a situation in which considerable inputs of work to the textile industry came from producers that were widely distributed throughout an agricultural territory, rather than concentrated in something akin to a factory. Although the textual and iconographical records regarding textiles and their production are unusually rich, the archaeological evidence for spinning and weaving in mainland Mycenaean sites is remarkably thin, insofar as substantial deposits of loomweights and spindle whorls are not commonly encountered (Sabatini 2016). Most of the well-excavated sites from the Aegean Late Bronze Age represent either major palatial centers or minor urban agglomerations, while only a few sites represent the kinds of isolated farmsteads or small villages where textile production in a distributed mercantile industry normally takes place. The smaller sites that have been excavated and published, e.g., Tzoungiza in the Nemea valley, do preserve evidence for spinning, weaving, and sewing in the form of small collections of textile tools (Dabney and Wright 2020: 1023, 1026). The absence of conspicuous agglomerations of textile tools in major centers and the presence of small collections of textile tools at other sites is therefore not inconsistent with what we might expect to see as material proxies for a devolved mercantile operation.

The *ta-ra-si-ja* system also governs some bronze production documented in Linear B tablets from Pylos (Killen 1987). In the case of bronze production, the distribution of raw materials and delivery of goods was managed by intermediaries called *qa-si-re-we*. Like collectors, *qa-si-re-we* are concerned with several stages of craft production: the requisition and delivery of materials to workers or workgroups, over whom they seem to have some authority, and the return of finished goods to the palace (Carlier 1995). Like collectors, they are called by personal name, although unlike collectors, they are always referred to by both name and title. They do not seem to be associated with a fixed toponym or a profession. Their main identifying task concerns supervising craft production taking place in work groups (Nakassis 2013: 13–14). As is the case with collectors, it seems that the palatial records regarding these figures generate a picture of their activities and status that is not incompatible with an interpretation that they acted in ways similar to firms, organizing activities across an industry through internal hierarchical systems.

A diverse organizational environment: Evidence for cooperatives and guilds

It is interesting to observe that the *ta-ra-si-ja* system governs the same industries — textiles and metalworking — that most commonly supported putting-out firms in other historical cases. As noted above, economic historians have observed that putting-out industries share certain material affordances conducive for organization in devolved mercantile firms: labor inputs are large compared to capital inputs, resources or technologies needed for production are easily distributed rather than fixed, and finished products are conducive to profitability for the entrepreneur. Perhaps such material logics may likewise produce some clarity regarding variation in organization across Mycenaean craft industries (Schon 2011).

In the spirit of thinking through this possibility, Figure 5.1 plots some Mycenaean industries on two axes: capital- vs. labor- inputs and relative fixity to a specific location. This makes clear how such differences would necessarily impact the design of economic organization. Different industries are conducive to management according to different systems, because each industry had different material characteristics. These material characteristics had determinative impacts on factors such as whether work had to be done in one place, the extent to which raw materials and finished products could be easily moved around, and how much profit could be obtained by organizing production to meet demand.

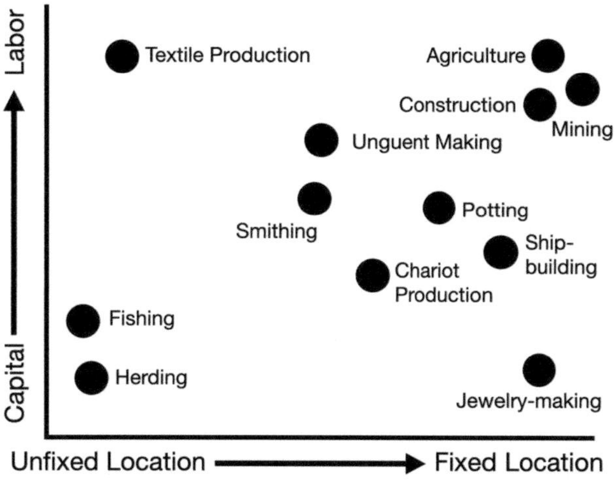

Figure 5.1. Schematic plot of industries based on the material requirements for production on two axes: ratio of capital to labor inputs required and flexibility in the location of production.

Even from such an abstract rendering, it becomes logically obvious that it would never benefit any organization to manage all categories of production or distribution according to a single system. The diversity of material affordances present in the various Mycenaean industries should lead us to expect exactly what we see in the evidence, which is diversity in production and distribution strategies. Even the transactions recorded in Linear B texts, which we might presume would be among the most regulated and regularized transactions in the Mycenaean economy, are characterized by variety. Complexity reigns not only across industries, but also within them. For example, palatial centers sourced textiles through numerous different extractive procedures simultaneously (Nakassis 2021: 110).

Organizational variety in the unguent boiling industry

Considering the organization of the unguent-boiling industry provides compelling insights along this vector. It has been observed that, although the term *ta-ra-si-ja* is not used in texts regarding unguent boiling, the unguent producing industry may have been organized, in some contexts, along similar lines: via a system of dispersed labor that involved supervisors overseeing disbursement of resources to producers and subsequently collecting finished goods for delivery to consumers (Nosch 2006; Schon 2011). For example, according to Palaima, a tablet from the palatial archive of Pylos, PY Vn 130, records quantities of vessels being boiled in Pylos' hither province under the general supervision of a man called Kessandros (Figure 5.2) (Palaima 2014: 86–89). The tablet lists the locations where the vessels are being boiled, the name of a local supervisor or boiler, and numbers of vessels being boiled at each location. These vessels seem to have been provided by Kessandros to individual unguent boilers, along with logs for the fire (Palaima 2014: 88).

If we accept Palaima's reading of this tablet, we may identify Kessandros as another individual in the Mycenaean economy who is behaving in a firm-like way: bringing logs and pots to rural producers and extracting finished products for delivery to consumers. However, variation in organizational logic within the regional unguent-boiling system is evident in the tablet's second-to-last line, which records unguents being boiled at the toponym of Lousos without an individual local supervisor. The variance evident between the norm,

PY Vn 130

Thus Kessandros is boiling with fire logs:
-vessels at *me-ta-pa*, Perins 1
-at *a-pi-no-we-jo,* Erussios 1
-at *a-pi-no-we-jo,* Aigiheus 4
-at *e-na-po-ro*, Wadomenos 9
-at *Salinwons*, Owotos 5
-at Sphagianes, Antanor 4
-at Kharadros, Throwos 1
-at Sphagianes, Eriweros 3
-at *e-wi-te-wi-jo,* Wisanthos 1
-at *me-te-to*, Koldos 3
-at [Lo]usos 24
-at *me-te-to*, Eug^{w}honis 3

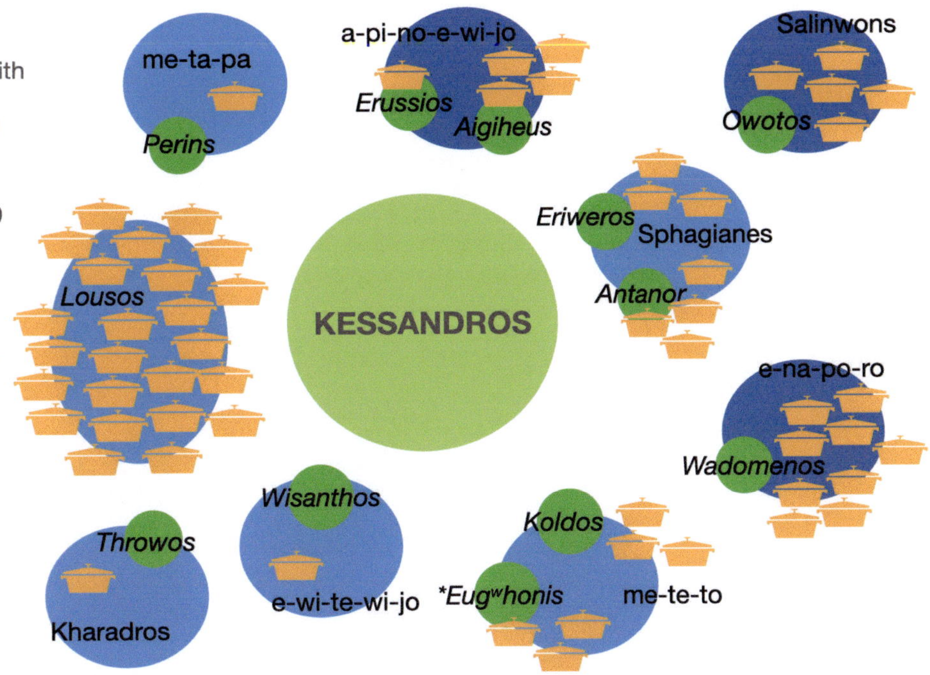

Figure 5.2. Diagram of unguent boiling under the supervision of Kessandros according to Palaima's (2014) reading of Linear B Tablet PY Vn 130.

where Kessandros interacts with an individual local intermediary, and the case at Lousos, where it seems the community itself operates as a single entity, is intriguing. In observing this variance, Palaima raised the possibility that the Lousos boilers are part of a "collective entity" (Palaima 2014: 89).

In institutional economic view, such a collective would be categorized as a cooperative. Firms and cooperatives are both defined as integrated economic organizations; they share some features, but are distinct in their aims and their internal organization. Both benefit from solidarity among members and organize many kinds of tasks up and down the chain of production to consumption. However, cooperatives usually focus on enhancing risk mitigation amongst groups of producers by coordinating inter-related activities in a geographically contiguous area and by pooling resources such as labor and equipment amongst a reasonably small cohort. Thus, like households, cooperatives are almost always more limited in scale than firms and they are also more likely to be fixed in space. Most economists therefore see cooperatives as significantly less desirable than firms (Cook, Klein, and Iliopoulos 2008: 301–304).

It is interesting to observe that while the people of Lousos may have experimented with the establishment of a cooperative that took part in unguent boiling, the rarity of such an arrangement could indicate that this was not a successful strategy for doing business in the unguent industry, or at least a sign that a cooperative form of organization in the unguent industry was not seen as optimal by the majority. More successful and also resembling historically defined cooperatives is the entity called a *damos* (Nakassis 2021: 101–102). It is not entirely surprising to find such an organization most evident in a Mycenaean entity that is closely associated with land management since, as discussed above, such cooperatives are most often seen to be useful in mitigating risk for groups of agricultural producers.

In any case, we can say with relative confidence that Kessandros engaged in transactions with both the collective entity at Lousos and individual supervisors with jurisdiction over local production. Extrapolating a larger point about economic systems from this observation, we can further conclude that the unguent production economy was characterized by organizational variety. Moreover, it seems likely that the organizational characteristics of this sector of the economy were dynamic rather than fixed over time. Lis's restudy of pottery from Pylos's room 60 led him to suggest that a "perfumed oil workshop was ... moved into the building complex", towards the end of its life, after a period of time when it was located somewhere else (Lis 2016: 531), perhaps a village like Zygouries, where evidence for perfumed oil production has likewise been documented (Thomas 1992). Lis's conclusions align with a general evidentiary picture that supports the possibility that some perfumed oil production became centralized or more closely controlled by palatial agents towards the end of the palatial period (Wright 1984, Shelmerdine 1987, Palaima 2014). If the text describing Kessandros' activities monitoring perfumed oil production at various locations was written down around the same time that perfumed oil production was being conducted within the

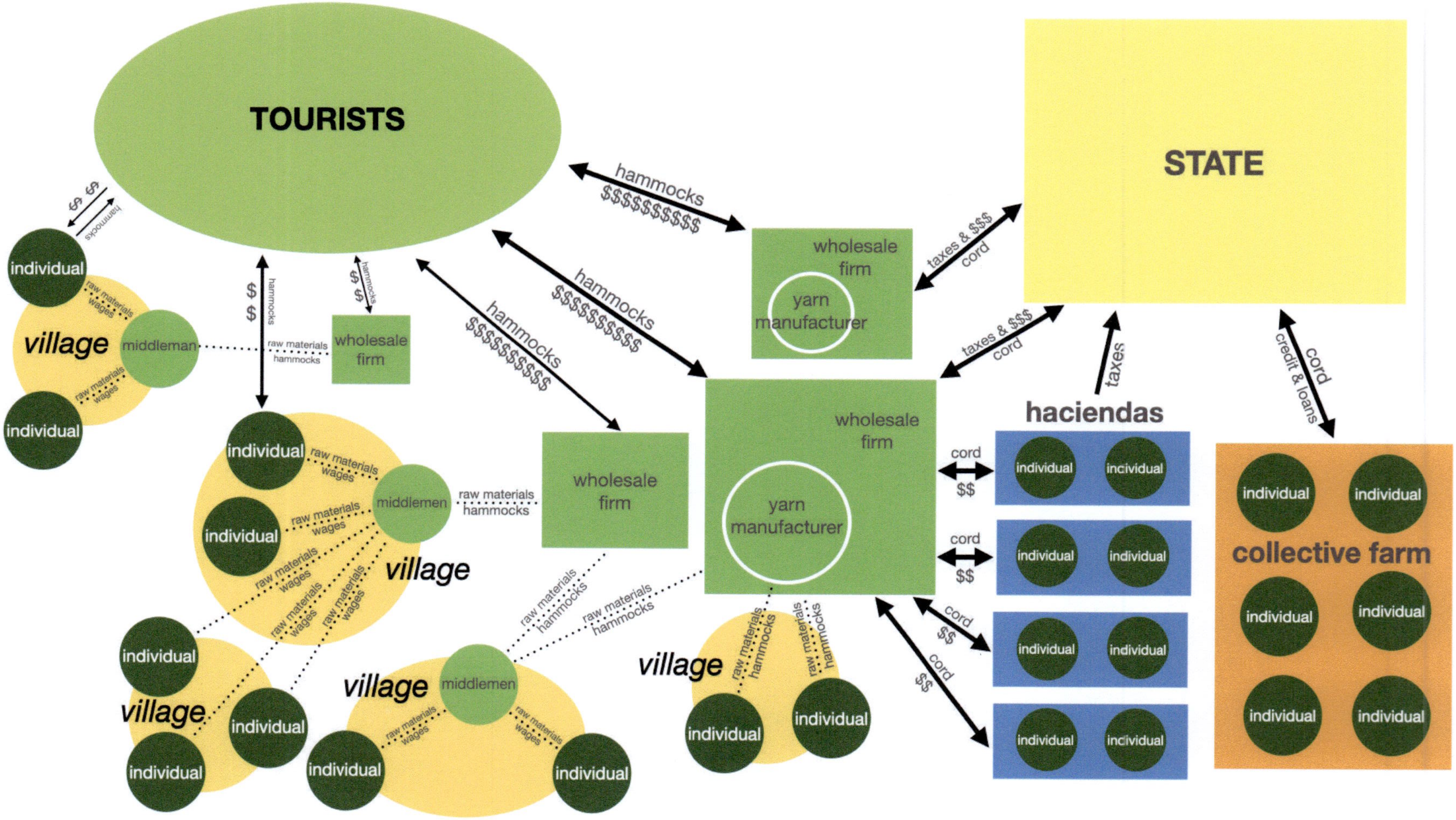

Figure 5.3. Diagram of the hammock production industry in the Yucatan peninsula following the introduction of tourism and increased demand in the 1980s.

palace, then we could reconstruct a scenario in which at least three different sorts of entities were involved in oil production by the end of the thirteenth century: states, cooperatives, and entrepreneurial individuals.

Such variation and diachronic evolution in economic organization reiterates the above point about the range of transactional types evident within individual industries. Taken in analytical view with comparable historical case studies, it also appears entirely ordinary. For example, the introduction of hammock firms in the Yucatan peninsula in the 1980s did not hinder or preclude the simultaneous existence of many other economic institutions and arrangements (Figure 5.3) (Littlefield and Reynolds 1990: 362–365). Tourists sometimes bought hammocks from hammock wholesale firms, but they also transacted directly with independent vendors. Local, village-scale demand for hammocks was still met through petty commodity trade or production to order. Many farmers worked on government supervised collective farms that produced cord for hammocks, earning advances for work performed or advantageous tax status. Pre-existing independent haciendas likewise produced cord, and both government and private cord were purchased and used by hammock firms. Envisioning Mycenaean industries as likewise layered mosaics of diverse, evolving organizations and older established structures seems helpful in smoothing a path to understanding their varied demeanors.

The organization of ceramic production

The question of ceramic production is also interesting to consider in coming to terms with the varying organizational entities that likely made up the Mycenaean economy. A variety of evidence provides reason to surmise that some conditions associated with the rise of firms might have been present within the ceramic industry. During the LH III period, the scale of Mycenaean pottery production increased. Presumably, this would not have occurred if there were not an increase in demand — perhaps not locally, but at the regional and supra-regional scale (Whitelaw 2001).

It seems certain that the organization of ceramic production in the Late Bronze Age Aegean was complex and multi-faceted. Some research makes clear that ceramic production was probably not completely controlled or governed by palatial centers (Whitelaw 2001; Galaty 2007, 2010). On the other hand, there is textual evidence for at least one "royal" potter working under the supervision of the Pylian palatial elite (Palaima 1997). Moreover, the preferential distribution of certain kinds of specialized shapes, e.g., for cooking *haute cuisine*, in palatial centers surely indicates that palatial agents played some role in requesting or directing potters to produce certain kinds of vessels to suit their needs (Hruby 2017). Thus, it is probably not accurate to state that palatial agents had no direct involvement in the ceramic production economy. On the other hand, the preponderance of the evidence makes it seem rather likely that many communities of ceramicists operated independently from direct palatial oversight, although their products were produced in considerable quantities and were an important component in both short- and long-distance exchange economies.

If it is agreed that some ceramic producing individuals or groups operated without palatial oversight, the question of their operational logic becomes important to address. That Late Bronze Age ceramic producers were organized and aware of broader dynamics within the Mediterranean economy seems self-evident from the characteristics of the archaeological record: production seems to have increased to meet demand, Mycenaean potters (especially in the Argolid) cultivated a distinctive and widespread "brand," different shapes seem to have flowed to individual regions based on different tastes among consumers (Papadimitriou 2012), and producers apparently moved around the Mediterranean effecting technology transfers that led to local imitations of desirable styles (Kiriatzi and Andreou 2016). It is difficult to imagine how such a situation could have arisen or been maintained without some kind of coordination across groups and relatively systematic communication between producers, merchants, and consumers.

If such coordination and communication were not being governed by the state, how did it work? If there were an integrated organizational structure in the Mycenaean ceramic industry, it does not seem likely that it would have resembled a system of distributed labor like the one that governed some textile production. Moving bulk quantities of raw clays and other material resources to dispersed producers would have been immensely inefficient, nor is it easy to imagine that subsequent overland trips around the territory to fetch small quantities of vessels from each producer's house would have provided an efficient or elegant strategy. Moreover, it is unlikely that most peasant households possessed the technical skill or equipment (e.g., the wheel) to produce Mycenaean decorated finewares. Instead, pottery production would be more logically concentrated in locations where suitable clays, water, and fuel, as well as specialized equipment and specialist knowledge, were all close to hand.

Thus, Mycenaean pottery firms, if they existed, probably had different logics and shapes than did organized systems for the production of textiles. What sort of organization might have been conducive to coordination and management within the ceramic industry? Returning to an Early Modern analogy, the notion of a guild provides a reasonably decent fit. Guilds are communities of craftworkers that may be geographically distributed, but dominate industries through strong control over what is known as instructional capital — the expertise required to make or do a certain, specialized kind of work (Kieser 1989; Epstein 1998). Guilds organize learning through apprenticeships. In order to proceed to being a master, an early modern guild member had to spend a certain amount of time as a journeyman, traveling around as a voyager for several years, during which they often communicated new methods and techniques abroad (Lis, Soly, and Mitzman 1994). Perhaps such a scenario could also help to explain the apparent commonality of mobile or migrant potters and other craftspeople and evidence for the blending of production methods and techniques across space and time (e.g., Abell 2014, 2020; Lis 2016; papers in Kiriatzi and Knappett 2016). For reasons of space, it is not possible to examine this possibility in detail in the current context. However, I suspect that there might be analytical value available from understanding the Mycenaean pottery industry as comprising various (and probably variously organized) entities akin to entreprenurial guilds in future work along these lines (see Shelton, chapter eight). In many ways, guilds and the archaeological concept of the community of practice share many characteristics, although inhabiting different areas of scholarly analysis.

Discussion: Mycenaean Aegean states as unexceptional, complex economic systems

Where, if anywhere, has thinking about Mycenaean institutions through the lens of theories of the firm gotten us? En route to a conclusion, I discuss four productive aspects. First, this intellectual exercise encourages us to recast political actors who accrue economic benefit from their political roles as something like the opposite. Second, it allows more scope for reconstructing self-interested actors beyond the elite register of society. Third, it confirms recent work that frames the Mycenaean economy as a complex and evolved system rather than a coherent and static structure, but does so within an established theoretical body of economic thought. Finally, it raises the possibility that the Mycenaean state itself operated, at least in some ways, as a vertically integrated firm-like state not dissimilar to those documented under categorically similar geopolitical conditions in Early Modern Europe.

Political and economic actors

Both categories of textually documented operators that I have identified as acting rather firm-like — "collectors" and *qa-si-re-we* — have traditionally been defined as primarily political actors whose authority and positions accrued due to their position in the state bureaucracy. Following Ventris and Chadwick, Nakassis suggests that the *qa-si-re-we* were probably chiefs who had politically powerful positions in their local communities as craft production supervisors (Nakassis 2013: 13–14). Likewise, Killen suggested that collectors were "prominent members of the ruling elite (members of the royal family, high palace officials, and the like) who have been assigned part of the productive capacity of the kingdoms for their own benefit" (Killen 1995: 213). Palaima considers the view of *qa-si-re-we* as a leader of a local guild — e.g., as an economic actor — as badly outdated, seeing them more likely as village level "big men" who became entangled in economic affairs haphazardly by virtue of their political positions (Palaima 2014: 88). Thus, both figures are understood through the lens of politics, with their roles in the economic system arising from their political positions.

I suggest that we might consider the possibility that these individuals were primarily economic actors whose political importance arose from a pre-existing entrepreneurial role, as was frequently the case among important merchants in the Early Modern European context discussed above (Tilly 1983). In that environment, many successful entrepreneurs began with relatively minor operations, but ultimately became immensely wealthy, powerful, and influential — the heads of huge families that generated prosperity for and controlled the fates of many (Munro 2003: 218–221; Munro 2015: 113–114). A single merchant in the Italian cloth industry, Francesco di Marco Datini, engaged about 1,000 workers, who conducted 6,088 cloth-producing transactions over a period of three years (Banaji 2020: 91). Such merchants sometimes financed expensive state ventures, such as wars and expeditions, and themselves often became influential members of the nobility. For example, an entrepreneur named Georg Fugger began operating a small business in the textile sector based in Augsberg, Germany in the late 15th century, then married into a smithing family. Soon, he had accrued sufficient wealth to expand his business into other sectors, including finance and mining. His son, Jakob Fugger, inherited the family firm and expanded its affairs even further. Fugger's career was a kaleidoscopic sequence of exciting economic adventures. He used the wealth accrued from the textile trade to finance the Habsburg regime's military adventures and the activities of the Roman Curia, then used the resulting influence to gain exclusive property rights over mineral deposits in Germany and Italy. These ultimately allowed his family to acquire a near-monopoly in European copper mining. The negative impacts of the monopoly led to government reforms to control pricing. When Fugger's business was threatened, he pivoted to the spice trade. The influence he gained through mercantile activities allowed him to impress his will upon political machinations among European royals, and he himself was ultimately inducted into the German nobility (Herre 2005; Kluger 2009).

Nakassis has observed that neither collectors nor *qa-si-re-we* fit neatly into the grid of palatial bureaucracy (Nakassis 2013: 13, 164–165). Thinking about firms encourages us to consider that palatially recorded transactions could reflect merely one sliver of these entrepreneurs' behavior, and that they were independent agents — like their Early Modern counterparts — who transacted with the state to the extent that it benefited their firms. Such comparisons reinforce the possibility that Mycenaean mercantile firms — should we agree they existed — could have developed separately from state institutions, with their leaders in turn earning political power and becoming integrated into state affairs due to their economic importance.

Agency, voluntarism and self-direction beyond the elite

A second useful point emerging from comparative analysis concerns the reconstruction of some strategy and agency amongst non-elite economic actors who engaged with the palatial economy. At the village and household level, the rise of distributed mercantile firms in early modern Europe is credited with (temporarily) raising standards of living in Europe. Households were offered the opportunity to make extra wages through craft work in the convenience of home, and as the agricultural calendar permitted. In other words, participation in entrepreneurially organized economic activity was both voluntary and beneficial to community members. If, by analogy, it is accepted that a firm in the Mycenaean context might have worked along similar lines, this generates some new avenues for thinking about the role of non-elites in the economic system. Rather than assuming that the workers mentioned in the texts were helpless "subjects" of the state, this allows us to identify agency and the pursuit of self-interest amongst even the most invisible members of Mycenaean society: rural producers that are nameless in the textual record and also usually elusive in archaeological contexts.

Seeing participation in Mycenaean economic organizations as voluntary also provides an apparent explanation for the seemingly random and variable distribution of participants in distributed production operations documented in the Linear B texts (Nakassis 2021: 109). The small and erratic quantities of raw materials distributed by palatial agents has been much discussed, e.g., in regard to the Jn tablets that document metal disbursements from the palace at Pylos (Blackwell 2018: 513–517). Variation in the quantities of material apparent in each set of tablets could reflect not the whims of an incoherent extractive state regime, but the entrepreneurial balancing of supply to demand, as organizers and producers coordinated to align the quantity of goods produced with perceived fluctuations in the scale of the market, as well as variation in the availability of laborers, who often had other concerns. Such variable scenarios in terms of entrepreneurial design and labor availability are also evident in the historical record. For example, records of membership in the ironworkers' guild (who manufactured guns and armor) in 16th century Brescia show constant fluctuations according to issues of demand, as workers would regularly move to and from neighboring towns and regions depending on where opportunities seemed greatest, as described by Braudel (1976: 434):

> "The situation at Brescia was much the same: The *Arte della Ferrarezza* which manufactured armour, side-arms, and arquebuses, was continually expanding and contracting according to the circumstances, losing its workers to neighbouring towns, then recovering them, and so on. At the end of the century under the impulsion of the newly appointed Capitano of the town, Francesco Molino, it recalled one of the master armourers from Brescia, who had gone to Saluzzo taking many *lavoranti* with him; workmen were recalled from Pistoia and Milan, and the number of *botteghe* immediately rose to twenty-three. Then there was a fresh crisis because of problems in the supply of iron and the scarcity of merchants."

Dynamism, evolution, and complexity

Institutional thinking is helpful, furthermore, because it offers a systematic framework through which to view the Mycenaean economy as the end product of evolving systems that developed over time, at the behest of thoughtful, entrepreneurial individuals that adapted to changing circumstances in establishing diverse economic arrangements. Many such arrangements probably preceded the establishment of hierarchical palatial states, rather than comprising elements devised or imposed by the palatial administration.

By extension, this encourages us to envision the palatial bureaucracies themselves as representing the culmination of a long process of integration. The development of institutions and their integration into a state bureaucracy (or not) clearly occurred in distinctive ways across regions and industries. It may have followed roughly similar contours across regions, as we know happened in historically documented contexts, where devolved mercantile firms are often widely but never universally operationalized, and the interplay between guilds, cooperatives, merchant-capitalists, and states always variable and complex. While some textiles were made through distributed work managed by firms, other textiles continued to be produced and used within households, or traded directly in markets. Viewed in evolutionary and comparative economic perspective, then, it is rather unsurprising to find that Mycenaean economic institutions contain multitudes.

If we accept that all economic systems are mixed artifacts of traditional structures and innovative entrepreneurial solutions, and accept that there is no reason to imagine the Mycenaean economy was different from any normal human economy, then we need not be surprised to observe that a wide variety of mechanisms and modes of exchange

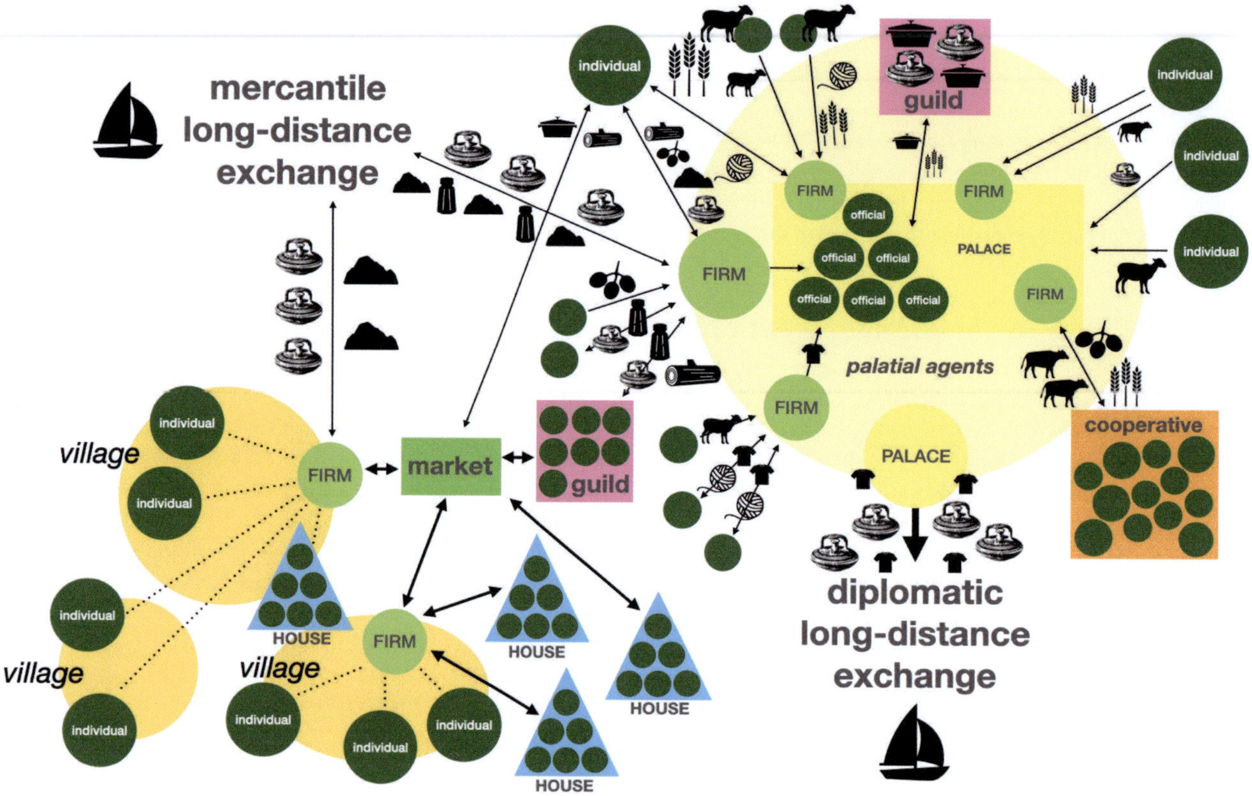

Figure 5.4. Schematic and hypothetical diagram of a complex and organizationally diverse Mycenaean economy.

are apparent in Late Bronze Age economies (Figure 5.4). This view is in keeping with recent trends, and encourages us to conceptualize the Late Bronze Age as witness to long-unraveling historical processes during which economic institutions and political institutions developed in tandem with, but also sometimes independently from one another (Shelmerdine 2001; Halstead 2011: 115).

The Mycenaean state as a vertically integrated economic organization

Thinking of the Mycenaean state as part business and part governance institution seems salutary, since this is consistent with general views of pre-modern states as always combining elements of both. As Lane observed long ago (1979: 38–39) in *Profits and Power*, "[w]hether we examine their motives, their methods, or their consequences, we find that the key innovating enterprises usually combined characteristics of government with characteristics of business." I propose re-imagining the mature Mycenaean state not as something separate to these economic institutions (state vs. non-state), but rather as a sort of super-institution that is at least in part compatible with the definition of a firm. It is often stated that a main aim of the Mycenaean state was to mobilize goods and labor in order to support the operations of the palace, which seem to have included generating value-added products such as textiles and perfumed oils that enabled its participation in long-distance diplomatic trade networks (Nakassis 2010, Schon 2011; Pullen 2013). Perhaps the process of state formation involved iterative episodes of opportunistic integration encouraged by the presence of conditions that usually precede the development of firms.

In his ambitious book *The Long Twentieth Century*, which traces the role of wealth accumulation in state formation over 700 years of the second millennium CE, Giovanni Arrighi reconstructed an antinomy between two logics of state power, one territorial, the other capitalist. The logic of the territorial state sees abstract economic command as an intermediate link in a process that primarily aims at the accrual of territory, while for the capitalist state territory is instead the link on a vector aiming ultimately at increasing additional means of payment (Arrighi 1994: 34). Calling on Giddens' notion of states as "containers of power," he distinguished territorial rulers, "who tend to increase their power by expanding the size of their container," and capitalist rulers, who tend to "increase their power by piling up wealth within a small container. They sometimes increase the size of the container, but only if it is justified" by the requirements of the accumulation of wealth (Arrighi 1994: 34–35, drawing from Giddens 1987). While territorial rulers identify power with the extent and population of their domains, and see wealth as a means or by-product of territorial expansion, capitalist rulers identify power with their command over scarce resources, and care about territory only insofar as it contributes to the accumulation of wealth. It seems to me that, given what we know of the primary activities of some Mycenaean states, their focus was often more squarely on wealth as opposed to territory.

In this view, the palace could have functioned as a large-scale integrator that bound together and partially swallowed numerous previously-integrated firms in order to muster sufficient raw materials and finished products to enable engagement with long-distance diplomatic trade networks, aiming also to reduce local transaction costs in ways that are typical for firms. These included selectively organizing production and delivery internally through contracts, with the ultimate aim of generating material sufficient for exchange on a high-risk, high-reward long distance exchange market. Since such a market would not have been static, nor should we imagine the Mycenaean commercial system that way. Rather, officials and individuals were always making careful choices and designing specific interventions based on changing adaptive strategies in response to perceived risks and opportunities.

Moving to a more synthetic view, based on the examples that I have covered in this paper, I tentatively posit a new proposal for the relationship of each palatial center to the others. As is the case within a single industry, genuine increasing returns in entire trade systems often accrue along with overall increases in the volume of trade handled. In this sense, any individual trading center within a regional group always benefits from coordination within that larger body of regional trading centers, provided that each occupies a distinct niche of supply, rather than competing with one another. As the variety and number of trading centers increases within a region, the array and quantity of goods that each can mobilize expands and becomes more profitable. Moreover, risk is mitigated by the accumulation of many traders who can share information amongst one another, thus reducing uncertainty and mitigating risk (Hicks 1969: 49). I propose, then, that the relationship amongst the Mycenaean centers could have resembled something like what Marx called an operating fraternity of trading centers, with each member specializing in distinct operations and cooperating to share information in order to minimize risk and maximize output (Marx 1962: 248).

Conclusions: The Mycenaean economy as a proto-industrial firm-rich environment

Overall, applying institutional ideas surrounding the growth and logic of firms to the Mycenaean economy seems somewhat helpful, because it encourages us to envision it as a cumulative, evolving system of organic, variable, historically contingent moving parts that developed gradually over time. Of course, many previous discussions of the Mycenaean economy have made this point from a variety of perspectives (e.g., Wright 2008; Dickinson 2010; Voutsaki 2010). An approach taking into account ideas about organizations from institutional economics is primarily productive insofar as it provides a flexible but established theoretical framework within which to parse the logic of some aspects of the Mycenaean economy that we may only view obliquely in the evidentiary record. It also provides some clues about the potential vectors of Mycenaean economic organizations' development over time and articulation with one another.

From this point of view, the Mycenaean economy comprises a complex, overlapping lattice of different types and sizes of organization, including, at least in theory, both previously recognized entities like the palatial state and households, but also organizations that share some structural characteristics with historically documented mercantile firms, agricultural cooperatives, and craft guilds. The organizations involved in different kinds of production vary considerably, because the relative material and skill-based affordances relevant to each industry are likewise variable, with some conducive to vertical integration and others more conducive to cooperative management or governance through closed single-craft organizations.

A major limitation of both the textual and archaeological data is that they do not bring into view a range of additional industries that were probably important but are not well-represented in the evidentiary record. It seems likely that maritime industries like shipbuilding, murex processing, or fishing could have required or benefited from some kind of organizational integration. Fishermen, for example, would need to consider aspects of demand and transportation when choosing whether to preserve and store or transport and market products, lest their harvests go to waste or fetch suboptimal prices. The construction of ships likewise involved a great deal of specialized knowledge and numerous resource types. If it were taking place at scale over time, shipbuilding would probably have benefited from some coordination across sectors. Additional research into comparative examples and possible archaeological correlates for organization in such industries seems like a promising topic for future investigation.

A final general concluding point is that thinking about firms is helpful because it discourages us from hiving off study of prehistoric economies from historical ones. A comparison between Marx's operating fraternity of industrial trading centers to Aegean prehistoric states may strike some as anachronistic and entirely inappropriate. Surely there were as many differences as similarities between these two historical contexts. While acknowledging such a criticism, I maintain that engaging the Bronze Age material in dialogue with historical examples is generally productive. It frees us from the flawed assumption that prehistoric people were fundamentally simpler or less entrepreneurial than modern ones and reveals commonalities in institutions that bridge the residual analytical gap between prehistory and history.

Bibliography

Abell, N., 2014. Migration, Mobility, and Craftspeople in the Aegean Bronze Age: A Case Study from Ayia Irini on the Island of Kea. *World Archaeology* 46: 551–568.

Abell, N., 2020. Rethinking Household-Based Production at Ayia Irini, Kea: An Examination of Technology and Organization in a Bronze Age Community of Practice. *American Journal of Archaeology* 124: 381–416.

Arrighi, G., 1994. *The Long Twentieth Century: Money, Power, and the Origins of our Times*. London: Verso.

Banaji, J., 2020. *A Brief History of Commercial Capitalism*. Chicago: Haymarket.

Bang, P., 2009. The Ancient Economy and New Institutional Economics. *Journal of Roman Studies* 99: 194–206.

Bennet, J., 1992. 'Collectors' or 'Owners'? An Examination of Their Possible Functions within the Palatial Economy of LM III Crete. In *Mykenaïka: Actes du IXe Colloque international sur les textes mycéniens et égéens*, edited by J.-P. Olivier, 65–101. Bulletin de correspondance hellénique, Supplément 25. Paris: de Boccard.

Bennet, J., and P. Halstead, 2014. O-no! Writing and Righting Redistribution. In *KE-RA-ME-JA: Studies Presented to Cynthia W. Shelmerdine*, edited by D. Nakassis, J. Gulizio, and S. A. James, 271–282. Philadelphia: INSTAP Academic Press.

Blackwell, N. G., 2018. Contextualizing Mycenaean Hoards: Metal Control on the Greek Mainland at the End of the Bronze Age. *American Journal of Archaeology* 122: 509–539.

Bowes, K., 2021. When Kuznets Went to Rome: Roman Economic Well-Being and the Reframing of Roman History. *Capitalism: A Journal of History and Economics* 2: 7–40.

Braudel, F., 1976. *The Mediterranean and the Mediterranean World in the Age of Philip II*. 2 vols, New York: Harper & Row.

Braudel, F., 1984. *The Perspective of the World*. New York: Harper & Row.

Burns, B., 2007. Life Outside a Mycenaean Palace: Elite Houses on the Periphery of Citadel Sites. In *Building Communities: House, Settlement, and Society in the Aegean and Beyond*, edited by R. Westgate, N. Fisher, and J. Whitley, 111–119. British School at Athens Studies 15. London: British School at Athens.

Calvet, Y., 2000. The House of Urtenu. *Near Eastern Archaeology* 63: 210–213.

Carlier, P., 1995. *Qa-si-re-u* et *qa-si-re-wi-ja*. In *Politeia: Society and State in the Aegean Bronze Age. Proceedings of the 5th International Aegean Conference, University of Heidelberg, Archäologisches Institut. 10–13 April 1994,* edited by R. Laffineur and W.-D. Niemeier, 355–364. Aegaeum 12. Liège: Université de Liège, Histoire de l'art et archéologie de la Grèce antique; Austin: University of Texas at Austin, Program in Aegean Scripts and Prehistory.

Casson, M., 1997. *Information and Organization*. Oxford: Oxford University Press.

Coase, R., 1937. The Nature of the Firm. *Economica* 4.16: 386–405.

Cook, M., and C. Iliopoulos, 2000. Ill-defined Property Rights in Collective Action: The Case of US Agricultural Cooperatives. In *Institutions, Contracts, and Organizations*, edited by C. Ménard, 335–348. Cheltenham: Edward Elgar.

Cook, M., P. Klein, and C. Iliopoulos, 2008. Contracting and Organization in Food and Agriculture. In *New Institutional Economics: A Guidebook*, edited by É. Brousseau and J.-M. Glachant, 292–304. Cambridge: Cambridge University Press.

Dabney, M., and J. Wright, 2020. Tools, Weapons, Figurines, and Personal Ornaments. In *Nemea Valley Archaeological Project. Volume III: The Mycenaean Settlement on Tsoungiza Hill. Part I: Context Studies*, edited by J. Wright and M. Dabney, 1023–1028. Princeton: American School of Classical Studies at Athens.

Dickinson, O. T. P. K., 2010. The 'Third World' of the Aegean? Middle Helladic Greece Revisited. In *Mesohelladika: La Grèce Continentale au Bronze Moyen*, edited by A. Philippa-Touchais, G. Touchais, S. Voutsaki, and J. Wright, 13–27. Bulletin de correspondance hellénique, Supplément 52. Athens: Ecole française d'Athènes.

Driessen, J., 1992. 'Collector's Items.' Observations sur l'élite mycénienne de Cnossos. In *Mykenaïka:. Actes du IXe Colloque international sur les textes mycéniens et égéens*, edited by J.-P. Olivier, 197–214. Bulletin de correspondance hellénique, Supplément 25. Paris: de Boccard.

Driessen, J., 2010. Spirit of Place. Minoan Houses as Major Actors. In *Political Economies of the Aegean Bronze Age: Papers from the Langford Conference, Florida State University, Tallahassee, 22–24 February 2007*, edited by D. J. Pullen, 35–65. Oxford: Oxbow Books.

Driessen, J., 2018. Beyond the Collective...The Minoan Palace in Action. In *From the Foundations to the Legacy of Minoan Archaeology: Studies in Honour of Professor Keith Branigan*, edited by M. Relaki and Y. Papadatos, 291–313. Sheffield Studies in Aegean Archaeology 12. Oxford: Oxbow Books.

Driessen, J., and Q. Letesson, 2023. The Gathering: Collectivity and the Development of Bronze Age Cretan Society. *Journal of Archaeological Research* 32: 1–58. DOI:10.1007/s10814-023-09183-1.

Earle, T., 2011. Redistribution in Aegean Palatial Societies. Redistribution and the Political Economy: The Evolution of an Idea. *American Journal of Archaeology* 115: 237–244.

Epstein, S., 1998. Craft Guilds, Apprenticeship, and Technological Change in Preindustrial Europe. *The Journal of Economic History* 58: 684–713.

Finley, M. I., 1973. *The Ancient Economy*. Berkeley: University of California Press.

Fischer, W., 1973. Rural Industrialization and Population Change. *Comparative Studies in Society and History* 15: 158–170.

Foss, N., and P. Klein, 2005. Entrepreneurship and the Theory of the Firm: Who Gains from Trade? In *Handbook of Entrepreneurship: Disciplinary Perspectives*, edited by R. Agarwal, S. Alvarez, and O. Sorenson, 55–80. New York: Kluwer.

Foss, N., and P. Klein, 2008. The Theory of the Firm and Its Critics: A Stocktaking and Assessment. In *New Institutional Economics: A Guidebook*, edited by É. Brousseau and J.-M. Glachant, 425–442. Cambridge: Cambridge University Press.

Galaty, M. L., 2007. Wealth Ceramics, Staple Ceramics: Pots and the Mycenaean Palaces. In *Rethinking Mycenaean Palaces II: Revised and Expanded Second Edition*, edited by M. L. Galaty and W. A. Parkinson, 74–86. Monograph 60. Los Angeles: University of California at Los Angeles, Cotsen Institute of Archaeology.

Galaty, M. L., 2010. Wedging Clay: Combining Competing Models of Mycenaean Pottery Industries. In *Political Economies of the Aegean Bronze Age: Papers from the Langford Conference, Florida State University, Tallahassee, 22–24 February 2007*, edited by D. J. Pullen, 230–247. Oxford: Oxbow Books.

Galaty, M. L., D. Nakassis, and W. A. Parkinson, eds., 2011. Forum: Redistribution in Aegean Palatial Societies. *American Journal of Archaeology* 115: 175–244.

Garrouste, P., and S. Saussier, 2008. The Theories of the Firm. In *New Institutional Economics: A Guidebook*, edited by É. Brousseau and J.-M. Glachant, 23–36. Cambridge: Cambridge University Press.

Giddens, A., 1987. *The Nation-State and Violence*. Berkeley: University of California Press.

Granovetter, M., 1985. Economic Action and Social Structure: The Problem of Embeddedness. *American Journal of Sociology* 91: 481–510.

Greif, A., 2006. *Institutions and the Path to the Modern Economy: Lessons from Medieval Trade*. Cambridge: Cambridge University Press.

Halstead, P., 2011. Redistribution in Aegean Palatial Societies: Terminology, Scale, and Significance. *American Journal of Archaeology* 115: 229–235.

Herre, F., 2005. *Die Fugger in ihrer Zeit*. Augsberg: Wißner Verlag.

Hicks, J., 1969. *A Theory of Economic History*. Oxford: Clarendon.

Hirschfeld, N., 2010. Cypro-Minoan. In *The Oxford Handbook of the Bronze Age Aegean (ca. 3000–1000 BC)*, edited by E. H. Cline, 373–384. Oxford: Oxford University Press.

Hruby, J., 2017. Finding Haute Cuisine: Identifying Shifts in Food Styles from Cooking Vessels. In *From Cooking Vessels to Cultural Practices in the Late Bronze Age Aegean*, edited by J. Hruby and D. Trusty, 15–26. Oxford: Oxbow Books.

Joskow, P., 2004. Vertical Integration. In *Handbook of New Institutional Economics*, edited by C. Ménard and M. Shirley, 319–48. Norwell, MA: Kluwer Academic Publishers.

Joskow, P., 2008. Introduction to New Institutional Economics: A Report Card. In *New Institutional Economics: A Guidebook*, edited by É. Brousseau and J.-M. Glachant, 1–19. Cambridge: Cambridge University Press.

Jung, R., 2016. Friede den Hütten, Krieg den Palästen! — In the Bronze Age Aegean. In *Arm und Reich: Zur Ressourcenverteilung in prähistorischen Gesellschaften* edited by H. Meller, H. Hahn, R. Jung, and R. Risch, 553–577. Halle: Tagungen deese Landesmuseums für Vorgeschichte Halle.

Kieser, A., 1989. Organizational, Institutional, and Societal Evolution: Medieval Craft Guilds and the Genesis of Formal Organizations. *Administrative Science Quarterly* 34: 540–564.

Kilian-Dirlmeier, I., 1997. *Das mittelbronzezeitliche Schachtgrab von Ägina*. Alt-Ägina 4.3. Mainz: Zabern.

Killen, J. T., 1987. Bronzeworking at Knossos and Pylos. *Hermathena* 143: 61–72.

Killen, J. T., 1995. Some Further Thoughts on 'Collectors.' In *Politeia: Society and State in the Aegean Bronze Age. Proceedings of the 5th International Aegean Conference / 5e Rencontre égéenne internationale, University of Heidelberg, Archäologisches Institut, 10–13 April 1994*, edited by R. Laffineur and W.-D. Niemeier, 213–226. Aegaeum 12. Liège: Université de Liège, Histoire de l'art et archéologie de la Grèce antique; Austin: University of Texas at Austin, Program in Aegean Scripts and Prehistory.

Killen, J. T., 2001. Some Thoughts on *Ta-ra-si-ja*. In *Economy and Politics in the Mycenaean Palace States: Proceedings of a Conference held on 1–3 July 1999 in the Faculty of Classics, Cambridge*, edited by S. Voutsaki and J. Killen, 161–180. Cambridge Philological Society Supplementary Volume 27. Cambridge: Cambridge Philological Society.

Kiriatzi, E., and S. Andreou, 2016. Mycenaean and Mycenaeanizing Pottery across the Mediterranean: A Multi-Scalar Approach to Technological Mobility, Transmission, and Appropriation. In *Human Mobility and Technological Transfer in the Prehistoric*

Mediterranean, edited by E. Kiriatzi and C. Knappett, 128–153. British School at Athens, Studies in Greek Antiquity. Cambridge: Cambridge University Press.

Kiriatzi, E., and C. Knappett, eds., 2016. *Human Mobility and Technological Transfer in the Prehistoric Mediterranean.* British School at Athens, Studies in Greek Antiquity. Cambridge: Cambridge University Press.

Kirzner, L., 1973. *Competition and Entrepreneurship.* Chicago: University of Chicago Press.

Klima, A., 1974. The Role of Rural Domestic Industry in Bohemia in the Eighteenth Century. *Economic History Review* 27: 48–56.

Kluger, M., 2009. *Die Fugger: Die Deutschen Medici in und am Augsberg.* Augsberg: Context Verlag.

Knapp, A. B., and N. Meyer, 2023. Merchants and Mercantile Society in Late Bronze Age Cyprus. *American Journal of Archaeology* 127: 309–338.

Kotsonas, A., 2016. Politics of Periodization and the Archaeology of Early Greece. *American Journal of Archaeology* 120: 239–270.

Kriedte, P., H. Medick, and J. Schlumbohm, 1981. *Industrialization before Industrialization: Rural Industry in the Genesis of Capitalism.* New York: Cambridge University Press.

Kyriakidis, E., 2010. 'Collectors' as Stakeholders in Mycenaean Governance: Property and the Relations between the Ruling Class and the State. *Proceedings of the Cambridge Philological Society* 56: 140–177.

Landes, D., 1969. *Unbound Prometheus.* Cambridge: Cambridge University Press.

Lane, F. C., 1979. *Profits from Power.* New York: SUNY Press.

Langlois, R., and P. Robertson, 1995. *Firms, Markets, and Economic Change: A Dynamic Theory of Business Institutions.* London: Routledge.

Lis, B., 2016. A Foreign Potter in the Pylian Kingdom? A Reanalysis of the Ceramic Assemblage of Room 60 in the Palace of Nestor at Pylos. *Hesperia* 85.3: 491–536.

Lis, C., H. Soly, and L. Mitzman, 2009. An Irresistible Phalanx: Journeyman Associations in Western Europe, 1300–1800. *International Review of Social History* 39, *Supplement S2: Before the Unions, Wage Earners and Collective Action in Europe, 1300–1850*: 11–52.

Littlefield, A., 1979. The Expansion of Capitalist Relations of Production in Mexican Crafts. *Journal of Peasant Studies* 6: 471–488.

Littlefield, A., and L. Reynolds, 1990. The Putting Out System: Transitional Form or Recurrent Feature of Capitalist Production. *The Social Science Journal* 27: 359–372.

Lo Cascio, E., 2018. Market Regulation and Transaction Costs in the Roman Empire. In *Trade, Commerce, and the State in the Roman World,* edited by A. Wilson and A. Bowman, 117–132. Oxford: Oxford University Press.

Lytle, E., 2016. Chaerephilus and Sons: Vertical Integration, Classical Athens, and the Black Sea Fish Trade. *Ancient Society* 46: 1–26.

Mantoux, P., 1961. *The Industrial Revolution in the Eighteenth Century.* New York: Harper & Row.

Marx, K., 1962. *Capital, Vol. III.* Moscow: Foreign Languages Publishing House.

Medick, H., 1981. The Structures and Function of Population-Development under the Proto-Industrial System. In *Industrialization before Industrialization: Rural Industry in the Genesis of Capitalism,* edited by P. Kriedte, H. Medick, and J. Schlumbohm, 74–93. New York: Cambridge University Press.

Ménard, C., 2004. The Economics of Hybrid Organizations. *Journal of Institutional and Theoretical Economics* 160.3: 1–32.

Monroe, C., 2010. Sunk Costs at Late Bronze Age Uluburun. *Bulletin of the American Schools of Oriental Research* 357: 19–33.

Moreno García, J. C., ed., 2022. *From House Societies to States: Early Political Organization from Antiquity to the Middle Ages.* Multidisciplinary Approaches to Ancient Societies 3. Oxford: Oxbow Books.

Munro, J., 2003. Medieval Woollens: Textiles, Technology, and Organization, c. 800–1500. In *The Cambridge History of Western Textiles,* edited by D. Jenkins, 181–227. Cambridge: Cambridge University Press.

Munro, J., 2015. The Dual Crisis of the Late Medieval Florentine Cloth Industry, c. 1320–c. 1420. In *Textiles and the Medieval Economy: Production, Trade, and Consumption of Textiles, 8th–16th Centuries,* edited by A. Huang and C. Jahnke, 113–148. Oxford: Oxbow Books.

Nakassis, D., 2010. Reevaluating Staple and Wealth Finance at Mycenaean Pylos. In *Political Economies of the Aegean Bronze Age: Papers from the Langford Conference, Florida State University, Tallahassee, 22–24 February 2007,* edited by D. J. Pullen, 127–148. Oxford: Oxbow Books.

Nakassis, D., 2013. *Individuals and Society in Mycenaean Pylos.* Mnemosyne Supplements 358. Leiden: Brill.

Nakassis, D., 2021. The Extractive Systems of the Mycenaean World. In *Ancient Taxation: The Mechanics of Extraction in Comparative Perspective,* edited by J. Valk and I. Soto Marín, 93–127. New York: New York University Press.

Nakassis, D., 2022. Communities, 'Houses', and Political Organisation in the Mycenaean World. In *From House Societies to States: Early Political Organization from Antiquity to the Middle Ages,* edited by J. C. Moreno García, 123–140. Multidisciplinary Approaches to Ancient Societies 3. Oxford: Oxbow Books.

Nakassis, D., 2024. Before the Economy? Growth, Institutions, and the Late Bronze Age. In *Models,*

Methods, and Morality: Assessing Modern Approaches to the Greco-Roman Economy, edited by S. Murray and S. Bernard, 151–184. Cham, Switzerland: Springer Nature: Palgrave/MacMillan. DOI:10.1007/978-3-031-58210-3_6.

Nakassis, D., M. L. Galaty, and W. A. Parkinson, eds., 2016. Discussion and Debate: Reciprocity in Aegean Palatial Societies: Gifts, Debt, and the Foundations of Economic Exchange. *Journal of Mediterranean Archaeology* 29: 61–132.

North, D., 1994. Economic Performance through Time. *The American Economic Review* 84: 359–368.

North, D., 2005. *Understanding the Process of Economic Change*. Princeton: Princeton University Press.

North, D., J. Wallis, and B. Weingast, 2009. *Violence and Social Orders: A Conceptual Framework for Interpreting Recorded Human History*. Cambridge: Cambridge University Press.

Nosch, M.-L., 2000. Acquisition and Distribution: *ta-ra-si-ja* in the Mycenaean Textile Industry. In *Trade and Production in Premonetary Greece: Acquisition and Distribution of Raw Materials and Finished Products. Proceedings of the 6th International Workshop, Athens 1996*, edited by C. Gillis, C. Risberg, and B. Sjöberg, 43–61. Studies in Mediterranean Archaeology Pocketbook 154. Jonsered: Paul Åströms Förlag.

Nosch, M.-L., 2006. More Thoughts on the Mycenaean *ta-ra-si-ja* System. In *Fiscality in Mycenaean and Near Eastern Archives: Proceedings of the Conference Held at Soprintendenza Archivistica per la Campania, Naples, 21–23 October 2004*, edited by M. Perna, 161–182. Studi egei e vicinorientali 3. Paris: de Boccard.

Nye, J., 2008. Institutions and the Institutional Environment. In *New Institutional Economics: A Guidebook*, edited by É. Brousseau and J.-M. Glachant, 67–80. Cambridge: Cambridge University Press.

Osborne, R., 1996. *Greece in the Making: 1200–479 BC*. Abingdon: Routledge.

Palaima, T. G., 1997. Potter and Fuller: The Royal Craftsmen. In *TEXNH: Craftsmen, Craftswomen, and Craftsmanship in the Aegean Bronze Age. Proceedings of the 6th International Aegean Conference/6e Rencontre* égéenne *internationale, Philadelphia, Temple University, 18–21 April 1996*, edited by R. Laffineur and P. Betancourt, 407–412. Aegaeum 16. Liège: Histoire de l'art et archéologie de la Grèce antique; Austin: University of Texas at Austin, Program in Aegean Scripts and Prehistory.

Palaima, T. G., 2014. Pylos Tablet Vn 130 and the Pylos Perfume Industry. In *KE-RA-ME-JA: Studies Presented to Cynthia W. Shelmerdine*, edited by D. Nakassis, J. Gulizio, and S. A. James, 83–90. Philadelphia: INSTAP Academic Press.

Papadimitriou, N., 2012. Regional or 'International' Networks? A Comparative Examination of Aegean and Cypriot Imported Pottery in the Eastern Mediterranean. *Talanta* 44: 92–136.

Parkinson, W. A., D. Nakassis, and M. L. Galaty, eds., 2013. Forum: Crafts, Specialists, and Markets in Mycenaean Greece. *American Journal of Archaeology* 117: 413–459.

Platteau, J.-P., 2008. The Causes of Institutional Efficiency: A Development Perspective. In *New Institutional Economics: A Guidebook*, edited by É. Brousseau and J.-M. Glachant, 443–462. Cambridge: Cambridge University Press.

Pullen, D. J., ed., 2010. *Political Economies of the Aegean Bronze Age: Papers from the Langford Conference, Florida State University, Tallahassee, 22–24 February 2007*. Oxford: Oxbow Books.

Pullen, D. J., 2013. Crafts, Specialists, and Markets in Mycenaean Greece: Exchanging the Mycenaean Economy. *American Journal of Archaeology* 117: 437–445.

Pullen, D. J., 2020. Merchants, Ports, and Market Exchange: Strategies for Coping in an Interconnected Mycenaean World. In *Communication Uneven: Acceptance of and Resistance to Foreign Influences in the Connected Ancient Mediterranean*, edited by J. Driessen, 189–202. Aegis 20. Louvain-la-Neuve: Presses universitaire de Louvain.

Rougement, F., 2009. *Contrôle économique et administration à l'époque des palais mycéniens (fin du IIe millénaire av. J.-C.* Bibliothèque des Écoles françaises d'Athènes et de Rome 332. Athens: École française d'Athènes.

Sabatini, S., 2016. Textile Tools from the East Gate at Mycenaean Midea, Argolis, Greece. *Opuscula* 9: 217–247.

Scheidel, W., R. Saller, and I. Morris, eds., 2007. *The Cambridge Economic History of the Greco-Roman World*. Cambridge: Cambridge University Press.

Schon, R., 2011. By Appointment to His Majesty the *Wanax*. Value-Added Goods and Redistribution in Mycenaean Palatial Economies. *American Journal of Archaeology* 115: 219–227.

Schumpeter, J., 1934. *The Theory of Economic Development: An Inquiry into Profits, Capital, Credit, Interest, and the Business Cycle*. Cambridge: Harvard University Press.

Shelmerdine, C. W., 1987. Architectural Change and Economic Decline at Pylos. In *Studies in Mycenaean and Classical Greek Presented to John Chadwick*, edited by J. Killen, J. Melena, and J. P. Olivier, 557–568. Salamanca: Ediciones Universidad.

Shelmerdine, C. W., 2001. The Evolution of Administration at Pylos. In *Economy and Politics in the Mycenaean Palace States: Proceedings of a Conference held on 1–3 July 1999 in the Faculty of Classics, Cambridge*, edited by S. Voutsaki and J. Killen, 113–128. Cambridge Philological Society Supplementary Volume 27. Cambridge: Cambridge Philological Society.

Sherratt, S., 2003. The Mediterranean Economy: "Globalization" at the End of the Second Millennium BCE. In *Symbiosis, Symbolism, and Power of the Past: Canaan, Ancient Israel, and their Neighbors from the Late Bronze Age through Roman Palaestina*, edited by W. Dever and S. Gitin, 37–62. Winona Lake: Eisenbrauns.

Snodgrass, A., 1986. Interaction by Design: The Greek City State. In *Peer Polity Interaction and Socio-Political Change*, edited by C. Renfrew and J. Cherry, 47–58. Cambridge: Cambridge University Press.

Terpstra, T., 2019. *Trade in the Ancient Mediterranean: Private Order and Public Institutions*. Princeton: Princeton University Press.

Tilly, C., 1983. Flows of Capital and Forms of Industry in Europe, 1500–1900. *Theory and Society* 12: 123–142.

Vetters, M., 2014. A Clay Ball with Cypro-Minoan Inscription from Tiryns. *Archaiologischer Anzeiger* 2011.2: 1–49.

Viglietti, C., 2021. Cultural Hegemonies, 'NIE-orthodoxy', and Social-Development Models: Classicists' 'Organic' Approaches to Economic History in the Early XXI Century. In *Antonio Gramsci and the Ancient World*, edited by E. Zucchetti and A.M. Cimino, 301–326. London: Routledge.

Voutsaki, S., 2001. Economic Control, Power, and Prestige in the Mycenaean World: The Archaeological Evidence. In *Economy and Politics in the Mycenaean Palace States: Proceedings of a Conference held on 1–3 July 1999 in the Faculty of Classics, Cambridge*, edited by S. Voutsaki and J. Killen, 195–213. Cambridge Philological Society Supplementary Volume 27. Cambridge: Cambridge Philological Society.

Voutsaki, S., 2010. Middle Bronze Age: Mainland Greece. In *The Oxford Handbook of the Bronze Age Aegean (ca. 3000–1000 BC)*, edited by E. H. Cline, 99–112. Oxford: Oxford University Press.

Voutsaki, S., and J. Killen, eds., 2001. *Economy and Politics in the Mycenaean Palace States: Proceedings of a Conference held on 1–3 July 1999 in the Faculty of Classics, Cambridge*. Cambridge Philological Society Supplementary Volume 27. Cambridge: Cambridge Philological Society.

Whitelaw, T., 2001. Reading between the Tablets: Assessing Mycenaean Palatial Involvement in Ceramic Production and Consumption. In *Economy and Politics in the Mycenaean Palace States: Proceedings of a Conference held on 1–3 July 1999 in the Faculty of Classics, Cambridge*, edited by S. Voutsaki and J. Killen, 151–179. Cambridge Philological Society Supplementary Volume 27. Cambridge: Cambridge Philological Society.

Williamson, O., 1975. *Markets and Hierarchies*. New York: Free Press.

Wright, J. C., 1984. Changes in Form and Function of the Palace at Pylos. In *Pylos Comes Alive: Industry and Administration in a Mycenaean Palace*, edited by C. Shelmerdine and T. Palaima, 19–29. New York: Archaeological Institute of America.

Wright, J. C., 2008. Early Mycenaean Greece. In *The Cambridge Companion to the Aegean Bronze Age*, edited by C. Shelmerdine, 230–257. Cambridge: Cambridge University Press.

Coastal Communities and Connectivity in the Late Bronze Age Aegean

Thomas F. Tartaron

Abstract

We often remark that communities inhabiting coastal anchorages, harbors, and ports linked terrestrial and maritime worlds. But the ways that these realms were linked, and the people who linked them, are typically obscure. In this paper, I first examine a range of Aegean Bronze Age coastal sites from uninhabited to seasonally occupied to fully sedentary, followed by discussion of the spectrum of resources that were exploited on them. I then shift my focus inland to explore strategies for investigating the linkages between coastal and interior sites, including Mycenaean palaces. In a case study, I investigate the relationships among the inland palatial site of Mycenae, the Saronic harbor settlement at Korphos-Kalamianos, and the Saronic Gulf. I highlight Kalamianos as a "weak tie" linking Mycenae with the Saronic Gulf, thus fulfilling a mediating role. This exercise draws evidence from excavations and surveys, archaeometric analyses, Linear B archives, and ethnography and cross-cultural ethnoarchaeology.

Introduction

In the context of Aegean Bronze Age maritime networks, it is often remarked that coastal communities linked, and mediated between, terrestrial and maritime worlds. But the characteristics of these communities, the ways these realms were linked, and the people who linked them, are often obscure. In this chapter, I reflect on the diverse types of coastal sites, the people and communities that inhabited them, and the practicalities of the links they facilitated and exploited. Previously, I focused on the maritime networks in which these communities participated (Tartaron 2013); here, I turn my gaze inland to scrutinize their connections to people and places in the interior (Figure 6.1). In the concluding section, I examine Korphos-Kalamianos, where Daniel Pullen and I worked together for several years, to illustrate these themes.

Coastal sites and the small worlds they comprised were realms of constant motion and connectivity (Broodbank 2000; Horden and Purcell 2000), but the coastscapes and communities that inhabited them were highly diverse. There were different kinds of coastal sites, in terms of size, infrastructure, and range of activities they witnessed. Simply by distinguishing landing sites with the labels anchorage, harbor, and port (Tartaron 2013: 4), we acknowledge a continuum of increasing infrastructural formality for accommodating subsistence, trade, or even naval fleets. Further, we can identify a range of activities as people exploited coastal and marine resources such as fish, shellfish, and salt, and wetland products such as clay, grasses, and waterfowl. Many coastal sites were not occupied continuously at all — such as

ORCID 0009-0002-8316-5785
Department of Classical Studies, University of Pennsylvania
tartaron@sas.upenn.edu

In *Social Groups and Production in Mycenaean Economies. Papers from the Langford Conference, Florida State University, Tallahassee, 24-25 February 2023*, edited by D. Pullen (2025), 79–100. Leiden: Sidestone Press.

Figure 6.1. Map of the Aegean region showing key sites mentioned in the text. Base map public domain, Wikimedia Commons.

Site type	Subtype	Activities
Uninhabited	Special purpose	Fishing; shellfish gathering; salt collection, wetland resources; ferry
	Opportunistic	Sheltered anchorage; offload agricultural and forest products
Seasonally inhabited	Subsistence; Special purpose	Fishing; herding ("goat island")
Inhabited year-round	Subsistence	Agriculture, pastoralism, hunting, gathering
	Node in ordered site hierarchy	Dependent harbor; administrative center
	Trade harbor/ emporion	Import/export
	Production site	agricultural, marine, metal, textiles, stone tools, etc.
	Ritual/sacred	Pilgrimage; sanctuary
	Military port	Defense; fleet storage
	Ferry port	Crossing point

Table 6.1. Hypothetical coastal type sites and activities. This typology is neither intended to be exhaustive of the range of variation, nor to suggest that sites could have only one purpose or kind of activity.

locations for harvesting shellfish or sea salt, or for picking up or dropping off agricultural products episodically. It is possible to propose a tentative typology for the kinds of coastal sites that might have existed (Table 6.1). There are many ways one could organize coastal sites conceptually; in Table 6.1, I have chosen to feature a continuum from uninhabited to seasonally inhabited to inhabited year-round. These types and subtypes are not exhaustive, and it is understood that a coastal place can slide along this continuum or accommodate multiple activities at the same time.

A coastal location need not be inhabited to be important economically or in some other way. Fishing and shell fishing grounds, as well as collection sites for salt and wetland resources, may be spatially detached from settlements and yet part of routine subsistence practices. Other uninhabited landing sites could be used opportunistically as anchorages, for example as occasional shelter for ships, or for loading/offloading of agricultural and forest products. Obviously, such locations are difficult or impossible to identify in the archaeological record, in view of coastal change over millennia and the light imprint humans left on them, unless there is an accumulation of material as for example in a shell midden. What we *can* do is point to the kinds of settings on modern coasts —

Figure 6.2. Examples of uninhabited coves that could serve as informal landing sites, Cyprus.

Figure 6.2 continued.

wetlands, small anchorages, etc. — as representative of the *types* of locations where non-settlement activities took place. In recent fieldwork in Greece and Cyprus, I have examined numerous small, uninhabited coves that could serve as informal anchorages (Figure 6.2).

Small seasonal and sedentary sites: Chryssi and Papadiokampos

Activity at some coastal sites involved seasonal occupation and exploitation of resources such as seafood or grazing land for livestock. Chryssi, a small island about 12 km off the south coast of Crete, is nearly waterless, windy, and hot. It has no permanent settlement today, but is used seasonally by shepherds and fishermen, as archaeologists believe was also the case in the Bronze Age (Brogan et al. 2019; Chalikias 2015). The Minoan site (MM II–LM IB) yielded massive amounts of crushed *Hexaplex trunculus* (murex) shell, a purple dye producer.[1] Building B1 on the site has been interpreted as a residence with an attached purple dye workshop. The site produced many other species of fish and shellfish, and a large number of hooks, floats, and net weights. The excavators suggest this was a seasonal site where people fished and produced purple dye for a textile industry at one of the palace centers on Crete, or more locally for an as yet unknown center on the southern coast of the Ierapetra Isthmus (Chalikias 2015: 43–44; Mylona 2020: 188–193). Another kind of seasonally occupied site is the so-called goat island, where herders brought livestock seasonally to graze on unexploited pasture (Constantakopoulou 2007: 200–214; Horden and Purcell 2000: 224–230). Starting with Homer's Thrinacia, the island where the cattle and sheep of Helios grazed (*Odyssey* 12.128–131), and the offshore island of the Cyclopes, inhabited only by goats (*Odyssey* 9.116–124), it has remained a popular trope among authors down to the present day. Ptolemy (*Geography* 3.15.28) and Pliny the Elder (*Natural History* 4.12.23) wrote of the small, uninhabited island of Polyaigos (literally, "many goats") off Melos, and in recent centuries numerous islets and islands have been described in this way (Constantakopoulou 2007: 203–204).

By contrast, Papadiokampos was a small, year-round seaside settlement on the north coast of Crete with a diversified economy (Mylona 2020: 195–201; Sofianou and Brogan 2009). The inhabitants of Building A1 (LM IB)

1 *Hexaplex trunculus* was formerly known as *Murex trunculus*, as it often appears in the archaeological literature. Closely related species such as *Murex brandaris* (now *Bolinus brandaris*) are also present in Bronze Age assemblages.

processed wine and olive oil, but really striking was the massive deposit of edible seashells, 50 kg spread around hearths in rooms 5 and 8. 98% of these were limpet and top shells. Archaeologists were fortunate because the site was abandoned hastily, and the occupants left the food refuse along with pottery, tools, and other items. While the inhabitants of A1 seemed occupied with subsistence featuring a seafood diet, those living in Building B1 on the same site appear to have been involved in the production and trade of metals and textiles (Sofianou and Brogan 2009: 9). Modern ethnographic examples similarly confirm that small coastal communities often adopt diversified economies. On the small, nearly waterless island of Dokos off the coast of the southern Argolid, in 1945 22 families herded sheep and goat, cultivated wheat and olives, collected wild plants, and stored water in cisterns for human and animal use (Kardulias 2000). Despite their risk-buffering strategies and attempts at self-sufficiency, they could persist on the island only by articulating with regional markets and resources on the larger island of Hydra and the mainland around Hermione. Islands like Dokos were enmeshed in networks of connectivity, both facilitating them and depending on them for survival.

The brief examples of Chryssi and Papadiokampos highlight some of the variability among small Bronze Age coastal sites. They give a vivid picture of resource exploitation and daily life, and there is much we can learn from them. Systematic surface reconnaissance is necessary to discover such tiny, unobtrusive sites, many of which will have been erased or otherwise rendered undetectable by millennia of coastal transformation by natural and anthropogenic means (e.g., Knodell et al. 2022). They reveal diverse strategies for subsistence, and in particular for the roles they played in regional maritime networks connected to the palaces and other intermediate nodes, with purple dye and metals just two examples of their productive output. Equally important are the meticulous methods of excavation, demonstrating that it is possible to recover and analyze fragile assemblages of fish and shellfish.

Larger sedentary sites and networks

As the size and complexity of coastal settlements increases, these communities may take on multiple roles in social, economic, and political organization at scales from small worlds to international world systems (Table 6.1). For example, Minoan Kommos on Crete may have functioned as the dependent harbor of the Phaistos palace, a center of production (pottery, purple dye) and trade in its own right with imports from throughout the Mediterranean, and a working town with evidence for vigorous daily life (Shaw 2006).

Following the organizational structure evident in the Pylian Linear B tablets, many archaeologists have favored top-down models of vertical regional integration with multi-tiered site hierarchies based on site size, complexity, or presence of certain features such as imports, elite tombs, or other monuments (e.g., Carothers 1992; Cosmopoulos 2006; Kilian 1988; Liko 2012). Cosmopoulos (2006: 208–215) drew upon archaeological and textual evidence to propose a four-tiered site hierarchy in Messenia in the 13th century B.C. with Pylos at the apex. This is a compelling model for that particular place and time, but there are alternative organizational structures that do not present clear hierarchies or even high levels of regional integration. One aspect of this is exploring the limits of the palaces' political and economic dominance of nearby territories, as well as the presence of non-palatial and nonstate forms of integration. Pullen and Tartaron argued that the northern Corinthian coastal plain developed a non-hierarchical pattern of similarly scaled peer polities beyond palatial reach during the Bronze Age (Pullen and Tartaron 2007; Tartaron 2010). Emiliano Arena (2015) envisioned loosely integrated chiefdoms (in the descriptive, not evolutionary sense) in LBA Achaia as an alternative to the palatial model. The political situation in the LH III Argolid is notoriously difficult to resolve in a hierarchical framework; Pullen recently argued for "...a situation of competition, not subordination, among those centers" (Pullen 2022: 83). Dimitri Nakassis, among others, has cautioned against reconstructing from the Linear B archives a rigidly hierarchical bureaucratic state (Nakassis 2013, 2023).

Network analysis is another source of alternative organizational models. It has been a quarter century since Cyprian Broodbank (2000) published his Proximal Point (network) Analysis (PPA) model of maritime interaction in the "small world" of the Cycladic islands for each phase of the Early Bronze Age. Using a simple method of connecting each site to its three nearest neighbors, the PPA identified the densest webs of connections as "interaction centers." Often, the islands that were more "central" in network terms were not the largest or most environmentally endowed, but those that were most strategically placed on communication corridors. Location is also a strong factor in the prominence of Kalamianos, as I discuss below.

Exploitation of marine resources in the Aegean Bronze Age: Fish and shellfish

For a long time, the received wisdom has been that Aegean Bronze Age people, both coastal and inland, avoided fish and other marine resources in their diet (e.g., Iezzi 2015: 101; Petroutsa and Manolis 2010). Negative evidence was drawn from two sources: the low quantities of archaeological remains; and stable isotope analyses that consistently failed to detect isotopic signatures for consumption of marine products. Regarding the first problem, recovery of very small remains like seeds, plant parts, and fish bones was poor in the Aegean until excavations made flotation of deposits standard procedure in recent decades. Judith

Powell (1996) was able to catalogue only modest remains of fish and associated material culture in the early 1990s. This change in field practice has resulted in the recovery of fish bones and shells that would have been missed before, though because of the fragility of the skeletal remains of small fish, at most sites they are poorly preserved and must represent only a fraction of the specimens once used and discarded (Theodoropoulou 2012: 301–304). Meticulous recovery at sites like Chryssi and Papadiokampos, along with a growing number of excavations using similar techniques, has yielded evidence of harvesting marine creatures for both dietary and industrial uses. Particularly striking is the expanding roster of Bronze Age sites, both large and small, with substantial deposits of crushed murex shells: Knossos, Kommos (Ruscillo 2006), Pefka (Apostolakou et al. 2016; Apostolakou, Brogan, and Betancourt 2020), Chryssi, Palaikastro (Reese 1987; Stieglitz 1994), Ayia Irini (Kea), Kolonna (Berger et al. 2020), Mitrou (Vykukal 2011), and many more (see also Betancourt, Brogan, and Apostolakou 2020; Burke 1999; Nuttall 2021: 155–162). Moreover, our understanding of the process and scale of purple dye manufacture has fundamentally changed. For decades it was believed that thousands of living murex were required to extract a mere gram or two of dye (Ruscillo 2005: 101), but recent experiments by Ruscillo (2005) and others have shown those estimates to be grossly overstated. Thus, while it was once believed that only sites with enormous piles of crushed murex shells could be involved in the production of purple dye, it now seems likely that dye could be produced on a more modest scale, and not necessarily for export (Apostolakou, Brogan, and Betancourt 2012). Future discoveries are likely to happen at a remove from habitation areas, in view of the infamous stench of the process.

The "stable isotope paradox"

Despite the progress in the recovery of marine resources at archaeological sites, the results of stable isotope studies consistently indicate that throughout Aegean prehistory, both coastal and inland dwellers avoided marine resources in their diet — a contradiction we might call a "stable isotope paradox." The stable isotopes of carbon and nitrogen are "fixed" in human teeth and bone collagen through the kinds of foods we consume. Plants like wheat or barley (C3) can be distinguished from maize or millet (C4) by their different photosynthetic pathways, which produce distinct carbon–nitrogen isotope ratios. In the same way, consumption of marine and terrestrial animals can be distinguished by the ratios of their stable isotopes; the segregation of terrestrial, marine, and mixed terrestrial/marine dietary practices was worked out for Atlantic fish and shellfish, and when these benchmarks were applied to Aegean prehistoric sites, marine animals were consistently absent in the diet. The problem is that Aegean marine species had not been measured for the Mediterranean. When Garcia-Guixé et al. (2010) and Vika and Theodoropoulou (2012) measured Mediterranean fish directly, they found that the ratios not only diverged from those of the Atlantic, but also varied within the Mediterranean and overlapped with terrestrial values. These findings could mean that marine exploitation is hiding in the stable isotope data. Because the scientific data seemed so conclusive, it had been possible to ignore the contrary data — particularly the rich marine iconography of the Aegean Bronze Age, such as Minoan Marine Style pottery, frescoes from Akrotiri, Knossos, and Phylakopi, and the octopus and nautilus motifs on Mycenaean painted pottery. Hence, paradoxically, the stable isotope data contradict emerging marine assemblages and the care with which Aegean artists expressed their engagement with marine life in art (Theodoropoulou 2012).

Textual evidence

More than 30 years ago, Tom Palaima stated unequivocally, "There are no references in the Linear B tablets to fish or fishermen" (Palaima 1991: 284), though that position may need to be modified somewhat (Mylona 2020; Nosch 2004; Palaima 2020). The different forms of the Linear B word *po-pu-re-jo*, which has been taken to refer variously to (female) purple dyers, purple-dyed cloth, or a purple dye workshop, might also refer to murex fishermen, who of course are implicit in the textile industry (Mylona 2020: 205; Nosch 2004: 33; Palaima 2020). Yet it could be that seafood was not consumed at the palaces, or that marine products (other than special dyes) were simply not among their administrative interests. Fish, we might conjecture, were ubiquitous and so not amenable to palace monopoly; and perishable so that routine delivery to the palaces — most of which were at least several kilometers inland — would not be practical. On the other hand, we now have solid evidence that at least some people consumed fish and shellfish at Mycenae, 50 or more kilometers from the coast. According to stable isotope analysis of skeletal material, elite individuals buried in Grave Circle A at Mycenae were apparently eating fish (Richards and Hedges 2007). More recently, an analysis of faunal remains from the well in Petsas House at Mycenae revealed a significant, though still minor, assemblage of shellfish (5.9% NISP) and fish (2.0% NISP) consumed during the palatial period (Meier, Price, and Shelton 2023). The shell belonged mainly to the bivalve *Arca noae* (Noah's Ark shell), an excellent source of nutrients including protein, fatty acids, and various vitamins and other essential elements. These findings raise a host of questions, not least of which center on who is transporting highly perishable resources tens of kilometers from the coast, and what was the nature of the transactions by which the inhabitants of Petsas House acquired them. Did they acquire them independently, or was the palace involved? Clearly, the story of exploiting marine resources in the Bronze Age Aegean is still being written.

Exploitation of marine resources in the Aegean Bronze Age: Salt

Like fish, salt is a fundamental marine resource that is elusive at Aegean Bronze Age sites, both coastal and inland. Salt was necessary for nutrition, for flavoring, and as a food preservative, along with medicinal and other uses. Salting was probably the main way to preserve highly perishable fish and other marine fauna meant for transport.

Salt could be produced in several ways. It could be mined at inland locations in terrestrial deposits or briny lakes (e.g., China: Flad et al. 2005), or extracted from sea water by various methods. It might simply be gathered in small quantities from rocks at the shoreline (Figure 6.3). In many places, salt water was boiled down in special salt production pottery known as *briquetage*. Some of the earliest evidence for this process comes from China, where such specialized vessels are known as early as the mid-third millennium B.C. (Li and Flad 2020). Hundreds of Maya salt production sites have been identified along the Caribbean coast, largely submerged with masses of broken briquetage; from there, salt was taken by canoe to be sold at inland markets (McKillop 2002, 2019).

In the Mediterranean, the main way to harvest salt is by solar evaporation, because of the sea's high salinity and extraordinarily high evaporation rate. It is a relatively simple matter to create shallow coastal pools to isolate sea water and allow it to evaporate in the hot sun, at scales from family production to massive industries. The western coast of the Peloponnese, with its extensive barrier-and-lagoon and wetland systems, was ideal for salt production. No place is better situated than Messolonghi, where vast saltpans today produce 120,000 tons of salt a year, as much as 60% of the country's production.

Direct evidence for salt harvesting in the Aegean Bronze Age is scant, both because of coastline change and the ephemeral nature of the materials used in the process (Harding 2013: 66; Mylona 2018: 426–428). It is estimated that 63% of Greek wetlands were lost in the 20th century, due to a combination of direct drainage, dam construction, irrigation, changing river morphology, and various coastal engineering projects (Zalidis, Mantzavelas, and Gourvelou 1997). A unique cache of sea salt stored in ceramic jars in Ourania Cave near Zakros, eastern Crete dates to the transition from the Protopalatial to the Neopalatial period (Kopaka and Chaniotakis 2003). As far as we know, salt as a commodity is not mentioned in any of the Linear B tablets despite the fact that it must have been essential to life at the palaces, and throughout history central authorities have sought to control its production and distribution (Carusi 2018; Kurlansky 2003). One possible explanation for the absence of salt in the Linear B texts refers to seasonality: salt collection is most efficient in summer, when hot, dry, sunny conditions create exceptionally high evaporation. Even today, salt production in Greece begins in March and ends in October. If, as some believe, the palace at Pylos was destroyed in the spring with an archive of six months to a year, it could mean that the tablets reflect the off-season for salt production.

Figure 6.3. Gathering salt from a rocky shore on the Aegean island of Ikaria. Buettner 2019: 188.

Linking maritime and inland economies and people

My second theme is how coastal people linked maritime and terrestrial worlds, turning our attention now to connections into the interior. The approaches we use to investigate these connections will vary, depending on a host of factors, including local terrain, coastline change, and preservation of archaeological sites and features. The following are sources of evidence we can exploit:

- Topography/least-cost models
- Archaeological site types and locations
- Walking experiments
- Texts: Linear B and subsequent written sources ancient to modern
- Ethnographies/oral histories

A first approximation of potential routes from the coast to the interior can be made by studying local topography. While in some cases a wide coastal plain offers access to the interior via numerous, undifferentiated routes, it is common in most of the Aegean to find narrow coastal plains backed by rugged, mountainous terrain that limited the possible routes inland. Eyeballing a topographic map can often suggest more and less likely paths based on slope and landscape features that might facilitate or obstruct progress. In recent decades, archaeologists have turned increasingly to least-cost analysis, or least-cost path, routines in GIS to derive statistically based routes that maximize efficiency and minimize effort for a person or a convoy of humans and animals traversing a given terrain. The assumption of least-cost analysis, that humans are rational actors who will always attempt to minimize the cost of movement when they travel, has been rightly criticized even if it is a logical starting-point. A host of reasons, such as ground cover, social relationships, or certain special places en route, might cause a person to deviate from the most energy-efficient path (Brysbaert, Vikatou, and Stöger 2020; Efkleidou 2019).

A second consideration is that most Bronze Age overland travel will have been on informal, unpaved roads and tracks. Although formal roads passable for cart traffic are known in the Aegean Bronze Age, notably around Mycenae, these would have been uncommon (Brysbaert, Vikatou, and Stöger 2020, with references). Instead, people walked from place to place on foot, or when transporting goods, they used human or animal power on tracks that could have been rough and seasonally impassible with rain and snow. The domesticated donkey (*Equus asinus*), introduced in the Aegean by the mid-third millennium at Lerna (Wiencke 2000: 44, 122), was the ideal pack animal for carrying loads in difficult terrain. Donkeys walk at about the same speed as humans, 3.5–4.0 kilometers per hour, with a similar need to rest every 4–5 hours or less, resulting in a daily range of 20–30 kilometers (Mitchell 2018). They presented significant advantages as cheaper, faster and more sure-footed than oxen, and before the adoption of the sail, even than maritime commerce (Brodie 2008). Long overland journeys would have required waystations as well as leaders and guides with knowledge of "...water sources, resting places, landmarks, and important passes" along the route (Brysbaert, Vikatou, and Stöger 2020: 42).

Overland routes from point A to point B have sometimes been mapped, at least partially, by linking a chain of intervening, known archaeological sites and features (e.g., traces of roadbeds) assumed to be contemporary. In his study of coast–hinterland interconnections in the Corinthian Gulf during Archaic to Early Hellenistic times, Anton Bonnier leans on topography but also states that "...the use of physical routes which connect coastal zones with hinterlands, and consequently developing patterns of communication, can be determined through the study of site development in connection with these routes" (Bonnier 2014: 12). There is a long tradition of walking the modern surface between destinations to discover intervening sites and features that may indicate where an ancient route passed. Sometimes this amounts to identifying places mentioned in Pausanias or other past travelers (for a recent example, see Windell and Webb 2021a, 2021b), but sites discovered as part of formal surface surveys or informal hikes in the countryside can begin to connect the dots (see Fachard and Knodell 2020).

The Linear B texts from Knossos and Pylos name hundreds of places, from which we can infer some sense of the geographical extent of the dominion of these *inland* palace centers in Late Bronze III. In the case of Knossos, we can derive a sphere of influence, if not direct control, extending north to the coast at Amnisos, east to the Lasithi massif, south to the Mesara plain and Phaistos, and west to Chania, during the mid-14th century (Bennet 2011: 148–151). Coastal sites are identified mainly by placenames that can be recognized in historical times (Phaistos, Kydonia, Amnisos).[2] These were classified as "second order" centers which, depending on distance, ranged from direct control (Amnisos, Tylissos) from Knossos to semi-independence (Kydonia) during the years of Mycenaean hegemony on the island (Bennet 1985). The Knossian archive famously records up to 100,000 sheep distributed in herds across central Crete, under direct control of the palace or indirectly through "collectors" as part of an expansive textile industry that supplied wool as well as meat and secondary products (Halstead 1993, 2003; Nosch 2014). Bennet (1985) shows that of approximately 100 herding sites indicated, most would have been actual settlements, meaning that, although it may prove impossible to match most Linear B names with specific archaeological sites, feasible routes for the movement of animals and their products can be proposed by joining the topographic, environmental, and archaeological records.

The Linear B archive at Pylos is more promising because of the repetitive patterning of place names across tablet groups in fixed-order lists that have been interpreted as "scribal itineraries." Combined with a small number of key identifications with later place names, it has been possible to construct a plausible political geography of the Pylian polity in LH IIIB (Bennet 2011; Cosmopoulos 2006; Hope Simpson 2014).[3] Some 17 or 18 second-order towns administered by a *ko-re-te*, a local or regional governor charged with overseeing agriculture, animal management, manufacturing, tax collection, and cult activity, can be discerned (Bennet 2011: 138). Among them, we can assume that several are coastal settlements. At least three occur on the *o-ka* tablets of the An series, referred to as the "coastguard" tablets for their references to troops stationed in coastal districts: *a-ke-re-wa* (modern Yialova: Palaiochori?), *ka-ra-do-ro* (modern Phoinikous?), and *ri-jo* (modern Charakopeio?). To these we should add a substantial number of Late Bronze Age coastal archaeological sites whose names are uncertain or unknown, such as at Kyparissia, Gargaliani, and Romanou on the Ionian Sea coast; and Nichoria, Kalamata, and Vigla-Ayios Ilias on

2 The built harbor installations (ship sheds and other infrastructure) that have been discovered at several coastal sites, including Kommos, Gournia, Poros-Katsamba, and Nirou Chani, were, except for Kommos, active mainly before the main Linear B archive at Knossos (Blackman 2011). Similarly, other coastal settlements involved in maritime trade, such as Mochlos and Pseira, were diminished or abandoned by the time that Mycenaean hegemony was firmly entrenched at Knossos.

3 Still, the only completely secure identification is *pu-ro*, the palace of Pylos itself at Ano Englianos.

the Gulf of Messenia (Hope Simpson 2014: Map 6). The scribal routes describe a logical way of organizing travel from a narrow administrative point of view, which would not make sense for other purposes. Notably, the actual movement of goods between the palace and the coast, or from farms and pastures to the palace, would have required more direct and timely routes — witness the transport of highly perishable seafood to Petsas House or to the occupants of Grave Circle A as examples. Similarly, there would be a strong incentive for high-value commodities such as imported raw metals to move directly and securely to their final destination. The Linear B archive offers far more than political geography alone — glimpses at social organization, the roles of named individuals, modes and scales of production, and specific transactions between the palace and subordinate communities are some examples (Nakassis 2013 and this volume). Combining the internal evidence of the tablets with topographic and archaeological information can help us suggest coast-inland itineraries with routes and waypoints.

Ethnoarchaeology can be a way to (literally) put flesh on the bones of these ancient activities. Ethnoarchaeologists have long recognized and acknowledged that the present cannot simply be grafted onto the past; when they record the places, actions, and ideas of living communities, they know they are not interacting with ancient people frozen in time, and they are aware of the changes separating modern people from the Bronze Age. Nonetheless, archaeologists can open their minds to a world of ideas about Bronze Age people by observing, interviewing, or participating in the lives of people who work(ed) with traditional practices, by which I mean unmechanized and not enhanced by recent technologies. In our day, this means finding the oldest members of a community, with the Second World War as a notional watershed in the Mediterranean before which traditional practices would have been widespread. Obviously, there is little time left to reach these living individuals.

We archaeologists write diligently about ancient farmers, herders, and fishers, but we should ask ourselves: Have I ever farmed? Have I ever led herds of sheep and goat looking for pasture? Have I ever relied on the daily catch for my existence and that of my family? Have I ever faced an existential crisis because of drought or blight? It seems perverse to tell our stories only from archaeological remains — which do not speak for themselves — or from elite ancient authors who themselves had little experience of these lifeways, while ignoring what one might learn from living people for whom these are day-to-day concerns. This is not to equate ancient with modern people, but to recognize that they may have faced similar challenges and opportunities with similar technologies and materials to address them. Relevant to the current topic, we might observe the moving parts that constitute regional economic networks. How do coastal inhabitants negotiate their landscapes to make connections with communities and markets in the interior? How do their movements diverge from optimized least-cost paths, and why? Who are the actors and the different roles they play in domestic life and territorial interactions? If we are fortunate, we may have some traces of ancient roads, as around Mycenae; an ambiguous list of subordinate sites as at Pylos; or a regional-scale roster of Bronze Age surface sites generated by intensive, systematic survey. These cases are rare, however.

Using ethnographic and oral history approaches, it is possible to build hypotheses and models based on living humans and living systems, which can then be considered in light of the ancient evidence. Under this rubric we should include observations made on traditional communities by ethnographers and travel writers of the last few centuries (e.g., Synge 1907; Lewis 1984). At times the convergence of archaeological and ethnographic evidence is striking and suggestive. One such example is the practice of beach seine fishing, which is still employed around the world and for which there is ample ancient substantiation. Called *karamadi* in Kerala state, South India (Figure 6.4a), and *gripos* in Greece, a broad net secured to extremely long ropes is taken offshore by swimmers or a small boat, and then slowly dragged back in to shore. This same practice is depicted on pottery in 12th century B.C. Greece (Figure 6.4b), and even earlier in Egypt (Figure 6.4c). The techniques and equipment of beach seine fishing are remarkably similar across time and space, reflecting universal subsistence pursuits and comparable raw materials and technologies. The only tangible remains may be fish bones and net sinkers, but iconographic representations show that it did happen in the Bronze Age, and details of the practice can be discerned by watching it in action.

Mycenae, the Saronic, and Korphos-Kalamianos

I turn finally to the coastscape of Korphos on the western shores of the Saronic Gulf, where Daniel and I co-directed the Saronic Harbors Archaeological Research Project (SHARP), as a case study to explore many of the themes outlined above (Figure 6.5). The Mycenaean harbor settlement of Kalamianos, situated 2.5 km southeast of Korphos village facing Aigina, was identified in 2001 by a team from the Eastern Korinthia Archaeological Survey during testing of a GIS-derived model for landing sites on the Saronic coast (Rothaus et al. 2003; Tartaron, Rothaus, and Pullen 2003). Daniel and I initiated and co-directed SHARP to study Kalamianos and its hinterland as a microregion within the context of the Bronze Age Saronic.

The archaeological site consists of an urban settlement preserved as exposed limestone architectural foundations and walls occupying approximately 4.5 hectares set within

a)

b)

Figure 6.4. Beach seine fishing, modern and ancient examples: (a) Kovalam Beach, Kerala state, India; (b) Aplomata, Naxos, Greece, LH IIIC; (c) Middle Kingdom Tomb 5, El Bersheh (Darby et al. 1977.1: 345 fig. 1.3).

c)

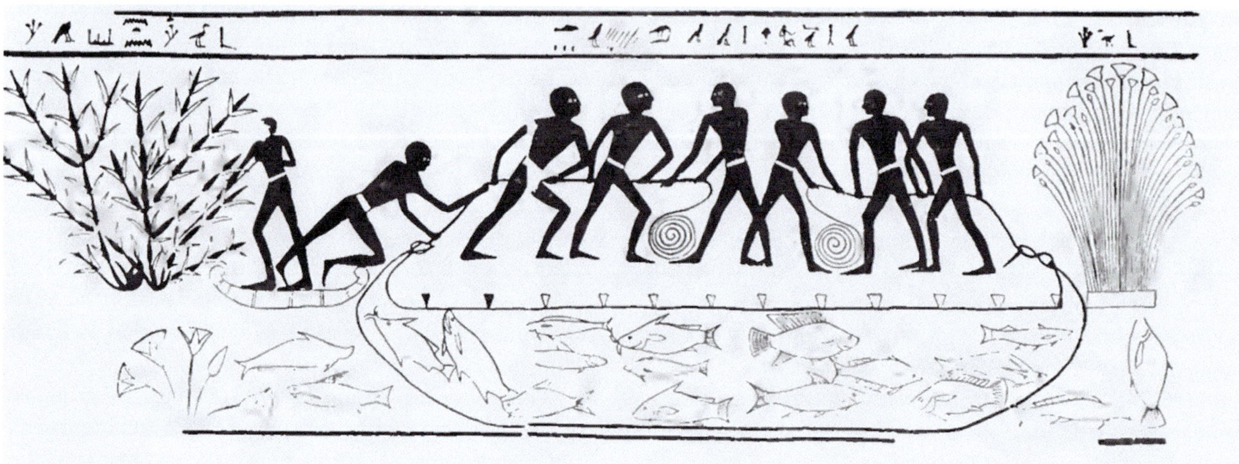

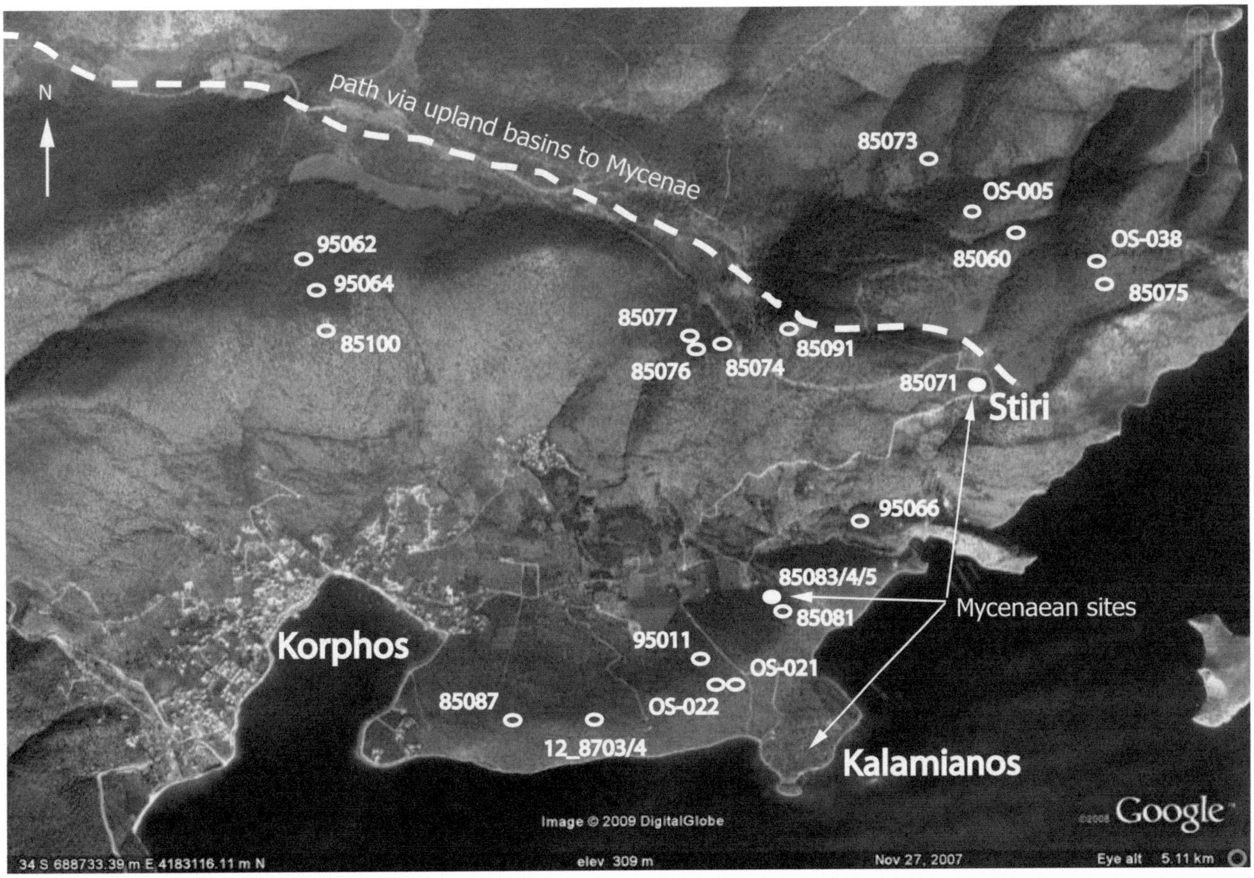

Figure 6.5. Google Earth image of the Korphos region with Late Bronze Age sites labeled. ©Google, 2009 DigitalGlobe.

a town wall enclosing around nine hectares (Figure 6.6).[4] The "empty" hectares appear to have accommodated stone agricultural terraces and a quarry that supplied the building stone. The exposure of the stone foundations is the result of a convergence of tectonism, erosion, and human action that is not fully understood (Tartaron et al. 2011: 568–569), but it enabled us to map and study a virtually complete plan of the Mycenaean town of the 13th century B.C. without excavation.[5] SHARP teams recorded over 1,200 walls and more than 50 buildings at Kalamianos between 2007 and 2010 (Pullen 2015; Pullen and Sapirstein 2020), collected artifacts, and engaged in geomorphological and underwater research (Tartaron et al. 2011). Simultaneously, surface survey in a zone of seven square kilometers in the hinterland of Kalamianos (Figure 6.7) revealed a second substantial Mycenaean architectural complex at Stiri and numerous agricultural terrace walls of probable Mycenaean date (Kvapil 2021; Tartaron 2015a). The broader survey aimed to contextualize Kalamianos in its wider microregional setting, in part to better understand how the harbor town was sustained by and connected to its interior hinterland.

A first realization about Kalamianos is that the architecture is surprisingly monumental. Wall blocks, typically composing inner and outer faces with a rubble core between them, are much larger than necessary for domestic dwellings, even if carrying a second story. The collapsed stone rubble of some buildings indicates that their walls were built higher in stone courses than the norm before receiving a mudbrick superstructure. Pullen and Sapirstein (2020) found the closest parallels for these masonry techniques in the Argolid, more specifically Mycenae. The use of ashlar blocks is absent, and the stones are smaller than those used for Mycenae's palatial buildings, but they are comparable to the "cyclopean" retaining walls of Mycenae's first fortification in late LH IIIA (Pullen and Sapirstein 2020: 378). Mycenaean painted pottery found built into the rubble cores of many buildings provides a *terminus post quem* that accords well with initial construction in late LH IIIA/early LH IIIB.

4 A part of the site, of unknown size, has been submerged in the sea due to tectonic subsidence.

5 No excavation has taken place on the site, in part because the exposure of much of the site to bedrock limits the opportunities for subsurface investigation.

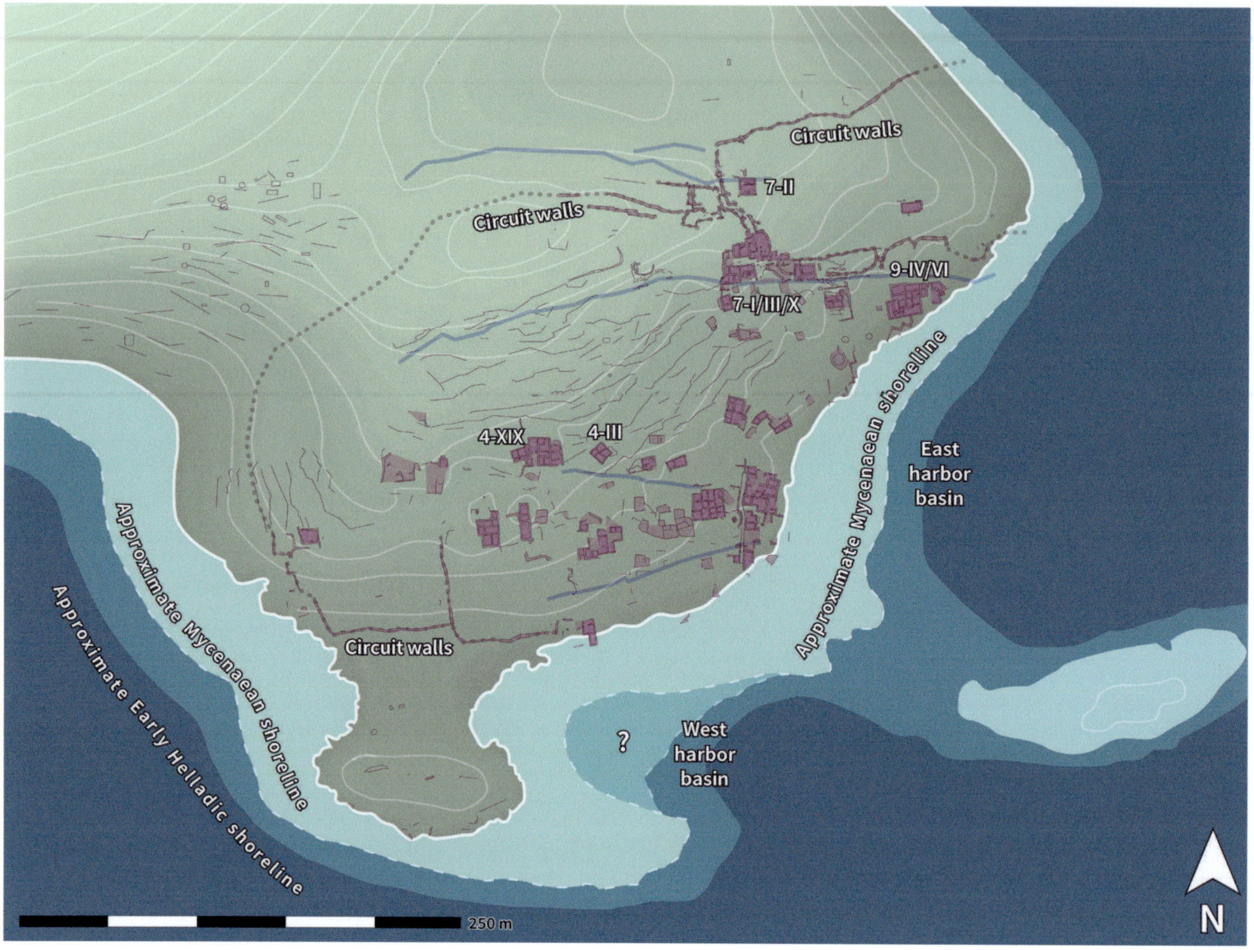

Figure 6.6. Plan of Kalamianos showing buildings, terraces, and other features.

Our working scenario has long been that colonists from Mycenae arrived at that time and founded the settlement at Kalamianos on a sparsely inhabited coast, as part of an economic and political expansion to tap into the connections and resources of the Saronic Gulf. The incursion of settlers into the Saronic, dominated by Kolonna on Aigina for the previous two millennia, placed Kalamianos in the interesting position of a potential "contested periphery" between a venerable and an emerging power. In recent years, I have moderated my initial depiction of this encounter as a titanic struggle between Mycenae and Kolonna for hegemony in the Saronic, because as the study of sites and artifacts progresses, a different picture emerges (Tartaron 2015b: 26–27; see Marabea 2019). At Kalamianos we see the hand of Mycenae in the architecture and in the expansion of settlement and intensification of agriculture in a new coastscape. At the same time, however, artifact assemblages give ample evidence at Kalamianos and in the Saronic generally for uninterrupted relations in a maritime small world centered on Kolonna. At Kalamianos and Stiri, the source of the coarse kitchen and storage pottery was determined, both macroscopically (Dill 2021: 240–250) and microscopically (Gilstrap 2015; Trusty and Gilstrap forthcoming), to be Aigina. Of 67 button-base jars and tripod cooking pots sampled for petrographic and chemical analysis, 66 were identified with an Aiginetan source; in a similar study of 266 coarse ware sherds from the Eastern Building Complex at Kanakia on Salamis, 260 were sourced to Aigina (Marabea 2019). These results are consistent with a scenario in which fineware exports from Aigina wound down in LH IIIA, presumably because of competition from Mycenaean exports, but Aeginetan cooking and kitchen ware continued to dominate the assemblages of places like Kanakia, Kontopigado, Kalamianos, and Stiri into LH IIIC Early. A petrographic and chemical analysis of Late Mycenaean fineware (c. 1300–1150 B.C.) around the Saronic revealed a complex picture of production and exchange (Gilstrap 2015; Gilstrap, Day, and Kilikoglou 2016). Kalamianos and Stiri imported fineware from Kontopigado in the Saronic, but also from extra-Saronic sources that may have included the region around Corinth. To the pottery

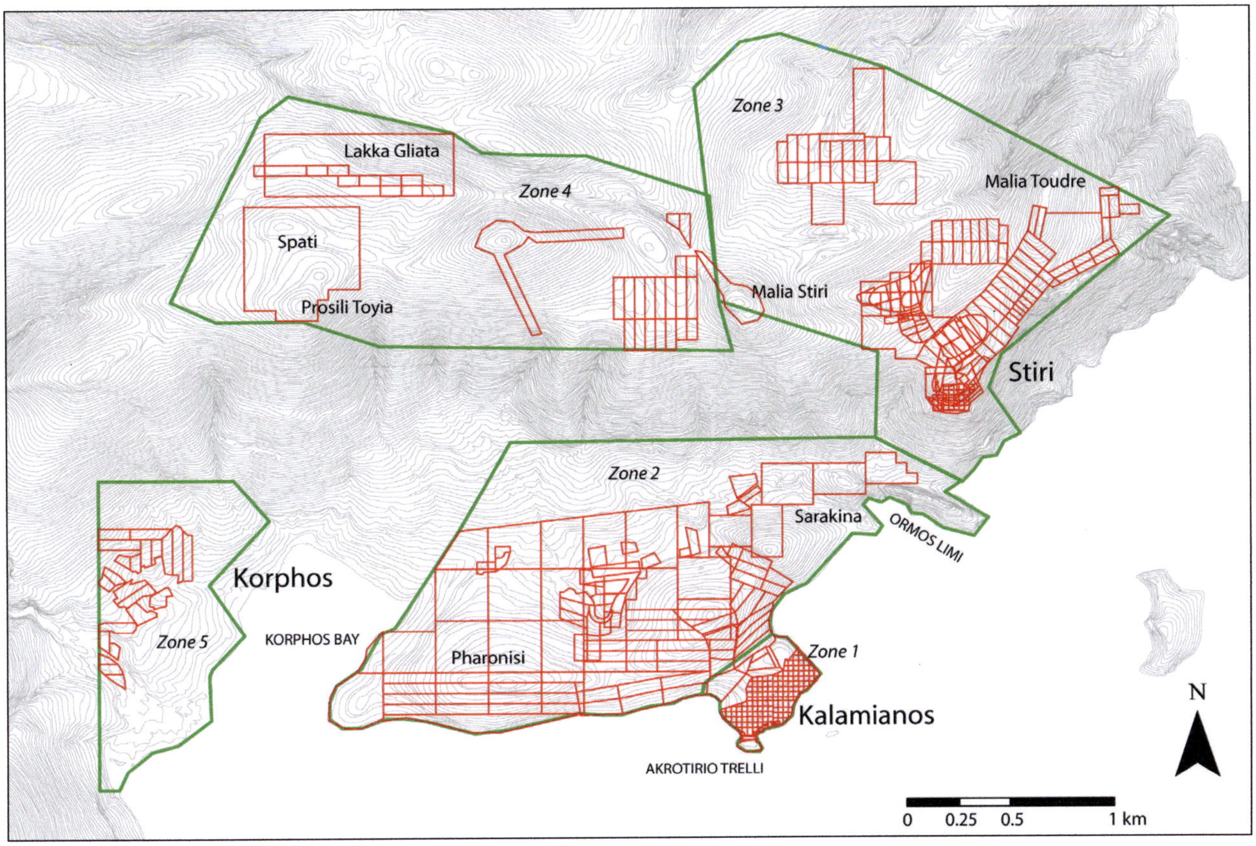

Figure 6.7. SHARP surface survey zones.

assemblages we can add that Aigina was the source of the ground stone collected at Kalamianos and Stiri.

What did Mycenae want?

If we are correct that Mycenae founded Kalamianos, the motivation was undoubtedly access to maritime networks. As a land-locked polity, Mycenae required coastal gateways through which exotic commodities, such as ivory and metals, could be secured. How and where this was accomplished? Proponents of a "Great Mycenae" (e.g., Kelder 2010; see Galaty and Parkinson, this volume) often cast Tiryns as the subordinate port of Mycenae, or maintain that Mycenae's control extended to the Corinthian Gulf (e.g., Salmon 1984). But others are skeptical of Mycenae's domination even of the Argolid, favoring instead a scenario of multiple, competing centers with little vertical integration (Pullen 2022). If Mycenae did not have unfettered access to the Argolic Gulf or to southern Saronic harbors such as Epidauros, Kalamianos may have been the closest and most accessible Aegean harbor. SHARP established that Kalamianos was a reasonably sheltered harbor by reconstructing the ancient coastline, identifying beach rock formations cemented with thousands of sherds of Bronze Age pottery, and locating ballast piles of volcanic stone (Tartaron et al. 2011: 569–575).

The question of how directly Mycenae controlled Kalamianos, if at all, is more difficult to answer. A top-down approach, modeled after the Linear B political geography of Knossos or Pylos, might portray Kalamianos as a "second order" center situated in a "Further Province." Bennet (1985) counted Phaistos and Kydonia (Chania) as second-order centers where "overseers" resided, through which Knossos administered smaller communities. But without a substantial archive, Mycenae's reach and political organization are less clear. There is the factor of distance over rugged, mountainous terrain, which is part of the logic we used to reject Mycenae's direct control over the northern Corinthian plain (Pullen and Tartaron 2007). While we should not expect perfect replication in material culture, it is not easy to explain the deviation of Kalamianos' built environment from Mycenaean standards: megara are absent and the building plans do not closely match any known Mycenaean site (Pullen and Sapirstein 2020: 378–382). Pullen (2019a: 147–149) addresses the direct-indirect question by pointing out the extraordinary outlay of labor, material, and expertise that would have been required to establish a modest-sized but monumentalized settlement along with robust agricultural terraces in a virtually uninhabited, and indeed somewhat isolated, coastal zone. With reference to Pylian Linear B tablets that assign groups of "wall builders," as well as the large-scale infrastructure projects at Mycenae, Gla/Lake Kopais, Tiryns and elsewhere, Pullen (2019a: 147, 2022) acknowledges the probability of palatial involvement in building and establishing a community at Kalamianos (see also Kvapil 2012: 205), but rejects any meaningful *direct* control over the 100–150 years of the coastscape's existence (Pullen 2019b: 227–231).[6] Instead, once Mycenae's presence on the Saronic Gulf was established and the desired commodities and connectivity were flowing, the microregion anchored at Kalamianos developed self-sufficiency and forged its main connections within the maritime small world of the Saronic Gulf. Archaeologically, this process can be appreciated in the expansion of agricultural potential on terraced slopes (Kvapil 2021), the construction of the slightly later architectural complex at Stiri (Tartaron 2015a: 395–399), and subsequent phases in some of the buildings at Kalamianos (Pullen and Sapirstein 2020).

Oral histories conducted by Lita Tzortzopoulou-Gregory in Korphos village between 2007 and 2009 offer insight on how a horizontally integrated economy can operate in a Saronic maritime small world (Dill 2021: 237–240; Tartaron 2013: 265–270, 2018: 83–88). She interviewed elder fishermen and women about their lives in the pre-World War II era and consulted local archives. There seem to have been some distinct social and economic groups and networks: around 90% of the male population of Korphos was engaged in a maritime pursuit, either fishing or as merchants on the Saronic Gulf. The fishermen worked the local waters, but the sea-traders of the village were more mobile, prosperous, and of higher status. In the early 20th century, Korphos was a major port in a vibrant Saronic maritime small world with nodes on coasts and islands and "strong ties" connecting them. There was no single dominant port in the Saronic, but instead a handful of bustling nodes of maritime connectivity in a heterarchical arrangement. The sea-traders purchased fish and agricultural and forest products locally and exported them to Saronic markets. Several interviewees recalled bringing wood, charcoal, resin, and manure to markets at Piraeus, Eleusis, Salamis, Aigina, Poros, Nea Epidauros, and elsewhere. In exchange, they imported water jugs, flour, fruits, vegetables, and other foods. Upon returning to Korphos, land-based merchants acquired some of these commodities and sold them at villages in the interior. The oldest informant, a 102-year-old woman, described how she traded cheese, meat, and other products for fish at Korphos and carried them on mule back to Sophiko and other villages as far as Angelokastro, an uphill trek of 3–4 hours. The people of Korphos had strong ties of kinship and intermarriage with Sophiko, but always contrasted themselves, as people of the sea, with Sophikites, whom they considered inland, "mountain" people. Many Korphiotes married into island families and emigrated after marriage, carrying on maritime traditions. These brief excerpts from a rich set of interviews shed light on the practicalities of a coastal settlement mediating between marine and terrestrial worlds.

With a foothold on the Saronic Gulf, we can begin to imagine the roles that the Korphos microregion may have assumed for Mycenae. The smaller settlement at Stiri is perched far above Kalamianos on a coastal ridge, with a fertile doline on its inland side, but more importantly offering a panoramic view of the Saronic Gulf, with Salamis and Athens, Aigina and other islands, and Methana and the coastal Argolid all in its viewshed. From Stiri, there is a relatively easy path along several basins to the interior of the southern Corinthia and the Argolid. Hence, Stiri was productive with upland grazing and limited agricultural potential, and strategically significant as a lookout point over the Gulf.

Intensive pedestrian survey at Kalamianos collected intriguing ceramic evidence for the residents' daily activities (Table 6.2). The fineware consists mainly of standard Mycenaean forms — kylikes, deep bowls (A and B), and stemmed bowls — dating from LH IIIA to LH IIIC Early but belonging overwhelmingly to LH IIIB. The coarser vessels include hydrias, jugs, belly-handled amphoras, and button-base and tripod-foot cooking pots. These forms indicate a domestic function for most structures, consisting of cooking/heating, drinking, pouring, serving, and small-scale storage. The rare forms — cups, pithoi, and stirrup jars — are equally informative. The scarcity of pithoi or other large-scale storage containers weighs against the kind of mass storage capacity that might imply redistribution or production for export. Similarly, the absence of transport stirrup jars indicates that the community was not geared to producing and exporting products like wine or olive oil. The petrographic and chemical analyses also seem to preclude pottery production, even on a household scale.

There is some evidence, however, for harvesting purple dye, at least at a modest level.[7] Murex shells were

6 It can be stressed that however the history of Mycenae's presence in the Saronic played out, Kalamianos was built for permanence with an expectation of longevity.

7 In Alberti's (2008: 74–76, table 2) paradigm for indicators of purple dye working, Kalamianos would qualify as indirect evidence, falling into her Group 3 ("dumps of purple-dye industry waste material: heaps of crushed murex shells found on the coast") or Group 4 (debris re-deposition: heaps of crushed murex shells found in settlements or construction sites [foundation or terrace fill]"), or both.

Abundant: Standard Mycenaean Forms	Rare: Standard Mycenaean Forms
Hydrias	Cups
Belly-handled amphoras	Stirrup jars
Jugs	Pithoi
Button-based cooking pots	Functions: mass storage, production and export of products like wine, olive oil
Tripod cooking pots	
Deep bowls (A and B)	
Kylikes	
Functions: cooking/heating, drinking, pouring, serving, small-scale storage	

Table 6.2. Pottery forms at LH III Kalamianos and Stiri.

the most common species recovered in collections from the buildings, present both within rooms and in the rubble cores; the latter were likely scooped up dead along with rock and soil to fill the walls. After our fieldwork at the site was completed, we learned about illicit digging that unearthed piles of crushed murex shell. As noted above, it is now recognized that murex were more productive of dye than earlier believed, and thus a household or small workshop mode of production was feasible for domestic needs. It is not possible on present evidence to contemplate a small industry for export or to supply Mycenae's needs, but we can speculate on the origin of the practice at Kalamianos. The earliest evidence for purple dye production is currently the enormous dye and textile industrial complex at MM IIB Alatzomouri Pefka on Crete (Betancourt, Brogan, and Apostolakou 2020). From Crete, the technology spread over the Aegean, and MH II was precisely the period that saw the most intensive Minoan influence at Kolonna (Kolonna IX), possibly including Cretan artisans. A steady increase in murex starting in MH II and carrying through LH III at Kolonna surely reflects the adoption of purple dye technology through Minoan connections (Berger et al. 2020; Galik et al. 2013: 167–168), and its subsequent transfer from Aigina to Kalamianos.

Even if we impute to Kalamianos a large measure of independence, it remains possible that Mycenaean agents resided at Kalamianos to ensure that commodities produced on the site (purple dye, seafood, salt, and taxes?) and imported at the harbor (Aiginetan coarse ware, metals?) made their way safely to the palace, and to maintain a watch over the Saronic from Stiri. If Mycenae's territorial administration was comparable to that recorded in the Linear B archives at Knossos and Pylos, a *ko-re-te* (a local official in charge of one of the administrative units within the realm) and his deputy *po-ro-ko-re-te* are likely figures — Palaima (2005: 274, n. 15) describes them as the palace's "agents in the field." Pullen and Sapirstein (2020: 372–377) give a detailed description of architectural complex 7-I/III/X at Kalamianos, situated at a commanding elevation within the town walls. They emphasize the unique masonry features that they interpret as "palatially inspired" and conjecture that Building 7-I may have served a public function. If a *ko-re-te* was active at Kalamianos at any time during the life of the site, this may have been his residence and headquarters.

Overland connections

Kalamianos must have been reasonably accessible by overland travel from the Argolid, to justify the considerable effort to found the settlement and maintain ties. The journey from Mycenae to Kalamianos is around 52 kilometers on foot, assuming a topographically efficient pathway that descends to the Berbati Valley, rises up through Limnes to Angelokastro, and then descends once again toward the Saronic coast at Kalamianos (Figure 6.8). A donkey train laden with goods, moving at 3–4 kilometers per hour and needing to rest every 4–5 hours, might cover about 25 kilometers in a single day. Thus, Mycenae to Kalamianos is a two-day trip, and this raises the question of where travelers might shelter for the night. The answer must lie in currently inconspicuous sites along the tracks that served as waystations where one could find food, drink, and shelter — rather like Bronze Age caravanserais.

I can point to two examples along this route (Figure 6.8). In the Berbati Valley, Findspot 14 (FS 14) was identified by the Berbati-Limnes Archaeological Survey (Wells, Runnels, and Zangger 1990: 227). FS 14 sits alongside a preserved section of the Mycenaean road just three kilometers east of Mycenae. The artifact scatter at Findspot 14 reaches 6 ha, so it may be more than a simple waystation, but it seems intimately associated with the road in some capacity and the artifacts date mainly to the 13th century B.C. A second example is at the other end of the Mycenae–Kalamianos pathway, discovered by members of the SHARP team during one of several experimental hikes between Kalamianos

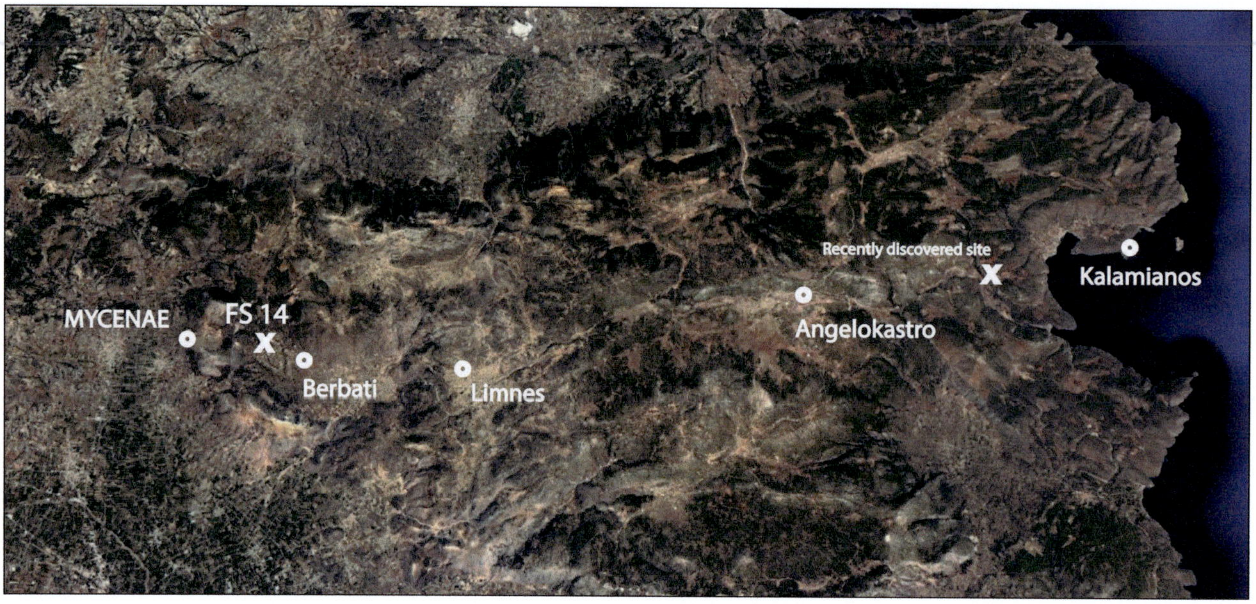

Figure 6.8. Hypothetical overland route from Mycenae to Kalamianos/Stiri. Source: Google Maps, Map data: ©2009 Cnes/ Spot Images, ©2008 Tele Atlas, Image ©2009 DigitalGlobe, ©2008 Basarsoft.

and Mycenae.[8] On a small hill overlooking the route, we encountered a walled enclosure with traces of several ruined buildings as well as pottery of the Mycenaean palatial period and perhaps earlier in the Late Bronze Age. These two sites could be waystations on the overland route, and I am confident that a dedicated search would turn up others, perhaps an entire system of stopping places en route.

Although there can be skepticism about Mycenae's relationship with such a distant satellite, a convenient way to envision a rationale is through the concepts and language of network theory. Specifically, we witness Kalamianos playing a dual role as a node among "strong ties" within the highly connected Saronic maritime small world, and simultaneously a "weak tie" bridging the palatial realm of Mycenae with the resources and opportunities of the Saronic Gulf sea-world. In sociology, weak ties typically involve individuals who are in occasional or sporadic contact (and may or may not be physically distant), but they often bridge different groups bound by strong ties that otherwise have no connection, thus giving the individuals access to the persons and resources in these different social networks (Granovetter 1973). The maritime small world model defines networks that are "constituted by habitual face-to-face interaction and cohesion based on shared origin, cultural traditions, language, economic ties, social networks, mutual protection arrangements, and so forth" (Tartaron 2018: 73), and this is a good description of the relationship of Kalamianos to other Saronic coastscapes in the Bronze Age, or of Korphos in the early 20th century. The role of Kalamianos as a weak tie providing Mycenae access to the Saronic instantiates the mediating role that we often attach to coastal settlements. It might also help to explain the foundational imprint of the Argolid at Kalamianos, followed by what seems like a highly localized development when the hand of Mycenae seems very light. We might imagine that to Mycenae, Kalamianos was an important gateway that could be exploited with a substantial initial investment, and subsequently the presence of a small cadre of administrative agents. One way to interpret the unusual monumentality of the architecture at Kalamianos is as an advertisement of Mycenae's power rather than the actual exercise of it.

Actors and activities in the Korphos microregion

We can begin to imagine diverse individuals and social groups at Kalamianos, and a range of roles they played and activities they performed (Table 6.3). The buildings may have begun as similarly scaled structures based on a cellular plan, but with time and growth of the settlement, some groups seem to have elaborated on the basic form, perhaps signaling elevated wealth and status relative to their neighbors (Pullen and Sapirstein 2020: 384). The identity of these groups is unknown. As I conjectured above, the best-appointed house complexes like 7-I/III/X may have housed a *ko-re-te* or similar official appointed by the palace. But there are other possibilities at a scale between individuals and societies, such as the extended family (*oikos*) or the so-called House

8 This site was discovered by Sarah Murray and Emily Anderson. Because it is situated outside our permit zone, we have informed the archaeological authorities of its existence, but we have not studied it further. For alternate pathways from Mycenae to the Saronic Gulf, see Newhard, Levine, and Phebus 2014.

Fishing, shell fishing (food)
Purple dye production (Murex shell)
Salt production (wetlands, seashore)
Farming (terrace farming and small patches of arable)
Forestry production (timber, fodder, charcoal)
Herding (local transhumance; grazing at higher elevations — Stiri)
Quarrying limestone (on Kalamianos and Stiri sites for wall building, lime plaster)
Construction (planners, engineers, work groups of construction workers)
Import/export at harbor
Maritime traders in the Saronic
Overland traders with donkey trains
Itinerant craftspeople
Palace agents (*ko-re-te* and *po-ro-ko-re-te* from Mycenae, or "collectors"?)

Table 6.3. Hypothetical activities in the Korphos coastscape, LH IIIA–IIIB.

societies, where physical dwellings become the enduring materialization of the corporate identity, memory, and status of the social groups with which they are associated (Driessen 2010). The initial planning and layout of those houses on a regular grid was performed by skilled planners, who oversaw the construction by groups of semi-skilled and unskilled workers (Harper 2016: 188–208, 303).

The activities listed in Table 6.3 imply a busy microregion brimming with activity, mobility, and connectivity. The stone for buildings and lime plaster at Kalamianos and Stiri was quarried onsite. The earth for making mudbricks was available in nearby dolines or wetlands from which reeds and grasses for roofing could also be harvested. The timber for structural beams had to be obtained from upland forests beyond Stiri. Fishermen were busy on the shore and inshore waters catching fish and shellfish, for food and possibly to produce purple dye. Domestic activities were supported by access to fresh groundwater from enlarged joints or fissures in the limestone (Pullen 2019a: 141, fig. 4; Tartaron et al. 2011: 566–567, figs. 7–8). Terrace farming was practiced at Kalamianos and in the low hills around it. Currently, there is little information about herding, but ample grazing was available in the hills above Kalamianos, raising the potential for local seasonal transhumance.

More mobile were the maritime traders plying the Saronic and the overland traders who articulated Kalamianos with interior routes to the Corinthia and Argolid. Kalamianotes imported pottery and ground stone from Aigina, and fineware seemingly from both inland (Argolid, northern Corinthia) and overseas (Kontopigado) sources. Aiginetans virtually ceased fineware production for export by 1400, but the cooking pottery continued to be exported to the interior of the Corinthia and Argolid into LH IIIC (Gauß et al. 2015).[9] Kalamianos may have been a key point of transshipment from the harbor to merchants traveling overland routes. Over these same pathways they might have encountered shepherds, itinerant craftspeople, and palace agents forging those connections.

Conclusions

More work is needed to sharpen our understanding of the oft-cited mediating and connective role of coastal communities in the Aegean Bronze Age. We must first delineate their diversity in scale, habitation status, range of activities and functions, and connections by sea and land. Recent attention to the maritime networks in which they participated has not been matched by equal efforts to flesh out the overland connections that would allow us to begin to reconstruct a full constellation of network connections. Only when this is accomplished can we convincingly demonstrate the mediation and articulation they ostensibly performed. A holistic suite of methods, as outlined above, will advance us toward this goal. In particular, walking experiments and ethnoarchaeology deserve to be more prominent features of our methodological toolkit.

A close reading of the evidence from the coastscape anchored at Korphos-Kalamianos illustrates the challenges and opportunities. While SHARP has collected a wealth of empirical evidence, the narrative of Mycenae's involvement in founding the settlement at Kalamianos and its interests in the Saronic Gulf remains speculative. Kalamianos seems unusual in some ways, but the diversity in architecture alone among contemporary sites such as Kanakia on Salamis (Lolos 2007) or Mitrou in East Lokris (Vitale and Van de Moortel 2020) demonstrates that there was no cookie-cutter approach to the built environment. Yet we are fortunate that construction techniques, ceramic fabrics, and volcanic stone can all be traced with some confidence to their sources. Kalamianos was just one kind of site in terms of it scale and mix of activities, but its geographical position makes it an ideal location to explore its dual role as a node among strong ties in a Saronic Gulf small world centered on Kolonna, and simultaneously a weak tie bridging that world with the inland center of power at Mycenae.

Acknowledgements

I am honored to be a part of the celebration of Daniel Pullen's retirement. I had long admired his work on the Early Bronze Age when I first had the opportunity to work alongside him on the Eastern Korinthia Archaeological Survey. The exciting discovery of the Mycenaean site at Korphos-Kalamianos in 2001 gave us the impetus to join forces to initiate the

9 Gauß and Knodell (2020: 253) note that Aiginetan sherds at many sites, including Mycenae, are undercounted because relevant contexts remain unpublished.

Saronic Harbors Archaeological Research Project, or SHARP. As we became closer colleagues and then good friends, this became for me a dream collaboration on a truly fascinating archaeological landscape that never ceased to produce interesting new revelations. To this day I marvel at Daniel's professionalism, integrity, and scholarly acumen, but I also want to emphasize that Daniel knew how to have fun while working hard, and I think all of our SHARP colleagues over the years would attest to that. It is hard to overestimate the positive effect that Daniel has had on my career: when I was building my case for tenure, he graciously allowed me to take the lead on EKAS and SHARP publications, and we continue to work together on future publications. I offer this chapter as a humble tribute to work done together and work still to come.

Bibliography

Alberti, M. E., 2008. Murex Shell as Raw Material: The Purple Dye Industry and Its By-Products. Interpreting the Archaeological Record. *Kaskal* 5: 73–90.

Apostolakou, V., P. Betancourt, T. Brogan, and D. Mylona, 2016. Chryssi and Pefka: The Production and Use of Purple Dye on Crete in the Middle and Late Bronze Age. In *Textiles, Basketry and Dyes in the Ancient Mediterranean World: Proceedings of the Vth International Symposium on Textiles and Dyes in the Ancient Mediterranean World, Montserrat, 19–22 March 2014*, edited by J. Ortiz, C. Alfaro, L. Turell, and M. J. Martínez, 199–208. Universitat de València.

Apostolakou, V., T. M. Brogan, and P. P. Betancourt, 2012. The Minoan Settlement on Chryssi and Its Murex Dye Industry. In *Kosmos: Jewellery, Adornment and Textiles in the Aegean Bronze Age. Proceedings of the 13th International Aegean Conference/13e Rencontre égéenne internationale, University of Copenhagen, Danish National Research Foundation's Centre for Textile Research, 21–26 April 2010*, edited by M.-L. Nosch and R. Laffineur, 179–182. Aegaeum 33. Leuven and Liège: Peeters.

Apostolakou, V., T. M. Brogan, and P. P. Betancourt, eds., 2020. *Alatzomouri Pefka: A Middle Minoan IIB Workshop Making Organic Dyes*. Philadelphia: INSTAP Academic Press.

Arena, E. 2015. Mycenaean Peripheries During the Palatial Age: The Case of Achaia. *Hesperia* 84: 1–46.

Bennet, J., 1985. The Structure of the Linear B Administration at Knossos. *American Journal of Archaeology* 89: 231–249.

Bennet, J., 2011. The Geography of the Mycenaean Kingdoms. In *A Companion to Linear B Mycenaean Greek Texts and their World*, Volume 2, edited by Y. Duhoux and A. Morpurgo Davies, 137–168. Bibliothèque des cahiers de l'Institut de Linguistique de Louvain 127. Louvain-la-Neuve: Peeters.

Berger, L., G. Forstenpointner, E. Kreuz, and J. Weilhartner, 2020. Purpur im Bronzezeitlichen Ägina: Archäologische und Archäozoologische Evidenz für die Frühe Herstellung von Purpurfarbstoff in Griechenland. In *Gedenkschrift für Wolfgang Wohlmayr*, edited by L. Berger, F. Lang, C. Reinholdt, B. Tober, and J. Weilhartner, 43–63. Schriften zur Archäologie und Archäometrie der Paris Lodron Universität Salzburg 13. Salzburg: ArchaeoPlus.

Betancourt, P. P., T. M. Brogan, and V. Apostolakou, 2020. Discussion and Conclusions. In *Alatzomouri Pefka: A Middle Minoan IIB Workshop Making Organic Dyes*, edited by V. Apostolakou, T. M. Brogan, and P. P. Betancourt, 129–138. Philadelphia: INSTAP Academic Press.

Blackman, D., 2011. Minoan Shipsheds. *Skyllis* 11(2): 4–11.

Bonnier, A., 2014. *Site Patterns, Microregions and Coast-Inland Interconnections by the Corinthian Gulf, c. 600–300 BC*. BAR International Series 2614. Oxford: Archaeopress.

Brodie, N., 2008. The Donkey: An Appropriate Technology for Early Bronze Age Land Transport and Traction. In *Horizon. Ορίζων: A Colloquium on the Prehistory of the Cyclades*, edited by N. Brodie, J. Doole, G. Gavalas, and C. Renfrew, 299–304. Cambridge: McDonald Institute for Archaeological Research.

Brogan, T. M., D. Mylona, V. Apostolakou, P. P. Betancourt, and C. Sofianou, 2019. A Bronze Age Fishing Village on Chryssi. In *Exploring a Terra Incognita on Crete: Recent Research on Bronze Age Habitation in the Southern Ierapetra Isthmus*, edited by K. Chalikias and E. Oddo, 97–110. Philadelphia: INSTAP Academic Press.

Broodbank, C., 2000. *An Island Archaeology of the Early Cyclades*. Cambridge: Cambridge University Press.

Brysbaert, A., I. Vikatou, and J. Stöger, 2020. Highways and Byways in Mycenaean Greece: Human-Environment Interactions in Dialogue. *Arctos: Acta Philologica Fennica* 54: 33–94.

Buettner, D., 2019. *The Blue Zones Kitchen: 100 Recipes to Live to 100*. Washington, D.C.: National Geographic.

Burke, B., 1999. Purple and Aegean Textile Trade in the Early Second Millennium BC. In *Meletemata: Studies in Aegean Archaeology Presented to Malcolm H. Wiener as He Enters His 65th Year*, edited by P. Betancourt, R. Laffineur, V. Karageorghis, and W.-D. Niemeier, 75–82. Aegaeum 20. Leuven: Peeters.

Carothers, J. J., 1992. The Pylian Kingdom. A Case Study of An Early State. Ph.D. dissertation, University of California, Los Angeles.

Carusi, C., 2018. Salt and Fish Processing in the Ancient Mediterranean: A Brief Survey. *Journal of Maritime Archaeology* 13: 481–490.

Chalikias, K., 2015. Chryssi Island: New Evidence on the Bronze Age Settlement Patterns of the Ierapetra Area.

In *Minoan Archaeology, Perspectives of the 21st Century: Perspectives for the 21st Century. Proceedings of the International PhD and Post-Doc Conference at Heidelberg, 23–27 March* 2011, edited by S. Cappel, U. Günkel-Maschek, and D. Panagiotopoulos, 37–51. Aegis 8. Louvain-la-Neuve: Presses universitaires de Louvain.

Constantakopoulou, C., 2007. *The Dance of the Islands: Insularity, Networks, the Athenian Empire and the Aegean World.* Oxford: Oxford University Press.

Cosmopoulos, M., 2006. The Political Landscape of Mycenaean States: A-pu$_2$ and the Hither Province of Pylos. *American Journal of Archaeology* 110: 205–228.

Darby, W. J., P. Ghalioungui, and L. Grivetti, 1977. *Food: The Gift of Osiris,* 2 vols. London: Academic Press.

Dill, A., 2021. An Analysis of the Application of Central Place Models in Mycenaean Archaeology. Ph.D. dissertation, Florida State University.

Driessen, J., 2010. Spirit of Place: Minoan Houses as Major Actors. In *Political Economies of the Aegean Bronze Age: Papers from the Langford Conference, Florida State University, Tallahassee, 22–24 February 2007,* edited by D. J. Pullen, 35–65. Oxford: Oxbow Books.

Efkleidou, K., 2019. Walking Your Way to Death. Exploring the Relation Between the Location of Mycenaean Chamber Tombs and Roads in the Argolid. *Open Archaeology* 5: 484–504.

Fachard, S., and A. R. Knodell, 2020. Out of Attica: Modeling Mobility in the Mycenaean Period. In *Athens and Attica in Prehistory: Proceedings of the International Conference, Athens, 27–31 May 2015,* edited by N. Papadimitriou, J. C. Wright, S. Fachard, N. Polychronakou-Sgouritsa, and E. Andrikou, 407–416. Oxford: Archaeopress.

Flad, R., J. Zhu, C. Wang, P. Chen, L. von Falkenhausen, Z. Sun, and S. Li, 2005. Archaeological and Chemical Evidence for Early Salt Production in China. *PNAS* 102(35): 12,618–12,622.

Galik, A., G. Forstenpointner, G. E. Weissengruber, U. Thanheiser, M. Lindblom, R. Smetana, and W. Gauß, 2013. Bioarchaeological Investigations at Kolonna, Aegina (Early Helladic III to Late Helladic III). In *Diet, Economy and Society in the Ancient Greek World: Towards a Better Integration of Archaeology and Science,* edited by S. Voutsaki and S.M. Voulamonti, 63–172. Leuven: Peeters.

Garcia-Guixé, E., M. E. Subirà, R. Marlasca, and M. P. Richards, 2010. δ13C and δ15N in Ancient and Recent Fish Bones from the Mediterranean Sea. *Journal of Nordic Archaeological Science* 17: 83–92.

Gauß, W., G., Klebinder-Gauß, E. Kiriatzi, A. Pentedeka, and M. Georgakopoulou, 2015. Aegina: An Important Centre of Production of Cooking Pottery from the Prehistoric to the Historic Era. In *Ceramics, Cuisine and Culture: The Archaeology and Science of Kitchen Pottery in the Ancient Mediterranean World,* edited by M. Spataro and A. Villing, 65–74. Oxford: Oxbow Books.

Gauß, W., and A. R. Knodell, 2020. Aeginetan Pottery in the Aegean World: Mapping Distributions Around an Island Hub. In *From Past to Present: Studies in Memory of Manfred O. Korfmann,* edited by S. W. E. Blum, T. Efe, T. L. Kienlin, and E. Pernicka, 245–262. Studia Troica 11. Bonn: Verlag Dr. Rudolf Habelt GMBH.

Gilstrap, W. D., 2015. Ceramic Production and Exchange in the Late Mycenaean Saronic Gulf. Ph.D. thesis, University of Sheffield.

Gilstrap, W. D., P. M. Day, and V. Kilikoglou, 2016. Pottery Production at Two Neighbouring Centres in the Late Bronze Age Saronic Gulf: Historical Contingency and Craft Organization. *Journal of Archaeological Science: Reports* 7: 499–509.

Granovetter, M., 1973. The Strength of Weak Ties. *American Journal of Sociology* 78: 1360–1380.

Halstead, P., 1993. Lost Sheep? On the Linear B Evidence for Breeding Flocks at Mycenaean Knossos and Pylos. *Minos* 25–26: 343–365.

Halstead, P., 2003. Texts and Bones: Contrasting Linear B and Archaeozoological Evidence for Animal Exploitation in Mycenaean Southern Greece. In *Zooarchaeology in Greece: Recent Advances,* edited by E. Kotjabopoulou, Y. Hamilakis, P. Halstead, C. Gamble, and P. Elefanti, 257–261. British School at Athens Studies 9. London: British School at Athens.

Harding, A. E., 2013. *Salt in Prehistoric Europe.* Leiden: Sidestone Press.

Harper, C. R., 2016. Laboring with the Economics of Mycenaean Architecture: Theories, Methods, and Explorations of Mycenaean Architectural Production. Ph.D. dissertation, Florida State University.

Hope Simpson, R., 2014. *Mycenaean Messenia and the Kingdom of Pylos.* Philadelphia: INSTAP Prehistory Press.

Horden, P., and N. Purcell, 2000. *The Corrupting Sea: A Study of Mediterranean History.* Oxford: Blackwell.

Iezzi, C. A., 2015. Existence and Subsistence in Mycenaean-era East Lokris: The Isotopic Evidence. In *Archaeodiet in the Greek World: Dietary Reconstruction from Stable Isotope Analysis,* edited by A. Papathanasiou, M. P. Richards, and S. C. Fox, 89–104. Hesperia Supplement 49. Princeton: American School of Classical Studies at Athens.

Kardulias, P. N., 2000. Adaptation on Arid Islands: A Study of Herders on Dokos, Greece. *Near Eastern Archaeology* 63(1): 35–44.

Kelder, J. M., 2010. *The Kingdom of Mycenae: A Great Kingdom in the Late Bronze Age Aegean.* Bethesda, MD: CDL Press.

Kilian, K., 1988. The Emergence of *Wanax* Ideology in the Mycenaean Palaces. *Oxford Journal of Archaeology* 7: 291–302.

Knodell, A. R., D. Athanasoulis, Z. Tankosić, J. F. Cherry, T. K. Garonis, E. I. Levine, D. Nenova, and H. Ç. Öztürk, 2022. An Island Archaeology of Uninhabited Landscapes: Offshore Islets near Paros, Greece (The Small Cycladic Islands Project). *Journal of Island and Coastal Archaeology* 17: 475–511.

Kopaka, K., and N. Chaniotakis, 2003. Just Taste Additive? Bronze Age Salt from Zakros, Crete. *Oxford Journal of Archaeology* 22: 53–66.

Kurlansky, M., 2003. *Salt: A World History*. New York: Penguin Books.

Kvapil, L. A., 2012. The Agricultural Terraces of Korphos-Kalamianos: A Case Study of the Dynamic Relationship Between Land Use and Socio-Political Organization in Prehistoric Greece. Ph.D. dissertation, University of Cincinnati.

Kvapil, L. A., 2021. Growth and Change in the Prehistoric Landscape: The Mycenaean Terraces of Kalamianos. In *Early Land Allotment in Europe: The Spread, Function and Social Implications of Field Systems across Europe in Prehistoric Times,* edited by S. Arnoldussen, M. Løvschal, and R. Johnston, 101–114. Cham, Switzerland: Springer.

Lewis, N., 1984. *Voices of the Old Sea*. London: Eland Publishing Ltd.

Li, S., and R. K. Flad, 2020. Archaeology of Salt in China. *Encyclopedia of Global Archaeology*: 789–799.

Liko, S. M., 2012. Second Order Centers and Regional Integration in the Late Bronze Age Aegean. Ph.D. dissertation, Florida State University.

Lolos, Y., 2007. Το Μυκηναϊκό άστυ της Σαλαμίνος. In *Επάθλον: Αρχαιολογικό Συνέδριο προς τιμήν του Αδώνιδος Κ. Κύρου*, edited by E. Konsolaki-Giannopoulou, vol. 1, 221–252. Athens: Demos Porou.

Marabea, C., 2019. Late Bronze Age Aiginetan Coarse Pottery at Kanakia, Salamis: A Macroscopic Study. *Hesperia* 88: 447–525.

McKillop, H., 2002. *Salt: White Gold of the Ancient Maya.* Gainesville: University Press of Florida.

McKillop, H., 2019. *Maya Salt Works*. Gainesville: University Press of Florida.

Meier J. S., G. C. Price, and K. Shelton, 2023. 'Well' Off in Animals: A Taphonomic History of Faunal Resources and Refuse from a Well Feature at Petsas House, Mycenae (Greece). *PLOS ONE* 18(3): e0280517.

Mitchell, P., 2018. *The Donkey in Human History: An Archaeological Perspective*. Oxford University Press.

Mylona, D., 2018. Fish Processing in the Mediterranean: Varying Traditions, Technologies and Scales of Production with Particular Reference to the Eastern Mediterranean. *Journal of Maritime Archaeology* 13: 419–436.

Mylona, D., 2020. Marine Resources and Coastal Communities in the Late Bronze Age Southern Aegean: A Seascape Approach. *American Journal of Archaeology* 124: 179–213.

Nakassis, D., 2013. *Individuals and Society in Mycenaean Pylos*. Mnemosyne Supplements 358. Leiden: Brill.

Nakassis, D., 2023. People Like Us? Individuals and Individualism in the Late Bronze Age Aegean. In *Πολυμήχανος: Man of Many Ways: Papers in Honour of Professor Jan Driessen*, edited by C. Langohr and Q. Letesson, 81–87. Aegis 25. Louvain-la-Neuve: Presses universitaires de Louvain.

Newhard, J. M. L., N. S. Levine, and A. D. Phebus, 2014. The Development of Integrated Terrestrial and Maritime Pathways in the Argo-Saronic Region, Greece. *Cartography and Geographic Information Science* 41: 379–390.

Nosch, M.-L., 2004. Red Coloured Textiles in the Linear B Inscriptions. In *Colour in the Ancient Mediterranean World*, edited by L. Cleland, K. Stears, and G. Davies, 32–39. British Archaeological Reports International Series 1267. Oxford: Archaeopress.

Nosch, M.-L., 2014. The Aegean Wool Economies of the Bronze Age. *Textile Society of America 2014 Biennial Symposium Proceedings: New Directions: Examining the Past, Creating the Future, Los Angeles, California, September 10–14, 2014*. http://digitalcommons.unl.edu/tsaconf/900.

Nuttall, C., 2021. Seascape Dialogues: Human-Sea Interaction in the Aegean from Late Neolithic to Late Bronze Age. Ph.D. dissertation, Uppsala University.

Palaima, T. G., 1991. Maritime Matters in the Linear B Tablets. In *Thalassa: L'Égée Préhistorique et la Mer. Actes de la troisième rencontre égéenne internationale de l'Université de Liège, Station de recherches sous-marines et océanographiques (StaReSo), Calvi, Corse, 23-25 avril 1990*, edited by R. Laffineur and L. Basch, 273–310. Aegaeum 7. Liège: Université de Liège, Histoire de l'art et archéologie de la Grèce antique.

Palaima, T. G., 2005. Mycenaean Ideograms and How They Are Used. In *Studi in Onore di Enrica Fiandra: Contributi di Archeologia Egea e Vicinorientale*, edited by M. Perna, 267–283. Studi egei e vicinorientali 1. Paris: de Boccard.

Palaima, T. G., 2020. *Porphureion* and *Kalkhion* and Minoan-Mycenaean Purple Dye Manufacture and Use. In *Alatzomouri Pefka: A Middle Minoan IIB Workshop Making Organic Dyes*, edited by V. Apostolakou, T. M. Brogan, and P. P. Betancourt, 123–128. Philadelphia: INSTAP Academic Press.

Petroutsa, E. I., and S. K. Manolis, 2010. Reconstructing Late Bronze Age Diet in Mainland Greece Using Stable Isotope Analysis. *Journal of Archaeological Science* 37: 614–620.

Powell, J., 1996. *Fishing in the Prehistoric Aegean*. Studies in Mediterranean Archaeology Pocketbook 137. Jonsered: Paul Åströms Förlag.

Pullen, D. J., 2015. How to Build a Mycenaean Town: The Architecture of Kalamianos. In *Mycenaeans Up to Date: The Archaeology of the Northeastern Peloponnese - Current Concepts and New Directions*, edited by A.-L. Schallin and I. Tournavitou, 377–390. Skrifter Utgivna av Svenska Institutet i Athen 4°, 56. Stockholm: Swedish Institute in Athens.

Pullen, D. J., 2019a. Agricultural Self-Sufficiency and Mycenaean Kalamianos on the Saronic Gulf. In *Country in the City: Agricultural Functions in Protohistoric Urban Settlements (Aegean and Western Mediterranean)*, edited by D. Garcia, R. Orgeolet, M. Pomadère, and J. Zurbach, 137–151. Oxford: Archaeopress.

Pullen, D. J., 2019b. If You Build It, Will They Come? Will They Stay? The Mycenaean Port Town of Kalamianos. In *Coming Together: Comparative Approaches to Population Aggregation and Early Urbanization*, edited by A. Gyucha, 215–238. IEMA Proceedings 8. Albany: State University of New York Press.

Pullen, D. J., 2022. The Political Geography of the Late Bronze Age Argolid: States and Territories. In *Political Geographies of the Bronze Age Aegean: Proceedings of the Joint Workshop of the Belgian School at Athens (EBSA) and the Netherlands Institute at Athens (NIA), May 28 to 31, 2019*, edited by G. J. van Wijngaarden and J. Driessen, 75–86. BABESCH Supplement 43. Leuven: Peeters.

Pullen, D. J., and P. Sapirstein, 2020. Materiality of Power through Masonry at Mycenaean Kalamianos. In *Ashlar: Exploring the Materiality of Cut-Stone Masonry in the Eastern Mediterranean Bronze Age*, edited by M. Devolder and I. Kreimerman, 365–397. Aegis 17. Louvain-la-Neuve: Presses universitaires de Louvain.

Pullen, D. J., and T. F. Tartaron, 2007. Where's the Palace? The Lack of State Formation in the Late Bronze Age Corinthia. In *Rethinking Mycenaean Palaces II: Revised and Expanded Edition*, edited by M. L. Galaty and W. A. Parkinson, 146–158. Monograph 60. Los Angeles: University of California at Los Angeles, Cotsen Institute of Archaeology.

Reese, D. S., 1987. Palaikastro Shells and Bronze Age Purple-Dye Production in the Mediterranean Basin. *Annual of the British School at Athens* 82: 201–206.

Richards, M. P., and R. E. M. Hedges, 2007. Stable Isotope Evidence of Past Human Diet at the Sites of the Neolithic Cave of Gerani; the Late Minoan III Cemetery of Armenoi; Grave Circles A and B at the Palace of Mycenae; and Late Helladic Chamber Tombs. In *Archaeology Meets Science. Biomolecular Investigations in Bronze Age Greece: The Primary Scientific Evidence, 1997–2003*, edited by Y. Tzedakis, H. Martlew, and M. Jones, 220–230. Oxford: Oxford University Press.

Rothaus, R. M., E. Reinhardt, T. Tartaron, and J. Noller, 2003. A Geoarchaeological Approach for Understanding Prehistoric Usage of the Coastline of the Eastern Korinthia. In *Metron: Measuring the Aegean Bronze Age. Proceedings of the 9th International Aegean Conference/ 9e Rencontre égéenne internationale, New Haven, Yale University, 18–21 April 2002*, edited by K. P. Foster and R. Laffineur, 37–47. Aegaeum 24. Liège: Université de Liège, Histoire de l'art et archéologie de la Grèce antique/Austin: University of Texas at Austin, Program in Aegean Scripts and Prehistory.

Ruscillo, D., 2005. Reconstructing Murex Royal Purple and Biblical Blue in the Aegean. In *Archaeomalacology: Molluscs in Former Environments of Human Behaviour. Proceedings of the 9th International Conference for Archaeozoology, Durham 2002*, edited by D. E. Bar-Yosef Mayer, 99–106. Oxford: Oxbow Books.

Ruscillo, D., 2006. Faunal Remains and *Murex* Dye Production. In *Kommos: An Excavation on the South Coast of Crete. Volume V: The Monumental Buildings at Kommos*, edited by J. Shaw and M. Shaw, 776–844. Princeton: Princeton University Press.

Salmon, J. B., 1984. *Wealthy Corinth: A History of the City to 338 B.C.* Oxford: Clarendon Press.

Shaw, J. W., 2006. *Kommos: A Minoan Harbor Town and Greek Sanctuary in Southern Crete*. Princeton: American School of Classical Studies at Athens.

Sofianou, C., and T. Brogan, 2009. The Excavation of House A.1 at Papadiokampos. *Kentro* 12: 6–9.

Stieglitz, R. R., 1994. The Minoan Origin of Tyrian Purple. *Biblical Archaeologist* 57: 46–54.

Synge, J. M., 1907. *The Arran Islands*. Dublin: Maunsel & Company.

Tartaron, T. F., 2010. Between and Beyond: Political Economy in Non-palatial Mycenaean Worlds. In *Political Economies of the Aegean Bronze Age: Papers from the Langford Conference, Florida State University, Tallahassee, 22–24 February 2007*, edited by D. J. Pullen, 161–193. Oxford: Oxbow Books.

Tartaron, T. F., 2013. *Maritime Networks in the Mycenaean World*. Cambridge: Cambridge University Press.

Tartaron, T. F., 2015a. Late Bronze Age Architecture and Regional Dynamics at Korphos in the Corinthia. In *Mycenaeans Up to Date: The Archaeology of the Northeastern Peloponnese - Current Concepts and New Directions*, edited by A.-L. Schallin and I. Tournavitou, 391–401. Skrifter Utgivna av Svenska Institutet i Athen 4° 56. Stockholm: Swedish Institute in Athens.

Tartaron, T. F., 2015b. The Settlement at Kalamianos: Bronze Age Small Worlds and the Saronic Coast of the Southeastern Corinthia. In *Bridge of the Untiring*

Sea: The Corinthian Isthmus from Prehistory to Late Antiquity, edited by E. R. Gebhart and T. E. Gregory, 25–38. Hesperia Supplement 48. Princeton: American School of Classical Studies at Athens.

Tartaron, T. F., 2018. Geography Matters: Defining Maritime Small Worlds of the Aegean Bronze Age. In *Maritime Networks in the Ancient Mediterranean World*, edited by J. Leidwanger and C. Knappett, 61–92. Cambridge: Cambridge University Press.

Tartaron, T. F., D. J. Pullen, R. K. Dunn, L. Tzortzopoulou-Gregory, and A. Dill, 2011. The Saronic Harbors Archaeological Research Project: Investigations at Mycenaean Kalamianos, 2007–2009. *Hesperia* 80: 559–634.

Tartaron, T. F., R. M. Rothaus, and D. J. Pullen. 2003. Searching for Prehistoric Aegean Harbors with GIS, Geomorphology, and Archaeology. *Athena Review* 3(4): 27–36.

Theodoropoulou, T., 2012. Searching for the Sea: The Exploitation of Marine Resources in Late Bronze Age Aegean. *Talanta* 44: 295–314.

Theodoropoulou, T., forthcoming. The Shells at Kalamianos. *The Saronic Harbors Archaeological Research Project: Engaging Land and Sea in the Saronic Gulf, Greece*, edited by in D. J. Pullen, P. Sapirstein, and T. F. Tartaron. Princeton: American School of Classical Studies at Athens.

Trusty, D. A., and W. D. Gilstrap, forthcoming. LBA Kitchen Ware Vessels from Kalamianos and Stiri. In *The Saronic Harbors Archaeological Research Project: Engaging Land and Sea in the Saronic Gulf, Greece*, edited by in D. J. Pullen, P. Sapirstein, and T. F. Tartaron. Princeton: American School of Classical Studies at Athens.

Vika, E., and T. Theodoropoulou, 2012. Re-investigating Fish Consumption in Greek Antiquity: Results from $d^{13}C$ and $d^{15}N$ Analysis from Fish Bone Collagen. *Journal of Archaeological Science* 39: 1618–1627.

Vitale, S., and A. Van de Moortel, 2020. The Late Helladic IIIB Phase at Mitrou, East Lokris: Pottery, Chronology, and Political Relations with the Palatial Polities of Thebes and Orchomenos/Glas. *Annuario della Scuola Archeologica di Atene e delle Missioni Italiane in Oriente* 98: 9–59.

Vykukal, R. L., 2011. *Purpurae Florem* of Mitrou: Assessing the Role of Purple Dye Manufacture in the Emergence of a Political Elite. M.A. thesis, University of Tennessee-Knoxville.

Wells, B., C. Runnels, and E. Zangger, 1990. The Berbati-Limnes Archaeological Survey: The 1988 Season. *Opuscula Atheniensia* XVIII (15): 207–238.

Wiencke, M. H., 2000. *Lerna IV: The Architecture, Stratification, and Pottery of Lerna III.* Princeton: American School of Classical Studies at Athens.

Windell, D. J., and R. A. Webb, 2021a. Following Pausanias: The Ancient Route from Argos to Epidaurus and its Archaeology. https://www.academia.edu/71921265/Following_Pausanias_The_Ancient_Route_from_Argos_to_Epidaurus_and_its_Archaeology, accessed 17 December 2023.

Windell, D. J., and R. A. Webb, 2021b. Kastraki/Kastro Foniskou: An Overlooked Multi-period, Walled Site in Argolis, Greece, Middle Helladic–Modern. *Academia Letters*, July 2021: 1–8.

Zalidis, G. C., A. L. Mantzavelas, and E. Gourvelou, 1997. Environmental Impacts on Greek Wetlands. *Wetlands* 17: 339–345.

Brokering Change in Southern Aegean Networks

A Comparison of Communities of Practice in the Cyclades and Mainland Greece in the Era of Minoanization

Natalie Abell

Abstract
The later Middle and early Late Bronze Age in the Cyclades and mainland Greece witnessed different patterns of adoption and adaptation of Cretan-style material culture as part of the so-called Minoanization phenomenon. In the Cyclades, the proliferation of Minoanizing material culture and practices can be considered as a kind of complex contagion, whereby new ideas spread widely among different social groups, including craftspeople as well as participants in new kinds of ritual and exchange activities. In the mainland, however, it has long been noted that the uptake of Minoanizing material culture and practice was more limited. Differences in the configuration of social networks, especially crafting communities and constellations of practice, probably played a role in the divergent ways that Cycladic and mainland communities responded to innovations associated with the Minoanization phenomenon.

Introduction
The application of formal network models has become increasingly common in studies of the ancient world, including in the Aegean. Qualitative, informal analysis of ancient networks can also provide useful insights into dynamics of interaction and socioeconomic change across sites and regions. Such analyses offer a framework for assessing communities and individuals as entities that are not coterminous with archaeological sites. This chapter explores how ideas derived from one kind of network — communities and constellations of practice — can contribute to our narratives of socioeconomic change in the Cyclades and mainland Greece during the later MBA and early LBA, that is, the era of Minoanization in the Cyclades or the shaft grave period in mainland Greece. After an introduction of key concepts, the dynamics of some communities and constellations of practice in the Cyclades are analyzed, in order to clarify how different social groups encouraged change in material culture and practice as part of the Minoanization phenomenon. Connections between Cycladic and mainland communities are then examined in order to highlight how different network dynamics in the two regions may have contributed to some of the well-known differences in material culture between the mainland and insular Aegean in this era.

ORCID 0009-0008-1693-4154
Department of Classical Studies
University of Michigan
ndabell@umich.edu

In *Social Groups and Production in Mycenaean Economies. Papers from the Langford Conference, Florida State University, Tallahassee, 24-25 February 2023*, edited by D. Pullen (2025), 101–128. Leiden: Sidestone Press.

Communities and constellations of practice

A community of practice is a group of people who interact with each other on a regular basis to do some *thing* together (Lave and Wenger 1991; Wenger 1998; Amin and Roberts 2008). The community is a social network, in which links are generated between members through repeated, in-person interaction to do whatever that thing is. The original formulation of the theory by Lave and Wenger (1991) focused on the social dynamics of learning and was influenced by ethnographic studies of craft apprenticeship. In a community of practice (Figure 7.1), craft-making or otherwise, new members are initiated and learn how to do whatever the thing is, whether it is how to tailor a suit or talk openly about alcoholism (two of the key case studies from Lave and Wenger's study). Non-members may encounter ideas and norms within the community through peripheral observation and participation, without fully learning all the skills, equipment, and other knowledge associated with whatever thing the community does. For example, children who are not potters may encounter tools, materials, and practices associated with potting as they play in or around the workspace or by being asked to perform simple tasks, like fetching water or raw materials. Adult non-potters may be able to observe some potting practices if they interact with potters working outside or if they participate in certain steps of the *chaîne opératoire*, like digging or transporting clay or making tools, which may not all be undertaken by the same people who form, finish, and fire pots. Some of these peripheral participants in a community of practice may eventually go on to become fully initiated, knowledgeable members of the community, but some will not, even if they may maintain other kinds of links to it.

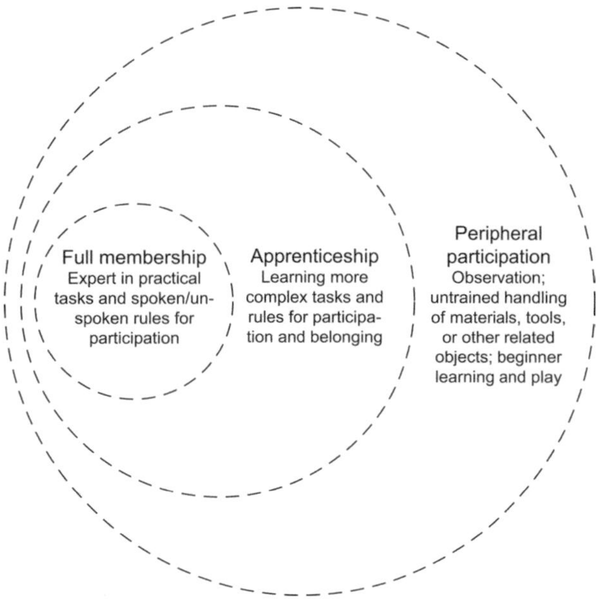

Figure 7.1. Types of membership in communities of practice, maintained through repeated interaction and vertical (expert-apprentice) and horizontal (peer-to-peer) learning. Drawing by the author.

Becoming a member of a community of practice includes learning social norms and values, especially as they intersect with participation in that community. Members of a community of practice create and enforce implicit and explicit rules about the correct ways to do the thing, as well as how the thing that is being learned fits into broader sociocultural norms, including ideas around gender, class, relative value, and so on. For example, if a mother only ever invites her daughter and never her son to work with clay, then both son and daughter learn that potting is work done by women and that the experience and identity of being a potter is intertwined with being a woman, a mother, a teacher, and an apprentice (Michelaki, Braun, and Hancock 2015: 785). The social bonds that develop between members of a community of practice can be very strong, especially when, as with craft apprenticeship, they are built up over months or years. At the same time, the community of practice is also constantly shifting, as new members are initiated, change status, gain or lose the power to influence others, and leave the group. More than one community of practice that does similar things (e.g., potting) can exist within the same settlement or area, while not all members of a community of practice have to be co-resident in the same settlement. Communities of practice should not be understood as spatially equivalent to "natural" or "geographical" communities, which comprise people who live in the same location (Isbell 2000; Varien and Potter 2008: 2–6).

Communities of practice are connected to other communities in networks called "constellations of practice" (Figure 7.2; Wenger 1998; Roddick and Stahl 2016). Connections within constellations of practice can be generated in many ways, such as the movement of people or finished products between communities, the exploitation of shared raw material sources or tools, or by short-lived encounters between members of different communities, for example at periodic events like markets or festivals. Every community in a constellation of practice does not necessarily engage in the same practice. A pot-making community of practice may be connected to other potting communities as well as metallurgical or weaving ones through the use of similar clay sources for making vessels and terracotta tools. That same potting community may be connected with other non-craft-making groups, including consumers, neighbors who interact with potters working outside, household members or relatives who are not themselves involved in potting, and so on. Each person in a community or constellation of practice also may have different identities and social roles, which means that they

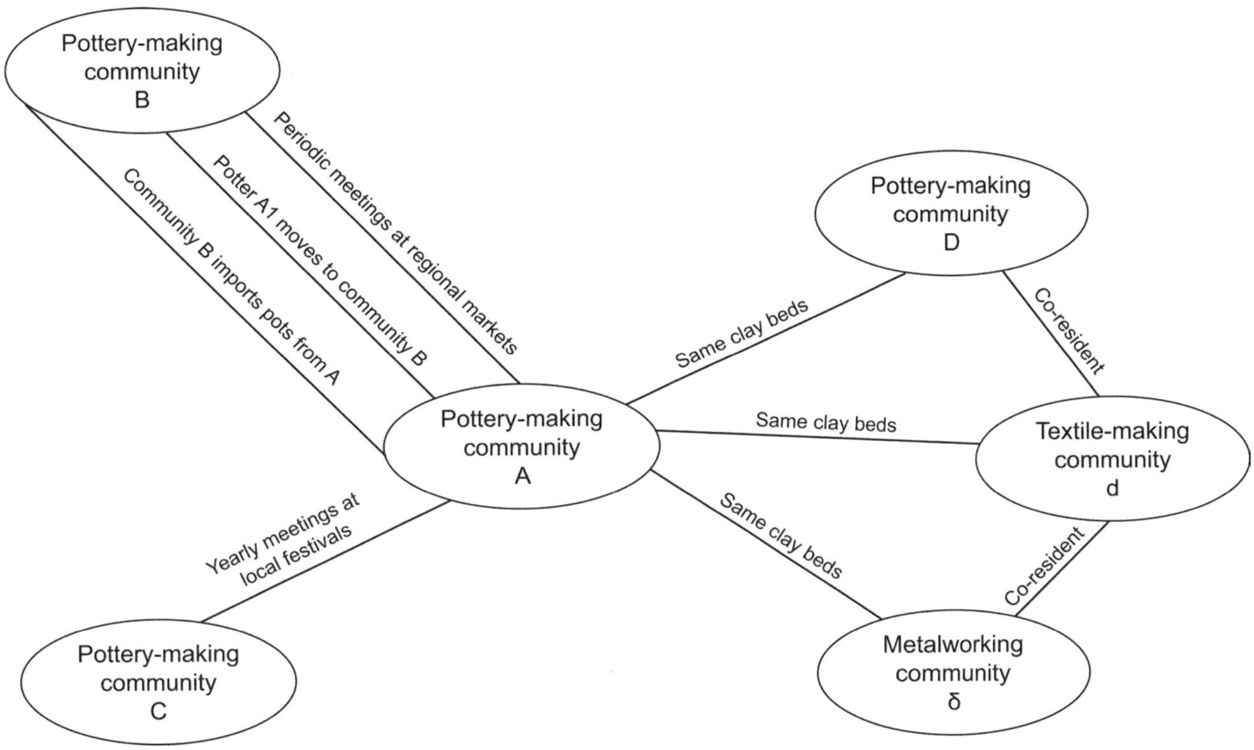

Figure 7.2. Different kinds of links connecting a hypothetical crafting constellation of practice. Drawing by the author.

themselves become nodes that connect different kinds of networks together. In a potting community of practice, for example, each potter is also a member of different kinds of social groups based on their non-potting activities, household and kin relationships, age, status, gender, and/or personal history. Different kinds of connections within constellations of practice have different dynamics in terms of the potential to transfer information. But the more links — and the more *kinds* of links — that exist within the constellation (i.e., within the broader network), the more potential avenues there will be for the flow of new information and the more opportunities for individuals to negotiate changing practices, styles, and ideas.

One particularly important kind of link within networks, including constellations of practice, is created by brokers.[1] Brokers fill structural holes in a network (Burt 1992). We can see examples in Figure 7.3. Each cluster (A, B, C, and D) may be considered as a relatively closed network, with strong ties generated by personal knowledge and trust linking most participants more closely to each other than to other network clusters. There is, however, a clear structural hole between clusters C and D, which have no direct connections to each other. Structural holes also separate most individuals in clusters A, B, and D. Cally and Saul have no connection with each other, nor do Diana and Kara. Laura and Lee provide the only connections between clusters A and B and so can be considered as brokers filling structural holes. Networks with abundant structural holes tend to be temporally fragile, since links across them tend to be maintained by comparatively few individuals in a society (Soda, Usai, and Zaheer 2004).

Structural holes are closely related to Granovetter's (1973) idea of weak ties (Burt 1992: 24–28; Granovetter 2005: 34–35). These ties are considered *weak* in the sense of being a link between acquaintances or people who do not know each other well; weak ties are also understood in a structural sense as ties between different clusters in a network (Granovetter 1973, 1983; Centola 2018: 21–24). The second, structural sense of the term is the more usual (e.g., Granovetter 2005: 35). New, nonredundant information is most likely to enter a network cluster through weak ties, especially when they connect distant clusters (e.g., Manzo et al. 2018, 1119–1120). Brokers are the agents who enable communication across weak ties and introduce new information. In Figure 7.3, Laura is a broker creating connections through structural weak ties, linking cluster A with distant clusters B and D. Her connection with Tom is strong in the sense that they know each other well and trust each other, in contrast to her connection with Lee, who is more of an acquaintance. The latter link is weak in both the structural and the social senses of the term. In

1 The concept of culture brokers has a long history outside explicitly network-oriented approaches (e.g., Wolf 1956).

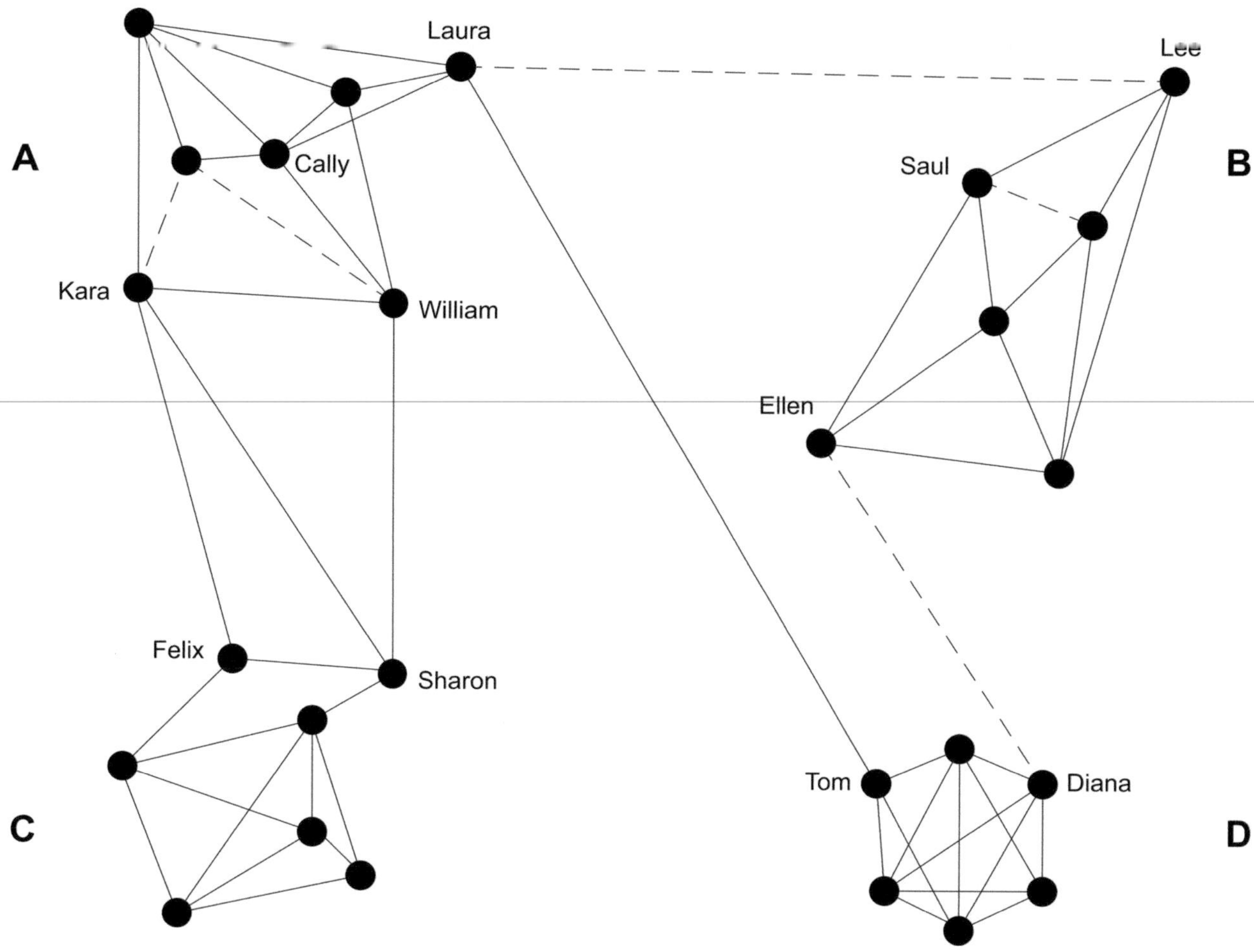

Figure 7.3. Connections between hypothetical network clusters (A–D), with solid lines representing strong ties and dashed lines representing weak ties. Drawing by the author.

network studies, so-called entrepreneurial brokers are often understood to gain a social or economic advantage by linking otherwise disconnected networks (Burt 1992; Xiao and Tsui 2007; Peeples and Haas Jr. 2013). The entrepreneurial broker is a familiar concept for archaeologists, in the form of middlemen who exploit special knowledge or access to resources in order to increase their own social capital and material wealth. This idea is echoed in influential theories like Hirth's (1978) concept of gateway communities.

The idea of brokering also can have other valences. Within constellations of practice, brokers may be understood as individuals who encourage the transfer of knowledge or techniques between members of different communities of practice. Transferring knowledge between two communities of practice requires that the broker has enough legitimacy in both in order to enable the productive sharing of knowledge between them. In the case of successfully introducing new technologies, this may take the form of recognized expertise (Roux, Bril, and Karasik 2018). Brokers may have to move physically between places where different communities of practice are operating, but this is not inherently necessary since brokering is about crossing social distances, not geographical ones. Although this kind of broker creates a link between different network clusters (i.e., the communities of practice), some of their links may be (or become) strong, especially if they become integrated with a new community of practice. Such brokers may also operate as part of "wide bridges" made up of multiple connections between different network clusters (Centola 2018). In Figure 7.3, for example, clusters A and C are linked by connections between Kara, Felix, and Sharon, as well as between William and Sharon. These links create a wide bridge and enable information circulating in cluster A to reach cluster C through different individuals. All of these individuals have the potential to act as brokers for the transfer of knowledge between network clusters. The fact that these individuals are connected by strong social ties also means that they are more likely to be trusted when they endorse an innovation, which may help the innovation to spread more widely in the network (Manzo et al. 2018).

In some contexts, brokering can be negatively perceived or even dangerous, especially when brokers provide links across weak ties between relatively closed networks, like Laura between clusters A and B or A and D in Figure 7.3. The sometimes socially peripheral status of brokers, which enables them to transfer ideas between groups, can mean that the trust that they are afforded is comparatively fragile, and they may be treated with suspicion (Xiao and Tsui 2007; Peeples and Haas Jr. 2013; see also Bowser and Patton 2008; Iorio 2023). Brokering is not inevitable. It relies on the existence of individuals capable of successfully negotiating dynamics between groups, as well as members of those groups who are open to accepting information from people at the peripheries of their own social networks.

Networks that are structured with high numbers of strong ties that enable mutual influence, a high number of ties in general, and a high number of different kinds of ties that enable the introduction of new, non-redundant information have been noted in modern contexts as particularly likely to encourage the adoption of innovations (Muller and Peres 2019; see also Soda, Usai and Zaheer 2004). These studies suggest that a network with a balance of closed configurations made up of many strong trusted ties and open ones with brokers making connections between different clusters is more structurally efficient for the spread of innovations than other kinds of network configurations (see also Burt 2005). The existence of multiple well-placed brokers might also be able to mitigate the temporal fragility that typifies networks with abundant structural holes, since the loss of one broker from the network would not prevent information from flowing between clusters.

Complex contagions and the Minoanization phenomenon

It has become common in Mediterranean archaeology to consider the "strength of weak ties" (Granovetter 1973, 1983) as part of small-world network dynamics in eras of major sociocultural change (e.g., Malkin 2011; Knodell 2021; see also Collar 2022). New information can spread quickly across a whole regional network through weak ties, which provide shortcuts between otherwise distant nodes. The transfer of new ideas in this kind of situation can be considered as a kind of simple contagion. Each individual or node that comes into contact with the idea may spread it on, like a virus.

Adopting some innovations, however, is costly in time, effort, or potential risks to social status, especially when it involves changing core beliefs or behaviors. For these kinds of innovations to spread, it is not enough for individuals to simply encounter them through one acquaintance, i.e., a weak link. Rather, people are more likely to take up a higher-risk innovation if they encounter it from multiple trusted sources, i.e., through multiple strong ties or wide bridges. This is a complex contagion (Centola and Macy 2007; Bond et al. 2012; Centola 2018; Collar 2022). When each individual encounters the same new ideas from a variety of directions, information and innovation can spread more readily through the network. Although complex contagions can be encouraged when new ideas are endorsed by opinion leaders, the process must ultimately operate from the bottom up and involve many different individuals. Otherwise, some combination of negative feedback and lack of positive reinforcement through multiple strong ties will halt the spread of the innovation (Centola 2018: 49–62; Manzo et al. 2018). For complex contagions to work, longer-distance ties in the network must take the form of wide bridges that are maintained by multiple kinds of connections (such as those between clusters A and C in Figure 7.3) rather than weak links maintained by single individuals (Centola 2018: 109–120). The development of multiple strong ties between network clusters can happen when geographical proximity enables regular communication and the development of strong ties between individuals who otherwise operate primarily in different network clusters, although other possibilities also exist (Rivera, Soderstrom, and Uzzi 2010: 105–107; Centola 2018: 30–33).

Knappett (2018) argued that Minoanization processes can be understood as a part of a complex contagion, given how varied and widespread the evidence is for participation in it by insular and coastal Aegean communities, including in the Cyclades. The adoption of a variety of Cretan-style forms of material culture and practice by Cycladic communities would have had significant impacts on how people lived, worked, and related to each other. These changes represent precisely the kind of high-risk innovations that we would expect to spread via the mechanisms of complex rather than simple contagion. As I will discuss further below, the multiple links that seem to have connected different kinds of geographically dispersed communities and constellations of craft, exchange, and ritual practice would have provided an excellent foundational structure for enabling the widespread changes associated with Minoanization in the archipelago.

Communities and constellations of practice in the MBA–LBA Cyclades

In the MBA–LBA Cyclades, ideas related to communities and constellations of practice have mostly been applied to craft production, especially in relation to the transfer of Cretan technologies into Cycladic towns during the era of Minoanization (Knappett and Nikolakopoulou 2005; Abell and Hilditch 2016; Gorogianni, Abell, and Hilditch 2016; Nikolakopoulou and Knappett 2016; Abell and Gorogianni 2019; Hilditch 2019; Cutler 2021; Abell forthcoming). The local uptake of Cretan-derived technologies, in at least some cases to make Cretan-style products, is a key feature of the phenomenon. It has con-

(Opposite page) Figure 7.4. Plan of published parts of Ayia Irini during (a) LC I and (b) LC II showing the distribution of craft tools and debris in chronologically unmixed deposits from inside architectural units. Objects from exterior spaces are not shown. Icons are not connected with specific findspots within rooms. Information on metallurgical objects reflects both published artifacts and unpublished data from archival documents. Data on published craft tools were compiled by Jami Baxley Craig, Theo Nash, Ashton Rodgers, and the author. Allison Densel created the phase plans (after Cummer and Schofield 1984, Schofield 2011, and Abell 2021). Jami Baxley Craig provided invaluable assistance in generating these distribution plans. Plan after unnamed architects' field sheets and site plan by R. L. Holzen, georeferenced by John Wallrodt and Anna Belza (courtesy of the Department of Classics University of Cincinnati).

tributed substantially to the general scholarly consensus that the Cyclades were more heavily "Minoanized" than mainland Greece during these centuries, even if what actual social, political, and/or economic phenomena are implied by this problematic term have been long debated (Wiener 1984, 2013; Broodbank 2004; Momigliano 2009; Abell 2023). People in the Cyclades adopted the Cretan-derived warp-weighted loom and potter's wheel; wall-painting, aromatic processing, and cooking techniques; Cretan metrological standards; and, to a limited degree, Linear A script. Cretan-derived technologies did not appear everywhere nor contemporaneously across the archipelago, and they continued to be used alongside other, non-Minoanizing techniques.

Several features of Cycladic craft-making communities of practice probably encouraged the widespread adoption of Cretan technologies and production of Cretan-style material culture in the archipelago, namely (1) that some specialized craft production took place in households and (2) that some craftspeople were mobile and could act as brokers (for more detail on these arguments, see Abell forthcoming). I will outline the evidence for these two hypotheses below, starting with the former.

Export patterns as well as the distribution of craft tools suggests the existence of specialized production (in the sense of production for exchange beyond the household) based in houses at Ayia Irini and Akrotiri, the two sites with the best evidence for domestic assemblages in the Cyclades. The widespread distribution of Cycladic products, especially pottery, in the southern Aegean in this period, demonstrates the existence of multiple communities involved in the production of pottery for export (Abell 2023: 369, 371–372 with references). At both Ayia Irini and Akrotiri, imported finished products, ceramic and otherwise, are widely distributed across different houses (Abell forthcoming with references). Evidence for craft production, however, is unevenly distributed and not found in all houses (Figures 7.4, 7.5). Even though the precise production spaces may be unclear, I assume that all craft tools found within a house were primarily used by people who lived or worked in that building. It is challenging to assess scale and intensity of production precisely on the basis of archaeological data, but evaluating the quantity of craft tools and debris across houses and sites provides at least some relative basis for comparison. The uneven distribution of evidence for craft production across houses strongly suggests that finished goods were produced by a smaller number of local specialists, and then exchanged within and perhaps beyond each town.[2] The assemblage of loomweights in the West House (around 450) and Complex Alpha (around 200) at Akrotiri is far larger than other deposits in the Aegean, even large, artifact-rich deposits like those from LC II Ayia Irini, where fewer than 100 weights were found in House A, and far fewer (usually <15) were found in other published buildings (Figures 7.4b, 7.5; Tzachili 1990; Cutler 2021: 182–216, 219–228). At Ayia Irini, the quantity of metallurgical tools and debris, including dozens of crucibles, is well beyond what is typical for Aegean sites, including Akrotiri, where such equipment is comparatively rare (Schofield 1990; Michailidou 1995, 2008a; Abell and Georgakopoulou forthcoming).[3] The textile industry at Akrotiri and the metallurgical industry at Ayia Irini were probably targeted for regional, rather than just local exchange, even though we cannot trace the destination of the final products, unlike pottery.

At both Ayia Irini and Akrotiri, analysis of the *chaînes opératoires* of local ceramic production in the later MBA suggests that there were multiple producers who made different choices about how to make pots, a pattern that continued into the LBA at least at Ayia Irini (Hilditch 2019; Abell 2020, 2021).[4] In addition to high levels of contemporary technical variability, the inconsistent application of marking and labelling systems on pottery suggests a lack of standardization and absence of

2 Karnava and Nikolakopoulou (2020: 251) see only the West House at Akrotiri as involved in "household industry" because of the large quantity of loomweights there. I would argue that the uneven distribution of evidence for all kinds of craft production is evidence for small-scale yet still specialized production, which was not undertaken by everyone in the community to fulfill their internal domestic needs and so probably targeted for exchange, at least in local networks.

3 Likewise, there are nearly 100 fireboxes from Ayia Irini, whereas most other sites have produced fewer than ten (Georgiou 1986, 7). Fireboxes may have been used for aromatic processing, although some argue that they were incense burners; for discussion with references, see Abell 2020: 390–391, fn. 60; see also Vitale et al. 2016: 261–263.

4 A study of *chaînes opératoires* like those that have been undertaken for MBA Akrotiri and MBA–LBA Ayia Irini has not yet appeared for LBA Akrotiri.

a)

Key:
Crucible
2
3
Litharge
2
7
Slag
1
Ingot
1
Firebox
1
Whorl
1
2
3
9
Loomweight
1-2
3
6
10
House J
House F
House EJ
House C
House B
House A
0
5
10 m

b)

Key:
Crucible
1
2
3
4
Metallurgical ceramic
1
Litharge
1
6
27
Slag
1
2
Mould
1
Ingot
1
Firebox
1
2
3
4
Whorl
1
2
3-4
6
9
Loomweight
1-2
3-5
6-12
15
25
32
House J
House F
House EJ
House C
House A
House B
0
5
10 m

Figure 7.5. Plan of Akrotiri, showing the general association of craft production tools with different architectural contexts. Distributional information is derived from synthetic publications of textile tools and metallurgical tools and debris (Tzachili 1990; Michailidou 1995, 2008a, 2008b; Sotiropoulou et al. 2010; Cutler 2021), as well as the publication of small finds from the West House (Doumas 2007). Michailidou (1995: 173) suggested that hammerstones and other objects from Building Gamma may also have been used in metallurgy; these are not included on the plan. Plan after Knappett and Nikolakopoulou 2008, fig. 2 (courtesy of the Akrotiri Excavations Archive).

centralized oversight over ceramic production (Bikaki 1984: 7–39; Nikolakopoulou 2019: 217–234; Abell 2020: 396–400, 404–406). Contemporary technical variety is also a feature of the Keian crucible assemblage, with different choices around the use of organic temper and how to create rocker grooves among otherwise morphologically similar vessels (Abell and Georgakopoulou forthcoming). Choices about how metallurgical tools should be made seem to have been open to some amount of interpretation, which is probably not what we would expect if production was overseen by a centralized authority that provided tools or imposed its own standards over production. This variety in tool manufacturing processes suggests that metallurgists on Kea, like potters, were relatively independent in at least some aspects of their production practices.

From a community and constellation of practice perspective, the centering of production activities within households, many of which were located in the main settlement centers on these islands is significant. Since several kinds of specialized craft production sometimes took place within a household, individuals who lived and worked in that space could have participated in multiple communities of practice as initiated members or peripheral observers. Broad similarities in tool types and finished products between houses demonstrate that craft producers across settlements were linked to each other, because they were making comparable technical and stylistic production choices; that is, they were members of the same or highly interconnected communities of practice. Day-to-day interactions that occurred in and around households at Ayia Irini and Akrotiri would have enabled the development of strong ties linking local communities of practice to each other and to their local constellations of practice. The evidence discussed also above suggests the existence of dense, overlapping networks of producers and consumers based in local households, in which many producers and local consumers probably would have had several different kinds of connections to each other. The probable strength and quantity of these ties suggests that these networks would have been capable of propagating innovation via wide bridges as part of a complex contagion.

In this context, it is worth emphasizing that not only was some specialized craft production situated in household contexts at Ayia Irini and Akrotiri, so too were specialized exchange practices. Cretan-derived metrological standards were adopted as tools to enable and regulate exchange. There are more standardized weights at Akrotiri and Ayia Irini than other Aegean sites, with Mochlos on Crete coming third (Figure 7.6; Petruso 1992; Alberti 1995; Brogan 2006; Michailidou 2006, 2008b). The relative abundance of weights at these sites suggests that residents were particularly heavily involved in transactions that had to be monitored in some way, presumably because they were occurring between people who did not know each other well enough to trust each other implicitly. At Ayia Irini and Akrotiri, these activities were not taking place in administrative centers, but rather in what appear to be independent houses, in addition to hypothesized trading posts at Akrotiri, in Complex Alpha, Delta-South, and Delta-East (Petruso 1992; Michailidou 2008b; Karnava 2018: 33–38, 144–145; Karnava and Nikolakopoulou 2020: 251). The distribution patterns of standardized weights strongly suggest that members of multiple households were relatively direct participants in exchange, rather than exchange being mediated primarily through a single elite individual or group.

The complexity of local systems of production and exchange and their connection with different households can be usefully illustrated by the textile industry at Akrotiri. Both the West House and Complex Alpha contained large numbers of loomweights as well as standardized weights, suggesting that they managed some exchange transactions — of raw materials and/or finished products — independently (Michailidou 2008b). Additional evidence for the textile industry comes from Delta-East, where Linear A tablets in local clay record 46 sheep and a very large number of textiles, at least 200 units (Boulotis 2008). Delta-East, which has been interpreted as an independent unit, has no evidence for textile production in the form of loomweights, so the registering of these products as well as the sheep themselves suggests a local exchange system involving the acquisition of finished textiles from another location, as well as some oversight over (presumably rural) sheep-keeping. Delta-East is also not the only building where recording of commodities seems to have taken place at Akrotiri, although it is the only one with Linear A-inscribed tablets (Karnava 2008). Over 30 (and perhaps as many as 50) unfired clay cylinders bearing impressed marks were found in Delta-North, with another from Delta-South (Tzachili 2002–2003). These have been interpreted by Tzachili as devices for counting goods. Firth (2016) argued more specifically that these objects were tally-sticks for recording commodities or livestock like sheep outside the settlement, given the portability of the cylinders. Unfired clay cylinders of similar morphology, but without markings, were found also in the West House, Delta-West, the House of the Ladies, the House of the Anchor, and Xeste 3, as well as the site of Potamos near Akrotiri and at Ftellos (Tzachili 2002–2003). The function of the uninscribed cylinders is less clear although their similarities to the marked cylinders suggests they may have had a related function. The appearance of unfired cylinders at Theran sites outside of Akrotiri and the existence of standardized lead weights at Raos near Akrotiri (Marthari 2019: 137) suggest that people outside the urban core were active participants in Theran production and exchange patterns, whether connected with textiles or not. This example highlights how craftspeople in local contexts would have been connected with complex networks of production, consumption, and exchange operating at both local and regional levels.

a)

Figure 7.6. Plans of (a) Ayia Irini and (opposite page) (b) Akrotiri showing the distribution of standardized lead weights and balance pans based on the data provided by Petruso (1992) and Michailidou (2008b). Objects reported from the pillar pits at Akrotiri are not shown. Plans after Schofield 2011, pl. 2 (courtesy of the Department of Classics University of Cincinnati) and Knappett and Nikolakopoulou 2008, fig. 2 (courtesy of the Akrotiri Excavations Archive).

b)

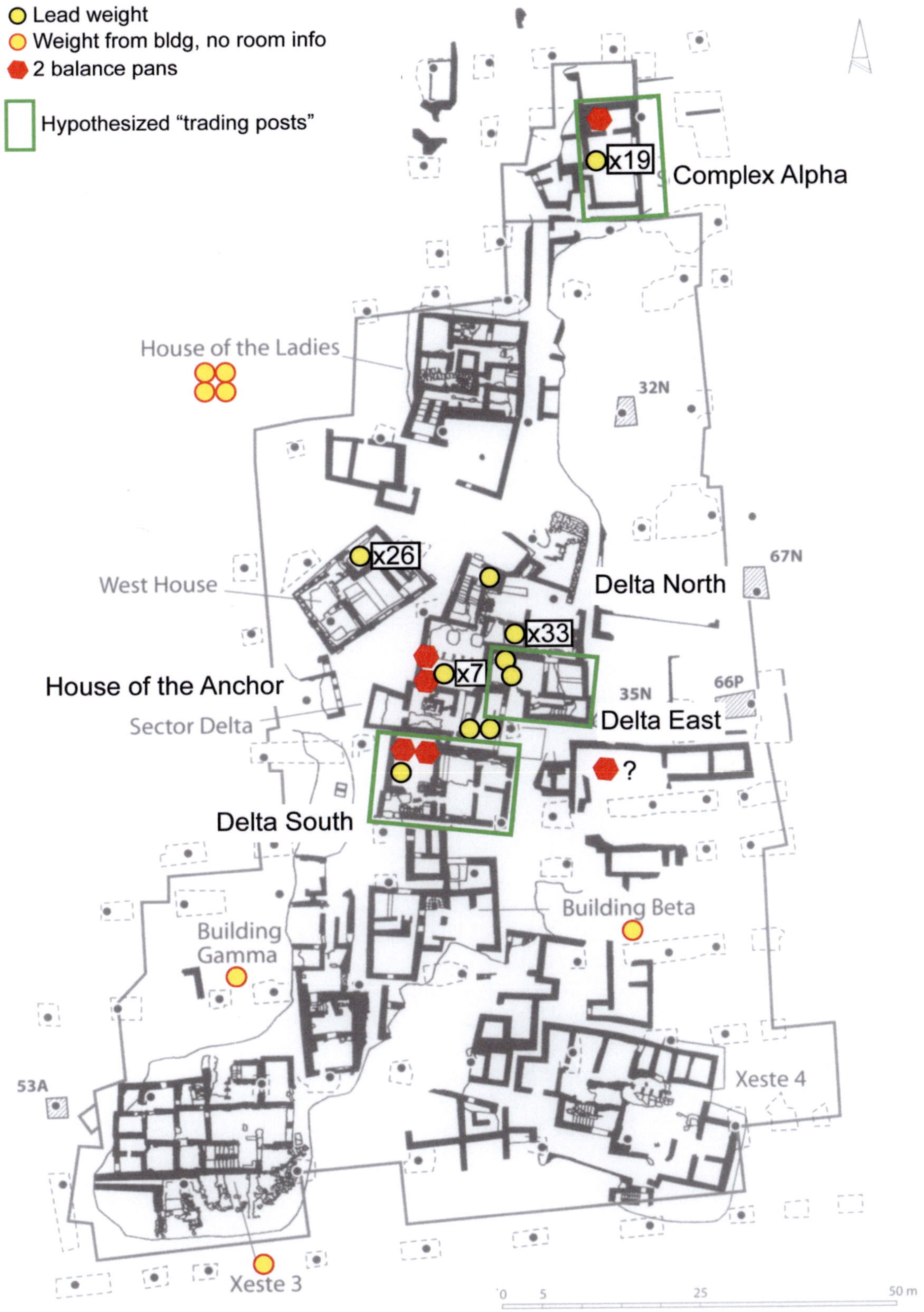
Lead weight
Weight from bldg, no room info
2 balance pans
Hypothesized "trading posts"
x19
Complex Alpha
House of the Ladies
32N
x26
West House
Delta North
67N
x33
x7
House of the Anchor
Sector Delta
35N
66P
Delta East
?
Delta South
Building Beta
Building Gamma
53A
Xeste 4
Xeste 3
0
5
25
50 m

	Ayia Irini, Kea	Akrotiri, Thera	Phylakopi, Melos	Kastri, Kythera
Potter's wheel	Earlier MBA (Period IV)	Later MBA (Phase C)	Later MBA (City II-iii)	Earlier MBA
Warp-weighted loom	Earlier MBA (Period IV)	Earliest MBA (Phase A)	MBA (City II)	Later MBA
Fireboxes	LBA I (Period VI)	LBA I	?	LBA I

Table 7.1. Overview of when some Minoanizing technologies were adopted in major Cycladic settlements and on Kythera (Georgiou 1986; Berg 2007; Kiriatzi 2010; Cutler 2012, 2021; Gorogianni, Abell, and Hilditch 2016).

One significant factor in enabling connections *between* insular southern Aegean craft-making communities of practice seems to have been the persistent small-scale mobility of craftspeople, at least some of whom were able to act as brokers. Mobile craftspeople acting as brokers may be recognized in cases of the transfer of complex craft technologies like weaving on a warp-weighted loom from one community to another. Since it is not possible to replicate such techniques on the basis of observing a finished product, these technologies are assumed to move through the mobility of trained practitioners. When mobile technologies become integrated into production practices in new locations, we can assume that mobile practitioners were able to share their knowledge with local communities of practice, i.e., they were able to act as brokers. At both Ayia Irini and Akrotiri, local potters clearly took up the wheel through interaction with potters trained in Cretan techniques (Knappett and Nikolakopoulou 2005; Gorogianni, Abell, and Hilditch 2016). Potters in these towns used the wheel to manufacture Cretan-style shapes, but they continued to use local clay recipes and firing practices for the most part (Hilditch 2019; Abell 2021).[5] These patterns suggest that the flow of information operated in both directions. Local potting communities allowed some novelties, but required all members, even those who arrived from abroad, to conform with certain traditional practices.

New technologies appeared at southern Aegean sites at different times throughout the Minoanization phenomenon, which suggests ongoing movement of craftspeople-brokers over time (Table 7.1). After the initial horizon of technological transfer, we need not assume that every mobile craftsperson came from Crete. As new technologies were adopted by Cycladic and other Aegean communities, individuals from those communities would have been as capable of sharing techniques as were those trained on Crete (Kiriatzi 2010; Cutler 2016; Kiriatzi and Broodbank 2021).

Evidence for mobile craftspeople comes also from imported craft tools, especially loomweights. Cutler (2019) argued that such objects were more likely to move with their probably female owners rather than as trade goods, because they have little inherent worth but a great deal of personal value. Imported loomweights have been recognized at many sites where people have looked for them (Table 7.2), and they were deposited in multiple periods, which strongly suggests that the movement of weavers was ongoing and multidirectional (Cutler 2012: 2019; 2021: 252–253; Knappett and Hilditch 2015b: 203–204; Vakirtzi 2019: 488; Morrison, Nodarou, and Cutler 2022: 161–162). Since craftspeople at least sometimes operated out of households in the Cyclades, mobile craftspeople would have been embedded in dense crafting and non-crafting networks similar to those of local producers. Mobile craftspeople, therefore, had significant potential to act as brokers linking geographically distant network clusters and encouraging new ways of thinking that could spread widely across settlements.

The existence of brokers among craft producers, especially mobile craft producers, is an important feature of the Minoanization phenomenon in the Cyclades. We might wonder whether people who could act as brokers in the realm of craft production might have been able to introduce and endorse new ideas in their other roles, too. The existence of mobile craftspeople acting as brokers also encourages us to consider the existence of mobile brokers in other domains too, even if it can be difficult to track them archaeologically.

Craftspeople, ritual, and regional gatherings in Cycladic constellations of practice

Knappett (2018) noted that one of the unusual features of Minoanization as a network phenomenon in the insular Aegean is that strong ties seem to have been maintained over relatively long geographical distances. Geographically dispersed networks are likely to develop structural holes, because frequent in-person interaction across long distances is difficult over time. He suggested that one reason for the strength of ties across the insular Aegean might be the spread of new religious and/or ritual practices that encouraged mutual recognition of shared values

5 Cooking pottery at Akrotiri provides one exception. Metamorphic temper began to be added to cooking pots of both Cretan and Cycladic traditions. This technique originated on Crete but experimental work suggests that it has no clear performance advantages for cooking vessels (Müller, Kilikoglou, and Day 2015).

Site	% imported	Origins, based on macroscopic analysis
Ayia Irini*	15%	Crete, Cyclades, eastern Aegean
Akrotiri*	?	Crete, Cyclades
Phylakopi	?	?
Miletus	14%	Crete, other locations
Kolonna	?	?
Serraglio	Rare	?
Mallia	?	?
Mochlos	?	Unknown, but including southeast Aegean

Table 7.2. Sites with imported MBA–early LBA loomweights (after Cutler 2012, 2016, 2021; Knappett and Hilditch 2015b; Vitale 2016; Vitale et al. 2016, p. 277; Vakirtzi 2019; Morrison, Nodarou, and Cutler 2022). *Imported spindle whorls are attested, which may also be evidence for mobile craftspeople.

across communities, lowering the costs of connections (Knappett 2018: 990; see also Kowalzig 2018).

Participating in ritual and communal events creates a different kind of community of practice, members of which come to understand the implicit and explicit rules for involvement — what is allowed and what is not, where value is created and where it is not, who can do what and when, and what the expected outcomes are meant to be. Mobile brokers with knowledge of new ritual practices and religious ideas must have existed, effectively sharing knowledge between geographically dispersed communities, parallel to the pattern discussed above with mobile craftspeople. Changing ritual practices could have created novel connections within regional networks in other ways as well, including by enabling new ritual calendars and opportunities for gathering between people who lived in geographically distant locations.

Crafting and ritual communities of practice intersected in ways that could have contributed to the formation and maintenance of wide bridges. Local craftspeople were linked with both cult spaces and communal events as producers of most of the equipment used in them, like the artifacts found in cult spaces such as the Temple at Ayia Irini or Xeste 3 at Akrotiri. Cycladic craftspeople also produced objects like rhyta and nippled jugs that may have been used in ritual or other marked drinking or pouring activities. Such vessels are found not only in possible ritual areas, but also in houses at Ayia Irini and Akrotiri; these objects link craftspeople with communities of ritual practice in domestic and non-domestic contexts.

Craft tools have also been found in cult spaces. On Kea, crucible fragments were recovered from Troullos, a hilltop shrine near Ayia Irini that is often compared with Cretan peak sanctuaries (Caskey 1971: 394). A miniature crucible, perforated pedestaled spreading bowl, perhaps for perfume manufacture, and fireboxes perhaps for aromatic processing were found in the Temple at Ayia Irini (Georgiou 1986: 16, 21–22, 35, nos. 29, 73, 88, 89, 150; Warren 1987: 143; Caskey 2009: 145). Connections between ritual deposits and craft tools have been drawn for a possible shrine in House A as well as several buildings at Akrotiri (Cummer and Schofield 1984: 39; Marinatos 1984). Craft production tools and debris have also been found at Stelida on Naxos and Ayios Yioryios on Kythera, both of which have been interpreted as peak sanctuaries (Sakellarakis 1996: 89–91; Banou 2018: 5; Carter et al. 2021; Carter 2022). The association of craft tools with cult spaces suggests that the relationships certain craftspeople had with those spaces and the activities focused on them were sometimes explicitly connected with their identities as craftspeople.[6] Although craftspeople probably participated in at least some ritual activities as part of their other social identities as well, the knowledge, values, and networks that they held as craftspeople would always have been present, entangled with the polyvalent identities carried within each individual.

The choices that were made for manufacturing objects used in ritual or communal activities may have been considered particularly significant by producers and perhaps consumers if the *process of making* and not just the final product was entangled with new ideologies. The adoption of some Minoanizing technologies, for example, may have been encouraged by their association with the production of objects used in communal and/or cult activities. As Knappett and Hilditch (2015a) suggested, the small open shapes that were the initial focus for wheel production at Cycladic sites, especially conical cups and ledge-rim bowls, were used in new group drinking or toasting activities that seem to have had ritualized components. The warp-weighted loom would have enabled the manufacture of elaborately patterned textiles like those that are common in depictions of women in ritual scenes on Crete and at Akrotiri.

As members of multicrafting households, some craftspeople could have been either involved in or witness to the production of objects used, worn, or interacted with at ritual events. In addition, as members of households, some craftspeople probably would have been involved in the manufacture and distribution of food and drink for special events, including those with ritual components. Evidence from both Ayia Irini and Akrotiri suggests that households hosted

6 The association of craft tools and ritual spaces is also attested on Crete; e.g., see Sakellarakis 1996: 89–91; Cutler 2021: 107, 157.

groups of people beyond their own household members, for example in special-purpose architectural spaces like the Minoan-style dining hall in the Northeast Bastion at Ayia Irini (Fitzsimons and Gorogianni 2017). Some houses have unusually large quantities of cooking equipment, which could have been used for industrial purposes or hosting events. Building Beta at Akrotiri contained more than 50 tripods (Georma, Nikolakopoulou, and Bitis 2017: 483). At Ayia Irini during LC I, tripods are unusually common in House EJ (nearly 30) and House A (over 60), while the LC II phase of House A contained over 300 tripods, an exceptional number when compared with other houses and other periods at the site (Cummer and Schofield 1984; Schofield 2011).[7]

Several lines of evidence suggest that non-local people may have participated in communal, potentially ritualized gatherings in Cycladic settlements. The miniature wall paintings of both Akrotiri and Ayia Irini depict voyagers arriving to coastal or island communities by boat, probably as part of a celebration (Akrotiri) and feast (Ayia Irini) (Morgan 1988, 2020; Televantou 1994). At Ayia Irini, the number of conical cups seems to far outstrip the needs of the entire local population, of 500 or fewer people (Wiener 1984, 2013; for discussion of population size, see Gorogianni 2016: 149 with references). LC I deposits in House EJ contained over 500 conical cups, for example, while those in House A contained over 800 (Cummer and Schofield 1984; Schofield 2011).[8] Large quantities of other tablewares in individual houses suggest that conical cups were not the only kind of equipment that could be deployed in communal events.

Although some exchange patterns probably resulted from the operation of specialized maritime traders in the Cyclades, it is possible that other kinds of exchange may have occurred during gatherings at settlements or ritual locations. The multicultural ceramic assemblage that typifies Ayia Irini from the earlier MBA through the era of Minoanization, for example, may have been an intentional creation meant to enable visitors to the site to participate in consumption activities that would be at least broadly recognizable to them (Abell 2021: 231, 237). Maintaining recognizability in consumption practices would have helped non-local visitors to the town to develop the trust necessary to enable trade, by creating a baseline of perceived shared values as enacted through shared consumption practices. Moreover, when Ayia Irini was refounded in the earlier MBA, one of the earliest buildings constructed was the Temple, which continued in operation throughout the LBA. Ritual events focused on the Temple also could have provided opportunities for exchange, since religious institutions can play an important role in lowering transaction costs. This evidence from Ayia Irini and analogy with other cultures suggest that some exchange in the Cyclades might have taken the form of periodic fairs or markets, perhaps tied with ritual or religious calendars (Hirth 2020: 284–287).

Communal gatherings, including events focused on cult spaces and especially those that involved nonlocal people, would have provided good opportunities to participate in exchange, identify possible marriage partners, develop new social relationships, and engage in competitive and/or collaborative behaviors at a more regional level. Investment in new locations for ritual practices, such as the newly founded peak sanctuary at Stelida on Naxos (Carter et al. 2021), possible cave shrines on Paros (Mavridis 2018: 3–4), or the hilltop of Troullos near Ayia Irini (Caskey 1971: 392–395; Davis 1984: 164–165) implies new calendars of visitation and ritual action in the islands. Events taking place in towns or in more rural locations would have provided opportunities to generate more kinds of links across geographically dispersed constellations of practice, enabling people from different areas to interact as part of ritual, crafting, and/or exchange activities. Regional gatherings create opportunities for network clusters to form that are not based on co-residence in the same geographical communities. They may play an important role in the generation and maintenance over time of strong links between groups of people who live in different locations (Kowalzig 2018; Williamson 2022).

In the Cyclades, practices associated with craft production, exchange, and ritual activities probably converged on some occasions. Those convergences would have provided key, repeated moments of connection between geographically dispersed communities. Over time, such events would have facilitated the development of the wide bridges necessary to enable the spread of ideas associated with the complex contagion of Minoanization.

Assessing mainland crafting communities and constellations of practice

The discussion above demonstrates how thinking through the lens of communities and constellations of practice can help to illuminate complex socioeconomic processes associated with horizons of material culture change. In this last section, I turn to the mainland Greece during the shaft grave era, where very different processes of Minoanization seem to have operated. The Minoanization phenomenon in the mainland during this period is intimately connected with the emergence of new forms of elite display (e.g., Wright 2004; Voutsaki 2010; Maran 2011; Galaty 2016; Davis 2022: 77–86). Processes of

7 I am grateful to the University of Cincinnati for allowing me to consult the excavation notebooks to clarify these numbers. Some tripods were not reported in the publications because they were discarded, but they are recorded in the notebooks. The number of tripod legs was divided by three to estimate the minimum number of tripods in each room.

8 As with tripods, excavation notebooks were consulted to clarify these numbers, since not all discarded conical cups were reported in the publications.

social and material culture change seem to have operated somewhat differently in different mainland regions (Voutsaki 1998; Galaty 2018; Eder and Zavadil 2021). Recent research has begun to consider more actively how members of society other than elite men would have been implicated in these processes, including through consensus-building around novel forms of displaying personal status and acquiring and demonstrating power (Voutsaki 2005; Dickinson 2021; Wright 2021).

From a crafting community of practice perspective, the networks linking mainland craft producers to each other and those in the wider Aegean, especially the Cyclades, are difficult to assess. Despite the abundance of wall painting in houses at Akrotiri and Ayia Irini, there is very limited evidence for it on the mainland during this era. The few examples appear mainly at Pylos, first in MH III and LH I and more abundantly in LH II and later (Egan 2021). The spread of wall painting technologies must be linked with the mobility of knowledgeable brokers, either from Crete or the Cyclades (Egan 2021; see also Nikolakopoulou and Knappett 2016).

The appearance of ashlar building techniques and the use of mason's marks suggests the mobility of Cretan masons, but there are only a few examples, primarily in early elite architecture in Messenia (Wright 2006: 17; Nelson 2017: 349–352). In addition, a wedge-shaped ashlar block with a double axe mason's mark was identified in a Late Roman wall at Kolonna (Niemeier 1995: 78). The block may originally have been part of the Large Building Complex (MH–LH I or early II), where Cretan imports and locally produced Minoanizing pottery, including some conical cups, were also found (Gauß, Lindblom, and Smetana 2011).

Pottery kilns have been found at several sites in central Greece, the northern Peloponnese, and Aigina dating from MH II–LH I, often connected with buildings that may be houses (Kapsali 2019 with references). In some cases, as at Plasi Marathon, kilns show evidence for technological changes that may have been aimed at increasing output or firing efficiency during the shaft grave era (Kapsali 2019: 45–50). Mainland kilns, however, cannot be readily compared with the Cyclades, as no kilns of either the MC or early LC period are known.

In the earlier MBA, the Cretan-derived potter's wheel was used at Kolonna, while the Cretan-derived vertical loom appeared at both Kolonna and Lerna (Banks 1967: 565–566; Gauß 2006: 438; Cutler 2012: 146–147; 2016: 175, 178). Wheel-using potters at Kolonna seem to have followed their own *chaîne opératoire* and were insulated from traditional local pottery-making techniques, which suggests that brokering between mobile potters with knowledge of the wheel and members of the local potting community of practice did not occur, unlike the situation in the Cyclades (Lindblom, Gauß, and Kiriatzi 2015: 228–232). Wheel technology was abandoned at Kolonna after less than a century, which demonstrates that the so-called economic efficiency of this technology was not a sufficient reason for local potters to adopt it permanently. There is no evidence for widespread adoption of the vertical loom at either Kolonna or Lerna, with only a handful of loomweights reported from few chronological phases (Carington-Smith 1992: 688; Gauß 2006: 438; Cutler 2012; 2016: 178). It is unclear whether or not brokering between mobile and local weavers occurred in these cases, or if the loomweights might instead reflect only the presence of mobile weavers. Elsewhere, Cretan-style loomweights are extremely rare in mainland contexts before LH II–IIIA1; even in that period, loomweights are rare compared with the situation on Crete or the Cyclades during the Neopalatial era (Carington-Smith 1992: 687–689; Cutler 2016: 178; 2021: 241–243). The lack of uptake of Cretan weaving technologies over the long-term in the mainland suggests that effective brokering between Cycladic/Cretan and mainland weaving communities of practice was very limited.

Of Cycladic settlements, Ayia Irini seems to have had the strongest connections with the mainland during the MBA and earlier LBA, based on ceramic exchange and production patterns. When the Cretan-derived potter's wheel was adopted at Ayia Irini in the earlier MBA, one of the largest classes of imported pottery was wheel-formed Gray Minyan ware from central Greece (Overbeck 1982; Crego 2007). Yet Keian potters did not adapt the mainland version of the potter's wheel and, moreover, did not use the Cretan-derived potter's wheel to make any mainland-style shapes until decades after the technology was initially introduced (Gorogianni, Abell, and Hilditch 2016). This pattern suggests a lack of permeability between mainland and Keian potting communities of practice. During the later MBA and early LBA, ceramic connections between Ayia Irini and the mainland are stylistic rather than technological, involving local production of shapes or decorative motifs popular on the mainland, like goblets with hollow stems or framed bands in red and black paint. These stylistic choices, however, could have been produced on the basis of familiarity with finished objects rather than through communication between potters. In LC II and III, the so-called Mycenaeanization phenomenon in the Cyclades seems to have operated primarily at the level of new consumption rather than production patterns, much different from the era of Minoanization (Abell and Hilditch 2016). These examples suggest that the difficulty of brokering between Keian and mainland potting communities was long-lived and perhaps structural.

On the mainland itself, major technological innovations attested among potting communities during the EBA and MBA do not seem to have spread quickly between them, as already noted for the Cretan-derived wheel at Kolonna. On Crete, when the potter's wheel was adopted in MM IB, it rapidly spread between communities on the island, and a convergence around particular wheel-forming practices for small vessels occurred already in MM II (Jeffra 2013). This pattern suggests regular communication and probably brokering between Cretan potting communities, despite the existence of clear regionalism in ceramic morphology and decorative style. On the mainland, however, the spread of the Anatolian-derived wheel, starting in the mid-EBA, seems to have been slower and to have involved less communication between potting communities, given a lack of rapid convergence around particular wheel-forming techniques and continued prevalence of hand-building in some locations even well into the Late Bronze Age (Choleva 2018: 51–65; 2020; Choleva, Jung, and Kardamaki 2020: 265–268). Likewise, wheel-forming techniques and effective reducing firing atmospheres used to make "true" Gray Minyan in some MBA potting communities in central Greece were imitated in such a way in other communities that it is clear the same practices were not in use, presumably because technical knowledge of the manufacturing methods was not widely shared between groups (Sarri 2010: 605; Pavúk 2012).

The production of Minoanizing Lustrous Decorated pottery by communities on Kythera and perhaps also in the Peloponnese starting early in the MBA must have been enabled through mobility of and/or intense communication with potters who were trained in Cretan communities of practice, given the close technical adherence to Cretan practices of clay processing and forming, the use of lustrous paint, and the creation of Minoanizing shapes and decorative styles (Kiriatzi 2010, with references; Lindblom, Gauß, and Kiriatzi 2015: 225–228). Such pottery seems to have been produced in very few locations during the MBA, and the technical practices associated with it were not taken up by mainland potting communities more broadly until the LBA. Technical differences exist between Laconia and the Argolid in the process of change from "Minoanizing" Lustrous Decorated to "Mycenaean" LH I Lustrous Painted ware, which have been attributed primarily to different geographical proximities to producers of Lustrous Decorated pottery on Kythera (Zerner 2008: 185; Lindblom, Gauß, and Kiriatzi 2015: 232–234; see also Rutter 2015). Convergences around some of the same technical features in LH I (e.g., fine pastes, potter's wheel, lustrous paints) suggests that mobility and brokering of technological knowledge between mainland potting communities occurred in LH I, although additional information about the *chaînes opératoires* associated with different production centers is necessary. New bichrome and polychrome wares were produced in Boeotia, possibly Euboea, Aegina, and the Corinthia during the shaft grave era and demonstrate an interest in generally similar styles of pottery, but differences in the *chaînes opératoires* associated with these wares suggest a lack of brokering between potting communities (Lindblom and Rutter 2021). In contrast, elemental analysis has shown that several production centers in Boeotia and possibly Euboea were producing polychrome painted pots that are technically very similar to each other (Lindblom and Rutter 2021: 555–556). Such technical similarities suggest that brokering occurred within these local networks, where close geographical proximity could have enabled the development of wide bridges and/or strong ties between communities. The stylistic details of the ceramic fashions that were adopted by mainland communities in LH I, in Lustrous Painted and bichrome and polychrome wares, suggest that this process of ceramic change was enabled primarily through interaction with communities of practice in Kythera and Aegina, rather than more broadly through the Cyclades or Crete (Dickinson 2014; Lindblom, Gauß, and Kiriatzi 2015: 233–234; Lindblom and Rutter 2021; Rutter and Lindblom 2022). Overall, crafting communities of practice on the mainland appear to have been less closely connected to each other and the wider Aegean over time than Cycladic ones were.

Crafting communities and Minoanization processes in a small(er) world?

The lack of evidence for brokering between Cycladic and mainland crafting communities in the MBA and early LBA is not entirely a matter of geographical location, given the close physical proximity of Kea to Attica and southern Euboea, which is certainly comparable to the positions of Kythera or Aegina to other mainland communities. The maritime coastscape connecting the northwestern Cyclades, including Kea, with Attica and southern Euboea could have been traversed relatively frequently by people living in this region, in different kinds of vessels including small, relatively simple boats (for the socioeconomic significance of accessible short-distance travel within local coastscapes, see Tartaron 2013). Some regular movement as part of exogamous marriage practices is probable given the small size of settlements in the region. Close relationships between Kea, Attica, and southern Euboea are attested in earlier periods, especially the Final Neolithic and EBA (e.g., Wilson 1987; Nazou 2017). During the MBA and early LBA, ceramic imports attest to the movement of goods between the Cyclades, including Kea, Attica, and Euboea (Gorogianni, Abell, and Hilditch 2020, with references; Philippa-Touchais and Balitsari 2020; Papadimitriou 2020a, 2020b; Tankosic and Mathioudaki 2011; Abell 2021: 176–177, 184–189, 193–197, 200–205, 213–215, 218–226; Kalogeropoulos 2021). Metals compatible with a Lavrion source were worked on Kea as well as in Attica and have a wide distribution in the Cyclades and broader Aegean (Gale, Stos-Gale, and Davis 1984; Stos-Gale and Macdonald 1991; Gale and Stos-Gale 2008; Georgakopoulou et al. 2020). Exchange networks clearly linked people living in this micro-region, and indeed, some of the first inhabitants of Ayia Irini when

Figure 7.7. Metallurgical objects and terracotta tubes from Ayia Irini. a: Schist mould (K1.411, Cummer and Schofield 1984, no. 558; Room A.17, mixed Period VI and VII deposit). b: Crucible (K.340, Cummer and Schofield 1984, no. 856; Room A.18, Period VI destruction deposit). c: Crucible showing built feet that create a rocker groove (K.4271, Schofield 2011, no. 1526; Room EJ.8, Period VI deposit). d. Terracotta tube (K1.616, Cummer and Schofield 1984, no. 252; Room A.10, Period VII fill). e. Terracotta tube (K4.278, Davis 1986, no. Y-11; beneath Room N.12, Period V). f. Tuyere fragment with blackening in one area (K7.136, Area J unpublished, Period VI + MBA). Photos by Thomas Loughlin.

the site was refounded in the earlier MBA are likely to have arrived from the mainland and/or Aegina (Overbeck and Crego 2008; Crego 2010; Abell 2014). Nevertheless, evidence for interaction between craft producers or participation in the Minoanization phenomenon as manifested on Kea and elsewhere in the Cyclades is limited in Attica and southern Euboea during the later MBA and early LBA, especially before LH IIB–IIIA1.

In the later MBA and earlier LBA, there are ceramic connections especially between Ayia Irini and Thorikos, where both mainland-style and some Minoanizing types of pottery have been found (although it is not clear whether all were imports or locally made); close parallels for several published vessels from Thorikos, such as Minoanizing pithoid jars, exist on Kea (Papadimitriou 2020a: 462–468; 2020b: 188). The only place where Minoanizing discoid loomweights exist in Attica or Euboea, to my knowledge, is Brauron, where two were found, unstratified. The smaller of these, on display in the Brauron Museum, comes from an area that suggests a date during the shaft grave era (Kalogeropoulos forthcoming).[9]

Some connections between Keian and Attic metallurgical communities of practice exist, although there are differences as well. At Thorikos, litharge fragments were found in a house, suggesting that there, as at Ayia Irini, metallurgical activities were linked to households (Servais 1967: 20–24). Bowl-shaped litharge suggests a particular process of silver cupellation that is first attested in EBA Attica and Akrotiraki on Siphnos, with a few examples also from Limenaria on Thasos (Georgakopoulou et al. 2020: 188–190, fig. 4). Bowl-shaped litharge also appears in contexts dating to the era of Minoanization in both Attica and Kea (Servais 1967: 22–23, fig. 16; Abell and Georgakopoulou forthcoming). This technique was presumably introduced to Kea from Attica.

The use of relatively soft schist for moulds is attested at both Brauron and on Kea, although not all moulds on Kea are made of the same materials (Figure 7.7a; Efstratiou 2004: 25, pl. 17α). Most well-preserved crucibles from Ayia Irini have rocker grooves and several also have bridge-spouts, comparable to crucibles known from Crete (Figures 7.7b, 7.7c; Evely, Hein, and Nodarou 2012). To my knowledge, no such crucibles have been identified in MH or early LH Attica, although there are only two published crucibles from the region. One from the MH period was found in the Athenian Agora (Immerwahr 1971: 91, no. 376, pls. 27, 71). It preserves no evidence for slag and so a function as a crucible must remain tentative, although the cracking of the clay at the surfaces is similar to the appearance of many crucible surfaces on Kea. In form, however, it differs from Keian crucibles, having a thick, flat base rather than a rocker groove and no bridge spout. The shape of a crucible from the Athenian Acropolis, from a disturbed context but perhaps dating to the MH or early LH periods, is not entirely clear (Venieri 2020). The published photograph does not appear to show a rocker groove or a spout, although the object is also not fully preserved (Venieri 2020: 425, fig. 9a). A possible tuyere fragment from a MH deposit on the Athenian Acropolis (which the author [Venieri 2020: 425, fig. 9b] describes as an ακροφύσιο, but which Papadimitriou and Cosmopoulos [2020: 375] seem to call a mould) is typologically unlike anything in the Keian metallurgical assemblage. At Thorikos, a clay tube has been interpreted as a bellows fragment, although it bears no traces of burning (Papadimitriou 2020b: 175–176). Papadimitriou compared the shape and fabric of this object to clay tubes from Ayia Irini (Cummer and Schofield 1984: 39, 60–61, nos. 252, 272, pl. 45; Georgiou 1986: 46: 50, no. 186, pl. 22; see also Davis 1986: 52, no. Y-11). Many of the tubes at Ayia Irini (Figures 7.7d, 7.7e) are also unburned, and they may also have a larger diameter and sometimes exterior ridges, which differs from tuyeres that preserve traces of burning (Figure 7.7f). Nevertheless, an industrial function

9 I thank Kostas Kalogeropoulos for confirming that these two loomweights are Minoanizing, with one preserving a groove at the top, and for providing information about their contexts.

of some kind, including a metallurgical one, is possible for the unburnt tubes. Despite some differences, Keian and Attic metallurgical communities seem to have been connected into a constellation of practice in ways unlike Keian and most mainland (including Attic) potting, wall painting, and weaving communities, presumably enabled in large part by geographical proximity.

The evidence for a lack of knowledge brokering between most Cycladic and mainland crafting communities of practice cannot be ascribed solely to a lack of exchange links or geographical distance. Rather, structural holes seem to have separated most Cycladic and mainland crafting communities of practice in ways that brokers were not able to cross effectively.

Connections between other kinds of mainland and Cycladic communities of practice

Knowledge and innovation moved between mainland and Cycladic networks in the realm of funerary culture. Similar elite tombs were constructed in this era at both Thorikos and Ayia Irini (Papadimitriou 2010: 250–252, with references). Built chamber tombs from late MC to LC I Agriokastro on Antiparos also have mainland parallels (Papadopoulou 2018). One of the Agriokastro tombs contained a marble pommel and miniature dagger (Papadopoulou 2018: 184), which suggests a connection between at least this Cycladic community and new ideas around "warrior burials" that appeared on the mainland during this era. If this funerary evidence is, in fact, indicative of brokering or consensus-building around new ideas across mainland and Cycladic communities, then it appears to have operated primarily through networks connecting elite or elite-striving individuals. An increase in imagery connected with warfare or hunting in the Cyclades, Crete, and the mainland similarly might reflect growing commonalities in ideas around elite (male) identity markers and/or the popularization of stories with such themes across regions (see papers in Kvapil and Shelton 2023).

As discussed above, new ritual equipment, locations, and practices were an important component of Minoanization processes in the Cyclades, which probably helped to create and maintain wide bridges between communities. These novelties, however, find only broad parallels on the mainland. Cretan-style ritual or potentially religious objects like Minoanizing plaster tables of offering and sealstones with ritual scenes have been found in mainland contexts, especially (although not exclusively) in elite tombs (Davis 2022: 79–81). Moreover, the symbolisms and ideologies associated with these objects on Crete do not seem to have been adapted in mainland contexts, most notably by appearing primarily in funerary rather than domestic or cult spaces (Voutsaki 1997: 46–47; Maran 2011: 288–289; Davis 2022: 84; for a contrasting view, see Kalogeropoulos 2015). Evidence for investment in non-funerary locations for participating in Minoanizing communal and/or cult practices is very limited, in contrast to the situation in the insular Aegean. Kynortion (Apollo Maleatas) in the Argolid is one possible exception, which has been compared with Minoanizing peak sanctuaries (Briault 2007). In Attica, Brauron also might be an exception. Kalogeropoulos (2019: 231–233, 240) has suggested that the acropolis was a ritual center, given a lack of evidence for domestic architecture and local pottery wares, plus the presence of some probable Minoanizing cult objects, including a plaster table of offerings and a kernos. Yet, no mainland site has produced evidence to suggest widespread adoption of communal drinking or toasting events that incorporated abundant conical cups, for which there is so much evidence on Crete and much of the insular Aegean. The adoption of Minoanizing and Cycladicizing pottery styles and especially tableware typologies suggest that one avenue by which people other than the elites buried in well-appointed tombs would have encountered new kinds of objects during this era was through consumption practices, perhaps especially around formalized mortuary, ritual, and/or feasting events (Wright 2004; Lindblom 2007; Lindblom and Rutter 2021; Rutter and Lindblom 2022; Dickinson 2021). Yet, observation of and interaction with those new objects may have been mediated by elites as an outgrowth of already established patterns of reciprocity within elite-sponsored, potentially diacritical drinking events (Pullen 2017: 62–64 with references).

Finally, the lack of uptake of tools for exchange in the form of Minoanizing balance weights, which appear only rarely on the mainland in tombs at Vapheio and Thorikos, as well as, possibly, at Mycenae and Malthi (Petruso 1978: 134–157), suggests that brokering across economic communities of practice was also apparently difficult beyond a few probably elite individuals. The deposition of weights in a few wealthy tombs rather than in houses also suggests that participation in new Minoanizing exchange practices was more limited on the mainland than in the Cyclades. The data are of course skewed, with very few funerary contexts known in the Minoanizing Cyclades and few domestic contexts in the mainland of the shaft grave era. Nevertheless, the lack of standardized weights so far even from domestic contexts at Thorikos, which was connected with Ayia Irini in other ways, may suggest that different patterns of participation in exchange by mainland *vs.* Cycladic communities is not entirely a mirage created by the nature of the archaeological record.

From a network perspective, early Mycenaean elites seem to have acted as entrepreneurial brokers who crossed weak links between their local geographic communities and the wider world of the Aegean (as argued e.g., by Wright 2021, with references). The operation of this model seems relatively straightforward in inland parts of the Peloponnese, but we would expect entrepreneurial brokers to face difficulty when they cannot maintain their unusual or exclusive access to the broader network. In coastal eastern Attica, small boats and simple technologies should enabled many people to access maritime travel within the coastscape, with the possibility of participating directly in exchange and interaction networks with Minoanizing communities, especially Ayia Irini. Indeed, strong enough links must have existed between Ayia Irini, Brauron, and Thorikos that there was some movement of craft and other knowledge between them. This sharing of knowledge was presumably enabled by brokering and the fact that geographical proximity allowed the development of wide bridges within the micro-region. Nevertheless, the spread of information and innovation through those links was highly selective at each Attic site, even though those same wide bridges could have increased awareness around many new ideas and practices that were circulating just off the coast. In Attica, differences in Minoanization processes cannot be the result solely of a lack of wide bridges and concomitant lack of information around new ideas circulating in the insular Aegean. Rather, the power that different kinds of brokers had to effectively endorse the adoption of new ideas as part of the complex contagion of Minoanization seems to have been more limited than in the Cyclades, perhaps because brokers were fewer, less well-placed, or regarded with greater suspicion within local networks.

Some concluding thoughts

Network structure is shaped by cultural, ethnic, political, and economic realities. Differences in how Minoanization operated in the islands compared with the mainland certainly may reflect cultural differences that led to more frequent rejection of Minoanizing innovations by mainland communities than Cycladic ones. But reframing Minoanization as a network phenomenon also encourages us to think about the changes of the shaft grave era in a different way. As older colonial models have been replaced by new perspectives on the insular and coastal southern Aegean, it has become clear that this era was marked by an economic boom in which more people and communities participated, not just Cretan palaces (Abell 2023). New exchange practices developed, based on widespread distribution patterns of exchanged objects and standardized weights, as well as the development of new social and/or religious institutions that could have lowered transaction costs and enabled more frequent exchange within and between communities. Yet, in the shaft grave era, mainland communities did not participate in this emerging new system as early or as actively as we might expect, given the potential economic advantages available to, especially, residents of coastal communities like Thorikos or Brauron.

Variation in processes of Minoanization seems to have been driven, at least in part, by distinct network configurations that either prevented the development of wide bridges between insular and mainland communities of practice or discouraged the spread of many of the innovations associated with the phenomenon between them. Mainland crafting communities seem to have been linked with other crafting communities, especially geographically distant ones, primarily by weak ties. Moreover, crafting communities seem to have been separated by structural holes that were difficult for brokers to cross, whether those other crafting communities were located on the mainland or not. Differences in the spatial and social organization of craft production in the Cyclades *vs.* the mainland, with respect to who was involved and how closely different kinds of crafts were connected with multiple households and settlements, may have inhibited effective communication between communities of practice. Such differences would affect the number and kinds of connections craftspeople-brokers had within networks, thus impacting their ability to endorse innovations (Manzo et al. 2018). A comparative lack of mobility among craftspeople, ritual specialists, and other kinds of individuals who had the potential to act as brokers may have played into this pattern on the mainland. Differences in the operation of communal events are also probably significant. If Pullen's (2017) arguments about the long-lived social significance of hospitality and reciprocity at mainland feasting events are correct, mobile craftspeople and/or ritual specialists may not have been able to play socially significant roles depending on the norms enforced by the host(s). Exchange practices that were allowable at communal events on the mainland may also have been more circumscribed than what I have hypothesized took place in at least at some cases in the insular Aegean.

As more evidence appears for exchange networks linking mainland settlements to each other and the wider Aegean during the shaft grave era, it is more possible to examine if and how members of society other than elite men were implicated in the major social changes of this era. Analyzing how networks connected different kinds of social agents, like those linked through participation in communities and constellations of practice, allows more detailed evaluation of how new information and ideas moved (and did not); what kinds of social groups were involved in promoting buy-in to similar forms of material culture, practice, and ideology; and how these processes operated as complex, multifaceted phenomena.

Acknowledgements

I thank Daniel Pullen for the invitation to participate in the Langford conference, the FSU Department of Classics for hosting us, and the other participants in the conference for stimulating discussion. This research was supported by the University of Michigan, American Council on Learned Societies, Loeb Classical Library Foundation, and the Kress Fellowship from the American School of Classical Studies at Athens (ASCSA). Sylvie Dumont and the ASCSA enabled me to examine published Bronze Age pottery from the Athenian Agora. Emily Egan, Shannon Lafayette Hogue, and Margarita Nazou provided valuable help with references. I am grateful to the University of Cincinnati Department of Classics, Jack Davis, Dimitris Athanasoulis, Maria Koutsoumbou, and the KA' Ephoriea for allowing me to study materials from Jack Caskey's excavations on Kea. Carol Hershenson, Eleftheria Morfoniou, and the staff of the Kea Archaeological Museum provided access and a great deal of logistical support. Finally, Myrto Georgakopoulou collaborated with me on the study of the metal and metallurgical assemblage from Caskey's excavations before her untimely death in 2022. Her insights, generosity, and kindness are deeply missed.

Bibliography

Abell, N., 2014. Migration, Mobility and Craftspeople in the Aegean Bronze Age: A Case Study from Ayia Irini on the Island of Kea. *World Archaeology* 46: 551–568.

Abell, N., 2020. Rethinking Household-Based Production at Ayia Irini, Kea: An Examination of Technology and Organization in a Bronze Age Community of Practice. *American Journal of Archaeology* 124: 381–416.

Abell, N., 2021. *Ayia Irini: Area B*. Keos XII. Atlanta: Lockwood Press.

Abell, N., 2023. The Myth of the Minoan Thalassocracy: A Review of Evidence for Maritime Interaction, Power, and Violence in the Insular and Coastal Aegean. In *Brill's Companion to Warfare in the Bronze Age Aegean*, edited by L. A. Kvapil and K. Shelton, 353–417. Leiden and Boston: Brill.

Abell, N., forthcoming. A Community of Practice Perspective on Craft Production and Culture Change in the Bronze Age Cyclades. In *Identities in Antiquity*, edited by V. Manolopoulou, J. E. Skinner, and C. Tsouparopoulou. London and New York: Routledge.

Abell, N., and M. Georgakopoulou, forthcoming. Metals and Metallurgy at Bronze Age Ayia Irini, Kea: A Preliminary Report. In *3rd International Cycladological Conference: The Cyclades through Time, Space-People, Syros*. Επετηρίς Εταιρείας Κυκλαδικών Μελετών.

Abell, N., and E. Gorogianni, 2019. The Past in Practice: Craft Producers and Material Culture Change at Ayia Irini, Kea. In *MNHMH/MNEME: Past and Memory in the Aegean Bronze Age. Proceedings of the 17th International Aegean Conference, University of Udine, Department of Humanities and Cultural Heritage, Ca' Foscari University of Venice, Department of Humanities, 17-21 April 2018*, edited by E. Borgna, I. Caloi, F. M. Carinci, and R. Laffineur, 655–658. Aegaeum 43. Liège and Leuven: Peeters.

Abell, N., and J. Hilditch, 2016. Adoption and Adaptation in Pottery Production Practices: Investigating Cycladic Community Interactions through the Ceramic Record of the Second Millennium BC. In *Beyond Thalassocracies: Understanding Processes of Minoanisation and Mycenaeanisation in the Aegean*, edited by E. Gorogianni, P. Pavúk, and L. Girella, 155–171. Oxford: Oxbow Books.

Alberti, M. E., 1995. Ayia Irini: les poids de balance dans leur contexte. *Quaderni ticinesi di numismatica e antichità classiche* 24: 9–37.

Amin, A., and J. Roberts, 2008. Knowing in Action: Beyond Communities of Practice. *Research Policy* 37.2: 353–369.

Banks, E. C., 1967. The Early and Middle Helladic Small Objects from Lerna. Ph.D. dissertation, University of Cincinnati.

Banou, E., 2018. Minoans Overseas: The Peak Sanctuary at Ayios Yeorgios sto Vouno, Kythera. In *Πεπραγμένα ΙΒ΄ Διεθνούς Κρητολογικού Συνεδρίου, Ηράκλειο, 21–25 Σεπτεμβρίου 2016*, edited by C. Mitzotaki and L. Tzedaki-Apostolaki, viewed December 19, 2023, https://12iccs.proceedings.gr/en/proceedings/category/38/32/343.

Berg, I., 2007. *Negotiating Island Identities: The Active Use of Pottery in the Middle and Late Bronze Age Cyclades*. Gorgias Dissertations 31. Piscataway, NJ: Gorgias Press.

Bikaki, A. H., 1984. *Ayia Irini: The Potters' Marks*. Keos IV. Mainz on Rhine: Philipp von Zabern.

Bond, R. M., C. J. Fariss, J. J. Jones, A. D. I. Kramer, C. Marlow, J. E. Settle, and J. H. Fowler, 2012. A 61-Million-Person Experiment in Social Influence and Political Mobilization. *Nature* 489: 295–298.

Boulotis, C., 2008. Οι πινακίδες Γραμμικής Α από το Ακρωτήρι (THE 7–12): όψεις της οικονομικής ζωής του οικισμού. In *Ακρωτήρι Θήρας: Τριάντα χρόνια έρευνες 1967–1997*, edited by C. G. Doumas, 67–94. Βιβλιοθήκη της εν Αθήναις Αρχαιολογικής Εταιρείας 257. Athens: Η Εν Αθήνας Αρχαιολογική Εταιρεία.

Bowser, B. J., and J. Q. Patton, 2008. Learning and Transmission of Pottery Style: Women's Life Histories and Communities of Practice in the Ecuadorian Amazon. In *Cultural Transmission and Material Culture: Breaking Down Boundaries*, edited by M. T. Stark, B. J. Bowser, and L. Horne, 105–129. Tucson: University of Arizona Press.

Briault, C., 2007. Making Mountains out of Molehills in the Bronze Age Aegean: Visibility, Ritual Kits, and the Idea of a Peak Sanctuary. *World Archaeology* 39: 122–141.

Brogan, T. M., 2006. Tipping the Scales: Evidence for Weight Measurement from the Wider Neopalatial

Community at Mochlos. In *Weights in Context: Bronze Age Weighing Systems of the Eastern Mediterranean Chronology, Typology, Material and Archaeological Contexts*, edited by M. E. Alberti, E. Ascalone, and L. Peyronel, 265–292. Rome: Istituto Italiano di Numismatica.

Broodbank, C., 2004. Minoanisation. *Proceedings of the Cambridge Philological Society* 50: 46–91.

Burt, R. S., 1992. *Structural Holes: The Social Structure of Competition*. Cambridge, Mass.: Harvard University Press.

Burt, R. S., 2005. *Brokerage and Closure: An Introduction to Social Capital*. Oxford: Oxford University Press.

Carington-Smith, J., 1992. Spinning and Weaving Equipment. In *Excavations at Nichoria in Southwest Greece*, vol. 2: *The Bronze Age Occupation*, edited by W. A. McDonald and N. C. Wilkie, 674–711. Minneapolis: University of Minnesota Press.

Carter, T., 2022. The Minoan-Type Peak Sanctuary at Stelida, Naxos: Preliminary Insights from the 2019/21 Seasons, lecture at the INSTAP Study Center East Crete, March 2, 2022, https://vimeo.com/783608796, viewed December 20, 2023.

Carter, T., K. Mallinson, V. Mastrogiannopoulou, D. A. Contreras, C. Diffey, C. Lopez, M. N. Pareja, G. Tsartsidou, and D. Athanasoulis, 2021. A New Minoan-Type Peak Sanctuary on Stelida, Naxos. *Journal of Greek Archaeology* 6: 60–99.

Caskey, J. L., 1971. Investigations in Keos: Part I: Excavations and Explorations, 1966–1970. *Hesperia* 40: 359–396.

Caskey, M. E., 2009. Dionysos in the Temple at Ayia Irini, Kea. In *ΔΩΡΟΝ: Τιμητικός τόμος για τον καθηγητή Σπύρο Ιακωβίδη*, edited by D. Danielidou, 143–163. Athens: Ακαδημία Αθηνών, Κέντρον Ερεύνης της Αρχαιότητος.

Centola, D., 2018. *How Behavior Spreads: The Science of Complex Contagions*. Princeton and Oxford: Princeton University Press.

Centola, D., and M. Macy, 2007. Complex Contagions and the Weakness of Long Ties. *American Journal of Sociology* 113: 702–734.

Choleva, M., 2018. Craft Behaviours during a Period of Transformations: The Introduction and Adoption of the Potter's Wheel in Central Greece during the Early Bronze Age. In *Technology in Crisis: Technological Changes in Ceramic Production during Periods of Trouble* edited by I. Caloi and C. Langohr, 19–74. Aegis 16. Louvain-la-Neuve: Presses universitaires de Louvain.

Choleva, M., 2020. Travelling with the Potter's Wheel in the Early Bronze Age Aegean. *Annual of the British School at Athens* 115: 59–104.

Choleva, M, R. Jung, and E. Kardamaki, 2020. Working on the Potter's Wheel: Technological Insights into Mycenaean Pottery Production. *Ägypten und Levante* 30: 219–282.

Collar, A., 2022. Strong Ties, Social Networks, and the Diffusion of New Ideas. Who Do You Trust? In *Networks and the Spread of Ideas in the Past: Strong Ties, Innovation and Knowledge Exchange*, edited by A. Collar, 1–27. London: Routledge.

Crego, D. M., 2007. Exchange in Period IV at Ayia Irini on Kea. In *Middle Helladic Pottery and Synchronisms. Proceedings of the International Workshop Held at Salzburg, October 31st – November 2nd, 2004*, edited by F. Felten, W. Gauß, and R. Smetana, 333–338. Österreichische Akademie der Wissenschaften Denkschriften der Gesamtakademie 42, Ägina - Kolonna Forschungen und Ergebnisse 1. Vienna: Verlag der Österreichischen Akademie der Wissenschaften.

Crego, D. M., 2010. Ayia Irini IV: A Distribution Center for the Middle Helladic World? In *Mesohelladika: La Grèce continentale au Bronze Moyen*, edited by A. Philippa-Touchais, G. Touchais, S. Voutsaki, and J. C. Wright, 841–845. Bulletin de correspondance hellénique, Supplément 52. Athens: École française d'Athènes.

Cummer, W. W., and E. Schofield, 1984. *Ayia Irini: House A*. Keos III. Mainz on Rhine: Philipp von Zabern.

Cutler, J., 2012. Ariadne's Thread: The Adoption of Cretan Weaving Technology in the Wider Southern Aegean in the Mid-Second Millennium BC. In *Kosmos: Jewellery, Adornment and Textiles in the Aegean Bronze Age. Proceedings of the 13th International Aegean Conference/13e Rencontre égéenne internationale, University of Copenhagen, Danish National Research Foundation's Centre for Textile Research, 21–26 April 2010*, edited by M.-L. Nosch and R. Laffineur, 145–154. Aegaeum 33. Leuven and Liège: Peeters.

Cutler, J., 2016. Fashioning Identity: Weaving Technology, Dress and Cultural Change in the Middle and Late Bronze Age Southern Aegean. In *Beyond Thalassocracies: Understanding Processes of Minoanisation and Mycenaeanisation in the Aegean*, edited by E. Gorogianni, P. Pavúk, and L. Girella, 172–185. Oxford: Oxbow Books.

Cutler, J., 2019. Arachne's Web: Women, Weaving and Networks of Knowledge in the Bronze Age Southern Aegean. *Annual of the British School at Athens* 114: 79–92.

Cutler, J., 2021. *Crafting Minoanisation: Textiles, Crafts Production and Social Dynamics in the Bronze Age Southern Aegean*. Ancient Textiles Series 33. Oxford and Philadelphia: Oxbow Books.

Davis, J. L., 1984. Cultural Innovation and the Minoan Thalassocracy at Ayia Irini, Keos. In *The Minoan Thalassocracy: Myth and Reality. Proceedings of the Third International Symposium at the Swedish Institute in Athens, 31 May–5 June 1982*, edited by R. Hägg and N. Marinatos, 159–166. Skrifter Utgivna av Svenska Institutet i Athen 4°, XXXII. Stockholm: Paul Åströms Förlag.

Davis, J. L., 1986. *Ayia Irini: Period V*. Keos V. Mainz on Rhine: Philipp von Zabern.

Davis, J. L., 2022. *A Greek State in Formation: The Origins of Civilization in Mycenaean Pylos*. Sather Classical Lectures 75. Oakland: University of California Press.

Dickinson, O. T. P. K., 2014. Late Helladic I Revisited: The Kytheran Connection. In *KE-RA-ME-JA: Studies Presented to Cynthia W. Shelmerdine*, edited by D. Nakassis, J. Gulizio, and S. A. James, 3–15. Philadelphia: INSTAP Academic Press.

Dickinson, O. T. P. K., 2021. The Significance of Developments in Peloponnesian Pottery over the Middle to Late Helladic Transition. In *(Social) Place and Space in Early Mycenaean Greece: International Discussions in Mycenaean Archaeology, October 5–8, 2016, Athens*, edited by B. Eder and M. Zavadil, 539–548. Mykenische Studien 35. Vienna: Austrian Academy of Sciences.

Doumas, C. C., ed., 2007. *Ακρωτήρι Θήρας. Δυτική Οικία. Τράπεζες, Λίθινα, Μετάλλινα, Ποικίλα*. Βιβλιοθήκη της εν Αθήναις Αρχαιολογικής Εταιρείας 246. Athens: Η εν Αθήναις Αρχαιολογική Εταιρεία.

Eder, B., and M. Zavadil, eds., 2021. *(Social) Place and Space in Early Mycenaean Greece: International Discussions in Mycenaean Archaeology, October 5–8, 2016, Athens*. Mykenische Studien 35. Vienna: Austrian Academy of Sciences.

Egan, E. C., 2021. Early Mycenaean Wall Paintings from the Palace of Nestor. In *(Social) Place and Space in Early Mycenaean Greece: International Discussions in Mycenaean Archaeology, October 5–8, 2016, Athens*, edited by B. Eder and M. Zavadil, 33–58. Mykenische Studien 35. Vienna: Austrian Academy of Sciences.

Efstratiou, K., 2004. Ανασκαφή Βραυρώνος. *Πρακτικά της εν Αθήναις Αρχαιολογικής Εταιρείας* 156 (2001): 21–25.

Evely, D., A. Hein, and E. Nodarou, 2012. Crucibles from Palaikastro, East Crete: Insights into Metallurgical Technology in the Aegean Late Bronze Age. *Journal of Archaeological Science* 39.6: 1821–1836.

Firth, R. J., 2016. The Clay Cylinders from Room Δ17, Akrotiri, Thera: Are They the Remains of Tally-Sticks? *Minos* 39: 401–405.

Fitzsimons, R. D., and E. Gorogianni, 2017. Dining on the Fringe? A Possible Minoan-Style Banquet Hall at Ayia Irini, Kea and the Minoanization of the Aegean Islands. In *Minoan Architecture and Urbanism: New Perspectives on an Ancient Built Environment*, edited by Q. Letesson and C. Knappett, 334–360. Oxford: Oxford University Press.

Galaty, M. L., 2016. The Mycenaeanisation Process. In *Beyond Thalassocracies: Understanding Processes of Minoanisation and Mycenaeanisation in the Aegean*, edited by E.Gorogianni, P. Pavúk, and L. Girella, 207–218. Oxford: Oxbow Books.

Galaty, M. L., 2018. Mycenaean Glocalism: Greek Political Economies and International Trade. In *Trade and Civilisation: Economic Networks and Cultural Ties, from Prehistory to the Early Modern Era*, edited by K. Kristiansen, T. Lindkvist, and J. Myrdal, 143–171. Cambridge: Cambridge University Press.

Gale, N. H., and Z. A. Stos-Gale, 2008. Changing Patterns in Prehistoric Cycladic Metallurgy. In *Horizon. Ορίζων: A Colloquium on the Prehistory of the Cyclades*, edited by N. Brodie, J. Doole, G. Gavalas, and C. Renfrew, 387–408. Cambridge: McDonald Institute for Archaeological Research.

Gale, N. H., Z. A. Stos-Gale, and J. L. Davis, 1984. The Provenance of Lead Used at Ayia Irini, Keos. *Hesperia* 53: 389–406.

Gauß, W., 2006. Minos auf Ägina — Beobachtungen zu den Beziehungen Äginas zu Kreta. In *Timelines: Studies in Honour of Manfred Bietak*, vol. 2, edited by E. Czerny, I. Hein, H. Hunger, D. Melman, and A. Schwab, 437–448. Orientalia Lovaniensia Analecta 149. Leuven: Uitgeverij Peeters en Departement Oosterse Studies.

Gauß, W., M. Lindblom, and R. Smetana. 2011. The Middle Helladic Large Building Complex at Kolonna. A Preliminary View. In *Our Cups Are Full: Pottery and Society in the Aegean Bronze Age. Papers Presented to Jeremy B. Rutter on the Occasion of his 65th Birthday*, edited by W. Gauß, M. Lindblom, R. A. K. Smith, and J. C. Wright, 76–87. Oxford: Archaeopress.

Georgakopoulou, M., K. Douni, M. Ginalas, O. Kakavogianni, and I. Bassiakos, 2020. Recent Finds from Final Neolithic and Early Bronze Age Silver Production Sites in Southeastern Attica. In *Athens and Attica in Prehistory: Proceedings of the International Conference, Athens, 27–31 May 2015*, edited by N. Papadimitriou, J. C. Wright, S. Fachard, N. Polychronakou-Sgouritsa, and E. Andrikou, 185–192. Oxford: Archaeopress.

Georgiou, H. S., 1986. *Ayia Irini: Specialized Domestic and Industrial Pottery*. Keos VI. Mainz on Rhine: Philipp von Zabern.

Georma, F., I. Nikolakopoulou, and I. Bitis, 2017. Το Κτήριο Βήτα στο Ακρωτήρι Θήρας. Τοιχογραφίες, κεραμική και αρχιτεκτονική. In *Το Αρχαιολογικό Έργο στα Νησιά του Αιγαίου: Διεθνές Επιστημονικό Συνέδριο, Ρόδος, 27 Νοεμβρίου–1 Δεκεμβρίου 2013*, vol. Β΄, edited by P. Triantafyllidis, 471–486. Mitilene: Υπουργείο Πολιτισμού και Αθλητισμού, Γενική Γραμματεία Αιγαίου και Νησιωτικής Πολιτικής.

Gorogianni, E., 2016. Keian, Kei-noanised, Kei-cenaeanised? Interregional Contact and Identity in Ayia Irini, Kea. In *Beyond Thalassocracies: Understanding Processes of Minoanisation and Mycenaeanisation in the Aegean*, edited by E. Gorogianni, P. Pavúk, and L. Girella, 136–154. Oxford: Oxbow Books.

Gorogianni, E., N. Abell, and J. Hilditch, 2016. Reconsidering Technological Transmission: The Introduction of the Potter's Wheel at Ayia Irini, Kea, Greece. *American Journal of Archaeology* 120: 195–220.

Gorogianni, E., N. Abell, and J. Hilditch, 2020. Kea and Attica: Revisiting Connections in the Middle and Late Bronze Age. In *Athens and Attica in Prehistory: Proceedings of the International Conference, Athens, 27–31 May 2015*, edited by N. Papadimitriou, J. C. Wright, S. Fachard, N. Polychronakou-Sgouritsa, and E. Andrikou, 627–636. Oxford: Archaeopress.

Granovetter, M., 1973. The Strength of Weak Ties. *American Journal of Sociology* 78: 1360–1380.

Granovetter, M., 1983. The Strength of Weak Ties: A Network Theory Revisited. *Sociological Theory* 1: 201–233.

Granovetter, M., 2005. The Impact of Social Structure on Economic Outcomes. *Journal of Economic Perspectives* 19: 33–50.

Hilditch, J., 2019. Phases B–C. In *Akrotiri, Thera: Middle Bronze Age Pottery and Stratigraphy*, vol. 2, by I. Nikolakopoulou, 377–470. The Archaeological Society at Athens Library 318. Athens: The Archaeological Society at Athens.

Hirth, K. G., 1978. Interregional Trade and the Formation of Prehistoric Gateway Communities. *American Antiquity* 43: 35–45.

Hirth, K. G., 2020. *The Organization of Ancient Economies: A Global Perspective*. Cambridge: Cambridge University Press.

Immerwahr, S. A., 1971. *The Neolithic and Bronze Ages*. The Athenian Agora: Results of Excavations Conducted by the American School of Classical Studies at Athens 13. Princeton: American School of Classical Studies.

Iorio, A., 2023. Brokers in Disguise: The Joint Effect of Actual Brokerage and Socially Perceived Brokerage on Network Advantage. *Administrative Science Quarterly* 67: 769–820.

Isbell, W. H., 2000. What We Should Be Studying: The "Imagined Community" and the "Natural Community." In *The Archaeology of Communities: A New World Perspective*, edited by M. A. Canuto and J. Yaeger, 243–266. London and New York: Routledge.

Jeffra, C., 2013. A Re-Examination of Early Wheel Potting in Crete. *Annual of the British School at Athens* 108: 31–49.

Kalogeropoulos, K., 2015. Perceptions of Minoan Religious Symbolism in Mainland Greece during Late Helladic I: Towards a Model. In *Ein Minoer im Exil: Festschrift für Wolf-Dietrich Niemeier*, edited by D. Panagiotopoulos, I. Kaiser, and O. Kouka, 163–185. Universitätsforschungen zur prähistorischen Archäologie 270. Bonn: Verlag Dr. Rudolf Habelt GmbH.

Kalogeropoulos, K., 2019. Reflections on Pilgrimage at the Acropolis of Brauron during the Late Helladic Period. In *Ascending and Descending the Acropolis: Movement in Athenian Religion*, edited by W. Friese, S. Handberg, and T. M. Kristensen, 221–252. Monographs of the Danish Institute at Athens 23. Aarhus: Aarhus Universitetsforlag.

Kalogeropoulos, K., 2021. Cultural Variation in Mycenaean Attica. A Mesoregional Approach. In *Sidelights on Greek Antiquity: Archaeological and Epigraphical Essays in Honour of Vasileios Petrakos*, edited by K. Kalogeropoulos, D. Vassilikou, and M. Tiverios, 227–298, Berlin and Boston: Walter de Gruyter GmbH.

Kalogeropoulos, K., forthcoming. *Η προϊστορική ακρόπολη της Βραυρώνας (The Prehistoric Acropolis of Brauron).*

Kapsali, P., 2019. Two Middle Bronze Age Pottery Kilns at Plasi, Marathon. *Athens University Review of Archaeology* 2: 19–63.

Karnava, A., 2008. Written and Stamped Records in the Late Bronze Age Cyclades: The Sea Journeys of an Administration. In *Horizon. Ορίζων: A Colloquium on the Prehistory of the Cyclades*, edited by N. Brodie, J. Doole, G. Gavalas, and C. Renfrew, 377–386. Cambridge: McDonald Institute for Archaeological Research.

Karnava, A., 2018. *Seals, Sealings and Seal Impressions from Akrotiri in Thera.* Corpus der Minoischen und Mykenischen Siegel 10. Heidelberg: Heidelberg University Library.

Karnava, A., and I. Nikolakopoulou, 2020. More Oikoi at Akrotiri, Thera. Physical and Social Landscape in the New North/North-West Neighbourhood of the LB I Settlement. In *Oikos: Archaeological Approaches to House Societies in Aegean Prehistory*, edited by M. Relaki and J. Driessen, 237–255. Aegis 19. Louvain: Presses universitaires de Louvain.

Kiriatzi, E., 2010. "Minoanising" Pottery Traditions in the Southwest Aegean during the Middle Bronze Age: Understanding the Social Context of Technological and Consumption Practice. In *Mesohelladika: La Grèce Continentale au Bronze Moyen*, edited by A. Philippa-Touchais, G. Touchais, S. Voutsaki, and J. C. Wright, 693–699. Bulletin de correspondance hellénique, Supplément 52. Athens: École française d'Athènes.

Kiriatzi, E., and C. Broodbank, 2021. Social Places and Spaces on and beyond Kythera during the Second Palace Period: Exploring the Island's Landscape and Connectivity. In *(Social) Place and Space in Early Mycenaean Greece: International Discussions in*

Mycenaean Archaeology, October 5–8, 2016, Athens, edited by B. Eder and M. Zavadil, 365–382. Mykenische Studien 35. Vienna: Austrian Academy of Sciences.

Knappett, C., 2018. From Network Connectivity to Human Mobility: Models for Minoanization. *Journal of Archaeological Method and Theory* 25: 974–995.

Knappett, C., and J. Hilditch, 2015a. Colonial Cups? The Minoan Plain Handleless Cup as Iconic Inter-Regional Object. In *Pots, Palaces and Politics: The Evolution and Socio-Political Significance of Plain Ware Traditions in the 2nd Millennium BC Near East and East Mediterranean*, edited by C. Glatz, 91–113. Walnut Creek: Left Coast Press.

Knappett, C., and J. Hilditch, 2015b. Milesian Imports and Exchange Networks in the Southern Aegean. In *Ein Minoer im Exil: Festschrift für Wolf-Dietrich Niemeier*, edited by D. Panagiotopoulos, I. Kaiser, and O. Kouka, 199–209. Universitätsforschungen zur prähistorischen Archäologie 270. Bonn: Verlag Dr. Rudolf Habelt GmbH.

Knappett, C., and I. Nikolakopoulou, 2005. Exchange and Affiliation Networks in the MBA Southern Aegean: Crete, Akrotiri, and Miletus. In *Emporia: Aegeans in the Central and Eastern Mediterranean. Proceedings of the 10th International Aegean Conference/10e Rencontre égéenne internationale, Athens, Italian School of Archaeology, 14–18 April 2004*, edited by R. Laffineur and E. Greco, 175–184. Liège: Université de Liège, Histoire de l'art et archéologie de la Grèce antique; Austin: University of Texas at Austin, Program in Aegean Scripts and Prehistory.

Knappett, C., and I. Nikolakopoulou, 2008. Colonialism without Colonies? A Bronze Age Case Study from Akrotiri, Thera. *Hesperia* 77: 1–42.

Knodell, A. R., 2021. *Societies in Transition in Early Greece: An Archaeological History*. Berkeley: University of California Press.

Kowalzig, B., 2018. Cults, Cabotage, and Connectivity: Experimenting with Religious and Economic Networks in the Greco-Roman Mediterranean. In *Maritime Networks in the Ancient Mediterranean World*, edited by J. Leidwanger and C. Knappett, 93–131. Cambridge: Cambridge University Press.

Kvapil, L. A., and K. Shelton, eds., 2023. *Brill's Companion to Warfare in the Bronze Age Aegean*: Leiden and Boston: Brill.

Lave, J., and E. Wenger, 1991. *Situated Learning: Legitimate Peripheral Participation*. Cambridge: Cambridge University Press.

Lindblom, M., 2007. Early Mycenaean Mortuary Meals at Lerna VI with Special Emphasis on their Aeginetan Components. In *Middle Helladic Pottery and Synchronisms: Proceedings of the International Workshop Held at Salzburg, October 31st – November 2nd, 2004*, edited by F. Felten, W. Gauß, and R. Smetana, 115–135. Österreichische Akademie der Wissenschaften Denkschriften der Gesamtakademie 42, Ägina - Kolonna Forschungen und Ergebnisse 1. Vienna: Verlag der Österreichischen Akademie der Wissenschaften.

Lindblom, M., W. Gauß, and E. Kiriatzi, 2015. Some Reflections on Ceramic Technology Transfer at Bronze Age Kastri on Kythera, Kolonna on Aegina, and Lerna in the Argolid. In *The Transmission of Technical Knowledge in the Production of Ancient Mediterranean Pottery: Proceedings of the International Conference at the Austrian Archaeological Institute at Athens 23rd–25th November 2012*, edited by W. Gauß, G. Klebinder-Gauß, and C. von Rüden, 225–237. Österreichisches Archäologisches Institut Sonderschriften Band 54. Vienna: Österreichisches Archäologisches Institut.

Lindblom, M., and J. B. Rutter, 2021. An Explosion of Polychromy: Establishing Localised Ceramic Identities at the Dawn of the Mycenaean Era. In *(Social) Place and Space in Early Mycenaean Greece: International Discussions in Mycenaean Archaeology, October 5–8, 2016, Athens*, edited by B. Eder and M. Zavadil, 549–569. Mykenische Studien 35. Vienna: Austrian Academy of Sciences.

Malkin, I., 2011. *A Small Greek World: Networks in the Ancient Mediterranean*. Oxford: Oxford University Press.

Manzo, G., S. Gabbriellini, V. Roux, and F. N. M'Mbogori, 2018. Complex Contagions and the Diffusion of Innovations: Evidence from a Small-N Study. *Journal of Archaeological Method and Theory* 25: 1109–1154.

Maran, J., 2011. Lost in Translation: The Emergence of Mycenaean Culture as a Phenomenon of Glocalization. In *Interweaving Worlds: Systemic Interactions in Eurasia, 7th to 1st Millennia BC*, edited by T. C. Wilkinson, S. Sherratt, and J. Bennet, 282–293. Oxford: Oxbow Books.

Marinatos, N., 1984. Minoan Threskeiocracy on Thera. In *The Minoan Thalassocracy: Myth and Reality. Proceedings of the Third International Symposium at the Swedish Institute in Athens, 31 May–5 June 1982*, edited by R. Hägg and N. Marinatos, 167–178. Skrifter Utgivna av Svenska Institutet i Athen, 4°, XXXII. Stockholm: Paul Åströms Förlag.

Marthari, M., 2019. Raos and Akrotiri: Memory and Identity in LC I/LM IA Thera as Reflected in Settlement Patterns and Ceramic Production. In *MNHMH/MNEME: Past and Memory in the Aegean Bronze Age. Proceedings of the 17th International Aegean Conference, University of Udine, Department of Humanities and Cultural Heritage, Ca' Foscari University of Venice, Department of Humanities, 17-21 April 2018*, edited by E. Borgna,

I. Caloi, F. M. Carinci, and R. Laffineur, 135–142. Aegaeum 43. Liège and Leuven: Peeters.

Mavridis, F., 2018. Cave Sanctuaries in the Bronze Age Cyclades? New Evidence from the Island of Paros, Greece. *Antiquity* 92.363, e4: 1–5.

Michailidou, A., 1995. Investigating Metal Technology in a Settlement. The Case of Akrotiri at Thera. *Αρχαιογνωσία* 8 (1993–94): 165–180.

Michailidou, A., 2006. Stone Balance Weights? The Evidence from Akrotiri on Thera. In *Weights in Context: Bronze Age Weighing Systems of the Eastern Mediterranean. Chronology, Typology, Material and Archaeological Contexts*, edited by M. E. Alberti, E. Ascalone, and L. Peyronel, 233–263. Rome: Istituto Italiano di Numismatica.

Michailidou, A., 2008a. Μετάλλινα εργαλεία και σκεύη στα κτήρια του οικισμού. "Οικοσκευή" και κοινωνικές σχέσεις παραγωγής. In *Ακρωτήρι Θήρας: Τριάντα χρόνια έρευνας 1967–1997*, edited by C. Doumas, 17–33. Βιβλιοθήκη της εν Αθήναις Αρχαιολογικής Εταιρείας 257. Athens: Η εν Αθήναις Αρχαιολογική Εταιρεία.

Michailidou, A., 2008b. *Weight and Value in Pre-Coinage Societies*. Vol. 2*: Sidelights on Measurement from the Aegean and the Orient*. Μελετήματα 61. Athens: National Hellenic Research Foundation and Research Centre for Greek and Roman Antiquity.

Michelaki, K., G. V. Braun, and R. G. V. Hancock, 2015. Local Clay Sources as Histories of Human-Landscape Interactions: A Ceramic Taskscape Perspective. *Journal of Archaeological Method and Theory* 22: 783–827.

Momigliano, N., 2009. Minoans at Iasos? In *The Minoans in the Central, Eastern and Northern Aegean, New Evidence: Acts of a Minoan Seminar 22–23 January 2005 in collaboration with the Danish Institute at Athens and the German Archaeological Institute at Athens*, edited by C. F. Macdonald, E. Hallager, and W.-D. Niemeier, 121–140. Monographs of the Danish Institute at Athens 8. Athens: Danish Institute at Athens.

Morgan, L., 1988. *The Miniature Wall Paintings of Thera: A Study in Aegean Culture and Iconography*. New York: Cambridge University Press.

Morgan, L., 2020. *Wall Paintings and Social Context: The Northeast Bastion at Ayia Irini*. Keos XI. Philadelphia: INSTAP Academic Press.

Morrison, J., E. Nodarou, and J. Cutler, 2022. Clay Vessels and Loomweights: Tracing Southeast Aegean Connections at Neopalatial Mochlos. In *Kleronomia: Legacy and Inheritance. Studies on the Aegean Bronze Age in Honor of Jeffrey S. Soles*, edited by J. M. A. Murphy and J. E. Morrison, 155–171. Prehistory Monographs 61. Philadelphia: INSTAP Academic Press.

Muller, E., and R. Peres, 2019. The Effect of Social Networks Structure on Innovation Performance: A Review and Directions for Research. *International Journal of Research in Marketing* 36: 3–19.

Müller, N. S., V. Kilikoglou, and P. M. Day, 2015. Home-Made Recipes: Tradition and Innovation in Bronze Age Cooking Pots from Akrotiri, Thera. In *Ceramics, Cuisine and Culture: The Archaeology and Science of Kitchen Pottery in the Ancient Mediterranean World*, edited by M. Spataro and A. Villing, 37–48. Oxford: Oxbow Books.

Nazou, M., 2017. Euboean Connections with Attica and Kea: A View from Final Neolithic and Late Early Bronze Age II Pottery. In *An Island between Two Worlds: The Archaeology of Euboea from Prehistoric to Byzantine Times*, edited by Ž. Tankosić, F. Mavridis, and M. Kosma, 111–120. Papers and Monographs from the Norwegian Institute at Athens 6. Athens: Norwegian Institute at Athens.

Nelson, M., 2017. The Architecture of the Palace of Nestor. In *The Minnesota Pylos Project 1990–98*, edited by F. A. Cooper and D. Fortenberry, 283–418. British Archaeological Reports International Series 2856. Oxford: BAR Publishing.

Niemeier, W.-D., 1995. Aegina - First Aegean 'State' Outside of Crete? In *Politeia: Society and State in the Aegean Bronze Age. Proceedings of the 5th International Aegean Conference. 5e Rencontre égéenne internationale, University of Heidelberg, Archäologisches Institut, 10-13 April 1994*, edited by R. Laffineur and W.-D. Niemeier, 73–80. Aegaeum 12. Liège: Université de Liège, Histoire de l'art et archéologie de la Grèce antique; Austin: University of Texas at Austin, Program in Aegean Scripts and Prehistory.

Nikolakopoulou, I., 2019. *Akrotiri, Thera: Middle Bronze Age Pottery and Stratigraphy*. 2 vols. The Archaeological Society at Athens Library 318. Athens: The Archaeological Society at Athens.

Nikolakopoulou, I., and C. Knappett, 2016. Mobilities in the Neopalatial Southern Aegean: The Case of Minoanisation. In *Human Mobility and Technological Transfer in the Prehistoric Mediterranean*, edited by E. Kiriatzi and C. Knappett, 102–115. British School at Athens, Studies in Greek Antiquity. Cambridge: Cambridge University Press.

Overbeck, J. C., 1982. The Hub of Commerce: Keos and Middle Helladic Greece. In *Trade and Travel in the Cyclades during the Bronze Age*, edited by P. P. Betancourt, 38–49. Temple University Aegean Symposium 7. Philadelphia: Temple University.

Overbeck, J. C., and D. M. Crego, 2008. The Commercial Foundation and Development of Ayia Irini IV (Kea). In *Horizon. Ορίζων: A Colloquium on the Prehistory of the*

Cyclades, edited by N. Brodie, J. Doole, G. Gavalas, and C. Renfrew, 305–309. Cambridge: McDonald Institute for Archaeological Research.

Papadimitriou, N., 2010. Attica in the Middle Helladic Period. In *Mesohelladika: La Grèce Continentale au Bronze Moyen*, edited by A. Philippa-Touchais, G. Touchais, S. Voutsaki, and J. C. Wright, 243–257. Bulletin de correspondance hellénique, Supplément 52. Athens: École française d'Athènes.

Papadimitriou, N., 2020a. Ceramic Material from Valerios Stais' Excavation at the Prehistoric Settlement of Thorikos: A Summary. In *Athens and Attica in Prehistory: Proceedings of the International Conference, Athens, 27–31 May 2015*, edited by N. Papadimitriou, J. C. Wright, S. Fachard, N. Polychronakou-Sgouritsa, and E. Andrikou, 457–470. Oxford: Archaeopress Publishing Ltd.

Papadimitriou, N., 2020b. Προϊστορική εγκατάσταση στον Θορικό Αττικής: Η συμβολή των ανασκαφών του Βαλέριου Στάη (1888, 1890, 1893). *Αρχαιολογική Εφημερίς* 159: 149–254.

Papadimitriou, N., and M. B. Cosmopoulos, 2020. The Political Geography of Attica in the Middle and the Late Bronze Age. In *Athens and Attica in Prehistory: Proceedings of the International Conference, Athens, 27–31 May 2015*, edited by N. Papadimitriou, J. C. Wright, S. Fachard, N. Polychronakou-Sgouritsa, and E. Andrikou, 373–385. Oxford: Archaeopress Publishing Ltd.

Papadopoulou, Z., 2018. Middle Cycladic Pictorial Pottery from Antiparos. The Case of the 'Nippled Jug with Birds.' In *Χρωστήρες. Paintbrushes: Wall-Painting and Vase-Painting of the Second Millennium BC in Dialogue*, edited by A. G. Vlachopoulos, 182–193. Athens: University of Ioannina and Hellenic Ministry of Culture and Sports – Archaeological Receipts Fund.

Pavúk, P., 2012. Zur Entwicklung, Gliederung und Verbreitung der Grauminyschen Ware in Griechenland. In *Mittel- und Spätbronzezeitliche Keramik Griechenlands*, by P. Pavúk and B. Horejs, 13–39. Vienna: Verlag der Österreichischen Akademie der Wissenschaften.

Peeples, M. A., and W. R. Haas, Jr., 2013. Brokerage and Social Capital in the Prehispanic U.S. Southwest. *American Anthropologist* 115: 232–247.

Petruso, K. M., 1978. Systems of Weight in the Bronze Age Aegean. Ph.D. dissertation, Indiana University.

Petruso, K. M., 1992. *Ayia Irini: The Balance Weights*. Keos VIII. Mainz on Rhine: Philipp von Zabern.

Philippa-Touchais, A., and A. Balitsari, 2020. Attica in the Middle: Middle Helladic Pottery Traditions and the Formation of Cultural Identity. In *Athens and Attica in Prehistory: Proceedings of the International Conference, Athens, 27–31 May 2015*, edited by N. Papadimitriou, J. C. Wright, S. Fachard, N. Polychronakou-Sgouritsa, and E. Andrikou, 387–398. Oxford: Archaeopress Publishing Ltd.

Pullen, D. J. 2017. Reciprocity and Exchange Relationships: Exploring the Dynamics of Bronze Age Social Structures through Feasting and Hospitality. In *Social Change in Aegean Prehistory*, edited by C. Wiersma and S. Voutsaki, 49–68. Oxford: Oxbow Books.

Rivera, M. T., S. B. Soderstrom, and B. Uzzi, 2010. Dynamics of Dyads in Social Networks: Assortative, Relational, and Proximity Mechanisms. *Annual Review of Sociology* 36: 91–115.

Roddick, A. P., and A. B. Stahl, eds., 2016. *Knowledge in Motion: Constellations of Learning Across Time and Place*. Tucson: University of Arizona Press.

Roux, V., B. Bril, and A. Karasik, 2018. Weak Ties and Expertise: Crossing Technological Boundaries. *Journal of Archaeological Method and Theory* 25: 1024–1050.

Rutter, J. B., 2015. Ceramic Technology in Rapid Transition. The Evidence from Settlement Deposits of the Shaft Grave Era at Tsoungiza (Corinthia). In *The Transmission of Technical Knowledge in the Production of Ancient Mediterranean Pottery: Proceedings of the International Conference at the Austrian Archaeological Institute at Athens 23rd–25th November 2012*, edited by W. Gauß, G. Klebinder-Gauß, and C. von Rüden, 207–223. Österreichisches Archäologisches Institut Sonderschriften Band 54. Vienna: Österreichisches Archäologisches Institut.

Rutter, J. B., and M. Lindblom, 2022. A Shape for Few Seasons: The Rapid Appearance and Disappearance of the Mainland Greek Panel Cup. *Hesperia* 91: 571–648.

Sakellarakis, Y. 1996. Minoan Religious Influence in the Aegean: The Case of Kythera. *Annual of the British School at Athens* 91: 81–99.

Sarri, K., 2010. Minyan and Minyanizing Pottery: Myth and Reality about a Middle Helladic Type Fossil. In *Mesohelladika: La Grèce Continentale au Bronze Moyen*, edited by A. Philippa-Touchais, G. Touchais, S. Voutsaki, and J. C. Wright, 603–613. Bulletin de correspondance hellénique, Supplément 52. Athens: École française d'Athènes.

Schofield, E., 1990. Evidence for Household Industries on Thera and Kea. In *Thera and the Aegean World III*, vol. 1: *Archaeology*, edited by D. A. Hardy, C. G. Doumas, J. A. Sakellarakis, and P. M. Warren, 201–211. London: The Thera Foundation.

Schofield, E., 2011. *Ayia Irini: The Western Sector*. Keos X. Mainz on Rhine: Philipp von Zabern.

Servais, J., 1967. Les fouilles sur le haut du Velatouri. In *Thorikos 1965: Rapport préliminaire sur la troisième campagne de fouilles*, edited by H. F. Mussche, J. Bingen, J. Servais, J. de Geyter, T. Hackens, P. Spitaels, and A. Gautier, 9–30. Thorikos III. Brussels: Comité des fouilles Belges en Grèce.

Soda, G., A. Usai, and A. Zaheer, 2004. Network Memory: The Influence of Past and Current Networks on Performance. *Academy of Management Journal* 47: 893–906.

Sotiropoulou, S., V. Perdikatsis, C. Apostolaki, A. G. Karydas, A. Devetzi, and K. Birtacha, 2010. Lead Pigments and Related Tools at Akrotiri, Thera, Greece. *Journal of Archaeological Science* 37: 1830–1840.

Stos-Gale, Z. A., and C. F. Macdonald, 1991. Sources of Metals and Trade in the Bronze Age Aegean. In *Bronze Age Trade in the Mediterranean*, edited by N. H. Gale, 249–288. Studies in Mediterranean Archaeology 90. Göteborg: Paul Åströms Förlag.

Tankosić, Ž., and I. Mathioudaki, 2011. The Finds from the Prehistoric Site of Ayios Nikolaos Mylon, Southern Euboea, Greece. *Annual of the British School at Athens* 106: 99–140.

Tartaron, T. F., 2013. *Maritime Networks in the Mycenaean World*. Cambridge: Cambridge University Press.

Televantou, C. A., 1994. *Ακρωτήρι Θήρας: Οι Τοιχογραφίες της Δυτικής Οικίας*. Βιβλιοθήκη της εν Αθήναις Αρχαιολογικής Εταιρείας 143. Athens: Η εν Αθήναις Αρχαιολογική Εταιρεία.

Tzachili, I., 1990. All Important yet Elusive: Looking for Evidence of Cloth-Making at Akrotiri. In *Thera and the Aegean World III*, vol. 1: *Archaeology*, edited by D. A. Hardy, C. G. Doumas, J. A. Sakellarakis, and P. M. Warren, 380–389. London: The Thera Foundation.

Tzachili, I., 2002–2003. The Clay Cylinders from Akrotiri, Thera. A Non Literate Alternative Way of Accounting. *Minos* 37–38: 7–76.

Vakirtzi, S., 2019. The Loomweights. In *Akrotiri, Thera: Middle Bronze Age Pottery and Stratigraphy*, vol. 1, by I. Nikolakopoulou, 485–491. The Archaeological Society at Athens Library 318. Athens: The Archaeological Society at Athens.

Varien, M. D., and J. M. Potter, 2008. The Social Production of Communities: Structure, Agency, and Identity. In *The Social Construction of Communities: Agency, Structure, and Identity in the Prehispanic Southwest*, edited by M. D. Varien and J. M. Potter, 1–18. Lanham: Rowman and Littlefield Publishers.

Venieri, I., 2020. "Rethink Middle Helladic Athens": Ανασύνθεση της μεσοελλαδικής κατοίκησης γύρω από την Ακρόπολη. In *Athens and Attica in Prehistory: Proceedings of the International Conference, Athens, 27–31 May 2015*, edited by N. Papadimitriou, J. C. Wright, S. Fachard, N. Polychronakou-Sgouritsa, and E. Andrikou, 417–426. Oxford: Archaeopress Publishing Ltd.

Vitale, S., 2016. Cultural Entanglements on Kos during the Late Bronze Age: A Comparative Analysis of "Minoanisation" and "Mycenaeanisation" at the "Serraglio", Eleona, and Langada. In *Beyond Thalassocracies: Understanding Processes of Minoanisation and Mycenaeanisation in the Aegean*, edited by E. Gorogianni, P. Pavúk, and L. Girella, 75–93. Oxford: Oxbow Books.

Vitale, S., I. Moutafi, E. Vika, I. Iliopoulos, J. E. Morrison, T. Marketou, K.-S. Passa, K. Moulo, E. Ballan, C. McNamee, C. Mantello, and N. G. Blackwell, 2016. The Serraglio, Eleona, and Langada Archaeological Project (SELAP): Report on the Results of the 2011 to 2015 Study Seasons. *Annuario della Scuola Archeologica di Atene e delle Missioni Italiane in Oriente* 94, series 3.16: 225–285.

Voutsaki, S., 1997. The Creation of Value and Prestige in the Aegean Late Bronze Age. *Journal of European Archaeology* 5.2: 34–52.

Voutsaki, S., 1998. Mortuary Evidence, Symbolic Meanings and Social Change: A Comparison between Messenia and the Argolid in the Mycenaean Period. In *Cemetery and Society in the Aegean Bronze Age*, edited by K. Branigan, 41–58. Sheffield Studies in Aegean Archaeology 1. Sheffield: Sheffield Academic Press.

Voutsaki, S., 2005. Age and Gender in the Southern Greek Mainland, 2000–1500 BC. *Ethnographisch-Archäologische Zeitung* 46: 339–363.

Voutsaki, S., 2010. From the Kinship Economy to the Palatial Economy: The Argolid in the Second Millennium BC. In *Political Economies in the Aegean Bronze Age: Papers from the Langford Conference, Florida State University, Tallahassee, 22–24 February 2007*, edited by D. J. Pullen, 86–111. Oxford: Oxbow Books.

Warren, P. M., 1987. Review of *Ayia Irini: Specialized Domestic and Industrial Pottery*. Keos VI, by H. S. Georgiou. *The Antiquaries Journal* 67: 142–143.

Wenger, E., 1998. *Communities of Practice: Learning, Meaning, and Identity*. Cambridge: Cambridge University Press.

Wiener, M. H., 1984. Crete and the Cyclades in LM I: The Tale of the Conical Cups. In *The Minoan Thalassocracy: Myth and Reality. Proceedings of the Third International Symposium at the Swedish Institute in Athens, 31 May–5 June 1982*, edited by R. Hägg and N. Marinatos, 17–26. Skrifter Utgivna av Svenska Institutet i Athen 4°, 32. Stockholm: Paul Åströms Förlag.

Wiener, M. H., 2013. Realities of Power: The Minoan Thalassocracy in Historical Perspective. In *Amilla: The Quest for Excellence*, edited by R. B. Koehl, 149–173. Prehistory Monographs 43. Philadelphia: INSTAP Academic Press.

Williamson, C. G., 2022. Ritual Ties, "Portable Communities," and the Transmission of Common Knowledge through Festival Networks in the Hellenistic World. In *Networks and the Spread of Ideas in the Past: Strong Ties, Innovation and Knowledge Exchange*, edited by A. Collar, 139–173. London: Routledge.

Wilson, D. E., 1987. Kea and East Attike in Early Bronze II: Beyond Pottery Typology. In *ΣΥΝΕΙΣΦΟΡΑ McGill: Papers in Greek Archaeology and History in Memory of Colin D. Gordon*, edited by J. M. Fossey, 35–49. Amsterdam: J. C. Gieben.

Wolf, E. R., 1956. Aspects of Group Relations in a Complex Society, Mexico. *American Anthropologist* 58: 1065–1078.

Wright, J. C., 2004. A Survey of Evidence for Feasting in Mycenaean Society. In *The Mycenaean Feast*, 133–178. Hesperia Special Issue 73.2. Princeton NJ: American School of Classical Studies at Athens.

Wright, J. C., 2006. The Formation of the Mycenaean Palace. In *Ancient Greece: From the Mycenaean Palaces to the Age of Homer*, edited by S. Deger-Jalkotzy and I. S. Lemos, 7–52. Edinburgh Leventis Studies 3. Edinburgh: Edinburgh University Press.

Wright, J. C., 2021. Mobility and Agency in the Context of Space and Place in Early Mycenaean Greece. In *(Social) Place and Space in Early Mycenaean Greece: International Discussions in Mycenaean Archaeology, October 5–8, 2016, Athens*, edited by B. Eder and M. Zavadil, 33–58. Mykenische Studien 35. Vienna: Austrian Academy of Sciences.

Xiao, Z., and A. S. Tsui, 2007. When Brokers May Not Work: The Cultural Contingency of Social Capital in Chinese High-Tech Firms. *Administrative Science Quarterly* 52: 1–31.

Zerner, C. W., 2008. The Middle Helladic Pottery, with the Middle Helladic Wares from Late Helladic Deposits and the Potters' Marks. In *Ayios Stephanos: Excavations at a Bronze Age and Medieval Settlement in Southern Laconia*, edited by W. D. Taylour and R. Janko, 177–298. British School at Athens Supplementary Volume 44. London: British School at Athens.

Petsas House:

Potters, The Workshop, and Ceramic Production in Mycenae's Society and Economy

Kim Shelton

Abstract

Petsas House, the 14thc BCE building complex in Mycenae's settlement, may serve as a case study for the socio-economic role/s of potters and pottery production, in this case on an almost industrial scale, within a domestic context during the palatial period. Pottery, its production, distribution, and consumption can give information on its role in the economy. Evidence from the workshop context may also provide evidence for the social roles of potters and the pottery they produced.

Since the 2007 Langford conference and its publication in 2010, Petsas House has been interpreted as an independent or semi-independent workshop producing pottery for a wide range of contexts, markets, and consumers — one of whom was certainly the palace. The depth and breadth of socio-economic entanglement that this indicates is examined along with the potential scales of social units involved in ceramic production. At this level of evidence, individuals can be identified while beyond the workshop, the group, the guild, and in this case, the household may be identified as the social and economic actor. Evidence of generational ceramic production, living and working contexts, access to specialized knowledge and special materials, along with household organization provisioning all contribute to our understanding of the social status of this group.

Pottery at Mycenae and its production both during and especially after the life of Petsas House may also provide clues to the social and economic organization of ceramic craftspeople and workshops and especially potentially significant changes over time.

Introduction

The level of specialization in pottery production has been used to examine the social complexity of cultures or societies, often using the socio-economic framework of household production to estate and factory manufacture (van Wijngaarden 1999b). And to some extent, changes in ceramics may correlate with socio-cultural developments in a broader sense and are related to the economic control of the production process (van Wijngaarden 1999a, 8). These models and the discussion that followed make the pottery the agents, out of necessity primarily due to available evidence (Sinopoli 1991: 124–125). What was the social role of the potters themselves? Of course, choices made by the potter determined the character of the manufacturing process, which in itself may have had social significance, while complexity in the system of circulation and exchange of pottery may be equivalent to the degree of specialization in its production (van Wijngaarden 1999b; Longacre 1999). Craft specialization is closely related to the economic control of the production process, yet interactive cross-craft sharing of technologies creates a complex

ORCID 0009-0005-4977-0430
Nemea Center for Classical Archaeology and Department of Ancient Greek and Roman Studies, University of California, Berkeley
sheltonk@berkeley.edu

In *Social Groups and Production in Mycenaean Economies. Papers from the Langford Conference, Florida State University, Tallahassee, 24-25 February 2023*, edited by D. Pullen (2025), 129–140. Leiden: Sidestone Press.

network or web of important social relationships (van Wijngaarden 1999b; Brysbaert 2011). The relationship of the potter's craft with other socio-economic activities (should) determines the place of the potter and his craft in society (van Wijngaarden 1999a; Matson 1972: 221–222; Thompson 1984: 7–9).

So, what was the social role of potters in the Mycenaean world and how do we access and assess this? Pottery was an essential element in every social situation of the Late Bronze Age (LBA). Feasts, funerals, religious rituals, and episodes of everyday life would not have been possible without ceramic vessels and other objects. It is well-known that pottery was not a major concern in the Linear B textual evidence (Shelmerdine 2008: 144; Galaty 1999; Knappett 2001; Whitelaw 2001), its production was not under palatial control, and only four or five potters appear as named individuals in the tablets; one of them at Pylos, pi-ri-ta-wo, is identified as wanakteros — "royal" or "wanax-serving" (Voutsa 2001: 159–160). The volume of pottery in circulation would suggest many more than four or five potters at work — even four or five workshops with multiple potters do not seem enough for any single site and its immediate region. And what social status did pi-ri-ta-wo the royal potter have? Did he actually make pottery, or did he manage or own a workshop? How intimately engaged with potting was necessary to be a ke-ra-me-us in the Mycenaean world?

I will return to these questions but for now, ceramic production was an industry that seemed to have operated outside of palatial supervision, evidenced by the few tablets associated with it and the lack of archaeological evidence for its in-house production (Hruby 2013; Whitelaw 2001), and potters were independent specialists who operated in primarily extra-palatial markets (Tournavitou 1997); these production centers would have been hubs of private commerce within local and possibly international markets (Shelton 2010; 2016). Hruby (2013) sees among the fabric types in Pylos' pantry evidence of four potters working within the palace's orbit. Lis (2016) identifies also a non-Mycenaean potter who produced partially handmade vessels among the pottery in storeroom 60. None of these workshops needed to produce fulltime for the palace since vessels were reused until they had to be replaced and the majority were undecorated. Yet certainly the palace was a consumer of pottery on an ad hoc basis, potentially requiring thousands of vessels on hand.

The Petsas House at Mycenae

Petsas House (Figure 8.1), a 14th century BCE building complex in Mycenae's settlement, may serve as a case study for the socio-economic role, or roles, of potters and pottery production, in this case on an almost industrial scale within a domestic context during the palatial period. Pottery, its production, distribution, and consumption can provide information on its role in the economy. Evidence from the workshop context may also give evidence for the social roles of the potters themselves along with the pottery they produced. Since the 2007 Langford conference and its publication in 2010, Petsas House has been interpreted as an independent (or semi-independent) workshop producing pottery for a wide range of contexts, markets, and consumers — one of which was certainly the palace (Shelton 2010; Pullen 2013; Meier, Price, and Shelton 2022; Tournavitou 1997). This relationship inverts that expected between craftsmen and the palace based on the tablets where individuals or groups held transactional power and the palace was the consumer (Shelmerdine 2011). Petsas House was a residential complex (Figure 8.2), which also functioned as a ceramic workshop and storage facility during the LH IIIA period. The structure was destroyed by an earthquake and subsequent localized fires towards the end of the period, and, after a short-lived attempt to clear the destruction debris, the site was abandoned (Shelton 2022). Ceramic evidence from the destruction debris indicates that the workshop was in operation during the LH IIIA2 ceramic period, or the second half of the 14th century, which makes it one of the few examples of multi-use space in a settlement context during the period of expansion and centralization of Mycenaean palatial power (Shelton 2016).

Potters are often thought of in quite simple terms, almost always anonymous, even though they produce such an important part of a society's daily needs. Perhaps it is due to the banality of the everyday consumables they produce, only ever elevated to a "minor art" at best. And for archaeologists it is so much easier to discuss the objects that survive rather than the somewhat invisible people responsible for their production and circulation (Tournavitou 1997). Pottery production is considered a craft and makes us imagine or reconstruct skilled craftsmen of modest means and status, often a cottage industry of local importance (Skibo 1999) — a potentially very false impression indeed when we look at the evidence for Mycenaean pottery in the palatial period, traded all over the Mediterranean, and the extent of foreign contact and specialist knowledge exhibited by the potters themselves (Shelton 2016; van Wijngaarden 2002). What is the significance of "specialist knowledge" for pottery production and of far-flung markets and what might this tell us about the socio-economic standing of the potters themselves? At Petsas House in LH IIIA2, we observe a significant amount of mass production and standardization of pottery, especially of a small range of shapes that must be significant to the needs of the community, or at least an interested segment of it, alongside a continued corpus of individual and original pieces, that often required a great output of labor; there are even new experimental shapes complimenting older traditional ones, rather than simply replacing them

Figure 8.1. Plan of Petsas House (N. Mitrovgeni and K. Chronis), © K. Shelton.

(Kvapil et al. 2022; Esposito and Zurbach 2014). Most remarkable is the variety of ceramics produced and stored here that exhibits a breadth of specialization (Figure 8.3): fineware both decorated and undecorated, but also kitchen and cook wares, and figures, all made on the wheel, together with coarse vessels built up at least initially from coils, and hundreds of figurines and many miniature vases all fashioned by hand. It seemed to have been necessary for thousands of vessels and objects to be in production, in storage, and available for consumption in any or all use contexts (Shelton 2008; 2016). The product variety and complex production choices at work indicate that the workshop operated with an independence that allowed the potters to respond in different ways to traditional needs, consumer demands, and their own desire to experiment.

Figure 8.2. Aerial photograph of Petsas House (K. Chronis), © K. Shelton.

Standardization may be one result of increased production of efficient and highly desired vessel types, as I have discussed elsewhere, yet may also be the consequence of a long or complex chain of trade between producer and consumer (van der Leuw 1999: 130), where direct contact and communication is irregular or even non-existent (see Abell this volume). However, elements of the vessels at Petsas House suggest a knowledge of market potential and consumer preferences. The amphoroid krater shape decorated in the pictorial style for the Cypriot market is a great example. Other details from outside the Helladic tradition are incorporated into Mycenaean ceramics — details which perhaps can be communicated only through first-hand observation or technical experience rather than through a merchant intermediary. Regardless of where this occurs, the transmission of these technical and stylistic elements indicates a depth and breadth of socio-economic entanglement. The innovation and experimentation in production exemplify terrifically changing relationships among strata of the society and the effects of production and consumer strategies in ceramics (Shelton 2010). This to me suggests a significant socio-economic status for the individuals responsible for the design, production, and distribution of such diverse market potential.

In the archaeological record, pottery must speak for the potters and the message is not as clear as we would like. The environment in which they lived, worked, and interacted played a crucial and active role in forging a wide range of social relationships (Brysbart 2011), however, so we may investigate the character and status of the inhabitants of Petsas House by examining their residence and business. The impression is that potentially there were various scales of social units involved in ceramic production. Our evidence derived from the pottery produced in the workshop identifies individuals — individual hands that form and decorate - while the workshop installation and adjacent domestic and storage areas indicate group activities and spaces. The nature of that group can be interrogated, whether family or craft guild, and in this case, I would suggest that the household may be identified as the social and economic actor.

Figure 8.3. Pottery types produced at Petsas House in LH IIIA2: undecorated fineware; decorated fineware; cooking ware. © K. Shelton.

Petsas house was a substantial building located on multiple ground levels, built into and on the Pezoulia slope (Figure 8.2), which carried an upper story on at least part of its ground floor as evidenced by materials collapsed downslope and onto ground floor spaces — wall paintings are the best evidence of that. The remains suggest that multiple spaces on the upper floor were decorated with wall paintings, most of them patterned, some certainly dados, others figural. And there was at least one room with a plastered and painted floor imitating conglomerate stone in a red-lined framework. Constructed of drystone masonry foundations with timber-framed mudbrick walls, ashlar blocks in conglomerate and poros limestone were incorporated into wall corners, flanking room openings, and as base supports for columns and piers. Rooms were arranged axially along the slope opening onto an internal corridor and onto open areas within and outside the building. The building design exhibits some consideration for the delivery and movement of goods with wide well-made stone stairs and a ramp for wheeled traffic or heavy loads at its entrance on the southwest; a strong indication that part of this structure, at least, was intended to be actively accessible, both from outside and from within, and was built potentially with craft accommodations and distribution in mind. This included a ground floor dominated by pottery storage, organized by vessel ware, style, shape, and size, and an interior workshop area with a convenient water-source that opened onto an open-air space, had a nearby facility for levigating clay, and a large yard flanking the building's exterior with at least one kiln at its edge.

The building was organized into functional units, which is not surprising in a Bronze Age context, that combined in a single architectural complex habitation, craft production, and storage. The domestic areas were of surprisingly different characters, as was also the juxtaposition of elements like grand architecture and grain stores. A purely domestic context was encountered in the building's interior at the ground floor level, Room Sigma, and abundant food storage was located near the entrance in Room Ypsilon, where a minimum of 11 pithoi were built into the room's clay floor and overwhelmed the space. Room Sigma, on the ground floor of the middle terrace, opposite the storerooms, was only partially preserved, however, its labor-intensive construction cut deep into the bedrock slope, on which were founded substantial stone and brick walls, would not have allowed for much light or air circulation. Yet, Room Sigma was a space for domestic use with color-plastered walls, evidence for cooking, and three meal kits of plain fineware cups and bowls (Shelton 2007: plates XLVII–XLVIII). The accommodations seem modest at best and were immediately accessible to workshop and pottery storage areas, appropriate for the labor force. Cut into the bedrock floor of this room was an infant burial in a shallow pit that had occurred soon after the construction of the building at the start of the 14th cent., perhaps as much as three quarters of a century before the final destruction of the building, several generations later (Shelton 2007: 173–174). The burial under the floor points to a domestic space for the room above it, and the presence of at least one woman, likely as part of a family or a craft group made up of women

Figure 8.4. Imported objects and materials found in Petsas House: gold and lapis lazuli beads; Canaanite jars; Minoan stirrup jar; faience plaque fragment with cartouche of Amenhotep III. © K. Shelton.

and men. The burial was anything but modest, however, with only a few surviving bone fragments along with three vases: a conical cup, miniature conical cup with linear decoration, and an exceptional miniature sippy-goblet. This custom-made piece suggests that the earlier inhabitants of this space also were involved in ceramic production, since the vessel was designed with tremendous thought for the needs of an infant or small child, and may have been given as a token of real emotion to accompany the lost member of this group, to provide eternal nourishment, and perhaps to represent a craft that this child would never grow up to produce. Together with the vases was a necklace of beads (Figure 8.4): gold spherical and ivy-shaped, decorated with granulation, lapis lazuli, and blue glass. The imported materials and advanced metalworking technology exhibited in the beads signal a rather unusual and extravagant gift for an infant and a marker of potential wealth and status for the parents. There are other objects of foreign origin found in the destruction debris of the house, for example West Cretan stirrup jars, Canaanite jars, and the Amenhotep III faience plaque (Figure 8.4), all of which could have originated from the upstairs as easily as the ground floor and may be objects of market exchange or reciprocity from outside the Argolid or even the mainland (Shelton 2007; Pullen 2017).

The habitation areas as reconstructed indicate several options for the make-up of the house's residents. On the one hand, there are construction characteristics and decoration associated with the affluence of an elite population and yet, there also are domestic spaces of very simple make-up with minimal architectural elaboration and few material objects. There is strong evidence for generations of craftsmen, and likely craftswomen, from the outset living and working in Petsas House, but there are also clear signs of heterogeneous levels of socio-economic status. We also have found architectural and material remains of an earlier building with a well under the early 14th cent. foundations, which provide evidence of pottery production on this slope already in LH II. The rebuilding of the house and its workshop on the same location suggests a line of succession within a family or possibly social group (Wiersma 2017: 72–73).

Relative to the space used for storage, the workshop's size was not especially large but was well-organized with particular zones necessary for the production steps (*chaîne opératoire*) and ample area immediately outside the core. The pottery indicates at least one master potter with several assistants or apprentices and perhaps additional decorators. The terracotta figurines also indicate that several different hands formed and decorated them (Shelton 2009; Gillespie and Shelton 2024). Potters often work in groups (guilds), yet descriptions and reputation usually concentrate on the individual at the expense of the group, and workshops require much additional labor from the clay beds to the delivery of finished products to consumers (Tournavitou 1997; Skibo 1999; Longacre 1995). There would certainly have been a division of labor among the laborers and craftsmen, so were there also divisions along social and gender lines? When a workshop was integrated into domestic space it likely involved family members — women and children — and close community ties (Wright 2006). And as production was industrialized, workshops may have expanded outside the settlement and even occurred in a craft-specific production quarter, like the Kerameikos in Athens from the Geometric period onwards (Crielaard 1999; Papadopoulos 1996). The proximity to residences must indicate some family involvement and engagement of the settlement since it makes much more sense to have workshops closer to clay sources and smelly smokey kilns far away from residential activities (Tournavitou 1997). Petsas House was also a pottery warehouse and possibly a point of sale. How should we interpret the *household* of Petsas House? Whose house, was it? Did the building, its installations, and resources, material and human, belong to a potter? Did potters have slaves? Were potters themselves slaves? Should we populate the house with technicians (free and/or enslaved) living and working (literally and figuratively) under an "owner" or "manager" who would have access to and control of resources — especially clay beds and fuel, but also food and other material resources required by the household and its potentially fulltime industry?

Based on the variety of pottery types produced, for example kitchen and cooking vessels, the potters at Petsas House most likely created vessels for at least two types of clients: elite/palatial authorities and the wider domestic market (Figure 8.3). This is supported by the zooarchaeological and isotopic evidence that also indicate different food sources: palatial and local or household subsistence production (Meier, Price, and Shelton 2022; Kvapil et al. 2019). Livestock resources comprised the majority of the household meat diet, supplemented with some small game such as waterfowl, fish, and hare, which reveal a diet that included diverse animal resources. Among domestic animals, pigs are the most abundant species (42.9% of the total NISP) followed by sheep and goats (30.8%). Evidence suggests access to both sheep-dominated and specialized herds granted the use of a wide range of grazing areas and water resources that may have been regulated by palatial authorities, some evidence for which comes from the textual accounts where large-scale caprine production strategies are suggested. Faunal evidence also supports the argument that some subsistence resources came from a more local source. The abundance of young domestic pigs points to a low-risk provisioning strategy, typical of small-scale production most typically practiced to support a household. Given that pigs reproduce and attain a large body size quickly, they are ideal livestock animals for maintaining household food security. Isotope analysis reinforces this interpretation with clear indicators of high cholesterol, the result of foddering the pigs with house scraps. Thus, the residents of Petsas House likely accessed these animals either directly from their own household stock or from that of other small-scale producers in Mycenae's settlement. Overall, access to external provisioning systems, involving the palace, trade partners, or possible markets, appears to have afforded the residents of Petsas House a high degree of subsistence resiliency. Through the application of faunal contextual taphonomy, our analysis defined sub-assemblages of possible carnivore interments, the contents of meals, and evidence of cleaning events. Our intra-context results also elucidated a faunal shift that may reflect times when the household received greater support from external sources who may have paid for ceramic vessels with food. The shifts may also reflect periods of subsistence stress around the time of the destruction event or changing availability of food and completed vessels in different seasons (Price, Shelton, and Meier 2024).

Who was the *ke-ra-me-us* at Petsas House? Evidence of generational ceramic production for more than a century, living and working contexts, access to specialized knowledge and special materials, along with household provisioning all contribute to our understanding of the possible social status or statuses of this group. I interpret the evidence from Petsas House to identify a social hierarchy *within* the house, and that different household groups likely had various roles in the economic activity of the workshop, warehouse, and product distribution, some of them as individual agents representing the household. The complex nature of this structure and the many activities related to it and its inhabitants exhibit characteristics of affluence alongside industrial production and distribution on a large scale. Its place in the society and economy of the center at Mycenae is still not entirely resolved, however. All indications point to builders and inhabitants of complex nature, with a hierarchy of roles and status, perhaps from mining labor to master potter to wealthy merchant. Pots that were designed for export to consumer markets in Cyprus and the presence of foreign exotica among the house debris also suggest a rather high status for at least some of these individuals (Figure 8.4); so does the clear connection to the palace suggested by the Linear B tablets from the destruction debris.

Still, the independent nature of the Mycenaean pottery industry is suggested by the archaeological evidence along with the limited references to potters in the tablets; they are, however, few but mighty. I return to the Pylian royal potter, *pi-ri-ta-wo*, who holds outright *ki-ti-me-na* (private) land that can be subleased, presumably for their own profit, and other named potters that the palace seems to consider as functionaries or specialized craft personnel. The potter *qe-ta-ko* was listed on tablet Cn 1287.4 in connection with other functionaries, while two potters were listed on An 207 in a catalogue of specialized crafts personnel (Voutsa 2001: 159–160; Shelmerdine 2008). *Pi-ri-ta-wo* was also a "telestas" (*te-re-ta*), which was a prestige position, a title given to individuals in diverse economic sectors — early and likely generational landholders who also may have provided service to the palace (Lupack 2008: 63–65). They had access to resources unrestricted by the palace, were successful in enterprises, and likely maintained a significant labor force which would have required provisions and sustenance. The telestai also may have held a significant position with the damos (Lupack 2008: 65–71). And although this reference to *pi-ri-ta-wo* the *te-re-ta* at Pylos dates a century later than the destruction of Petsas House, it may describe a comparable situation. Our *ke-ra-me-us*, potentially *wanakteros* too, likely had existing and important exchange relationships across the social spectrum with their resources and their products. The artifact and ecofact evidence excavated in this household indicates socio-economic relationships with most segments of the local population, with settlements, the destination for most of the pottery produced, with a smaller percentage of the corpus in special shapes for the elite and the palatial administration, as well as for wider spheres of interest and export markets: regionally and internationally.

Exchange relationships are central to the establishment and maintenance of social relationships (especially where power and status are unequal), with reciprocal exchange a foundation of economic and social organization on which could be built further expanded networks of social relations, alliances, and exchange through significant interaction (Pullen 2017; Galaty, Nakassis, and Parkinson 2016), cooperative action including the pooling of resources and labor, and reciprocal obligations (like *pi-ri-ta-wo*). Social relationships can be reproduced or changed through multiple venues, feasting for instance is an often-cited example. To quote Nakassis (2012: 25), "feasts are active arenas in which participants with differential access to resources create, maintain, manipulate, and legitimize social and political power through personal relationships, contributions of feasting material, and presence as consumers of the food and drink." The *kerameus* or *kerameis* of Petsas House impacted others in the community, at the very least, as a supplier of essential feasting equipment — for cooking, serving, and communal consumption (Shelton 2008; Pullen 2017; Hruby 2013: 424). Some of the faunal material that made its way into the household may also be evidence for participation in feasts as well, where exchange relationships would be formed and negotiated (Pullen 2022; Galaty and Parkinson 2007).

Surely, Petsas House was not the only pottery workshop at Mycenae and in its environs during LH IIIA. Loads of LH IIIA2 pottery, made in the Argolid, has been found which macroscopically and stylistically does not seem to have been produced by this household group. Petsas House was destroyed completely in late LH IIIA2 by an earthquake and localized fires that resulted from the natural disaster. Even though there followed a huge clean-up effort, the attempt was abandoned with most storage areas still relatively full of broken pottery and building debris. Unlike elsewhere in the settlement that suffered significant destruction at this time and were completely built over at the start of the next period — like the House of the Wine Merchant (Wace 1953: 17) further southwest on the same slope — the area of Petsas House was not fully reclaimed, the house was not rebuilt, and nothing was constructed over it during the remainder of the Bronze Age. It is clear from the state of the excavated remains that the ruins of this building were left visible and exposed to the elements for a very long time.

Like Petsas House, the workshop at Berbati seems to have made pottery from LH II, but so far, they were the only producer in the north Argolid during LH IIIB and were using the clay from the exact same clay beds as the Petsas workshop in the Longaki pass, just off the road between Mycenae and Berbati (Schallin 1997; 2002; Pullen 2022; Mommsen, Beier, and Hein 2002). So little of Mycenae's settlement has been excavated so far that a 13th cent. pottery workshop could still be lurking out there somewhere. However, this may be a case where the decentralization of production was pushed even further, beyond Mycenae's settlement, and advantage was taken of the power vacuum following the destruction of the Petsas workshop towards the end of LH IIIA2. No palatial subsidy here — a multi-generational production area, in use for over a century and a half, was left in ruins.

The Petsas House pottery corpus itself seems to signal a transitional period from production for the home, the settlement, and the general population, to one of a partially mandated or more restricted industry with more specialized vessels and focused consumer needs. The demographics of the workshop may have been at a time of transition too, from multi-generational family members to a stratified group of professional craftsmen and businessmen. Petsas House was an impressive architectural and industrial complex that continued to be a residence for a family with social complexity of its own. It appears that this was not just any family of Mycenae's settlement. The pottery production, the tablets, and the connections to foreign markets indicate a significant relationship not only to other community members, but to other communities, to the palace, and to the wider socio-economic landscape of the Late Bronze Age Mediterranean. But not everyone who lived and worked in the Petsas household may have had the same social status or access to further opportunities for status and landed wealth.

Bibliography

Brysbaert, A., 2011. Introduction. Tracing Social Networks through Studying Technologies. In *Tracing Prehistoric Social Networks through Technology*, edited by A. Brysbaert, 1–11. London: Routledge.

Crielaard, J. P., 1999. Production, Circulation and Consumption of Early Iron Age Greek Pottery (Eleventh to Seventh Centuries BC). In *The Complex Past of Pottery: Production, Circulation and Consumption of Mycenaean and Greek Pottery (Sixteenth to Early Fifth Centuries BC)*, edited by J. P. Crielaard, V. Stissi, and G. J. Wijngaarden, 49–81. Amsterdam: J. C. Gieben.

Esposito, A., and J. Zurbach, 2014. Technological Standardization and Cultural Contact: Some Methodological Considerations and Two Case Studies. In *Understanding Standardization and Variation in Mediterranean Ceramics: Mid 2nd to Late 1st Millennium BC*, edited by A. Kotsonas, 39–47. Leuven: Peeters.

Galaty, M. L., 1999. *Nestor's Wine Cups: Investigating Ceramic Manufacture and Exchange in a Late Bronze Age 'Mycenaean' State*. British Archaeology Reports, International Series, 766. Oxford: J. and E. Hedges.

Galaty, M. L., and W. A. Parkinson, 2007. Introduction: Mycenaean Palaces Rethought. In *Rethinking Mycenaean Palaces II: Revised and Expanded Edition*, edited by M. L. Galaty and W. A. Parkinson, 1–17. Monograph 60. Los Angeles: University of California at Los Angeles, Cotsen Institute of Archaeology.

Galaty, M. L., D. Nakassis, and W. A. Parkinson, 2016. Introduction. In *Discussion and Debate: Reciprocity in Aegean Palatial Societies: Gifts, Debt, and the Foundations of Economic Exchange*, edited by D. Nakassis, M. L. Galaty, and W. A. Parkinson. *Journal of Mediterranean Archaeology* 29: 61–70.

Gillespie, M., and K. Shelton, 2024. Στα ίχνη της θεάς. Terracotta Figurine Production at Petsas House, Mycenae in LH IIIA2. In *IXNH: Walking in the Footsteps of the Pioneer of Aegean Archaeology in Celebration of the 200th Anniversary of the Birth of Heinrich Schliemann, 19th International Aegean Conference, Oristano, Italy, May 2022*, edited by M. Perna and R. Laffineur, 175–184. Aegaeum 49. Leuven: Peeters.

Hruby, J., 2013. Crafts, Specialists, and Markets in Mycenaean Greece. The Palace of Nestor, Craft Production, and Mechanisms for the Transfer of Goods. *American Journal of Archaeology* 117: 423–427.

Knappett, C., 2001. Overseen or Overlooked? Ceramic Production in a Mycenaean Palatial System. In *Economy and Politics in the Mycenaean Palace States. Proceedings of a Conference held on 1–3 July 1999 in the Faculty of Classics, Cambridge*, edited by S. Voutsaki and J. T. Killen, 80–95. Cambridge Philological Society Supplementary Volume 27. Cambridge: Cambridge Philological Society.

Kvapil, L. A., J. Meier, G. Price, and K. Shelton, 2019. Beyond City and Country at Mycenae: Urban and Rural Practices in a Subsistence Landscape. In *Country in the City: Agricultural Functions of Protohistoric Urban Settlements (Aegean and Western Mediterranean)*, edited by D. Garcia, R. Orgeolet, M. Pomadère, J. Zurbach, 122–136. Oxford: Archaeopress.

Kvapil, L. A., M. W. Kimpel, R. R. Jayasekare, and K. Shelton, 2022. Using Gaussian Mixture Model Clustering to Explore Morphology and Standardized Production of Ceramic Vessels: A Case Study of Pottery from Late Bronze Age Greece. *Journal of Archaeological Science: Reports*, 45. DOI:10.1016/j.jasrep.2022.103543.

Lis, B., 2016. A Foreign Potter in the Pylian Kingdom? A Reanalysis of the Ceramic Assemblage of Room 60 in the Palace of Nestor at Pylos. *Hesperia* 85: 491–536.

Longacre, W. A., 1995. Why Did They Invent Pottery Anyway? In *The Emergence of Pottery: Technology and Innovation in Ancient Societies*, edited by W. K. Barnett and J. W. Hoopes, 277–280. Washington DC: Smithsonian Institution Press.

Longacre, W. A., 1999. Standardization and Specialization: What's the Link? In *Pottery and People: A Dynamic Interaction*, edited by J. M. Skibo and G. M. Feinman, 44–58. Salt Lake City: The University of Utah Press.

Lupack, S. 2008. *The Role of the Religious Sector in the Economy of Late Bronze Age Mycenaean Greece*, British Archaeological Reports International Series 1858. Oxford: Archaeopress.

Matson, F. R., 1972. Ceramic Studies. In *The Minnesota Messenia Expedition: Reconstructing a Bronze Age Regional Environment*, edited by W. A. McDonald and G. R. Rapp, 200–224. Minneapolis: University of Minnesota Press.

Meier, J., G. Price, and K. Shelton, 2022. Distinguishing Palatial from Autonomous Subsistence Provisioning with Zooarchaeological and Isotopic Analyses at Petsas House, Mycenae (Late Helladic IIIA2). In *Food Provisioning in Complex Societies*, edited by L. Atici and B. Arbuckle, 45–70. Denver: University Press of Colorado.

Mommsen, H., T. Beier, and A. Hein, 2002. A Complete Chemical Grouping of the Berkeley Neutron Activation Analysis Data on Mycenaean Pottery. *Journal of Archaeological Science* 29: 613–637.

Nakassis, D., 2012. Prestige and Interest: Feasting and the King at Mycenaean Pylos. *Hesperia* 81: 1–30.

Papadopoulos, J. K., 1996. The Original Kerameikos of Athens and the Siting of the Classical Agora. *Greek, Roman, and Byzantine Studies* 37: 107–128.

Price, G., J. Meier, and K. Shelton, 2024. Revitalizing the Vittles: Recent Advances in the Study of Animal Subsistence at Mycenae. In *IXNH: Walking in the Footsteps of the Pioneer of Aegean Archaeology in Celebration of the 200th Anniversary of the Birth of Heinrich Schliemann, 19th International Aegean Conference, Oristano, Italy, May 2022,* edited by M. Perna and R. Laffineur, 199–206. Aegaeum 49. Leuven: Peeters.

Pullen, D. J., 2013. Crafts, Specialists, and Markets in Mycenaean Greece: Exchanging the Mycenaean Economy. *American Journal of Archaeology* 117: 437–445.

Pullen, D. J., 2017. Reciprocity and Exchange Relationships: Exploring the Dynamics of Bronze Age Social Structures through Feasting and Hospitality. In *Social Change in Aegean Prehistory,* edited by C. Wiersma and S. Voutsaki, 49–68. Oxford: Oxbow Books.

Pullen, D. J., 2022. The Political Geography of the Late Bronze Age Argolid: States and Territories. In *Political Geographies of the Bronze Age Aegean: Proceedings of the Joint Workshop of the Belgian School at Athens (EBSA) and the Netherlands Institute at Athens (NIA), May 28 to 31, 2019,* edited by G. J. van Wijngaarden and J. Diessen, 75–86. BABESCH Supplement 43. Leuven: Peeters.

Schallin, A.-L., 1997. The Late Bronze Age Potter's Workshop at Mastos in the Berbati Valley. In *Trade and Production in Premonetary Greece: Production and the Craftsman,* edited by C. Gillis, C. Risberg, and B. Sjöberg, 73–88. Studies in Mediterranean Archaeology and Literature Pocketbook 143. Jonsered: Paul Åströms Förlag.

Schallin, A.-L., 2002. Pots for Sale: The Late Helladic IIIA and IIIB Ceramic Production at Berbati. In *New Research on Old Material from Asine and Berbati, in Celebration of the Fiftieth Anniversary of the Swedish Institute of Athens,* edited by B. Wells, 141–155. Acta of the Swedish Institute at Athens 8°, 17. Stockholm: Swedish Institute.

Shelmerdine, C. W., 2008. Mycenaean Society. In *A Companion to Linear B: Mycenaean Greek Texts and their World. Volume 1,* edited by Y. Duhoux and A. Morpurgo Davies, 115–158. Bibliothèque des cahiers de l'Institut de Linguistique de Louvain 120. Louvain-la-Neuve: Peeters.

Shelmerdine, C. W., 2011. The Individual and the State in Mycenaean Greece. *Bulletin of the Institute of Classical Studies* 54: 19–28.

Shelton, K., 2007. Foot Soldiers and Cannon Fodder: The Underrepresented Majority of the Mycenaean Civilization. In *EPOS: Reconsidering Greek Epic and Aegean Bronze Age Archaeology. Proceedings of the 11th International Aegean Conference / 11e Rencontre égéenne internationale, Los Angeles, UCLA - The J. Paul Getty Villa, 20–23 April 2006,* edited by S. Morris and R. Laffineur, 169–175. Aegaeum 28. Liège: Université de Liège, Histoire de l'art et archéologie de la Grèce antique and Austin: University of Texas at Austin, Program in Aegean Scripts and Prehistory.

Shelton, K., 2008. Drinking, Toasting, Consumption and Libation: Late Helladic IIIA Pottery and a Cup for Every Occasion. In *Dais: The Aegean Feast: Proceedings of the 12th International Aegean Conference,12e Rencontre égéenne internationale, University of Melbourne, Centre for Classics and Archaeology, 25–29 March 2008,* edited by J. Crowley, L. Hitchcock, and R. Laffineur, 221–228. Aegaeum 29. Liège: Université de Liège, Histoire de l'art et archéologie de la Grèce antique and Austin: University of Texas at Austin, Program in Aegean Scripts and Prehistory.

Shelton, K., 2009. The Figurines from Petsas House and Other Find-Spots at Mycenae. In *Encounters with Mycenaean figures and figurines: Papers presented at a seminar at the Swedish Institute at Athens, 27–29 April 2001,* edited by A.-L. Schallin and P. Pakkanen, 55–60. Acta of the Swedish Institute at Athens 8°, 20. Stockholm: Swedish Institute at Athens.

Shelton, K., 2010. Citadel and Settlement: A Developing Economy at Mycenae, the Case of Petsas House. In *Political Economies of the Aegean Bronze Age: Papers from the Langford Conference, Florida State University, 22–24 February 2007,* edited by D. J. Pullen, 184–204. Oxford: Oxbow Books.

Shelton, K., 2016. Petsas House, Pottery Production, and the Mycenaean People in LH IIIA2. In *RA-PI-NE-U: Studies on the Mycenaean World offered to Robert Laffineur for his 70th Birthday,* edited by J. Driessen, 317–326. Aegis 10. Louvain-la-Neuve: Presses universitaires de Louvain.

Shelton, K., 2022. On Shaky Ground: Petsas House and Destruction at Mycenaean LH IIIA 2. In *Synchronizing the Destructions of the Mycenaean Palaces,* edited by R. Jung and E. Kardamaki, 35–48. Mykenische Studien 36. Vienna: Austrian Academy of Sciences Press.

Sinopoli, C., 1991. *Approaches to Archaeological Ceramics.* New York and London: Plenum Press.

Skibo, J. M. 1999. Pottery and People. In *Pottery and People: a Dynamic Interaction,* edited by J. M. Skibo and G. M. Feinman, 1–8. Salt Lake City: University of Utah Press.

Thompson, H., 1984. The Athenian vase painters and their neighbors. In *Pots and Potters. Current Approaches in ceramic archaeology,* edited by P. M. Rice, 7–19. Los Angeles: Cotsen Institute of Archaeology.

Tournavitou, I., 1997. The Social and Economic Position of Artisans in the Mycenaean World. In *Trade and*

Production in Premonetary Greece: Production and the Craftsman, edited by C. Gillis, C. Risberg, and B. Sjöberg, 29–41. Studies in Mediterranean Archaeology and Literature 143. Jonsered: Paul Åströms Förlag.

Van der Leuw, S. E., 1999. Exchange and Trade in Ceramics: Some Notes from the Potter's Point of View. In *The Complex Past of Pottery: Production, Circulation and Consumption of Mycenaean and Greek Pottery (Sixteenth to Early Fifth Centuries BC)*, edited by J. P. Crielaard, V. Stissi, and G. J. van Wijngaarden, 115–136. Amsterdam: J. C. Gieben.

van Wijngaarden, G. J., 1999a. The Complex Past of Pottery: An Introduction. In *The Complex Past of Pottery: Production, Circulation and Consumption of Mycenaean and Greek Pottery (Sixteenth to Early Fifth Centuries BC)*, edited by J. P. Crielaard, V. Stissi, and G. J. Wijngaarden, 1–19. Amsterdam: J. C. Gieben.

van Wijngaarden, G. J., 1999b. Production, Circulation and Consumption of Mycenaean Pottery (Sixteenth to Twelfth Centuries BC). In *The Complex Past of Pottery: Production, Circulation and Consumption of Mycenaean and Greek Pottery (Sixteenth to Early Fifth Centuries BC)*, edited by J. P. Crielaard, V. Stissi, and G. J. Wijngaarden, 21–47. Amsterdam: J. C. Gieben.

van Wijngaarden, G. J., 2002. *The Use and Appreciation of Mycenaean Pottery in the Levant, Cyprus and Italy (c. 1600–1200 BC)*. Amsterdam: Amsterdam University Press.

Voutsa, K., 2001. Mycenaean Craftsmen in Palace Archives: Problems in Interpretation. In *Manufacture and Measurement: Counting, Measuring and Recording. Craft Items in Early Aegean Societies*, edited by A. Michalidou, 145–165. Meletemata 33. Athens: Research Centre for Greek and Roman Antiquity.

Wace, A. J. B., 1953. Mycenae 1939–1952. *Annual of the British School at Athens* 48: 3–18.

Whitelaw, T., 2001. Reading Between the Tablets: Assessing Mycenaean Palatial Involvement in Ceramic Production and Consumption. In *Economy and Politics in the Mycenaean Palace States. Proceedings of a Conference held on 1–3 July 1999 in the Faculty of Classics, Cambridge*, edited by S. Voutsaki and J. T. Killen, 51–79. Cambridge Philological Society Supplementary Volume 27. Cambridge: Cambridge Philological Society.

Wiersma, C., 2017. Domestic Architecture: A Means to Analyse Social Change on the Bronze Age Greek Mainland. In *Social Change in Aegean Prehistory*, edited by C. W. Wiersma and S. Voutsaki, 69–97. Oxford: Oxbow Books.

Wright, J. C., 2006. Social Production of Space and the Architectural Production of Society in the Bronze Age Aegean During the 2nd Millennium B.C.E. In *Constructing Power: Architecture, Ideology and Social Practice*, edited by J. Maran, H. Schwengel, U. Thaler, and C. Juwig, 49–74. Hamburg: LIT Verlag.

Potting Communities during the Mycenaean Palatial Period

Peter M. Day
Eleftheria Kardamaki

Abstract

Consideration of pottery production in the Mycenaean world has often been overshadowed by the assumed role of palaces in value-added craft products, even though pottery itself seems not to have been of major concern to the central authorities, at least on the basis of the Linear B records. A more recent turn assesses consumption by those monuments/institutions of prodigious amounts of pottery vessels to facilitate the commensality which underpinned their authority, and the containers which allowed the movement of organic goods over long distances. What is sometimes missing from these reworkings of our perspectives is new diachronic, bottom-up data on where pottery was produced, its varied production technology and patterns of consumption in different regions.

This paper offers examples from four case studies: Kontopigado, Alimos and the LH IIIB2 Saronic Gulf; Late Bronze Age Lakonia; a class of Cretan style transport stirrup jars from LH IIIB2 Tiryns and Midea; and a window on the production of LH IIIA2 Mycenaean fine table-wares on the island of Lemnos. Through these cases we address issues of the longevity of some specific production locations, evidence for continuity and change in technological practice and the indications of mobility and long-distance connections between craftspeople and their communities. The social roles of accepted 'ways of doing', patterns of teaching and transmission, and the importance of reputation play an important role in the historical contingency of production patterns during this period, which suggests that extended families and communities of practice should be central to our understanding of ceramic production units.

ORCID 0000-0002-3954-2603
Ceramics and Composite Materials Research Group, Institute of Nanoscience and Nanotechnology, NCSR "Demokritos" *and* School of History, Philosophy and Digital Humanities, University of Sheffield
p.m.day@sheffield.ac.uk

ORCID 0000-0003-3450-3784
Institute for Prehistory, Protohistory and Near Eastern Archaeology, Heidelberg University
elkardamaki@yahoo.gr

Introduction

In this workshop, we were engaged in a timely effort to go beyond the regular focus on social groups exercising political power in the Mycenaean world, to highlight those involved in everyday practices of craft production, an important component of the material world of the Late Bronze Age Aegean. Our own offering concentrates on pottery vessels, presenting a range of new evidence concerning their technology, location and social context of production, as well as changes in their consumption. Our case studies concentrate on long-lived traditions, mobilities of people and objects, and the changes in demand that illuminate the different contexts and scales of pottery production at this time. Such a bottom-up approach holds the potential to reveal a ceramic spectrum, a regional and chronological diversity in fundamentals of the

In *Social Groups and Production in Mycenaean Economies. Papers from the Langford Conference, Florida State University, Tallahassee, 24-25 February 2023*, edited by D. Pullen (2025), 141–172. Leiden: Sidestone Press.

production of pottery vessels, which both facilitates and embodies the relations between central authorities and their subject populations.

Making pots in the Bronze Age Aegean

Most of our expectations about pottery production in the prehistoric Aegean have their roots deep within a social evolutionary perspective. This pertains both to the relationship between the specifics of crafting ceramic products and ideas of "specialization," and to the relationship of any mode of ceramic production that we care to define with the political economy of a specific society. This is notable in the often essentialist use by archaeologists of "household" and "specialized" as contexts of production, as a measure of emergent complexity (in craft production, as well as economic and political organization).

For example, in the classification of Sander van der Leeuw (1984) and a similar model by David Peacock for the Roman world (1983) components of pottery systems were identified whose presence, absence and combination were used to characterize modes of production. Rather than being seen as heuristic tools to interrogate variability in ceramic production, to see different pathways taken by potters, these became popular as a guide to spotting variables which might identify a single "system state," a convenient de-historicized label as a measure of technical progress or socio-economic complexity. This was despite van der Leeuw's own ethnographic examples in the same paper stressing the frequent co-existence of differing modes at the same time and place (1984: 748–763).

As another example, in the face of the wealth of insights from Dean Arnold's publications on pottery in Yucatan and Peru (1985; 1993; 2000; 2008; 2015; 2018), the tendency of archaeologists has been to quote his work on resource thresholds and ecological observations, in a desire for law-like propositions and re-assuring determinism. This is perhaps easier than acknowledging that he and other anthropologists (e.g. Bowser 2000; Gosselain 1998; 2002) reveal the complex, historicized and essentially social world of ceramics. In developing typologies of specialization, despite an increasing sophistication of approach, the hope has been to recognize different system states of crafting that could themselves be used as proxies of economic and political organization (see useful discussion by Costin 2007 and other papers in the same volume). Understandings of production have indeed developed to incorporate an emphasis on scale, intensity and other variables, but more recently the study of the crafting of material culture has undergone a welcome, more radical change to considering a dynamic picture of these relationships — in terms of our subject — between potters, their materials, practices and the pottery vessels they produce (e.g. Barrett 2014; 2021; Ingold 2000; 2007; 2013; Kiriatzi and Knappett 2016; Kozatsas 2018; Malafouris 2013). Those aspects pertaining to pottery have included detailed technological reconstructions, especially through new approaches to vessel forming (e.g. Choleva, Jung, and Kardamaki 2020; Knappett 2016). This and the regular integration of analytical insights into technology have brought a welcome movement away from the strictures of our ceramic typologies to a more nuanced appreciation of how we can use pots to think about the past.

Regarding the prehistoric Aegean, expectations of a development from initial, relatively simple, subsistence-oriented, household based ceramic production has been challenged by consideration of contexts of the first appearance of pottery, which showed patterns of wide exchange between different production locations (e.g. Dimoula 2017; Tomkins 2008; Tomkins and Day 2001). This impeded the vision of a gradual or stepped path from simplicity towards a perceived complexity of production and consumption, ultimately to some more centralized control of pottery making. Analytical insight into pottery of the Bronze Age has involved targeted attempts to emphasize the wide distribution of pottery, of both utilitarian pottery and highly decorated finewares and their production in a variety of contexts, some clearly linked to major centers (e.g. Poursat and Knappett 2006; Gauß and Kiriatzi 2011) and others rather more peripheral. The Mesara Plain of Crete has been important in such considerations, not only as its high-quality pottery was consumed in North-central Crete from at least the mid-third millennium BCE, but also due to its clear continuity of technological practice from at least the end of the fourth millennium throughout the Bronze Age (Shaw et al. 2001; Day and Wilson 1998; Day, Relaki, and Faber 2006; Todaro 2013; 2017). The latter case forms but one example where it is possible to trace patterns of production over the *longue durée*, to see the longevity of ways of doing, as well as the indicators of disruption and transformation.

The importance in the latter case, of Phaistos as a place of gathering (Day, Relaki, and Todaro 2010; Todaro 2013), generating demand for vessels of consumption and display, is something we see in a range of central places, including the Mycenaean world. Ethnographic examples also exist for the importance of centers of ritual and pilgrimage in other contexts. In twentieth century Mallorca, a large part of one potter's output was destined to be broken in the ceremonies on the name day of Santa Margalida (Day et al. 2015), while substantial parts of the output of some workshops on Lesvos were tied to places of pilgrimage on the island and in northern Chios (Day, work in progress). The supply of pottery for such religious observance was not always through markets or commercial peddling as, further afield in India, the *asmani / jajmani* system tied specific potters to clients of other castes to provide suitable vessels for specific festivals throughout the year (Miller 1985:

82–84; Kramer 1997: 25–27). Such obligations, and their reciprocation, were inherited, binding social ties. These demands for pottery vessels, therefore, are often satiated by craftspeople working in rather different contexts and scales, even within the same political or geographical units.

Potters, communities and consumption

If we are to release our models of production from an umbilical link with the concept of political and economic complexity, to accept neither that pots equate with people, nor that their production only somehow represents a system state of the centralization of power, then we need to acknowledge the diversity and historical contingency that characterized the production of pottery. It has become a commonplace to observe that — for instance — the uptake of wheel technology for pottery forming is often a drawn-out process, if not completely rejected, and that different units in the same region will adopt, reject or modify new ways of producing pottery (Abell and Hilditch 2016; Lindblom, Gauß, and Kiriatzi 2015). Yet pottery forming, though seen by some as a privileged link in the *chaîne opératoire*, is only one aspect of the variation in the make-up and practices of potting groups.

Sometimes these persistent traits and differences are stark, such as the combination of slabs of quite different composition in the production of pottery in the Mesara Plain of southern Crete (Day, Relaki, and Faber 2006; Todaro 2017) or the contrast between the high-fired, quality pottery of the red slipped EH I products of Talioti, near Nauplio (Burke, Day, and Kossyva 2020) and the contemporary low-fired and rather coarse red slipped ware in Attica (Tsai 2021). Local histories and trajectories of production are clearly diverse across areas which share their political and economic character, some even within the same polity.

As analytical understandings of pottery technology have developed, we have witnessed a decoupling of production and consumption, which previously were bound by a top-down vision of palatial economies. The appreciation of the multi-faceted nature of Mycenaean economy, with the interests of the palace extending into only certain spheres, has prompted bottom-up approaches that challenge the dominance of models of redistributive economies and a view based on the Linear B evidence. A crucial landmark in this revision was Susan Sherratt's re-thinking (2001) of the basis for Mycenaean palatial phenomenon and a move to acknowledge choice in the consumption of material culture. This in turn has highlighted crafting spheres that have long histories in the areas where palaces briefly emerged, with the consideration of key issues such as skill, training, and reputation. The series of papers focusing on the different forms of redistribution (Galaty, Nakassis, and Parkinson 2011) and the relevance and nature of markets (Parkinson, Nakassis, and Galaty 2013) in the Mycenaean world have built on these challenges to lead to a radical re-think over the different sectors of Late Bronze Age economies.

In this reassessment, research on ceramic production has concentrated on the palace at Pylos, with its substantial, well-preserved stores of pottery and the detail of its Linear B archive. The sheer diversity of the rather ordinary ceramic tools of commensality at palatial Pylos have been analyzed to explore not only the implications of their use and spatial implications of their place of storage (Bendall 2004; Hruby 2006), but also for what they have to tell us about ceramic production units and the mechanism of pottery supply to the palace (Galaty 1999b; Knappett 2001; Whitelaw 2001). The Linear B tablets, at Pylos and elsewhere, encourage us to de-couple the production of most types of pottery from the palaces themselves, both as locations and in some cases from economic overview of production, as there is only a small amount of evidence in the Linear B tablets for much interest, though clearly the ceramic drinking sets that were central to Palatial ceremonies mean that the *procurement* and *consumption* of such vessels was of no little interest to those imbibing and hosting.

Boulotis's excellent contextualized discussion of epigraphical and other evidence for potters in the Late Bronze Age Aegean (Boulotis 2014) is vital here. He suggests that we are most likely looking at a variety of levels and types of production, from utilitarian, perhaps seasonal, production to those responding to major orders, such as those suggested by the KN K 700 tablet, which mentions 1800 transport stirrup jars, a not insubstantial number. He debates whether we might expect the finest painted pottery, such as that represented by the Pictorial Style workshop at Mastos, Berbati, to be produced in specialist workshops with strict hierarchies and systems of apprenticeship. Boulotis also joins Palmer (1963) and Palaima (1997) in discussing the reference in a Linear B tablet from Pylos, which gives the epithet "royal" to a specific potter, in agreeing that a "Royal Potter" might be more in charge of procurement of pottery supplies than its actual production (see also Petrakis 2010). In other words, that their links to the palace and the politico-religious leader give them a status as intermediaries or privileged entrepreneurs in ensuring the availability of the ceramic tools of ceremony. Overall it seems clear that there is no easy view of a top-down control of pottery production, but at the same time it is improbable that the arrival of the palatial system did not transform some aspects of the crafting of ceramic vessels. Nakassis (2021) has reminded us that the means of extraction of goods and labor is likely to have been multi-faceted and particularly historically contingent and Zeman (2018) usefully discusses the probably varied ceramic landscape with specific relation to Pylos.

Those works that drew on the detailed textual and material remains from Pylos were able to discuss the demarcation of palatial and non-palatial contexts of production and consumption, to examine titles, roles, status and locations of production. Even then, the symbiosis of different crafting and agricultural worlds is clear (Nakassis 2021). Elsewhere this is a far more difficult challenge, as we navigate what are likely to have been rather pervious boundaries. In the range of case studies to be discussed here, we emphasize the markedly varied nature of pottery production units in the Mycenaean World and the substantially different, historically contingent patterns of production and consumption in different regions.

Michael Galaty has spearheaded an effort in Messenia to integrate petrographic and chemical analyses in the examination of the groups involved in and the locations of pottery production (Galaty 1999a; 1999b), building on pioneering work by Matson (1972). Importantly for our present comparative topic, in a previous Langford Conference, Galaty (2010) addressed such regionalism by comparing Messenia with the Argolid, concluding that pottery production in these major centers was quite different, with that from Messenia being de-centralized, based on a few units that supplied both the palace and other settlements. Based on analysis of material he suggested the existence of various smaller peripheral workshops in the region. His contention that some villages, such as Koukounara, largely consumed pottery that was produced in smaller peripheral workshops hints at competition between different potting centers or workshops and the possible contrast in the production of "wealth" and "staple" ceramics (Galaty 1999b; 2010). This element of hierarchy and perhaps even competition between units of production and social groups is fundamental, yet the specific nature of his example seems not to have generated re-examination in other regions. We hope to contribute here to such a re-consideration.

Our contention is that it is unhelpful to consider the crafting of "Mycenaean Pottery" as a unit. The label itself belies the radical differences that exist between the main pottery categories of consumption/display, storage, transportation and cooking. Even the technology behind "Mycenaean" finewares is accepted as practices and style imported to the Mainland from Crete, yet it is Handmade Burnished pottery at the end of LBA that holds a special place of representing "the other." These are mostly matters of perspective and of our biases and imposed categories. While recent analytical work has produced what now seems a critical mass of data to aid this process, there are still habits that need to be shed. For example, it was studies of pottery in the perceived "peripheries" of a Mycenaean world that were more instrumental in promoting an appreciation of the sheer diversity present in the crafting of pottery vessels. Vangelio Kiriatzi's doctoral research in Macedonia comes immediately to mind (Kiriatzi et al. 1997). But we need to do the same in what might be considered the "Mycenaean heartlands," in and around the Peloponnese.

In being tasked, as we are in this workshop, with considering social groups involved in production, we are aided by the fact that most current work is based on an understanding that technology itself is fundamentally social and the *chaîne opératoire* concept and methodology holds the potential to move from detailed technological reconstruction to insights into crafting communities of the past (Dobres 2000; Lemonnier 1993; see Roux 2019, Chapter 1 for a concise introduction). While this approach has its roots in French anthropology and especially the production of lithics, which lend themselves perhaps more readily to a study of bodily gesture, its application to ceramics has a long history (e.g. Balfet 1965; 1973; van der Leeuw 1977). While in North American studies there was a tendency to link detailed study of technical sequences to an evolutionary and perhaps optimizing viewpoint, Pfaffenberger (1992) has argued for the reinstatement of the study of *sociotechnical systems* against the background of the "standard view" of technology and there has been effective adoption of a practice-based approach by a number of scholars (e.g. Eckert 2008).

"Ways of doing" are social acts that include and exclude, which form the basis of communities of practice (Wenger 1998), of identity and of belonging in a group. Derived from studies of the *chaîne opératoire* these approaches emphasize embodied gesture and choices in production and consider the transmission of knowledge as a social process that forms the basis of technical traditions. Such traditions can be very long-lived, indeed specific practices can well outlive fluctuations in political and economic organization. It is this interplay between patterns of learning, skills and identity that has much to teach us about craftspeople negotiating their place with changing power relationships and transformations in demand.

There is a wealth of ethnographic information regarding the tendency of potters to train within the family (e.g. Arnold 2018: 220–221), usually the nuclear or extended family, and more rarely collateral family (Gosselain 1998: 92–104). This often starts during childhood, but even in cases where potters are trained a little later in life, when parents might have passed away, in several cases their training is still carried out within the extended family (e.g. Miller 1985: 77–78; Day 2004). Such family-centered apprenticeships not only reproduce specific operational sequences, but ensure that potters learn their place and develop a strong sense of identity and belonging (Wallaert 2008; Herbich and Dietler 2008).

Even when changes take place through the entry of entrepreneurs into production in Ticul, Mexico, Arnold shows that trainees from outside the household were still trained within a family-based unit of production (2015: 14–15). Similarly, in the case of the Siphniot

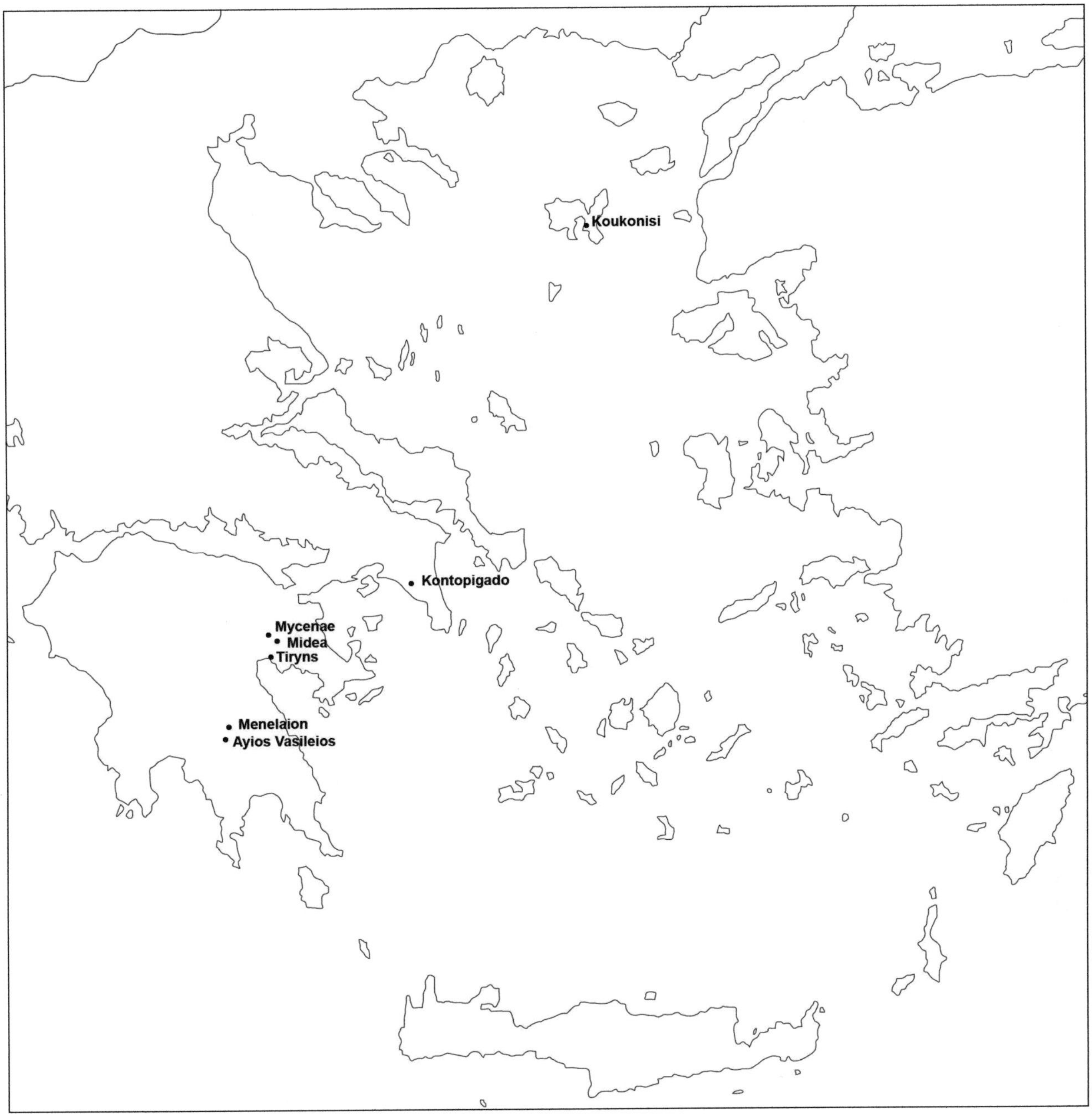

Figure 9.1. Map of case study areas and main sites.

diaspora in Greece, local labor was often trained within a close, family-based unit, as part of the deal of providing labor (Matson 1973: 120–121). Even substantial moves from a domestic mode of production through to the commoditization of labour still usually see training within a strong group environment (Goody 1989: 233–256). Of course there are always exceptions, and the Japanese practice in some places of sending young members out of the family for training with a Master Potter who may not be kin, before returning to the family unit for their professional life, takes place within a strong tradition and specific manufacturing practices (Singleton 1989).

This is particularly relevant to the case of the Mycenaean world, to examine whether transformations happened in pottery production, servicing the demand of palatial centers and the importance of commensality in the changing world of social differentiation and power. As the Mycenaean "palatial" system is itself relatively short-lived in a long-lived ceramic landscape, the degree to which groups of potters were affected by either direct control,

Figure 9.2. After Kaza-Papageorgiou et al. 2011: 205 fig. 3, photo by L. Valsamis.

by intermediaries and entrepreneurs, indeed perhaps themselves took advantage of changes in demand, or even rejected change, has much to tell us about how potters found their way through changing material conditions of their craft.

With this in mind, our aim here is to present some "bottom-up" information on the location and methods of production during the Mycenaean palatial period from four case studies and then to contemplate the implications for the central theme of the conference (Figure 9.1). We first examine the broader area of Athens and the Saronic Gulf, concentrating on Kontopigado-Alimos. Turning to Laconia and the marked change in pottery types produced over the course of the Late Bronze Age, we consider the new palace site of Agios Vasileios in relation the Menelaion and Agios Stephanos. Our third example comes from the Argive Plain and a specific fabric of Transport Stirrup Jar, the type of vessel known in some cases to bear Linear B painted inscriptions, explicitly linked to palatial accounting. Finally, we visit the North Aegean and the island of Lemnos to further examine the production of Mycenaean painted wares in a rather different context.

Pottery production at Kontopigado-Alimos, Attica

The Late Bronze Age phase of this important site, excavated by Konstantina Kaza-Papageorgiou on behalf of the Ephorate of Piraeus and the Islands, has been central to our analytical study of the Saronic Gulf during LH IIIB to earliest IIIC, which featured in William Gilstrap's doctoral research (Gilstrap 2015; Gilstrap, Day, and Kilikoglou 2016). Kontopigado in Alimos is best known as perhaps the most substantial industrial facility recovered of this period: an extensive system of rock-cut channels, basins and work surfaces, most likely used in the retting of flax (Kaza-Papageorgiou et al. 2011: 201). The installation was built approximately 500 m to the south of the settlement that was occupied from at least LH IIIA1 to LH IIIC Early 1 (Kardamaki and Kaza-Papageorgiou 2018). The toponym itself refers to the wells of the areas and presumably the plentiful water source, something vital for the process of retting. We know from Linear B that flax production was within the interests of the palace at Knossos and Pylos, most obviously because textiles were of such high social value (Killen 1985). Here, near the west coast of the Attic peninsula, it may have had an added importance: the production of sailcloth for the Mycenaean fleets (Kaza-Papageorgiou et al. 2011: 232). While this area on the west of the Attic peninsula was an important industrial zone from at least the Final Neolithic, notably concerned with metallurgical activity, the link to flax might be another that encourages us to envisage the possibility of the political and economic control of craft production by a powerful elite in Athens, only 5 km distant, where Papadimitriou (2023) has presented evidence of an extensive Mycenaean town around the Acropolis.

In the same complex there was substantial pottery production, testified by wasters discovered both in the area of the installation and in the nearby settlement, with heavily warped vessels and a fragment of a potter's wheel-head discovered in one of the refuse areas in the settlement (Kaza-Papageorgiou et al. 2011: 205 fig. 3; 206 fig. 4) (Figure 9.2). Although most of the wasters are found in later contexts of the site (LH IIIB2 Late and LH IIIC Early 1), ceramic production in the Late Bronze Age is likely to have taken place there at least from LH IIIA1, as pottery of that phase is identical in terms of fabric and manufacture with that of later phases, and there is continuity even in some shapes, such as the *hydriae*. While the date of construction of the rock-cut channels and basins is more difficult to establish, there is substantial evidence that the Mycenaean installation was built in late LH IIIA2 or early LH IIIB. Thus, these specific Kontopigado workshop facilities may have been in operation from at least the late 14th to the early 12th century.

Many of the wasters are complete enough to allow their typological characterization from both macroscopic and analytical examination. The site produced all sorts of painted and plain table ware (fineware), cooking pots and utensils like baking trays, lids, griddles and a range of coarse pottery from jug/jars through to storage jars and bathtubs in a range of closely related recipes. This very broad range of vessels was made through the manipulation and mixing of an unusually restricted range of raw materials, the recipes differentiated by different combinations according to the ware being produced (Gilstrap, Day, and Kilikoglou 2016). We have very detailed information on the range of wares and vessel types produced in this workshop (Kaza-Papageorgiou et al. 2011: 234–262; Kaza-Papageorgiou and Kardamaki 2012: 186–187 figs. 22:62–63; 23:65; 190 fig. 24:75). The production of bathtubs at Kontopigado appears to have been a specialty, and has yielded one of the largest accumulations of large and medium size tubs known in Mycenaean Greece, suggesting that the use of these vessels went beyond that known from a typical household (see Kardamaki and Kaza-Papageorgiou 2018: 130–131 fig. 6.35), perhaps for dyeing textiles.

The pottery products of the Kontopigado workshops are present in, and sometimes dominate, assemblages in sites around the Saronic Gulf (Gilstrap 2015; Gilstrap, Day, and Kilikoglou 2016, 2021). In rescue excavations at 4 Ragkava Street in Plaka, Athens (Papadimitriou 2023), the Kontopigado fabrics are the most common in fineware vessels, while at the important LH IIIB harbor settlement of Kanakia on Salamis, Christina Marabea's detailed macroscopic study suggested the consumption of pottery from Attica and our analyses demonstrate that pottery manufactured at Kontopigado makes up the majority of the assemblage, as well as that of the nearby Cave of Euripides (see Marabea 2010; 2012; 2021; Gilstrap, Day, and Kilikoglou 2021).

At first, then, Kontopigado would appear to be a prime candidate for some sort of centralized control of ceramic production, because of its location in an important crafting complex. The substantial industrial remains for flax production and the sheer size and labor invested in hewing the two-meter wide, 30–60 cm deep channels from the rock, preserved to a length of up to 64 m, would indicate substantial mobilized (enslaved?) labor and the possible involvement of those in power in Central Athens, or localized dispersed elites (cf. Nakassis 2008; 2021). In addition, the pottery from the workshop(s) in the same location is widely distributed, showing its importance in the local everyday economy.

Another aspect makes the pottery produced at Kontopigado stand apart. The closely related fabrics of pots of different function also paint a different picture to that prevalent in other regions and, in fact, to practices during earlier and later periods in Attica itself. We usually see a more stark distinction of the fabrics used for table wares, different from those of cooking pots, and from coarser jars. The classic difference between these categories often includes the use of low-calcareous, low-fired coarse materials for cooking pots and higher fired, calcareous base clays for the other two categories, with an added coarse-fraction distinguishing the coarser jars from the fine table wares. In many instances these different technological choices are accompanied by indications of different forming techniques and separate places of production. Yet, at Kontopigado, we have evidence for three main clay-rich earths that are combined to produce fabrics that differ only slightly according to pottery type (Gilstrap, Day, and Kilikoglou 2016). The range of pottery produced there shares remarkably similar firing regimes (Gilstrap, Day, and Kilikoglou 2016: 505–506), in all cases appearing to be kiln fired, which is not always the case for cooking pottery of this period (see below for Laconia). We know from the production debris that all the main types, from painted fine ware, through storage jars and cooking pots, are produced at this important potting center.

However, it should be noted that Kontopigado was already a substantial production center in Early Bronze II, *one and a half millennia* before our time period, with numerous wasters in classic shapes of that period, such as sauceboats, bowls and collared jars, from substantial fills and floor deposits at the site (Tsai 2021; Tsai et al. 2023: 95–98). Even in the third millennium BCE, its products have a wide distribution, mainly linked to drinking sets and collared jars, the early amphorae, through the Cyclades (Ayia Irini-Kea; Phylakopi-Melos; Akrotiri-Thera) to the gateway Cretan port of Poros-Katsambas and further inland at Knossos (Day and Wilson 2016). Important and large-scale pottery production clearly has a long history at the site.

In the Mycenaean period at Kontopigado, there is intriguing detail about the complexity of the pottery tradition and output. Until LH IIIA1, ceramics produced here were characterized by distinctive regional pottery classes of solidly painted burnished and unburnished wares, well known from previous work on the Acropolis, the so-called Acropolis burnished ware or monochrome "matt" wares (Kaza-Papageorgiou and Kardamaki 2018; Mountjoy 1981; Maran 1992). Large scale production of the types of vessels used in palatial and other contexts of large-scale

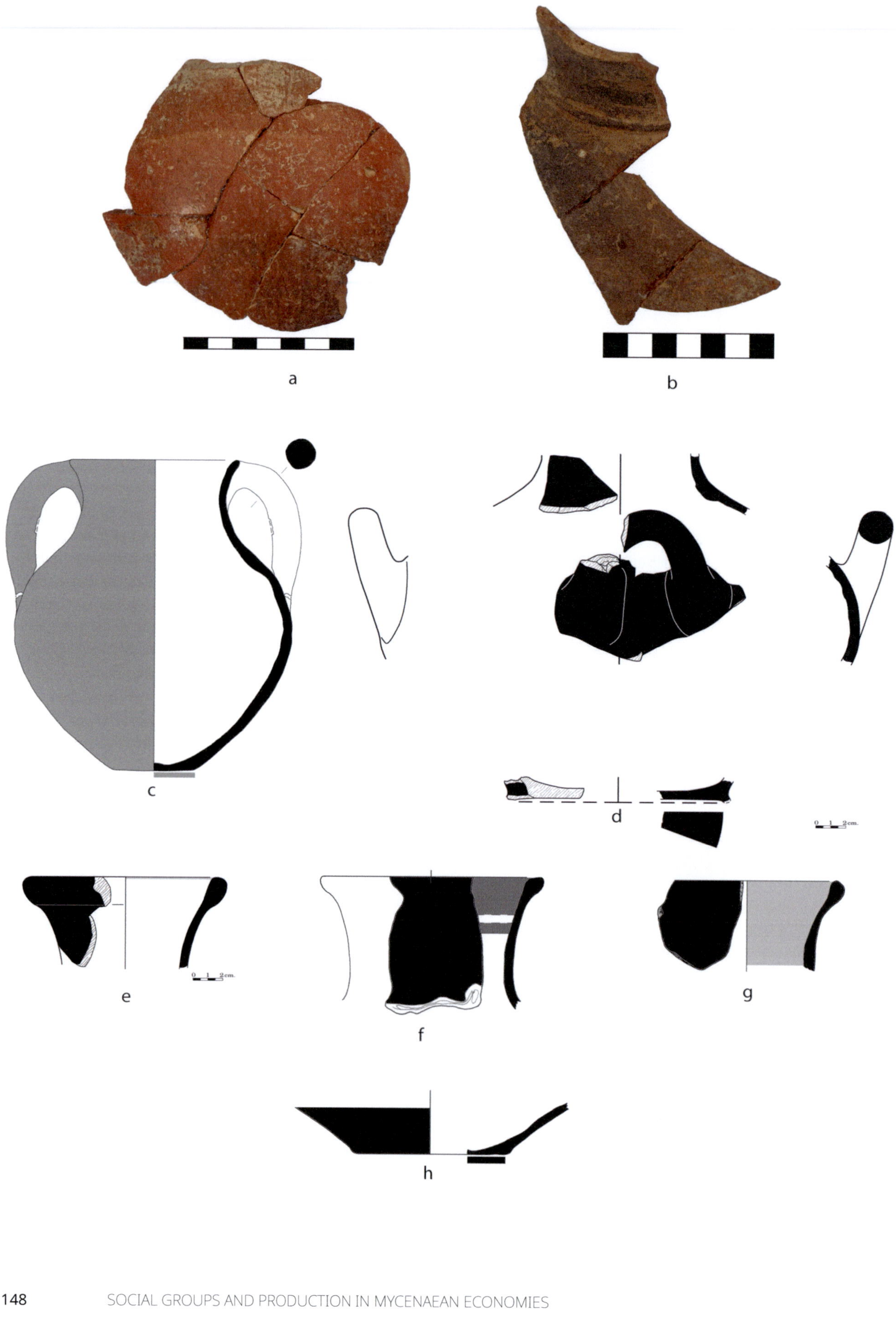
a
b
c
d
e
f
g
h

(Opposite page) Figure 9.3. Monochrome and painted pottery vessels produced at Kontopigado, Alimos. (a–c) after Kaza-Papageorgiou and Kardamaki 2018: 41 fig. 15,5 (a); 45 fig. 16,3 (b); 14 fig. 5,1 (c), photos E. Kardamaki, drawing V. Hachtmann; (d–e) after Kaza-Papageorgiou and Kardamaki 2017: 51 fig. 29,131 (d); 54 fig. 30,151 (e), drawings by B. Konnemann; (f–h) after Kaza-Papageorgiou et al. 2011: 252 fig. 16, 112 (f), 113 (g), 116 (h), drawings E. Kardamaki.

commensality started at Kontopigado in the late 14th century (LH IIIA2) with standardized, intensive production of the common universal table ware, such as plain *kylikes* (Kaza-Papageorgiou and Kardamaki 2018 for discussion). However, at the same time, production of the distinctive regional pottery shapes and styles of surface treatment continued there uninterrupted, in the form of *monochrome burnished drinking/closed sets*, that were among the most common vases produced at Kontopigado (Kardamaki and Kaza-Papageorgiou 2018). This pottery class represents a local or northern Saronic Gulf tradition in late MH or early LH, and continues without interruption, although modified, up to the late 13th century. Unlike in LH IIIA1, the focus later was mainly on closed monochrome vessels and less on open forms (Figure 9.3). So, while LH IIIB saw the large-scale production of standard plain and dark-on-light painted Mycenaean types with lustrous or semi-lustrous paint, the monochrome burnished/sporadically burnished tradition not only continues, but is dominant at Kontopigado (Kardamaki and Kaza-Papageorgiou 2018).

Interestingly, while the monochrome burnished pottery from Kontopigado was in extensive use and quite popular in Kanakia (see Marabea 2012), this seems not to have been in demand in the extensive Mycenaean center around the Acropolis, according to recent studies by Trevor van Damme (2023). In addition to this, the sporadic or more intensive burnishing of the vase surfaces — one of the hallmarks of local manufacturing techniques — was also applied during LH IIIB in standard Mycenaean vessel types (e.g. deep bowls, stemmed bowls, kylikes). One of the most common Kontopigado shapes with burnished surfaces is represented by the plain large or medium sized closed vases like *hydriae* and *amphorae*. These had a wide distribution and are well documented in the contexts of Kanakia (Marabea 2012) and the Athenian Acropolis (Gauß 2003).

From this it seems that the potters in LH IIIB Kontopigado might belong to, or be riding on the tails of, a long-established production center with a strong reputation for its products. However, the seemingly relative homogenization of clay recipes and firing regimes at Kontopigado in the later Mycenaean period may well hint at changes in the repertoires and practices of craftspeople in a long-lived crafting community.

Such changes in production practices are far from general in the region and, even if made at the level of the producers, are dependent on the preferences of consumers. The island of Aegina with its substantial, long-lived tradition as a potting center, had been in business for several more millennia than even Kontopigado, with little change in the clay choice and even in some trademark surface finishes, such as the thick burnished red slip, which can be found certainly as far back as the Early and Middle Neolithic, in the sixth and fifth millennia BCE (Vitelli 1993: 112, 129 for andesite wares). With regard to Aegina, clear evidence for customer loyalty exists at LBA Kanakia on Salamis, where not one example of cooking pottery from Kontopigado has been found, despite the rest of the assemblage (from fine pottery to domestic wares, bathtubs and storage jars) being dominated by products from that center (Marabea 2019). The cooking pots in Kanakia are imported from Aegina, products of an unchanged tradition, well after the abandonment of Kolonna. These choices of consumption give an even stronger flavor of a fragmented landscape of pottery production, reputation, demand and preferential consumption, which is always based on, reproduces and alters social ties between neighboring and even more distant communities. Similarly, until the Late Bronze Age the Saronic Gulf hosted potting communities that are surely linked to continued production in the same locations over millennia, to established communities of practice, most likely with systems of apprenticeship which relied on family structure, inter-marriage and post-marital residence patterns.

Despite this background, and a long history of pottery production in the same location, Kontopigado provides strong evidence for a different level of organization. Essentially, it appears to be a workshop that integrates the production of a wide range of pottery not only spanning the traditional functional divides such as cooking, tableware and storage, but also across stylistic divides, from the "traditional" LH IIIA1 burnished/unburnished pottery to plain and lustrous painted standard Mycenaean wares. Not only are the choices of raw material and firing practice shared across the repertoire, but recent work on the forming techniques employed at Kontopigado point to an unusual consistency across all types (Choleva pers. comm. 2024). After all, it seems that pottery manufacture was also only one activity in a center which comprises the largest known Mycenaean crafting complex, with possible large scale linen production. Similarly, the standardized large-scale production of the whole range of pottery from *kylikes* to bathtubs is certainly a strong candidate for production which differs from that before and, indeed, after this period, when certainly the manufacture of finewares and cooking pottery often represents rather different technical and perhaps social worlds.

At the end of the LBA, the scale of the complex at Kontopigado suggests substantial investment and a large

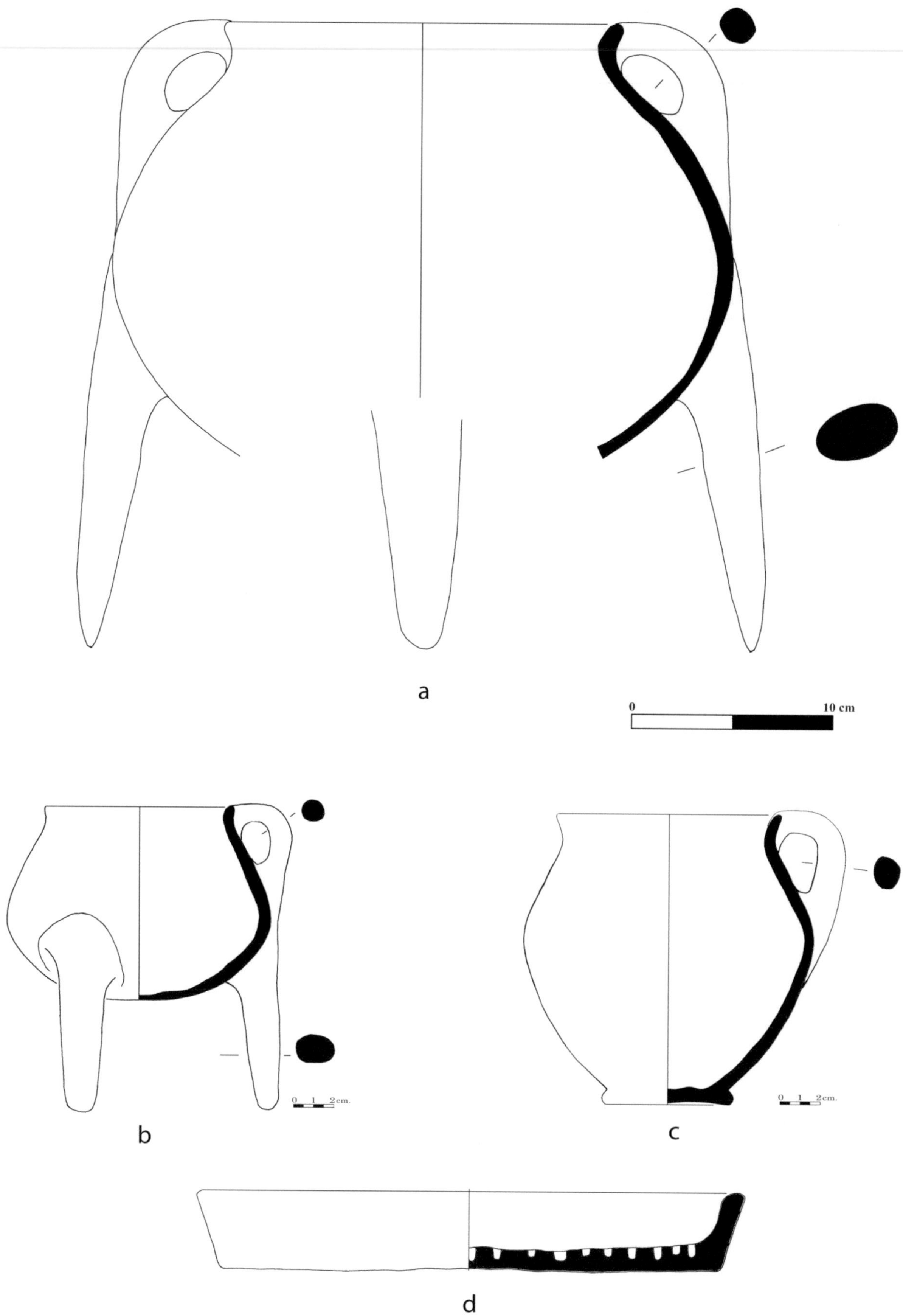
a
0
10 cm
b
0 1 2cm.
c
0 1 2cm.
d

(Opposite page) Figure 9.4. Cooking wares produced on Aegina (a) and at Kontopiagdo (b–d). After Kaza-Papageorgiou and Kardamaki 2017: 60 fig. 36,175 (a), drawing E. Kardamaki; 22 fig. 16,43; 62 fig. 37,183 (b–c), drawings V. Hachtmann; after Kaza-Papageorgiou et al. 2011: 260 fig. 24,155 (d), drawing E. Kardamaki.

output, arguing for the likelihood of control by local authorities, linked to the major center around the Acropolis. In this light, it is also worth returning to the remarkable patterns of the consumption of the center's products, which we linked above to consumer choice. Perhaps the absence at Kanakia of cooking pottery manufactured at Kontopigado, when all other of its products find their way to Salamis, is not just about customer loyalty, as the majority of the cooking range from the Attic center is rather different in nature, with smaller vessels and intended for more refined and special food preparation (Figure 9.4). Perhaps these are better suited to the tastes and commensal contexts that interest an urban elite, the production of a range in great demand in a palatial center in Athens?

This example of a production site in Mycenaean Attica raises a range of questions, and it demonstrates the sheer level of detail that we now possess, through integrated analytical approaches, to learn about the location of production, patterns of technological practice and the distribution and consumption of such products. It certainly takes us away from a false picture of homogeneity of pottery practice within and between regions. With this in mind, we turn to the example of Laconia, another area where ceramic networks were more diverse than previously acknowledged for the Mycenaean period

Gritty Wares and cooking pottery in Late Bronze Age Laconia

New information from ceramic study and analytical programs, focused on the recently discovered palatial center of Ayios Vasileos, offers increased definition in the chronology of the area, of the architectural phasing of the Menelaion and Agios Vasileios, as well as the changes in their generally shared material culture (see also Vasilogamvrou, Kardamaki, and Karadimas 2021).

When typical fineware Mycenaean pottery is established in an area, we tend to see it as "normal," when in fact it itself is an intrusive technology that we use to define a period, sometimes side-stepping acknowledgement of the veritable range of very different pottery types and production technologies at that time. Thus, the rather heterogeneous world of pottery in Laconia comprises our next example, illustrated by consideration of two pottery types: the so-called Gritty Ware and the range of cooking vessels.

Gritty Ware, made in a distinctive fabric, is handmade by coil building. The characteristic fabric, calcareous and tempered with fine sand particles, is used in Laconia to produce common vessels for the consumption of food and drink from late Middle Helladic times. The fabric is consistent, with a pale-firing, often birefringent clay groundmass, usually with microfossils and fossil shell and a consistent range of sand grains of sedimentary and metamorphic rocks (Figure 9.5c, d). The bimodal distribution of inclusions demonstrates the deliberate addition of the coarse fraction (Menelaion: Lis 2017b; Agios Stephanos: Whitbread and Jones 2008). The gritty fabric appears in goblets, as well as in other open shapes and jugs, both plain and matt painted (Rutter and Rutter 1976; Zerner 2008; Hachtmann 2023: 292–295). When the Mycenaean period is heralded by new fine table wares, formed with the use of the wheel (Choleva, Jung, and Kardamaki 2020) with highly fired calcareous clays and the skillful use of iron-rich paints, it is informative to see changes that took place in the products of the single potting center that produced the distinctive Gritty Ware fabric.

From its former dominant position (Hachtmann 2023: 263 tab. 6; 292; 364–370 fig. 13–19), in the period marked by phases LH IIB to LH IIIA2, this long-lived handmade tradition shifts its focus to the production of water jars with a matt or semi-lustrous paint (Kardamaki 2017). It appears to be a reaction to being usurped in the market for tableware by the popularity of what has been seen as the new-fashioned "true" Mycenaean pottery, itself probably the legacy of the importation of Cretan technology during the Middle Bronze Age. While the Gritty Ware is less common after LH IIA, in comparison to the standard Mycenaean fine wares, it has a wide distribution across Laconia and is well represented at both Ayios Vasileios and the Menelaion. At Ayios Stephanos, on the southern Laconian coast, there is good evidence for the existence of the Gritty Ware after LH IIA, though the relevant deposits (LH IIB and LH IIIA1) are poorly preserved (Mountjoy 2008). Though Gritty Ware occurs as a relatively smaller proportion of the total assemblage, in post LH IIA deposits, and especially in LH IIB most large and medium sized storage and transport vases (amphorae and hydria) occur in this ware (Figure 9.5a, b).

While this distinctive ware was not recognized and quantified in LH I–IIIA1 deposits from Building A at Ayios Vasileios (Kondyli and Mathioudaki 2022: 155, note 5), it is present at the site in these early LBA phases and is well testified in the central Laconian assemblage of the Menelaion (LH IIB/LH IIIA). At the latter site, a group of handmade and plain water pots was found *in situ* in Mansion 1, among what seems to be a rather typical Mycenaean assemblage. Catling (2009: 422) has discussed these in detail, emphasizing their distinctive manufacture, hand forming method and the characteristic fabric, which he described as varying from "quite fine with little inclusion to much sand/or grit". Although he correctly suggests that these vessels continued a

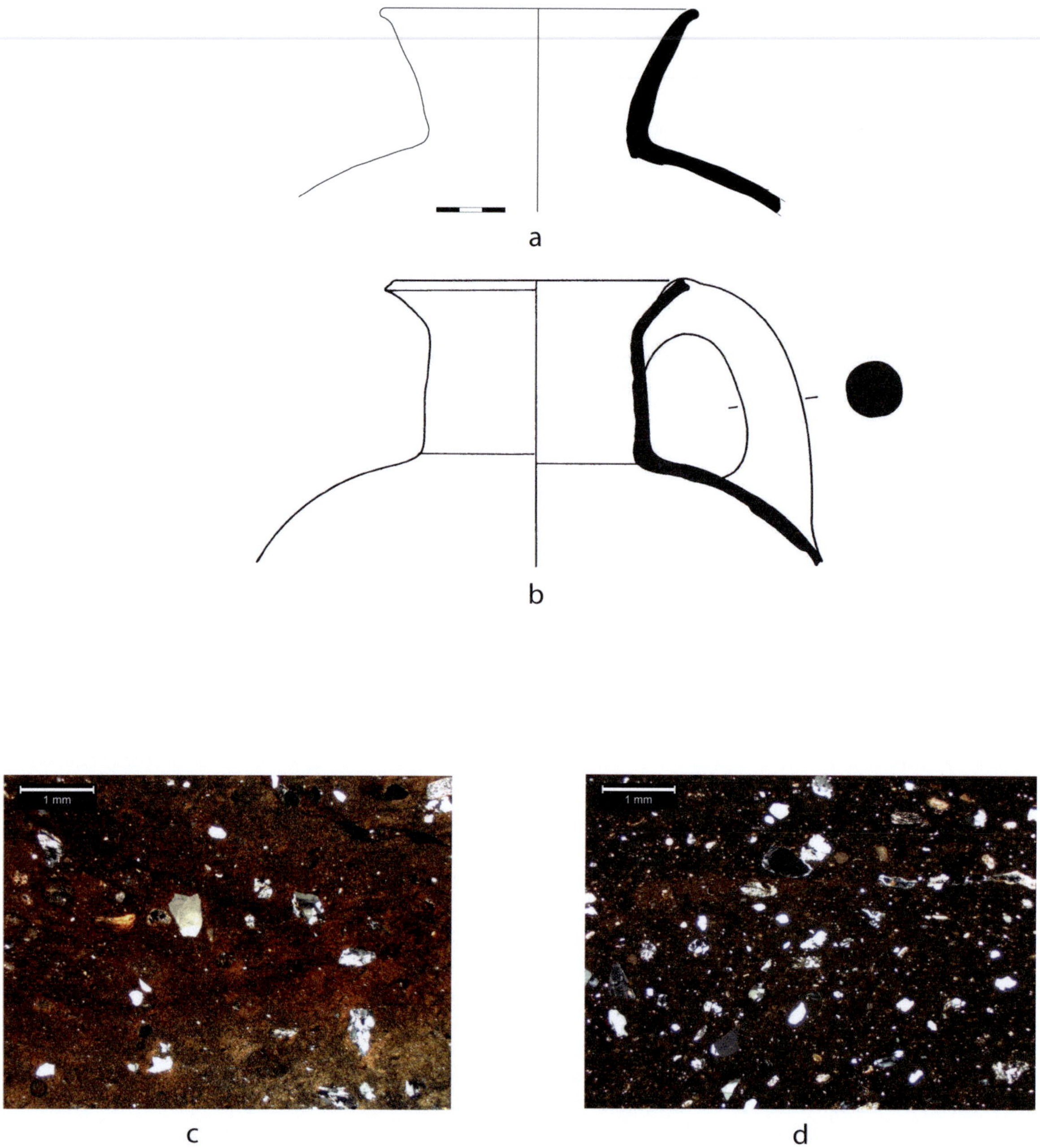

Figure 9.5. Laconian Gritty Ware shapes and thin section photomicrographs. (a) drawing A. Poelstra; (b) after Catling 2009: fig. 102, ET 179. scale 1:3. (c) Ayios Vasileios 16/7 (d) Ayios Vasileios 16/35, photomicrographs P.M. Day.

MH III and LH IIA tradition, and seeks similar phenomena in Athens and Kea, he did not associate them with the MH plain Gritty Wares from elsewhere in Laconia, as found in Ayios Stephanos. However, we suggest that their fabric, details of manufacture, and shape suggest that the water pots from the Menelaion belong to the same types as the MH III and LH IIA pots from Ayios Stephanos and Ayios Vasileios. Such a comparison of Gritty Ware across these three major (published) sites is aided through valuable new information provided by Lis (2017b) in a petrographic study of plain and painted water pots from the Menelaion. Although Lis is right to assign the plain vessels of the Menelaion to a local pottery tradition, he too does not associate these with the gritty plain or "gritty yellow Minyan" of Ayios Stephanos.

Even later examples of closed vessels in Gritty Ware are well documented in LH IIIA2 deposits of Ayios Vasileios (Kardamaki 2017), although by this phase they are rarer. Interestingly, at Ayios Vasileios the fabric of some of the "Gritty Ware vessels tends to become less coarse in

LH IIIA1 and LH IIIA2, in assemblages dominated by fine Mycenaean pottery.

We contend that the distinctive *chaîne opératoire* of the Gritty Wares denotes a crafting community wedded to a long-lived tradition, competing for its place in a changing ceramic landscape. The basis for suggesting that we are dealing with a community in a consistent location is the continuing specific fabric indicating not only sand temper, but the same distinctive petrological composition of the sand grains, accompanied by the same calcareous, fossiliferous base clay. We see the craft practice not only as embodied action, passed down through close, extended apprenticeship or training, but as an activity focused on a community consisting of practitioners and non-practitioners whose village or area was linked explicitly to the craft. In this case, the potters do not immediately adopt the new practices of production, but instead comprise a separate community that, based on its reputation, looks to survive by exploiting other spheres of demand and consumption.

This picture of diversity in the potting communities of Laconia and the positioning of crafting groups within a rapidly changing material world can be addressed by a second example, that of cooking wares from late Middle Helladic through to the end of the palatial period in LH IIIB. Around the time of settlement expansion and the first monumental building programs at the palace of Ayios Vasileios, in LH IIB and LH IIIA1, a new cooking shape makes its appearance at the site and across central Laconia in general, namely the *tripod* (Catling 2009: 425–426; Day et al. 2022: figs. 7, 8 and 9) (Figure 9.6a). The tripod cooking pot marks the beginning of new culinary practices in Mycenaean Greece and quickly became popular, perhaps also due to its suitability for outdoor cooking, which played a major role in consumption practices of the early Mycenaean elites (Wright 2004; also Lis 2017a). By at least LH IIIA1 the tripod, together with a whole new set of specialized cooking equipment such as baking trays, braziers, ladles and lamps at Ayios Vasileios, are made in a new fabric for the area, which is micaceous and coarse, and which has affinities in its choice of materials to practices on Kythera and Crete (Day et al. 2022: 370–377; 371 fig. 4). It is interesting to consider the reaction to these innovations by the local potting community that made handmade cooking pots in a characteristic style known as *button-based cooking jugs* (cf. Zerner 2008: 284 fig. 5.50:2195–2196 for Ayios Stephanos, and Hachtmann 2023: 263 tab. 6; 290–292; 362–363 fig. 11–12 for Ayios Vasileios).

Button-based cooking jugs were produced without interruption from the late Middle Helladic period, when they represented the main cooking vessel, to LH IIB and LH IIIA1, after which they are present, but more rare (Kardamaki 2017; Hachtmann 2023: 290–292, 361 fig. 10:137–145; 362–363 figs. 11–12 for button-based cooking jugs in a LH IIA deposit at Ayios Vasileios). The vessels were made in a characteristic schistose fabric that can be traced both at Ayios Vasileios and the Menelaion. Around LH IIB, when the tripod cooking pot was starting to gain popularity, this workshop changed its production strategies, adopting the new shape (Day et al. 2022: 376–377 for discussion) (Figure 9.6b).[1] However, this was the only new vessel adopted in the long-established schistose fabric, ignoring the other Cretan-influenced components of the intrusive culinary repertoire. Although reflecting the new trend for tripod vessels, these pots were still produced with "traditional" Middle Helladic techniques. They still had a round base, in contrast to the "Cretan-style" flat bases of those in the new micaceous fabric, and they continued with schistose sand tempering. Such diachronic persistence in cooking vessels is seen in crafting communities elsewhere, such as the Aeginetan potters and their handmade cooking pots, consistent from the Middle Bronze Age to the early 12th century (Gauß and Kiriatzi 2011) and the contrast of their products with the vessels reflecting newly introduced cuisine and cooking practices, as was discussed in the Kontopigado example above.

These are but a couple of examples from our work in Laconia, which indicate the existence of very distinct ways of producing ceramic vessels during the Mycenaean period, with substantial differences between broad functional types, but also diversity within functional categories. These testify to groups of potters reacting to the changing ceramic landscape, ostensibly re-positioning their products. Dare we say that this change takes place "as they compete for market share"? The establishment of a palace at Ayios Vasileios no doubt affected the consumption of pottery in the area. While we also see the broad use of wheel-coiling in the production of the Mycenaean fine-wares, there are slight variations which testify to differences in specific learned gestures and, therefore, to communities of potters (Choleva, Jung, and Kardamaki 2020). Equally, although chemical analysis suggests at least a *chemical* consistency in fineware pottery after LH IIB (Hein et al. 2021) this does seem to represent a consistency of the broad type of clay-rich materials selected in the region, rather than one source, as members of the group demonstrate clear compositional variability in thin section. Overall, these changes are consistent with the ebb and flow of influence and movement, especially in Laconia, which could be characterized as a border area between two cultural zones in the Bronze Age. In other words, such variability and dynamism are not restricted to the palatial period, though of course, with palatial consumption in mind, we await Vasilis Petrakis's study of the Linear B

1 Kondyli and Mathioudaki (2022: 161 fig. 11: a – b) date tripods found in the LH IIA – LH IIIA1 Deposit 3 of Building A at Ayios Vasileios to LH IIA. However, corresponding evidence for the shape is lacking from the substantial LH IIA deposit in the area of the cemetery at the site (Hachtmann 2023) and only comes in during LH IIB.

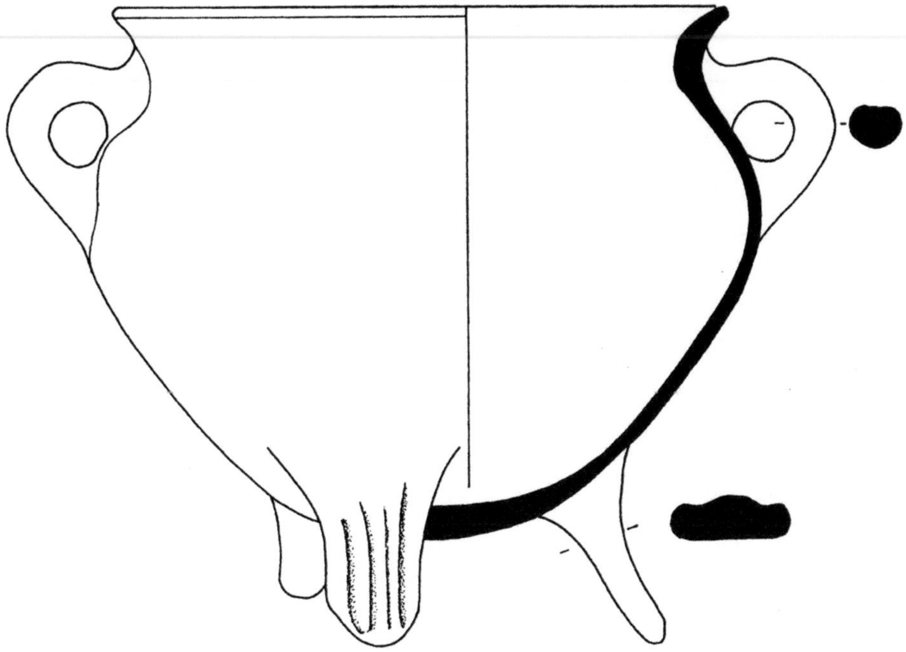

a

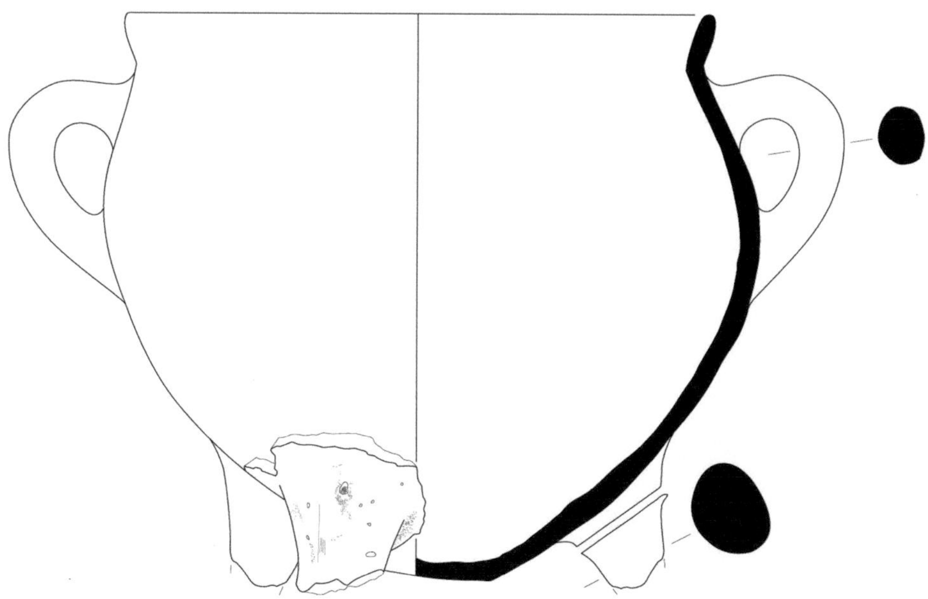

b

Figure 9.6. Cooking tripods from Laconia. (a) rounded based tripod cooking pot in long-lived schistose fabric, after Day et al. 2022: 371 fig. 3.2, drawing A. Poelstra. (b) flat-based cooking tripod in micaceous fabric, after Catling 2009: fig. 120, scale 1:3, CLO 57.

archive at Ayios Vasileios for insight into the activities of this most Cretan of mainland palaces.

Therefore, in these two Laconian examples, we witness both the adoption and rejection of pottery shapes and techniques that were newly introduced to everyday life and commensal practice. In both cases changes are made to the products of the crafting communities, one by making a version of the new shape, the other by changing the focus of their production. So, what does this case tell us about the Laconian potting communities in the Mycenaean period? In both instances, the practices of these specific existing potting communities, from the choice and manipulation of raw materials, through their forming techniques and firing practices, do not change substantially, if at all, in the face of the introduction of the characteristic fineware.

What does change is the range of shapes produced by the groups we discussed. This leaves us with the impression of a dominance of certain "ways of doing," even when a product repertoire is altered to service changing demands by consumers. In other words, there seems to be a "negotiated outcome" which balances acceptable change to the importance of continuity in long-lived technological choices and craft practices. Placing importance on the way things are done in the production of pottery, these crafting groups prioritized *inclusion* and *identity* through their everyday actions in a changing material and political landscape. In both cases, these are indeed the actions of communities of practice, seemingly wedded to place, rather than reflecting the control of the emergent political elites.

Of course, these actions are in response to the introduction of the classic repertoire of Mycenaean finewares, which clearly represent intrusive pottery technology and show us that production does indeed change. However, Choleva and co-workers, in their important study based on detailed analysis of forming methods, concur about the co-existence in Laconia of different potting communities with varied traditions and patterns of apprenticeship. The variability in Method 3 wheel-coiling forming methods, in terms of their detail and complexity, reflects differential demands in skill, with more complex methods gradually becoming dominant. Even so, by LH IIIA2 handmade vessels are very rare (Choleva, Jung, and Kardamaki 2020: 268, n. 167). The wheel-coiling method, which is to some extent "standardized" and effective in enabling an increase in output, in Laconia has variants, which indicate slightly different ways of mastering the potter's wheel, learned bodily gestures and, therefore, perhaps even marginalized potting communities (Choleva, Jung, and Kardamaki 2020: 271–272). The variation in the ostensible scale of production in groups represented by the slightly different forming methods, most likely indicates marked differences in their output, in a similar fashion to that suggested by Galaty for Messenia (1999b; 2010).

A transport stirrup jar group in the Argolid

If we are to suggest that potters in specific communities developed reputations and customer bases, indeed that their products would be recognized and carry a range of meanings, then the skill set, and the possible mobility of its practitioners is of importance. Sometimes the mobility of craftspeople of a specific tradition can be posited from rather detailed case studies and to illustrate this we now turn to the final palatial Argive Plain in LH IIIB2, to the sites of Tiryns and Midea and the occurrence of a specific type of transport stirrup jar.

Transport stirrup jars (TSJs) have long been the focus of analytical research, as they provide not only material evidence of the interactions between Crete and the Mycenaean Mainland in the Late Bronze Age, but also in some cases had inscriptions in Linear B that testify to their importance in the system of obligation that was central to palatial administration in both regions (Haskell et al. 2011; Maran 2005; Kardamaki et al. 2016). The establishment of their provenance, their place of production, became important in the reconstruction not only of economic links, but more especially of the balance of political power after the destructions of LM IB in Crete. Tablet KN K 700 from Knossos refers to 1800 TSJs, showing a palatial interest in large numbers of these large vessels, which are convincingly linked to the transportation of a value-added commodity, that of perfumed oil (Chadwick et al. 1986; Shelmerdine 1985). In terms of the TSJs, although the nature of the link between potters of these rather special jars and a centralized administration remains unknown, the fact that the inscriptions were painted *before* the pots were fired, in a script which is only used for centralized administration, would seem to demonstrate official involvement of the political authority in their manufacture (Boulotis 2014: 26; Kardamaki et al. 2016).

Previous work has concentrated on interpreting the Cretan provenance of some of these jars found on the Mainland (Haskell et al. 2011: 109–124). Tiryns was among the sites thought to have a large proportion of TSJs made in the Chania Plain of Crete and a recent project has aimed to look at a wider set of deposits to examine the provenance of the spectrum of TSJ types (Kardamaki et al. 2016). As we have discussed previously, it was estimated that around 6% of the TSJs at Tiryns are probably mainland products, mainly medium coarse in fabric, often standing out in terms of their shape from their Cretan counterparts (Kardamaki et al. 2016). In addition to these, however, amongst the vessels initially classified macroscopically as Cretan, is a very distinctive group (Kardamaki et al. 2016: 150–151 fig. 6; 152), and which comprise c. 15% of all TSJs, whose members have an ovoid shape and double zone decoration, with a deep wavy painted line motif on the main body and wavy line on the shoulder (Figure 9.7).

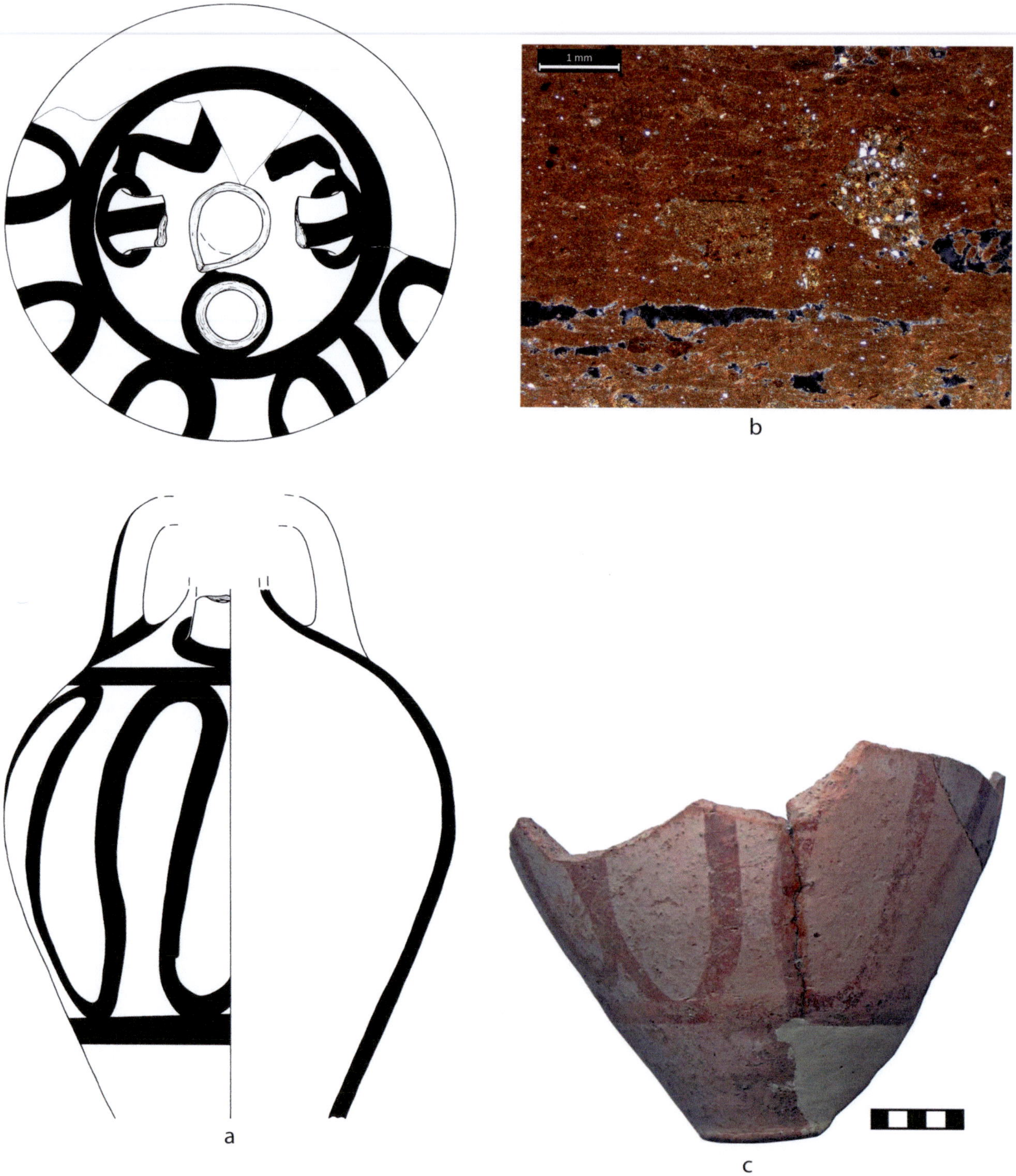

Figure 9.7. Argive Transport Stirrup Jars from Tiryns in the style discussed here. (a) after Podzuweit 2007: pl. 93, scale 1:3; (b) Mudstone breccia fabric, crossed polars, photomicrograph by P. M. Day, (c) photo E. Kardamaki.

All these features are very common in Central Crete (Haskell et al. 2011: 9–22). They have thick walls, being rather different from the "overgrown" fine ware jars that Haskell and others have argued are characteristic of Mainland jars (2011: 19–22). Furthermore, some details of their method of forming are even more suggestive of a link with Crete, namely a characteristic way of the joining of sections or coils in the lower body of the jars. At the join of the base coil to the central section, there is a marked thickening of the vessel wall, present in most examples made on Crete, but previously unknown in Mainland vessels. This specific way of joining the coils is clearly used by a number of different producers on Crete, as it occurs in a range of fabrics from the island (Haskell et al. 2011: 3, illustration 1.3). Such a shared practice that reflects learned gestures, through the specific detail of forming, gives us insight into apprenticeship and learning within communities, acquired through observation and imitation of repeated bodily movement.

The fabric of these vessels is also rather characteristic (Kardamaki et al. 2016: 151, fig. 6). They feature mudstone breccia (Figure 9.7b), which appears in fabrics produced in Corinth (Whitbread 1995: 273, 334–336; Burke and Day 2023: 16–17) and in Hellenistic Nemea (Graybehl 2015: Fabric 5), but also in long-lived fabrics in the Tiryns/Midea area, from the Final Neolithic onwards (Burke et al. 2018: Fig. 2). However, it is possible to distinguish this Argive fabric from the other two, as it has more frequent orange translucent silt and sand grains, despite it being a shared recipe across the Argolo-Korinthia (Burke et al. 2018: 148). Therefore, this distinctive group of TSJs, with its clearly intrusive influence in terms of forming technique, shape and decoration, all of which have strong links with Cretan pottery traditions, is made in a fabric local to the Argive Plain, which indeed has a long history from at least the late fourth millennium BCE.

With a production technology which has intrusive elements, distinctive to Crete, but a place of manufacture in the Tiryns/Midea area, these vessels indicate the movement in the late palatial 13th century, perhaps even earlier, of potters of the Cretan tradition producing TSJs, one of the shapes clearly of interest to the palace in terms of value-added goods and long-distance exchange. Of course, nothing is ever so simple, and displacement usually comes with some changes in practice, often familiar in consideration of processes of acculturation. The jar group does have slight morphological and stylistic differences, such as the slightly flatter cross-section of the handles, (when Cretan jars usually have more oval cross sections). In addition, the almost exclusive use of a linear decorative system, consisting of a single band on the shoulder and lower body, differs from the usual double or triple bands on Cretan jars (cf. Kardamaki et al. 2016: 154–155 figs. 8–9 for south central Cretan TSJs from Tiryns; Haskell et al. 2011: fig. 9, MYC78, MYC83 for West Cretan TSJs from Mycenae). However, we would suggest that these are minor details, equivalent to the slightly different motifs and syntax of elements in different ceramic workshops. On the other hand, the details of forming and coil joins and characteristic ovoid shape indicates the movement of an individual or individuals trained in practices developed on Crete, producing pottery in a long-lived production center and presumably potting community in the Tiryns/Midea area, at the very least sharing their specific clay sources and recipes.

While labelling the craftspersons that produced these TSJs as Cretan or Mainlanders seems rather a fruitless endeavor, it is clear that the embodied practice the objects reveal testifies to the movement of craftspeople from post-palatial Crete to the Argolid at the height of the Mycenaean period. Furthermore, it is surely of interest that — in this case — such mobility is associated with a type of vessel linked to the palatial economy and perhaps the specifics of the relationships between Crete and the Argolid. Linear B tells us of the movement of craftspeople, such as the (possibly enslaved) female Lemnian textile workers (Killen 1985), which opens the possibility of elite sponsorship of such migration. Yet this mobility is likely also to have occurred by individual initiative, and there are both archaeological and ethnographic examples of the diaspora of potters through problems in their home communities. Although the island of Aegina had a wide influence throughout the Bronze Age, with the suggestion of the movement of its potters to new production locations (Lis, Rückl, and Choleva 2015), it also suffered from a mass movement of its potters when the island population was exiled as a result of the Peloponnesian Wars (Klebinder-Gauß and Strack 2015: 90–92). Similarly, in the twentieth century CE the potters of Siphnos (Spathari-Begliti 1992) established workshops throughout the Aegean after the near-collapse of their distribution system due to the occupation in World War II and the economic collapse in the civil war. Whatever the particulars of these examples, our Argive Bronze Age potters using these distinctive clays are also involved in the production of basins and other coarse ware that closely match Cretan products (Demakopoulou 2009).

Southern Aegean crafting on Late Bronze Age Lemnos

For our final example in discussing social groups in the world of Mycenaean ceramics, we leave the perceived "heartland" and head to the island of Lemnos in the Northeast Aegean. This strategic location opposite the Dardanelles has produced a wealth of evidence that suggests such movement of craftspeople between distant regions was a long-lived phenomenon, leading to important links between potters across the Aegean. Our comments

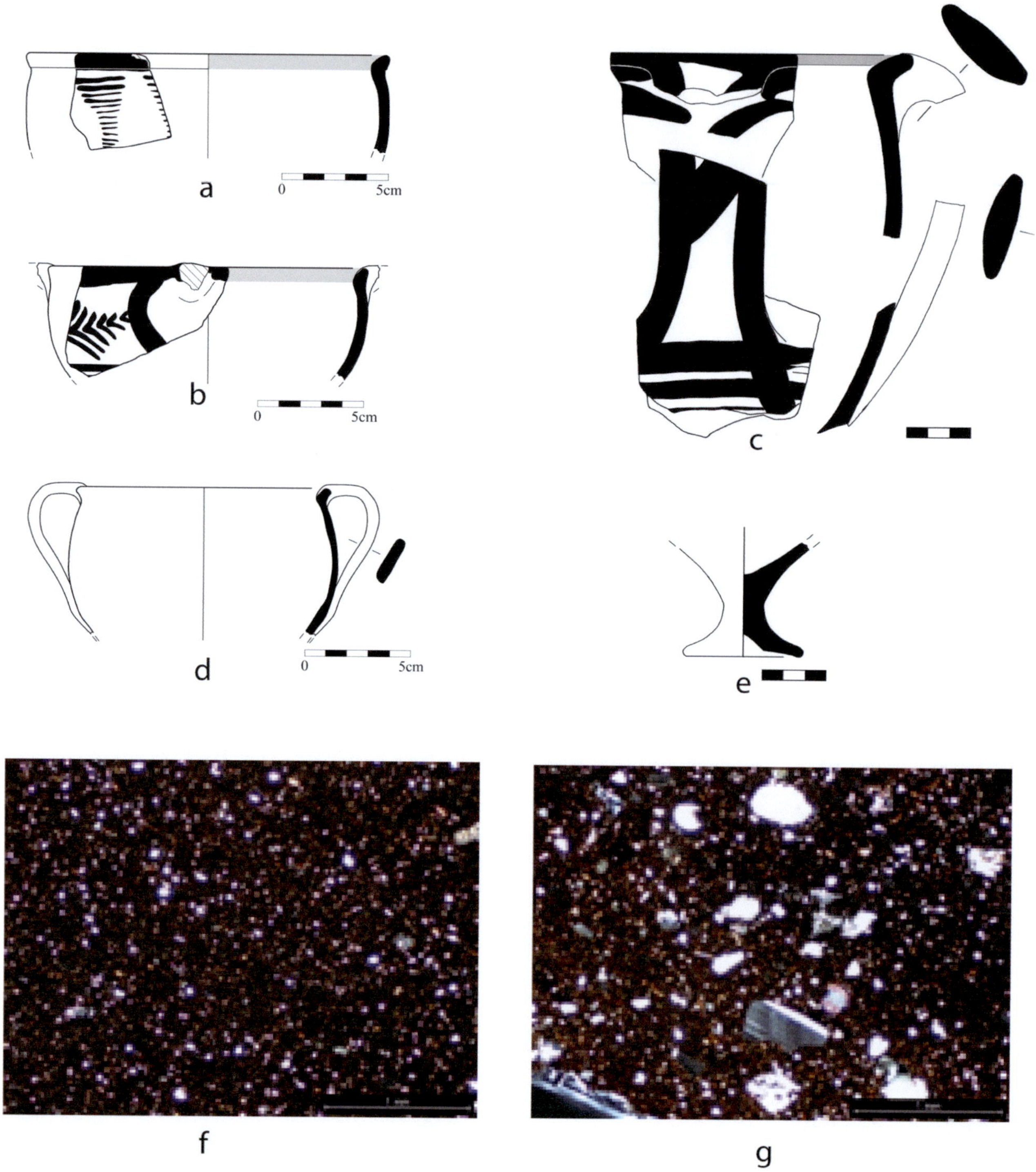

Figure 9.8. Examples of painted and plain Mycenaean pottery produced on Lemnos. (a–b) after Boulotis and Kardamaki 2021: 694 fig. 2, 1–2; (c) after Boulotis, Kardamaki, and Boloti 2017: 52 fig. 9,2, drawings V. Hachtmann; (e) photomicrograph of painted crater KOU 15/43, crossed polars; (f) photomicrograph of plain kylix KOU 15/25, crossed polars, photomicrographs by P.M. Day.

are based upon an analytical study of the substantial Late Bronze Age assemblages from Koukonisi on Lemnos (Boulotis, Kardamaki, and Boloti 2017; Boulotis and Kardamaki 2021), notably its rich Mycenaean phase.

The site of Koukounisi testifies to a strong local tradition of pottery production on the island, most notably the red slipped ware that appears there in the Middle Bronze Age and continues to the Late Bronze Age (Boulotis 2009: 183; 1997: 248; Boulotis, Kardamaki, and Boloti 2017: 49; Boulotis and Kardamaki 2021: 692). This ware group appears in other Lemnian sites, but seems to be rarer. It is a very distinct ceramic feature of the Koukonisi area and clearly represents diachronic continuity in ceramic production, through its consistent fabric, characterized by a range of volcanic inclusions, the wheel-aided forming practices in later phases and its distinctive slipped and burnished surface finish, sometimes with incised decoration (Boulotis 2009). Yet this rich pottery sequence is anything but a testament to isolation. On the contrary, it provides strong evidence of a closely connected world, with the appearance of clearly Minoan shapes in red slipped ware (Boulotis 2009: 187–188; Boulotis and Kardamaki 2021) and, later still, the rarer imitation of Mycenaean vessels. The reproduction of Cretan or southern Aegean shapes in local wares and fabrics has been observed also on the islands of Lesvos and Samothrace during what has been characterized by Girella and Pavúk (2015; 2016: 21) as a hybrid stage regarding the adoption of southern Aegean pottery features and other parts of Cretan material culture in the northern Aegean.

Besides the red slipped and burnished pottery, the earlier part of the Late Bronze Age (contemporary with LM IA and LM IB) sees the local production on Lemnos of a range of Minoanising vessels, including plain conical cups, tumblers, and semi-globular cups, both plain and painted, but also braziers, lamps and even rarer forms such as oval-mouthed amphorae (see also Boulotis, Kardamaki, and Boloti 2017). This Cretan-style pottery uses the same type of raw materials, and indeed possibly sources, as the red slipped and burnished pottery production. It is common across all the settlement excavated so far, and Boulotis has pointed to a distinct concentration of metallurgical activity that he argues may represent a "Minoan Sector," where there is evidence for the casting of objects which themselves have strong links to the Southern Aegean (Boulotis 2009).

In contrast to the Minoanising pottery, by Mycenaean times the ceramic assemblage of Koukonisi comprises a radical departure, with vessels in the style current in the Southern Aegean. Beyond imitations of Mycenaean shapes in the local red-slipped wares, in LH IIIA1 and especially LH IIIA2 there is a plethora of canonical fineware Mycenaean plain and decorated pottery at Koukonisi (Boulotis and Kardamaki 2021), but also animal and human figurines familiar on the Mycenaean mainland (Boulotis 1997: 265 fig. 28). This comprises a very substantial assemblage, with up to 30% of some "Mycenaean" levels made up of this fineware, notably in the LH IIIA2 deposit A, a refuse context (Boulotis, Kardamaki, and Boloti 2017). Amongst this pottery, there are large numbers of vessels that seem to comprise imported NE-Peloponnesian and other mainland finewares. However, a larger proportion, though in common Mycenaean shapes, manufacture techniques, surface treatments and styles, have a slightly different appearance, with a fine micaceous fabric (Figure 9.8a–d).

Petrographic and chemical analysis, the latter by neutron activation analysis, of these fineware Mycenaean vessels enables the distinction of clear groups, several of which have compositional matches with the Mycenaean mainland and especially the northeast Peloponnese. The majority of the Mycenaean vessels in the very fine micaceous fabrics are clearly separated and are compatible in both petrographic and chemical terms with a Lemnian source, notably the relatively fine, calcareous Neogene clays such as those in the area around Lychna and Varos, north of Koukonisi (Figure 9.8e). The choice of fine Neogene clay, its forming on the wheel in classic Mycenaean shapes and its high firing and use of lustrous red paint on a light ground comprise an important change in Lemnian pottery products. This represents more than the adaptation of the local practices, as could be argued from the point of view of fabric in the earlier Minoanising pottery. Plain Mycenaean vessels tend to be slightly coarser (Figure 9.8f), though there is some overlap between the two tableware categories. We suggest that these different raw material choices, and the rather different technological sequence and knowledge base in the local production of classic Mycenaean pottery suggests the movement of craftspeople versed in the Southern Aegean pottery traditions to Lemnos.

The question of Lemnian Mycenaean pottery produced from clays in the area north of the Moudros Bay becomes even more interesting when the material is placed in the wider context of the Northern Aegean and especially Troy, the well-known site on the Asia Minor coast where Mycenaean pottery has been well documented (Blegen, Caskey, and Rawson 1953; Mountjoy 2017). A hypothesized local production in the Troad of Mycenaean decorated pottery, which admittedly represented only a small portion of the Trojan assemblages, had been considered to go back to early in the Mycenaean period (LH II: Mountjoy and Mommsen 2006; Mountjoy 2017). Such an early local production of Mycenaean pottery was recently questioned and instead dated to a more advanced date namely LH IIIB (Pavúk et al. 2023).

Macroscopic comparisons of our Lemnian group with the Trojan material are very strong in terms of morphology, decoration and the distinctive fine micaceous fabric. Perhaps more importantly, comparative chemical compositional data suggest that our main Lemnian group from Koukonisi is compatible with the chemical profile of a pottery group of Mycenaean pottery from Troy dated to LH II, LH IIIA2 and especially LH IIIB (Troy Group-D). The sherds of this Troy Group-D were thought to represent production *in the Troad* of Mycenaean pottery in LH IIIA2 (five out of 30 samples dating to LH IIIA2 in Troy belong to Troy Group-D, Mountjoy and Mommsen 2006: 99 Tab. 1). The fact that the new Lemnian wares match the composition of the main fabric of Mycenaean pottery found at Troy, suggests the latter were instead produced on Lemnos. It shows that our group of potters on Lemnos was outward facing, producing not only for Koukonisi, Hephestia and other centers on the island, but also for exchange with the Asia Minor coastline. The techniques of production of these northern Aegean Mycenaean finewares in Lemnos are so specific and so different from the long-lived local traditions of pottery production, that they indicate the arrival of a different group of potters, who chose new types of raw material, innovative decorative techniques and a very specific firing process. Based on the sampled material at Koukonisi, local production of painted and the later plain Mycenaean pottery may have started here as early as LH IIB/IIIA1, reaching its peak in LH IIIA2, and the workshop seems to represent a production place of central significance in the Northern Aegean.

This mobility of potters was at least in response to a demand in the northeast Aegean for such highly decorated table ware, with population elements from the southern Aegean clearly present. The technological links across such long-distances testify to the diaspora of a crafting community, bound by tradition, training and apprenticeship. Again, we should ask whether the movement of such specialists to the Mycenaean outpost of Lemnos concerned palatial centers, as much as the movement of Lemnian women to the Peloponnese referred to in Linear B archives? Or whether, in common with documented diasporas of potters throughout the Aegean in the 19th and 20th centuries, this did not involve a central authority, but opportunistic or enforced migration, usually through family ties?

Comment

Longevity of traditions and local histories

To consider the implications of these observations, our contention is that through the reconstruction of raw material choices, forming, morphology, surface treatment and firing, integrated analytical programs characterize specific technological practices, provide insight into whether these are conducted in different locations and — in the best circumstances — may establish the locations of these production centers. If, as here, we add a diachronic dimension, it immediately becomes obvious that some of these practices last for long periods of time in the same place, not infrequently over millennia.

Given that such practices are the product of an often long learning process, they reflect the social groups that host such transmission of knowledge. Technical traditions, therefore, become more than an act of producing ceramic objects, instead being fundamental to belonging and community. As these groups and acts of production may be tied to specific locations and resources, group membership is often negotiated and maintained through skill, pride and the development of reputation for place and product. Of course, such practices are dynamic: tradition is not a given, but instead is performed, negotiated and at times transformed within the practice of technical sequences. It is this which lies at the basis of our consideration of social groups, as we discuss the production of pottery. In thinking of the reproduction of both the crafting of pottery vessels and the social group, we therefore acknowledge the situated, historical contingency of the activities. Local histories and trajectories are likely to be crucial to understanding the nature of ceramic production in the Mycenaean period, tied to regional variation rather than simply a reflection of a "palatial" economy (Figure 9.9).

Within the sometimes long-lived traditions, we might see the Mycenaean palatial phenomenon as a rather short-term disruption. Yet that it has an appreciable effect is seen in our case studies, in elements of marked change and other reactions of communities to fight for continuity of practice. The most radical change takes place in the Mycenaean finewares that have acted as an important guide to the transformations in and chronology of the period. The clearly intrusive elements of technical practice and ceramic style that epitomize Mycenaean pottery have, at once, masked a diversity in ceramic production and also provided us with the chance to examine the reactions of different potting groups to changes in demand and consumption. The above case studies provide evidence both for continuity in ceramic practices and for clear transformation in production. We will take the former first in looking at elements of resistance and reaction.

"That's the way to do it"

In our selected examples, evidence for the adaptation of repertoires, but based on retaining fundamental elements of the production sequence, are clearest in Laconia in the production of Gritty Ware and handmade cooking pots. We see the retention of forming practices and continuity in raw material sources and recipes. However, these strategies are increasingly challenged over the Mycenaean period. In the case of the Gritty Wares, it appears that a shift in the production strategies by the community is ultimately unsuccessful, as the vessels from that center become increasingly rare.

In both Laconian cases, characteristic fabrics are maintained, showing the strong link to place, resources and presumably to community, reputation and perhaps

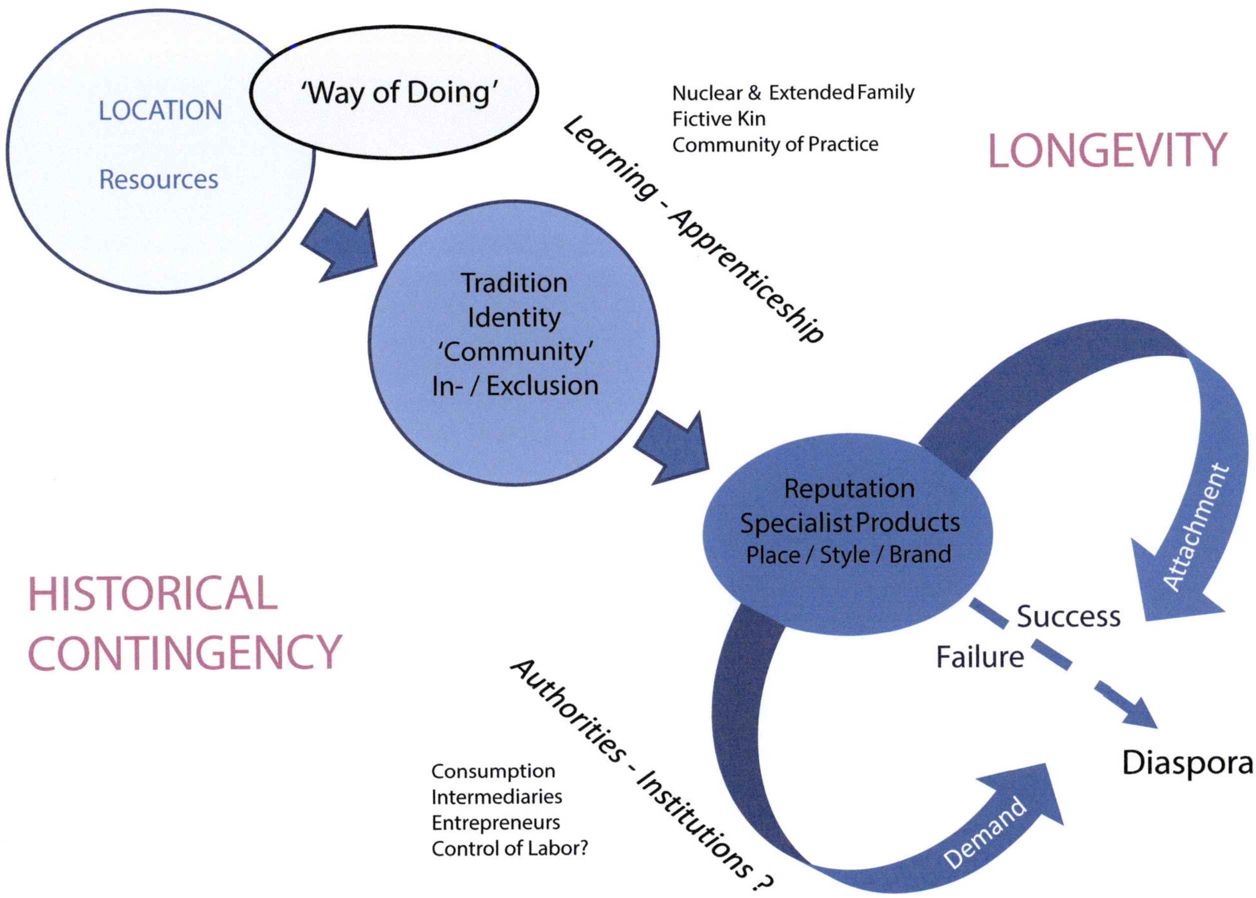

Figure 9.9. Graphic of longevity, historical contingency and transformation in Mycenaean pottery production. Graphic by P.M. Day.

to a consuming population. In material terms, continuity in clay sources and recipes is a common feature and their use in the intrusive shapes, like Laconian cooking tripods, and in the Argive TSJs challenges us to consider acculturation, hybrid practice and, ultimately the place of potters clearly trained in intrusive forming techniques or the introduction of new shape repertoires within local craft communities. Similarly, at Koukonisi on Lemnos, while there is substantial change in terms of a completely new choice of raw materials, pottery types, decoration and firing techniques in the production of Mycenaean finewares, elements of continuity exist in the red slipped ware and cooking wares.

What, then, determines such varied reactions to the change in pottery types, technologies and demand? In these crafting communities, sometimes over the *longue durée*, we see that practice is historically contingent, in terms of tradition and patterns of learning. Indeed, there are important practical considerations that would be fundamental to these social groups, perhaps most obviously in patterns of gendered labor and seasonality. Handmade vessels, such as the coiled Gritty Ware and schistose cooking pots of Laconia, involved less investment in facilities such as the potter's wheel and, perhaps more importantly, in terms of the extended and intensive apprenticeship often associated with wheel assisted manufacture (Roux and Corbetta 1990). The specialized nature of craftspersons trained in manufacture of pottery on the wheel perhaps curtails their potential commitment to agricultural practice, although that would have depended on the seasonality of production. In other words, the social costs of altering a pattern of less intensive production within households may be unacceptable to the community of potters. This is especially the case in terms of female labor within pottery production, balanced with domestic tasks, childcare and food production within a close range of the homestead. The change in these "ways of doing" that dovetail with other aspects of life is disruptive beyond ceramic craft practice, in a way which is fundamental to the coherence of family and transmission through generations.

These elements of continuity in the face of change, over the relatively short period of time of the Late Bronze Age, only serve to emphasize the endurance and adaptability of some of these "ways of doing." As clay recipes and raw materials tie some of these groups to a consistent location, specific areas and probably settlements must have developed traditions of ceramic craft production, reputations which may have underpinned demand, and the maintenance of long-term networks of distribution and consumption. In many ethnographic cases where such communities exist, it is the extended family that is the vehicle of learning and apprenticeship, forming the very basis of the community of practice, its rules of belonging and — ultimately — identity. It is also the case that when potters move, they take with them the practices of the communities in which they were trained, whose traces can be identified (Day 2004; 2022a). While the introduction of Mycenaean pottery, reflecting changes in commensal practice, is intrinsically tied to changes in technology, specialist products, scales of production and consumption, it would seem to us that the palaces in LH IIIA1 must have plugged into the output of existing potting communities for the majority of their ceramic needs. This is most characteristic in the region of the Argolid, where the production of Mycenaean pottery goes back to the very early stages of the LBA with the establishment of pottery production, both painted in LH I and plain in LH IIA (Rutter 2015). This was a source of expertise and skill base that would be increasingly exploited for the substantial consumption demands of the palaces. In Messenia, it has been argued convincingly that there is even a regional hierarchy of quality of *kylikes* produced in the workshops or centers supplying the palace at Pylos and surrounding settlements, linking this to "wealth" and "staple" pottery vessels and to differential interest of the palace in their production (Bendall 2004; Galaty 2010).

There are many Mediterranean ethnographic comparatives that show the degree to which craft practice is used to include and exclude, forming the very basis of identity in such communities. As Natalie Abell (2020; see also this volume) has argued recently for Kea, it is not a matter of the normal criteria for identifying specialism, of male labor, of the narrow factors of specialization, nor of the evolutionary schemes of production. These are intrinsically linked to social evolution and the colonialist roots of comparative ethnography. Kornos in Cyprus shows that female labor in households can form the basis of a major center of production and island-wide reputation for excellence (Ionas 2000; London, Egoumenidou, and Karageoghis 1990; London 2020: 55–56). In Cyprus, female labor in the last 200 years was valued very differently than, for example, in Crete, a product of the very different system of landholding and inheritance. The more such ethnographic cases are studied, the more it is clear that some items in our checklists to identify modes of production are of less importance than we think. What is undeniable is that the transmission of technical traditions and practices show, if not identity, a "groupness" (Roux 2019: 6) based on training within social groups which is often family based.

Contexts of Change

Regardless of the above, change characterizes the pottery landscape from LH I and IIA onwards, with the appearance of fineware lustrous painted vessels for display, and particularly the standard Mycenaean plain tableware for the consumption of food and drink (Kardamaki, forthcoming). Innovative in terms of their quality and sophistication of firing, and exploiting wheel-coiling, the scale of production of pottery is clearly increased, as palatial settings and large-scale ritual commensality increase demand for such vessels. While this is by no means a homogeneous phenomenon over time, the shared choice and manipulation of fine calcareous clays, the types produced and the firing form part of a very specific technical sequence, which was based on an extended period of training within potting communities. Nevertheless, there are differences between regions in key details of forming, which may point to differential skill and training.

It is apprenticeship and learning that form the basis of these very clearly different technological packages involved in the production of pottery within most regions. We know that the *chaîne opératoire* of a fine, painted kylix is usually very different to that of a cooking pot in Bronze Age Greece, the differences being so deep that they indicate specific communities of potters being responsible for each of the different products. Yet our example from Laconia shows differences *within* regions amongst pottery of the same type, most clearly the cooking pots. Choleva and co-workers' (2020) insights from forming show that, even within the intrusive fineware package and the wheel-coiling method that is pervasive, there are indications of variation in forming. Though slight, these are important enough to reflect bodily gesture that must have been the product of different training, and therefore of a different potting community. Thus even the fineware production quickly became a somewhat fractured landscape which reflects different groups and, probably, locations.

Amongst our case studies, Kontopigado provides the most convincing evidence for production in a workshop that might be linked to some centralized authority. Production is located in an important industrial complex, and its different pottery classes are clearly linked, almost "variations on a theme." Finewares, cooking vessels, storage jars and tubs differentially mix the same, restricted set of earths, using a very similar firing sequence for such diverse types (Gilstrap, Day, and Kilikoglou 2016), and remarkably consistent forming methods not observed in other studies (Choleva pers. comm. 2024). All indicate an unusual consistency in its large-scale production and distribution of the full range of pottery vessels in one location. What is of interest here is that, despite this homogenization of production, there are still strong elements of regional specialties, with the Saronic Gulf monochrome burnished wares continuing to be produced in the same workshop servicing a continued regional demand.

Here too, however, there is evidence for pottery production in the same location in Early Helladic II, which may indicate the existence of a community of potters whose technical tradition was passed down through learning and apprenticeship in extended families, or at least through fictive kin groups. It is worth asking whether the organization of a more centralized production unit would involve training outside of kinship groups and the family, while acknowledging that it is unlikely that Kontopigado would be chosen without the intention of exploiting an already long-established local base of skill and expertise.

Potters moving, especially when moving away from the raw materials they have been trained with, are presented with technical challenges of a magnitude that are sometimes difficult to overcome (Day 2004; 2022a; 2022b). Furthermore, the managed integration of potters with different technical traditions is far from simple. In a study on the Balearic island of Mallorca (Day et al. 2015), in the village of Portol, best known for cooking pots, an entrepreneur in the mid 20th century set up a factory employing potters of different traditions who were suffering a declining market for their products. He took on both specialist *ollers*, the potters who made cooking pots from red clays, and *gerrers*, who made water jars and other shapes from pale calcareous clays, the stark differences between the two traditions (and their specialist products) noted in their professional labels. When locals were asked how potters with very different technical traditions, honed over centuries, were integrated, we were told that they weren't integrated. The potters reproduced their division within the same business, by continuing to produce separately in different parts of the same building, adhering to their familiar well-suited and contrasting clays.

Perhaps some of the same obstinacy existed in the Mycenaean world, the same adherence to tradition. However, we have outlined clear evidence for skilled communities with an established knowledge base adapting to new technologies, to fit into new ceramic trends. As in the case of Kontopigado, it may have been a strength of these communities that they were wedded to specific locations, even with new demands and the introduction of new technical sequences.

Perhaps we find it easiest to consider such change when it is combined with obvious mobility of craftspersons, such as that we have suggested in the cases of both the Argive TSJs and Lemnos. In the latter case, the intrusive technology is so different from the local technical traditions and so close to those of fineware pottery in the Peloponnese that we believe that potters moved to the island from the Mainland of Greece, far away from their communities and locations of training. While this provides an example of relatively long-distance re-location, it is clear that such mobility of potters and other craftspeople was present at least throughout the Bronze Age and probably since the introduction of pottery vessels in the area.

Choleva and co-workers' Laconian study allows us to appreciate the implications of detailed reconstructions of forming techniques. Following Roux, they stress that the substantial additional training required in wheel assisted manufacture suggests that this, in essence, speaks to levels of specialization. But, in addition to variability within Laconia, they make an inter-regional comparison with the products of the Argolid. Though dealing with only a small sample of Argive or NE Peloponnesian pottery, some of which was found outside of its home region, and interpreting the NAA compositions in terms of micro-provenance, they show that there are preliminary indications of another forming technique, using higher RKE speeds, perhaps akin to Roux's Wheel-coiling Method 4 (Choleva, Jung, and Kardamaki 2020: 273) present in Argive pottery, which is not found, for example, in Laconia. Such a technique is more demanding and may have required a longer apprenticeship, though it is not entirely clear whether this would increase productivity (Roux and Courty 1998).

This chimes with a range of evidence of a particular intensification of production in the Argive Plain during the Mycenaean period, such as the prodigious quantities of pottery produced for palatial events and extensive trade at Petsas House (Shelton this volume). Even more specialized is the production of Pictorial style pottery at Mastos (Åkestrom 1987; Galaty 2010: 240–241). We take Mastos and the Pictorial Style to represent elite, market-orientated production of the highest quality pottery whose technical sophistication itself made it stand out as a value-added prestigious craft product. It seems likely that such production, in the hands of entrepreneurs, or perhaps less likely a political authority, would still require the active support of kin-based groups, given the length of apprenticeship. The alternative would be for a guild system of training, which if it ever existed was indeed short-lived and rare. It is worth remembering that already in LH IIB, Mastos hosts a potting community, demonstrated by the finding of a kiln structure of that period (Åkestrom 1987).

Social Groups and Historical Contingency

Against this mixed background of mitigated change, clear continuity, mobility of potters and regional diversity, what of the social groups that underlie ceramic production? Our reconstruction of the way in which pots were made, the choices and practices, reveal encapsulated gesture and consistencies in all links in the *chaînes*. In that way, while pots may not equal people, to a great extent they do equal potters (Roux 2019). Such production sequences are the product of training in activities that become second nature, an inherited body of knowledge that defines a community of practice, of belonging to a crafting group.

In most regions considered here, the wide range of pottery manufactured features different choices of raw materials, forming and firing. At times these different technical sequences correlate with the intended use of the vessels, or indeed are analogous to the size of the vessel. But it is also the case that many of these technical sequences are, instead, alternative ways of making a similar product.

We argue that it is the nuclear and extended family that often provides the framework for training in and the reproduction of these practices. In many historical contexts in Greece, pottery production has been primarily a seasonal occupation, most often combined with agricultural and other activities. Family often forms a broad and flexible labor base integrating training by older generations, as a source of continuity in their crafting livelihood. While it might be tempting to see mobility and transformation of practice as centrally driven by palatial interests in the Mycenaean world, there is little evidence of such, in the context of an already varied picture of pottery production.

Instead, in bottom-up studies we see a negotiation of change by production groups and the stepped transformation of practice in certain aspects of the pottery craft, and we note that it is not always the same components that change across workshops and regions. The support and experience of the extended family may have been even more importance in the case of restructuring of any aspect of production due to palatial demand. It should be remembered that, even amongst the fineware producers in Laconia, there are subtle differences in forming which testify to different learned gestures, beyond the more obvious variability across the ceramic spectrum in the area.

It could be argued that in accepting the possibility of specific centralized workshops, such as Kontopigado or those connected to Mycenae, we cannot discount corvée labor, yet Linear B does not give any hint of rations being given to practitioners. Ceramic vessels, unlike textile working and metallurgy, do not involve valuable raw materials being supplied, having value added by the craftsperson, and then returned to the center. Instead, the length of time involved in training potters in the manufacture of such everyday objects would suggest a continuation of the extended family as the core of training with place, production and tradition binding these families together. There is no evidence that this broke down, even with new demands in the length of training and skill level over the course of the Late Bronze Age, with the introduction of new techniques of forming, decorating and firing. Indeed, post-collapse from LH IIIC onwards, we witness marked continuity in pottery production which demonstrates the continuation of pottery traditions and presumably crafting communities after the demise of the palatial monuments and institutions.

This variability across regions, pottery types and craft communities, reveals a dynamic social and political world, with changes in economies of scale and consumption practice. It emphasizes the clear *historical contingency* of production in different regions. This is not to negate change, but that change occurs with reference to such traditions, reputations and the communities. Even our best candidate here for the status of centralized production related to a palatial elite — Kontopigado — is in a location which hosted large scale production already in the mid third millennium BCE. Of course, one can look at the production of Pictorial Painted pottery in the Mastos production site in the Argolid and recognize the specialist production of a high-quality, skilled product which is made with export in mind. While we may accept that such a workshop might be under the control of a central authority, or perhaps more likely of entrepreneurial individuals connected to the palace, it is the accumulated knowledge to produce such wares, the traditions and transfer of skilled practice in communities, that underlies such exploitation, which is ultimately temporary.

Within this scenario it seems likely that it was the nuclear and extended families, and their agglomerations, which continued to form the basis of training and continuity of practice. We find it intriguing that there are signs of these units and communities jockeying for position, trying to keep their livelihood going, as the changes in demand and the movement of craftspeople in an increasingly connected LBA world demanded that they tempered tradition with flexibility in a dynamic world of ceramics.

Acknowledgements

We would like to thank Daniel Pullen for the invitation to participate in this workshop, giving us the opportunity to celebrate the substantial achievements — thus far — of someone whom one of us (PMD) met all of 40 years ago in Athens and who was a beacon, in what was then at times a theoretical desert in the British and American Schools. In the mid-80s, as subsequently, Daniel stood out for his informed, critical, stance, at its best dripping with sarcasm, and his generosity of spirit and true collegiality. We are grateful to the Langford Endowment and the Department of Classics at Florida State University for the opportunity to attend such a fruitful workshop and to the participants whose stimulating papers showed not only new approaches on a variety of evidence, but produced a surprising convergence of viewpoints which belied the rather novel nature of what was argued. PD would like especially to thank Bill Parkinson and Michael Galaty for their consistent support and friendship.

As requested by the editor, this paper draws on the authors' fruitful collaboration over recent years examining Mycenaean pottery from a number of key sites, to examine what we can say about the social groups involved in the production of pottery during the Mycenaean period. On a topic that is often approached top-down, we have presented a selection of summary case studies to illustrate the range and indeed the depth of new analytical evidence, in the belief that we are now beginning to reach a critical mass of data that enables hitherto unthinkable detail on production patterns and regional variability. We believe that integrated analytical frameworks, especially those that value the social context of technology are now clearly an invaluable tool in allowing detailed data-driven, social and economic insights into the Late Bronze Age Aegean.

For access to pottery assemblages whose study and analysis have facilitated this study, we are indebted to Eva Alram-Stern, Christos Boulotis. Michael Cosmopoulos, the late Katie Demakopoulou, Nota Demopoulou-Rethemiotaki, Konstantina Kaza-Papageorgiou, Vasco Hachtmann, Nektarios Karadimas, Eleni Konsolaki, Yannos Lolos, Christina Marabea, Joseph Maran, Alkestis Papadimitriou, Apostolos Papadimitriou, Daniel Pullen, Naya Sgouritsa, Colin Renfrew, Tom Tartaron, Adamantia Vasilogamvrou, and David E. Wilson.

We have drawn on a variety of analytical research conducted over a number of years, through the fruitful collaboration of the Sheffield-Demokritos ceramics team, now based in the Ceramics and Composite Materials Research Group, Institute of Nanoscience and Nanotechnology at NCSR "Demokritos," Athens. We are grateful to Clare T. Burke, William D. Gilstrap, Heather Graybehl, Anno Hein, Vassilis Kilikoglou, Marta Tenconi and Evin Che-Hsien Tsai for analytical insights. We are indebted to Maria Choleva for allowing us to refer to her unpublished study of forming at Kontopigado.

Permission to take samples and analyze pottery has been granted and facilitated by the Conservation Directorate of the Hellenic Ministry of Culture, the Ephorates of Antiquities of Piraeus and the Islands, Argolida, Korinthia, the Cyclades, Heraklion, and Lesvos.

Ethnographic work referred to in the paper has benefited from the expertise and collaboration of Miguel-Angel Cau Ontiveros, Cati Mas Florit, and Noémi S. Müller, whom we thank warmly. Research described here draws on projects funded by the Marie Sklodowska–Curie Actions of the European Commission ("NARNIA: New Archaeological Research Network for Integrating Approaches to ancient material studies" — NARNIA ITN, Project no. 265010) and "COMEX: Transport Jars and Commodity Exchange in the Late Bronze Age Argolid, Tiryns and Midea"). The study of pottery from Kontopigado, Lemnos and Tiryns was supported by the Institute of Prehistory; that from Ayios Vasileios was conducted in the framework of the Austrian Science Fund (FWF) project "Studies on the new Mycenaean Palace of Ayios Vasileios in Laconia" (P28023-G25); pottery from Kontopigado through FWF project "Kontopigado: A Mycenaean Industrial Area South of Athens" (P31938-G25); and through the support of an Institute of Aegean Prehistory Post-Doctoral fellowship (2014/2015). For this support, we are immensely grateful.

Bibliography

Abell, N., 2020. Rethinking Household-Based Production at Ayia Irini, Kea: An Examination of Technology and Organization in a Bronze Age Community of Practice. *American Journal of Archaeology* 124: 381–416.

Abell, N., and J. Hilditch, 2016. Adoption and Adaptation in Pottery Production Practices: Investigating Cycladic Community Interactions through the Ceramic Record of the Second Millennium BC. In *Beyond Thalassocracies: Understanding Processes of Minoanisation and Mycenaeanisation in the Aegean*, edited by E. Gorogianni, P. Pavúk and L. Girella, 154–171. Oxford: Oxbow Books.

Åkerstrom, A., 1987. *Berbati 2: The Pictorial Pottery*. Skrifter utgivna av Svenska Institutet i Athen 4°, 36:2. Stockholm: Paul Åströms Förlag.

Arnold, D. E., 1985. *Ceramic Theory and Cultural Process*. Cambridge: Cambridge University Press.

Arnold, D. E., 1993. *Ecology of Ceramic Production in an Andean Community*. Cambridge: Cambridge University Press.

Arnold, D. E., 2000. Does the Standardization of Ceramic Pastes Really Mean Specialization? *Journal of Archaeological Method and Theory* 7: 333–375.

Arnold, D. E., 2008. *Social Change and the Evolution of Ceramic Production and Distribution in a Maya Community*. Boulder: University Press of Colorado.

Arnold, D. E., 2015. *The Evolution of Ceramic Production Organization in a Maya Community*. Boulder: University Press of Colorado.

Arnold, D. E., 2018. *Maya Potter's Indigenous Knowledge: Cognition, Engagement and Practice*. Boulder: University Press of Colorado Press.

Balfet, H., 1965. Ethnographical Observations in North Africa and Archaeological Interpretation: The Pottery of the Maghreb. In *Ceramics and Man*, edited by F. R. Matson, 161–177. New York: Viking Fund Publication in Anthropology.

Balfet, H., 1973. A propos du tour de potier. L'outil et le geste technique. In *L'Homme, Hier et Aujourd'hui: Recueil d'études en Hommage à André Leroi-Gourhan*, edited by Collectif, 109–122. Paris: Editions Cujas.

Barrett, J. C., 2014. The Material Constitution of Humanness. *Archaeological Dialogues* 21: 65–74

Barrett, J. C., 2021. *Archaeology and its Discontents: Why Archaeology Matters*. London: Routledge.

Bendall, L. M., 2004. Fit for a King? Hierarchy, Exclusion, Aspiration and Desire in the Social Structure of Mycenaean Banqueting. In *Food, Cuisine and Society in Prehistoric Greece*, edited by P. Halstead and J. C. Barrett, 105–135. Sheffield Studies in Aegean Archaeology 6. Oxford: Oxbow Books.

Blegen, C. W., J. L. Caskey, and M. Rawson, 1953. *Troy: Excavations Conducted by the University of Cincinnati, 1932–1938, III. The Sixth Settlement*. Princeton: Princeton University Press.

Boulotis, C., 1997. Κουκονήσι Λήμνου. Τέσσερα Χρόνια Ανασκαφικής Ερευνας: Θέσεις και Υποθέσεις. In *Poliochni e l'Antica Età del Bronzo nell'Egeo Settentrionale: Convegno Internazionale, Atene, 22–25 Aprile 1996,* edited by C. Doumas and V. La Rosa, 230–272. Athens: Scuola Archeologica Italiana di Atene/ University of Athens.

Boulotis, C., 2009. Koukonisi on Lemnos: Reflections on the Minoan and Minoanising Evidence. In *The Minoans in the Central, Eastern and Northern Aegean: New Evidence. Acts of a Minoan Seminar 22–23 January 2005 in collaboration with the Danish Institute at Athens and the German Archaeological Institute at Athens,* edited by C. F. Macdonald, E. Hallager and W.-D. Niemeier, 175–218. Monographs of the Danish Institute at Athens 8. Athens: Danish Institute in Athens.

Boulotis, C., 2014. Κεραμεύς (*ke-ra-me-u*) και κεράμεια (*ke-ra-me-ja*) στις μυκηναϊκές πινακίδες Γραμμικής Β. In Εγραφσεν και Εποίεσεν. *Μελέτες Κεραμικής και Εικονογραφίας προς Τιμήν του Καθηγητή Μιχάλη Τιβέριου. Essays on Greek Pottery and Iconography in Honour of Professor Michalis Tiverios,* edited by P. Valavanis and E. Manakidou, 19–34. Thessaloniki: Εκδόσεις Επιστημονικών Βιβλίων και Περιοδικών.

Boulotis, C., E. Kardamaki, and T. Boloti, 2017. Κουκονήσι Λήμνου: Πρώτες παρατηρήσεις από τη μελέτη της μυκηναϊκής κεραμικής. In Το Αρχαιολογικό Εργο στα *Νησιά* του Αιγαίου. Διεθνές επιστημονικό συνέδριο, Ρόδος, 27 Νοεμβρίου–1 Δεκεμβρίου 2013, edited by P. Triandaphyllides, 45–62. Mytilene: Υπουργείο Πολιτισμού και Αθλητισμού, Γενική Γραμματεία Αιγαίου και Νησιωτικής Πολιτικής.

Boulotis, C., and E. Kardamaki, 2021. Το Κουκονήσι της Λήμνου και τα χαρακτηριστικά της μυκηναϊκής περιφέρειας στο βόρειο Αιγαίο. In *3rd International Interdisciplinary Colloquium: The Periphery of the Mycenaean World. Recent Discoveries and Research Results, 18–21 May, Lamia 2018*, edited by E. Karantzali, 691–702. Athens: Υπουργείο Πολιτισμού και Αθλητισμού / Οργανισμός Διαχείρισης και Ανάπτυξης Πολιτιστικών Πόρων.

Bowser, B. J., 2000. From Pottery to Politics: An Ethnoarchaeological Study of Political Factionalism, Ethnicity and Domestic Pottery Style in the Ecuadorian Amazon. *Journal of Archaeological Method and Theory* 7: 219–248.

Burke, C., and P. M. Day, 2023. Strategies for Success: Early Helladic Pottery Production in Corinth, Greece. *Archaeological and Anthropological Sciences* 15:77 DOI:10.1007/s12520-023-01776-7.

Burke, C., P. M. Day, E. Alram-Stern, K. Demakopoulou, and A. Hein, 2018. Crafting and Consumption Choices: Neolithic – Early Helladic II Ceramic Production and Distribution, Midea and Tiryns, Mainland Greece. In *Pottery Technologies and Sociocultural Connections Between the Aegean and Anatolia During the 3rd Millennium BC,* edited by E. Alram-Stern and B. Horejs, 145–159. Oriental and European Archaeology 10, Vienna: Verlag der Österreichischen Akademie der Wissenschaften.

Burke, C., P. M. Day, and A. Kossyva, 2020. Early Helladic I and Talioti Pottery: Is It Just a Phase We're Going Through? *Oxford Journal of Archaeology* 39: 19–40.

Catling, H. W., 2009. *Sparta: Menelaion I. The Bronze Age.* Annual of the British School at Athens Supplement 45. Athens: British School at Athens.

Chadwick J., L. Godart, J. T. Killen, J. P. Olivier, A. Sacconi, and I. A. Sakellarakis, 1986. *Corpus of Mycenaean Inscriptions from Knossos. Vol I.* Incunabula Graeca 88. Rome: Instituto per gli studi micenei ed egeo-anatolici del consiglio nazionale delle ricerche.

Choleva, M., R. Jung, and E. Kardamaki, 2020. Working on the Potter's Wheel: Technological Insights into Mycenaean Pottery Production. *Ägypten und Levante* 30: 219–282.

Costin, C. L., 2007. Thinking about Production: Phenomenological Classification and Lexical Semantics. In *Special Issue: Rethinking Craft Specialization in Complex Societies: Archaeological Analyses of the Social Meaning of Production. Archaeological Papers of the American Anthropological Association* 17 (1): 143–162.

Day, P. M., 2004. Marriage and Mobility: Tradition and the Dynamics of the Pottery System in Twentieth Century East Crete. In *Pseira* VIII: *The Archaeological Survey of Pseira Island. Part 1*, edited by P. P. Betancourt, C. Davaras, and R. Hope Simpson, 105–142. Prehistory Monographs 11. Philadelphia: INSTAP Academic Press.

Day, P. M., 2022a. You Can Take the Potter Out of the Plain, but You Can't Take the Plain Out of the Potter. In *Kleronomia: Legacy and Inheritance. Studies on the Aegean Bronze Age in Honor of Jeffrey S. Soles,* edited by J. M. A. Murphy and J. E. Morrison, 319–329. Prehistory Monographs 61. Philadelphia: INSTAP Academic Press.

Day, P. M., 2022b. Kilns, Kin and Calcite: Potters with Problems in Twentieth Century Palaikastro. In *Megistos Kouros: Studies in Bronze Age and Greek Archaeology in memory of L. Hugh Sackett*, edited by J. Driessen and C. Knappett, 114–127. Aegis. 23. Louvain-la-Neuve: Presses universitaires de Louvain.

Day, P. M., M.-A. Cau-Ontiveros, C. Mas-Florit, and N. S. Müller, 2015. A Contextual Ethnography of Cooking Vessel Production at Pòrtol, Mallorca (Balearic Islands). In *Ceramics, Cuisine and Culture, the Archaeology and Science of Kitchen Pottery in the Ancient Mediterranean World*, edited by M. Spataro and A. Villing, 55–64. Oxford: Oxbow Books.

Day, P. M., V. Hachtmann, E. Kardamaki, and A. Vasilogamvrou, 2022. Pottery Production and Consumption at Ayios Vasileios during LH II–IIIA and the Cretan Connections. In *One State, Many Worlds: Crete in the LM II – IIIA2 Early Period. Proceedings of the International Conference held at Khania,* Μεγάλο Αρσενάλι, *21st – 23rd November 2019*, edited by L.-A. D'Agata, L. Girella, E. Papadopoulou and D. G. Aquini, 365–386. Studi micenei ed egeo-anatolici, n.s., Supplemento 2. Rome: Edizioni Quasar.

Day, P. M., M. Relaki, and E. W. Faber, 2006. Pottery Making and Social Reproduction in the Bronze Age Mesara. In *Pottery and Society: The Impact of Recent Studies in Minoan Pottery. Gold Medal Colloquium in Honor of Philip P. Betancourt. 104th Annual Meeting of the Archaeological Institute of America, New Orleans, Louisiana, 5 January 2003*, edited by M. H. Wiener, J. L. Warner, J. Polonsky, and Erin Hayes, 22–72. Boston: Archaeological Institute of America.

Day, P. M., M. Relaki, and S. Todaro, 2010. Living from Pots? Ceramic Perspectives on the Economies of Prepalatial Crete. In *Political Economies of the Aegean Bronze Age: Papers from the Langford Conference, Florida State University, Tallahassee, 22–24 February 2007*, edited by D. J. Pullen, 205–229. Oxford: Oxbow Books.

Day, P. M., and D. E. Wilson, 1998. Consuming Power: Kamares Ware in Protopalatial Knossos. *Antiquity* 72 (276): 350–358.

Day, P. M., and D. E. Wilson, 2016. Dawn of the Amphora: The Emergence of Maritime Transport Containers in the Early Bronze Age Aegean. In *Maritime Transport Containers in the Bronze–Iron Age Aegean and Eastern Mediterranean*, edited by S. Demesticha and A. B. Knapp, 17–37. Studies in Mediterranean Archaeology and Literature-Pocketbook 183. Uppsala: Paul Åströms Förlag.

Demakopoulou, K., 2009. Οι αποθηκευτικοί ψευδόστομοι αμφορείς της Μιδέας. Νέα στοιχεία για τις σχέσεις Κρήτης και Αργολίδας κατά τον 13ο αι. π.Χ. In *ΔΩΡΟΝ: Τιμητικός τόμος για τον καθηγητή Σ. Ιακωβίδη*, edited by D. Daniilidou, 243–259. Σειρά Μονογραφιών 6. Athens: Academy of Athens.

Dimoula, A., 2017. Early Pottery Mobility: The Case of Early Neolithic Thessaly, Greece. *Journal of Archaeological Science: Reports* 12: 209–218.

Dobres, M.-A., 2000. *Technology and Social Agency: Outlining a Practice Framework for Archaeology*. Oxford: Blackwell.

Eckert, S. L., 2008. *Pottery and Practice: The Expression of Identity at Pottery Mound and Hummingbird Pueblo*. Albuquerque: University of New Mexico Press.

Galaty, M. L., 1999a. *Nestor's Wine Cups. Investigating Ceramic Manufacture and Exchange in a Late Bronze Age "Mycenaean" State*. British Archaeological Reports International Series 766. Oxford: BAR.

Galaty, M. L., 1999b. Wealth Ceramics, Staple Ceramics: Pots and the Mycenaean Palaces. In *Rethinking Mycenaean Palaces: New Interpretations of an Old Idea*, edited by M. L. Galaty and W. A. Parkinson, 49–59. Monograph 41. Los Angeles: Cotsen Institute of Archaeology at UCLA.

Galaty, M. L., 2010. Wedging Clay. Combining Competing Models of Mycenaean Pottery Industries. *Political Economies of the Aegean Bronze Age: Papers from the Langford Conference, Florida State University, Tallahassee, 22–24 February 2007*, edited by D. J. Pullen, 230–247. Oxford: Oxbow Books.

Galaty, M. L., D. Nakassis, and W. A. Parkinson, eds. 2011. Forum: Redistribution in Aegean Palatial Societies. *American Journal of Archaeology* 115: 175–244.

Gauß, W., 2003. The Late Mycenaean Pottery from the North Slope of the Athenian Akropolis. In *LH III C Chronology and Synchronisms: Proceedings of the International Workshop held at the Austrian Academy of Sciences at Vienna, 7–8 Mai 2001*, edited by S. Deger-Jalkotzy and M. Zavadil, 93–104. Österreichische Akademie der Wissenschaften philosophisch-historische Klasse Denkscriften 310. Vienna: Verlag der Österreichischen Akademie der Wissenschaften.

Gauß W., and E. Kiriatzi, 2011. *Pottery Production and Supply at Bronze Age Kolonna, Aegina: An Integrated Archaeological and Scientific Study of a Ceramic Landscape*. Ägina-Kolonna Forschungen und Ergebnisse 5; Österreichische Akademie der Wissenschaften Denkschriften der Gesamtakademie 65; Contributions to the Chronology of the Eastern Mediterranean 27. Vienna: Verlag der Österreichischen Akademie der Wissenschaften.

Gilstrap, W. D., 2015. Ceramic Production and Exchange in the Late Mycenaean Saronic Gulf. Ph.D. thesis, University of Sheffield.

Gilstrap, W. D., P. M. Day, and V. Kilikoglou, 2016. Pottery Production at Two Neighbouring Centres in the Late Bronze Age Saronic Gulf. Historical Contingency and Craft Organization, *Journal of Archaeological Science Reports* 369: 499–509.

Gilstrap, W. D., P. M. Day, and V. Kilikoglou, 2021. Compositional Analysis of LH IIIB–IIIC Early

Ceramics from the Cave of Euripides, Salamis, Greece. (Appendix 2). In Σαλαμίς ΙΙ: Το Σπήλαιο του Ευριπίδη στα Περιστέρια Σαλαμίνας. Η Μυκηναϊκή χρήση, by C. Marabea, 215–243. Δωδωη 84. Ioannina: University of Ioannina.

Girella, L., and P. Pavúk, 2015. Minoanisation, Acculturation, Hybridisation: The Evidence of the Minoan Presence in the North East Aegean between the Middle and Late Bronze Age. In *NOSTOI. Indigenous Culture, Migration, and Integration in the Aegean Islands and Western Anatolia during the Late Bronze and Early Iron Age*, edited by N. Stampolidis, Ç. Maner and K. Kopanias, 387–420. Archaeology 58. Istanbul: Koç University Press.

Girella, L., and P. Pavúk, 2016. The Nature of Minoan and Mycenaean Involvement in the Northeastern Aegean. In *Beyond Thalassocracies: Understanding Processes of Minoanisation and Mycenaeanisation in the Aegean*, edited by E. Gorogianni, P. Pavúk and L. Girella, 15–42. Oxford: Oxbow Books.

Goody, E. N., 1989. Learning, Apprenticeship, and the Division of Labour. In *Apprenticeship: From Theory to Method and Back Again*, edited by M. W. Coy, 233–256. Albany: State University of New York Press.

Gosselain, O. P., 1998. Social and Technical Identity in a Clay Crystal Ball. In *The Archaeology of Social Boundaries*, edited by M. T. Stark, 78–106. Washington DC: Smithsonian Institution.

Gosselain, O. P., 2002. Poteries du Cameroun méridional. Styles techniques et rapports à l'identité. Paris: CNRS Editions.

Graybehl, H., 2015. The Production and Distribution of Hellenistic Ceramics from the Northeast Peloponnese at the Panhellenic Sanctuary at Nemea: A Petrographic Study. Ph.D. thesis: University of Sheffield.

Hachtmann, V., 2023. Late Helladic I to IIA pottery from Ayios Vasileios at Xirokambi, Laconia. The "Platform Deposit" in the North Cemetery Area. Αρχαιολογική Εφημερίς 162: 247–382.

Haskell H. W., R. E. Jones, P. M. Day, and J. T. Killen, 2011. *Transport Stirrup Jars of the Bronze Age Aegean and East Mediterranean*. Prehistory Monographs 33. Philadelphia: INSTAP Academic Press.

Hein, A., R. Jung, E. Kardamaki, and V. Kilikoglou, 2021. Pottery Production in Mycenaean Laconia: NAA Results from the Palace of Ayios Vasileios. *Praehistorische Zeitschrift* 96 (2): 464–484.

Herbich, I., and M. Dietler, 2008. The Long Arm of the Mother-in-law: Learning, Postmarital Resocialization of Women, and Material Culture Style. In *Cultural Transmission and Material Culture: Breaking Down Boundaries, edited by* M. T. Stark, B. J. Bowser, and L. Horne, 223–244. Tucson: University of Arizona Press.

Hruby, J., 2006. Feasting and Ceramics. A View from the Palace of Nestor at Pylos. Ph.D. dissertation, University of Cincinnati.

Ingold, T., 2000. *The Perception of the Environment: Essays on Livelihood, Dwelling, and Skill*. London: Routledge.

Ingold, T., 2007. Materials against Materiality. *Archaeological Dialogues* 14 (1): 1–16.

Ingold, T., 2013. *Making: Anthropology, Archaeology, Art and Architecture*. London: Routledge.

Ionas, I., 2000. *Traditional Pottery and Potters in Cyprus: The Disappearance of an Ancient Craft Industry in the 19th and 20th Centuries*. Birmingham Byzantine and Ottoman Monographs Volume 6. Aldershot: Ashgate.

Kardamaki, E., 2017. The Late Helladic IIB to IIIA2 Pottery Sequence from the Mycenaean Palace from Ayios Vasileios, Laconia. *Archaeologia Austriaca* 101: 73–172.

Kardamaki, E., forthcoming. Argive Style Pottery as a Benchmark? Distribution and Consumption of Painted Styles Deriving from the Argive Workshops in Three Case Studies from Laconia, Attica and Lemnos. In *Regional Variation in Mycenaean Pottery: International Workshop, 27–28 October 2022, Institute of Archaeology and Ethnology, Polish Academy of Sciences*, edited by B. Lis. Warsaw.

Kardamaki, E., P. M. Day, M. Tenconi, J. Maran, and A. Papadimitriou, 2016. Transport Stirrup Jars in Late Mycenaean Tiryns: Maritime Transport Containers and Commodity Movement in Political Context. In *Maritime Transport Containers in the Bronze–Iron Age Aegean and Eastern Mediterranean, edited by* S. Demesticha and B. Knapp, 145–167. Studies in Mediterranean Archaeology and Literature-Pocketbook 183. Uppsala: Paul Åströms Förlag.

Kardamaki, E., and K. Kaza-Papageorgiou, 2018. Change and Continuity in the Pottery Tradition at Kontopigado, Athens, During the Late 13th and the Early 12th Century BC. In *Technology in Crisis. Technological Changes in Ceramic Production during Periods of Trouble, edited by* I. Caloi and C. Langohr, 111–138. Aegis 16. Louvain-la-Neuve: Press universitaires de Louvain.

Kaza-Papageorgiou, K., and E. Kardamaki, 2012. Κοντοπήγαδο Αλίμου. Ο Οικισμός των ΥΕ χρόνων. Αρχαιολογική Εφημερίς 151: 141–199.

Kaza-Papageorgiou, K., and E. Kardamaki, 2018. A LH IIIA1 Deposit from Kontopigado, Alimos and Processes of Mycenaeanization at Athens. *Athenische Mitteilungen* 133: 1–58.

Kaza-Papageorgiou, K., E. Kardamaki, P. Koutis, N. Mouka, and E. Markopoulou, 2011. Κοντοπήγαδο Αλίμου Αττικής. Οικισμός των ΠΕ και ΥΕ χρόνων και ΥΕ εργαστηριακή εγκατάσταση. Αρχαιολογική Εφημερίς 150: 197–274.

Killen, J. T., 1985. The Linear B Tablets and the Mycenaean Economy. In *Linear B: a 1984 Survey. Mycenaean Colloquium of the VIII Congress of the International Federation of the Societies of Classical Studies*, edited by D. Morpurgo Davies, A. Duhoux, and Y. Duhoux, 241–305. Bibliothèque des Cahiers de l'Institut de Linguistique de Louvain 26. Louvain-la-Neuve: Cabay.

Kiriatzi, E., S. Andreou, S. Dimitriadis, and K. Kotsakis, 1997. Co-existing Traditions: Handmade and Wheelmade Pottery in Late Bronze Age Central Macedonia. *TEXNH: Craftsmen, Craftswomen and Craftsmanship in the Aegean Bronze Age. Proceedings of the 6th International Aegean Conference/6e Rencontre* égéenne *internationale, Philadelphia, Temple University, 18–21 April 1996*, edited by R. Laffineur and P. P. Betancourt, 361–367. Aegaeum 16. Liège: Histoire de l'art et archéologie de la Grèce antique; Austin: University of Texas at Austin, Program in Aegean Scripts and Prehistory.

Kiriatzi, E., and C. Knappett, eds., 2016. *Human Mobility and Technological Transfer in the Prehistoric Mediterranean.* British School at Athens, Studies in Greek Antiquity. Cambridge: Cambridge University Press.

Klebinder-Gauß, G., and S. Strack, 2015. An Aeginetan Potters' Workshop in Athens? *The Transmission of Technical Knowledge in the Production of Ancient Mediterranean Pottery, Proceedings of the International Conference at the Austrian Archaeological Institute at Athens 23rd–25th November 2012*, edited by W. Gauß, G. Klebinder-Gauß, and C. von Rüden, 77–95. Österreichisches Archäologisches Institut Sonderschriften Band 54. Vienna: Österreichisches Archäologisches Institut.

Knappett, C., 2001. Overseen or Overlooked? Ceramic Production in a Mycenaean Palatial System. In *Economy and Politics in the Mycenaean Palace States: Proceedings of a Conference held on 1–3 July 1999 in the Faculty of Classics, Cambridge*, edited by S. Voutsaki and J. T. Killen, 80–95. Cambridge Philological Society Supplementary Volume 27. Cambridge: Cambridge Philological Society.

Knappett, C., 2016. Resisting Innovation? Learning, Cultural Evolution and the Potter's Wheel in the Mediterranean Bronze Age. In *Cultural Phylogenetics: Concepts and Applications in Archaeology*, edited by L. Mendoza Straffon, 97–111. Berlin.

Kondyli, D., and I. Mathioudaki, 2022. Throwing Some Light on the Early History of the Mycenaean Palace at Ayios Vasileios, Laconia. Three Early Mycenaean Pottery Deposits from Building Alpha. In *Middle and Late Helladic Laconia: Competing Principalities*, edited by C. Wiersma and M. P. Tsouli, 151–166. Publications of the Netherlands Institute at Athens 7. Leiden: Sidestone/Netherlands Institute at Athens.

Kozatsas, J., 2018. *The Dialectic of Practice and the Logical Structure of the Tool: Philosophy, Archaeology and the Anthropology of Technology.* Praehistorica Mediterranea 7. Oxford: Archaeopress.

Kramer, C., 1997. *Pottery in Rajasthan: Ethnoarchaeology in Two Indian Cities.* Washington DC: Smithsonian Institution Press.

Lemonnier, P., 1993. *Technological choices: Transformation in Material Cultures since the Neolithic.* London/New York: Routledge.

Lindblom, M., W. Gauß, and E. Kiriatzi, 2015. Some Reflections on Ceramic Technology Transfer at Bronze Age Kastri on Kythera, Kolonna on Aegina, and Lerna in the Argolid. In *The Distribution of Technical Knowledge in the Production of Ancient Mediterranean Pottery: Proceedings of the International Conference at the Austrian Archaeological Institute at Athens 23rd–25th November 2012*, edited by W. Gauß, G. Klebinder-Gauß, and C. von Rüden, 225–237. Österreichisches Archäologisches Institut Sonderschriften Band 54. Vienna: Österreichisches Archäologisches Institut.

Lis, B., 2017a. Foodways in Early Mycenaean Greece: Innovative Cooking Sets and Social Hierarchy at Mitrou and Other Settlements on the Greek Mainland. *American Journal of Archaeology* 121: 183–217.

Lis, B., 2017b. Variability of Ceramic Production and Consumption on the Greek Mainland During the Middle Stages of the Late Bronze Age: The Waterpots from the Menelaion, Sparta. *Oxford Journal of Archaeology* 36: 243–266.

Lis, B., S. Rückl, and M. Choleva, 2015. Mobility in the Bronze Age Aegean: The Case of Aeginetan Potters. In *The Transmission of Technical Knowledge in the Production of Ancient Mediterranean Pottery: Proceedings of the International Conference at the Austrian Archaeological Institute at Athens 23rd–25th November 2012*, edited by W. Gauß, G. Klebinder-Gauß and C. von Rüden, 63–76. Österreichisches Archäologisches Institut Sonderschriften Band 54. Vienna: Österreichisches Archäologisches Institut.

London, G., 2020. *Wine Jars and Jar Makers of Cyprus: The Ethnoarchaeology of Pitharia.* Nicosia: Astrom Editions.

London, G., F. Egoumenidou, and V. Karageoghis, 1990. *Traditional Pottery in Cyprus.* Mainz am Rhein: Verlag Philipp Von Zabern.

Malafouris, L., 2013. *How Things Shape the Mind: A Theory of Material Engagement.* Cambridge, Mass. / London: MIT Press.

Marabea, C., 2010. *Το Ανατολικό Κτηριακό Συγκρότημα ΙΑ-ΙΒ-ΙΔ στη Μυκηναϊκή* Ακρόπολη *στα Κανάκια Σαλαμίνας: Περιεχόμενο και λειτουργία* (The Eastern Building Complex on the Mycenaean acropolis at

Kanakia, Salamis: Content and function). Ph.D. thesis, University of Ioannina.

Marabea, C., 2012. Η εγκατάλειψη της Μυκηναϊκής Ακρόπολης στα Κανάκια Σαλαμίνας: Μαρτυρίες από το Ανατολικό Συγκρότημα και άλλα οικοδομήματα. In ΣΑΛΑΜΙΣ Ι: Συμβολή στην Αρχαιολογία του Αργοσαρωνικού, edited by Y.G. Lolos, 161–217. Επιστημονική Επετηρίδα του Τμήματος Ιστορίας και Αρχαιολογίας της Φιλοσοφικής Σχολής του *Πανεπιστημίου Ιωαννίνων* 83. Ioannina: University of Ioannina.

Marabea, C., 2019. Late Bronze Age Aiginetan Coarse Pottery at Kanakia, Salamis: A Macroscopic Study. *Hesperia* 88: 447–525.

Marabea, C., 2021. Σαλαμίς ΙΙ: Το Σπήλαιο του Ευριπίδη στα Περιστέρια Σαλαμίνας: Η Μυκηναϊκή χρήση. (Salamis II. The Cave of Euripides at Peristeria, Salamis: The Mycenaean use). Δωδώνη Παράρτημα Αρ. 84. Ioannina: University of Ioannina.

Maran, J., 1992. *Kiapha Thiti: Ergebnisse der Ausgrabungen II2 (2.Jt.v.Chr.: Keramik und Kleinfunde).* Marburger Winckelmann-Programm 1990. Marburg: Philipps-Universität Marburg.

Maran, J., 2005. Late Minoan Coarse Ware Stirrup Jars on the Greek Mainland. A Postpalatial Perpective from the 12th Century BC Argolid. In *Ariadne's Threads: Connections between Crete and the Greek Mainland in Late Minoan III (LM III A2 to LM III C). Proceedings of the International Workshop, Scuola Archeologica Italiana, Athen, 5. – 6. April 2003,* edited by A. L. D'Agata, J. Moody, and E. Williams, 415–431. Tripodes 3. Athens: Scuola Archeologica Italiana di Atene.

Matson, F. R., 1972. Ceramic Studies. In *The Minnesota Messenia Expedition: Reconstructing a Bronze Age Regional Environment,* edited by W. A. McDonald and G. Rapp, Jr., 200–224. Minneapolis: University of Minnesota Press.

Matson, F. R., 1973. The Potters of Chalkis. In *Classics and the Classical Tradition: Essays Presented to Robert E. Dengler on the Occasion of His Eightieth Birthday,* edited by E. N. Borza and R. W. Carrubba, 117–142. University Park PA: Pennsylvania State University.

Miller, D., 1985. *Artefacts as Categories: A Study of Ceramic Variability in Central India.* Cambridge: Cambridge University Press.

Mountjoy, P. A., 1981. *Four Early Mycenaean Wells from the South Slope of the Acropolis at Athens.* Miscellanea Graeca 4. Ghent: Comité des Fouilles Belges en Grèce.

Mountjoy, P. A., 2008. Chapter 6. The Late Helladic Pottery. In *Ayios Stephanos: Excavations at a Bronze Age and Medieval Settlement in Southern Laconia,* W. D. Taylour and R. Janko, 299–387. British School at Athens Supplementary Volume 44. London: British School at Athens.

Mountjoy, P. A., 2017. *Troy VI Middle, VI Late and VII. The Mycenaean Pottery.* Studia Troica Monographien 9. Bonn: Verlag Dr. Rudolf Habelt GmbH.

Mountjoy, P. A., and H. Mommsen, 2006. Neutron Activation Analysis of Mycenaean pottery from Troia (1988–2003 Excavations). *Studia Troica* 16: 97–123.

Nakassis, D., 2021. The Extractive Systems of the Mycenaean World. in *Ancient Taxation: The Mechanics of Extraction in Comparative Perspective,* edited by J. Valk and I. Soto Marín, 93–127. New York: New York University Press.

Palaima, T. G., 1997. Potter and Fuller: The Royal Craftsmen. In *TEXNH: Craftsmen, Craftswomen, and Craftsmanship in the Aegean Bronze Age. Proceedings of the 6th International Aegean Conference/6e Rencontre égéenne internationale, Philadelphia, Temple University, 18–21 April 1996,* edited by R. Laffineur and P. P. Betancourt, 407–412. Aegaeum 16. Liège: Histoire de l'art et archéologie de la Grèce antique; Austin: University of Texas at Austin, Program in Aegean Scripts and Prehistory.

Palmer, L. R., 1963. *The Interpretation of Mycenaean Greek Texts.* Oxford: Clarendon Press.

Papadimitriou, A., 2023. Παρά την οδό Τριπόδων. Ανασκαφή στο Οικόπεδο επί της Οδού Ραγκαβά 4 στην Πλάκα. Paper presented at conference: *Η βόρεια κλιτύς της Ακρόπολης: ένα αρχαιολογικό παλίμψηστο,* Pavlos and Alexandra Kanellopoulos Museum, Athens, 19–21 October 2023.

Parkinson, W. A., D. Nakassis, and M. L. Galaty, eds. 2013. Forum: Crafts, Specialists, and Markets in Mycenaean Greece. *American Journal of Archaeology* 117: 413–459.

Pavúk, P., L. Girella, M. Pieniążek, and F. Franković, 2023. The Upper Interface Twenty-five Years Later. The Northeast Aegean Islands and the West Anatolian Coast during the Late Bronze Age. In *The Lady of Pottery. Ceramic Studies Presented to Penelope A. Mountjoy in Acknowledgment of Her Outstanding Scholarship,* edited by A. L. D'Agata and P. Pavúk, 121–147. Studi micenei ed egeo-anatolici n.s. Supplemento 3. Rome: Edizioni Quasar.

Peacock, D. P. S., 1983. *Pottery in the Roman World: An Ethnoarchaeological Approach.* London: Longman.

Petrakis, V. P., 2010. *Wa-na-ka-te-ro. Σπουδὲς στὴν οἰκονομικὴ 'οργάνωση καὶ πολιτικὴ γεωγραφία τῆς Ὑστερομινωικῆς ΙΙΙ Κρήτης μὲ ἀφορμὴ τὴ συνθετικὴ ἀνάλυση τῶν ἐνεπίγραφων ψευδόστο4φμων ἀμφορέων ποὺ μνημονεύουν τὸν ἡγεμονικὸ τίτλο.* Ph.D. dissertation, University of Athens.

Pfaffenberger, B., 1992. Social Anthropology of Technology. *Annual Review of Anthropology* 21: 491–516.

Poursat, J.-C., and C. Knappett, 2006. Fouilles exécutées à Malia. Le Quartier Mu IV. La poterie du Minoen

Moyen IIII: production et utilisation. Études crétoises 33, École Française d'Athènes. Paris: de Boccard.

Roux, V., 2019. *Ceramics and Society: A Technological Approach to Archaeological Assemblages*. Springer.

Roux, V., and D. Corbetta, 1990. *Le Tour du Potier: Spécialisation artisanale et compétences techniques*. Monographie du Centre du CRA 4. Paris: Editions de CNRS.

Roux, V., and M.-A. Courty, 1998. Identification of wheel-fashioning: technological analysis of 4th–3rd millennium B.C. Oriental Ceramics. *Journal of Archaeological Science* 25: 747–763.

Rutter J. B., 2015. Ceramic Technology in Rapid Transition. The Evidence from Settlement Deposits of the Shaft Grave Era at Tsoungiza (Corinthia). In *The Transmission of Technical Knowledge in the Production of Ancient Mediterranean Pottery. Proceedings of the International Conference at the Austrian Archaeological Institute at Athens, 23rd–25th November 2012*, edited by W. Gauß, G. Klebinder-Gauß and C. von Rüden, 207–23. Österreichisches Archäologisches Institut Sonderschriften 54. Vienna: Österreichisches Archäologisches Institut.

Rutter, J. B., and S. H. Rutter, 1976. *The transition to Mycenaean: a Stratified Middle Helladic II to Late Helladic IIA Pottery Sequence from Agios Stephanos in Lakonia*. Monumenta Archaeologica 4. Los Angeles: University of California Institute of Archaeology.

Shaw, J. W., A. Van der Moortel, P. M. Day, and V. Kilikoglou, 2001. *A Late Minoan IA Ceramic Kiln from South-Central Crete: Function and Pottery Production*. Hesperia Supplement 30. Princeton NJ: American School of Classical Studies at Athens.

Shelmerdine, C. W., 1985. *The Perfume Industry in Mycenaean Pylos*. Studies in Mediterranean Archaeology Pocketbook 34. Göteborg: Paul Åstöms Förlag.

Sherratt, S. 2001. Potemkin Palaces and Route-based Economies. In *Economy and Politics in the Mycenaean Palace Statess. Proceedings of a Conference held on 1–3 July 1999 in the Faculty of Classics, Cambridge, edited by* S. Voutsaki and J. T. Killen, 214–238. Cambridge Philological Society Supplementary Volume 27. Cambridge: Cambridge Philological Society.

Singleton, J., 1989. Japanese Folkcraft Pottery Apprenticeship: Cultural Patterns of an Educational Institution. In *Apprenticeship: From Theory to Method and Back Again, edited by* M. W. Coy, 13–30. Albany: State University of New York Press.

Spathari-Begliti, E., 1992. *Οι Αγγειοπλάστες της Σίφνου: Κοινωνική συγκρότηση, παραγωγή, μετακινήσεις.* Διδακτορική διτριβή. Athens: Arsenidis Editions.

Todaro, S. V., 2013. *The Phaistos Hills before the Palace: A Contextual Repraisal*. Praehistorica Mediterranea 5. Milan: Polimetrica.

Todaro, S., 2017. Forming Techniques and Cultural Identity in Early and Middle Minoan Crete: Multi-layered Vessels from a Pottery Production Area at Phaistos. *Annuario della Scuola Archeologica di Atene e delle Missioni Italiane in Oriente* 95: 129–143.

Tomkins, P., 2008. Time, Space and the Reinvention of the Cretan Neolithic. In *Escaping the Labyrinth: The Cretan Neolithic in Context*, edited by V. Isaakidou and P. Tomkins, 21–48. Sheffield Studies in Aegean Archaeology 8. Oxford: Oxbow.

Tomkins, P., and P. M. Day, 2001. Production and Exchange of the Earliest Ceramic Vessels in the Aegean: A View from Early Neolithic Knossos, Crete. *Antiquity* 75: 259–260.

Tsai, C.-H., 2021. Times of Change: Transformations in Pottery Production and Exchange at Early Bronze Age Kontopigado-Alimos, Attica. Ph.D. thesis, University of Sheffield.

Tsai, C.-H., K. Kaza-Papageorgiou, D. E. Wilson, and P. M. Day, 2023. 青銅器時代早期愛琴海運輸罐的來源與技術研究: 以阿提卡半島的 Kontopigado 遺址為例 (A Provenance and Technological Study of the Transport Jars from the Early Bronze Age Kontopigado in Attica, Greece). *Journal of Archaeology and Anthropology* 98: 89–120.

Van Damme, T., 2023. The Mycenaean Fountain and the Transformation of Space on the Athenian Acropolis: 1200 to 675 B.C. *Hesperia* 92: 111–190.

van der Leeuw, S. E., 1977. Towards a Study of the Economics of Pottery Making. *Ex Horreo* 4: 68–76.

van der Leeuw, S. E., 1984. Dust to Dust: A Transformational View of the Ceramic Cycle. In *The Many Dimensions of Pottery: Ceramics in Archaeology and Anthropology*, edited by S. E. van der Leeuw and A. C. Pritchard, 707–773. Amsterdam: Institute for Pre- and Protohistory.

Vasilogamvrou A., E. Kardamaki, and N. Karadimas, 2021. The Foundation System at the Palace of Ayios Vasileios, Xirokambi, Laconia. In *(Social) Place and Space in Early Mycenaean Greece: International Discussions in Mycenaean Archaeology, October 5–8, 2016, Athens*, edited by B. Eder and M. Zavadil, 341–64. Mykenische Studien 3. Vienna: Austrian Academy of Sciences.

Vitelli, K. D., 1993. *Franchthi Neolithic Pottery. Volume 1: Classification and Ceramic Phases 1 and 2.* Bloomington: Indiana University Press.

Wallaert, H., 2008. The Way of the Potter's Mother: Apprenticechip Strategies Among Dii Potters from Cameroon, West Africa. In *Cultural Transmission and Material Culture: Breaking Down Boundaries*, edited by M. T. Stark, B. J. Bowser, and L. Horne, 178–198. Tucson: University of Arizona Press.

Wenger, E., 1998. *Communities of Practice: Learning, Meaning and Identity*. Cambridge: Cambridge University Press.

Whitbread, I. K., 1995. *Greek Transport Amphorae: A Petrological and Archaeological Study*. Fitch Laboratory Occasional Paper 4. Athens: British School at Athens.

Whitbread I. K., and R. E. Jones, 2008. Appendix 2. Petrographic and Chemical Analysis of Middle and Late Helladic I–II Pottery. In *Ayios Stephanos: Excavations at a Bronze Age and Medieval Site in Southern Lakonia*, edited by W.D. Taylour and R. Janko, CD 89–117. British School at Athens Supplementary Volume 44. London: British School at Athens.

Whitelaw, T., 2001. Reading between the Tablets. Assessing Mycenaean Palatial Involvement in Ceramic Production and Consumption. In *Economy and Politics in the Mycenaean Palace States. Proceedings of a Conference held on 1–3 July 1999 in the Faculty of Classics, Cambridge*, edited by S. Voutsaki and J. T. Killen, 51–79. Cambridge Philological Society Supplementary Volume 27. Cambridge: Cambridge Philological Society.

Wright, J. C., 2004. A Survey of Evidence for Feasting in Mycenaean Society. In *The Mycenaean Feast*, 133–178. Hesperia Special Issue 73.2. Princeton NJ: American School of Classical Studies at Athens.

Zeman, P., 2018. Strategies of Pottery Acquisition in the Mycenaean Palace at Pylos. *Studia Hercynia* XXII/1: 31–55.

Zerner, C. W., 2008. The Middle Helladic Pottery, with the Middle Helladic ware from Late Helladic deposits and the potters' marks. In *Ayios Stephanos. Excavations at a Bronze Age and Medieval Settlement in Southern Laconia*, edited by W. D. Taylour and R. Janko, 177–298. British School at Athens Supplementary Volume 44. London: British School at Athens.